"Why Should White Guys Have All the Fun?"

"Why Should White Guys Have All the Fun?"

How Reginald Lewis Created a Billion-Dollar Business Empire

Reginald F. Lewis
and
Blair S. Walker

John Wiley & Sons, Inc.
New York • Chichester • Brisbane • Toronto • Singapore

Copyright © 1995 by Loida Nicolas Lewis and Blair S. Walker.
Published by John Wiley & Sons, Inc.

Library of Congress Cataloging-in-Publication Data:

Lewis, Reginald F., 1942–1993.
    "Why should white guys have all the fun?" : how Reginald Lewis
created a billion-dollar business empire / Reginald F. Lewis and
Blair S. Walker.
        p.   cm.
    Includes bibliographical references.
    ISBN 0-471-04227-7 (acid-free paper)
    1. Lewis, Reginald F., 1942–1993. 2. Afro-Americans in business—
Biography. 3. Millionaires—United States—Biography. I. Walker,
Blair S. II. Title.
HC102.5.L493A3 1995
338'.04'092—dc20
[B]   94-17864

Printed in the United States of America

10 9 8 7 6 5 4 3 2 1

This book is dedicated to the memory of Reginald F. Lewis, my husband, lover, counselor, best friend, role model, and devoted father to our children, Leslie Lourdes and Christina Savilla. It is also dedicated to Carolyn E. Cooper Lewis Fugett, Reginald Lewis's mother, whose fortitude and wisdom strengthen us all.

—LOIDA NICOLAS LEWIS

This book is dedicated to my daughters, Blair and Bria. May the two of you grow up in a world where accomplished African-American entrepreneurs are the rule, rather than the exception.

It is also dedicated to my wife, Felicia, and to my parents, Dolores Pierre and James Walker: I owe the two of you a debt of gratitude for cultivating in me a respect for—and love of—the written word.

—BLAIR S. WALKER

Publisher's Note

"Why Should White Guys Have All the Fun?" was the title of a partial autobiography written by Reginald F. Lewis shortly before his death in January 1993. His words are compelling and provide insight into the success he achieved and the personality and intellect that facilitated that success. Blair S. Walker used Lewis's autobiography as a guide to write a complete biography, based on hundreds of interviews Walker conducted with Lewis's family, friends, colleagues, business partners, associates, and employees. This unique book includes Reginald Lewis's own words, here set in italic type, and Blair Walker's account, which together tell the full story of how Reginald Lewis built a billion-dollar business empire.

Acknowledgments

I approached this project with a vague sense of trepidation, knowing it would require collaboration with Reginald Lewis's wife, Loida Lewis. Was she after a full and frank accounting of her late husband's life, or did she have a lengthy Valentine in mind? Would her involvement lead to a manuscript bearing little relation to reality?

I needn't have fretted. Loida Lewis proved to be a facilitator of the first order. Her candor and forthrightness were invaluable, as were the insights that only a spouse could provide about someone as intensely private as Reginald Lewis. Whether accompanying me to the Paris restaurant that she and her husband adored, or providing access to Reginald Lewis's school grades, Loida Lewis consistently strove to make this book as complete as possible, in lieu of Reginald Lewis penning it himself.

The other woman who played an instrumental role in bringing this book to fruition was Ruth Mills, my editor. Every first-time author should be so fortunate as to have Ruth walk them through the intricacies of book writing.

Someone whose thoughts move at the speed of light, and talks nearly as fast, Ruth is a walking clearinghouse when it comes to suggestions and ideas for sharpening prose. She was consistently upbeat and encouraging throughout this project and juggled the roles of editor, psychologist, and confidante with panache.

Another individual deserving of special mention is Rene (Butch) Meily, the spokesman for TLC Beatrice International Foods. From a business standpoint, no one spent more time with Reginald Lewis than Butch. Butch traveled frequently with Reginald Lewis and the two of them spent countless hours hatching strategies for dealing with the press.

Butch went over the manuscript with an eye toward ensuring that events were accurate. Butch was also helpful when it came to defining some of the nuances of his late boss's personality.

—BLAIR S. WALKER

Contents

Prologue   xiii

Chapter 1   A Kid from East Baltimore   1

Chapter 2   Lewis's "Demon Work Ethic": The High School Years   16

Chapter 3   "I'm Going to Be a Millionaire": Lewis at
             Virginia State   32

Chapter 4   No Application Needed: Breaking Down the
             Doors of Harvard Law   50

Chapter 5   Building His Own Law Practice: The Years of Struggle   72

Chapter 6   "Masterful" Man: Winning Loida Nicolas   97

Chapter 7   "I Was Not Ready"   110

Chapter 8   Drexel, the Bear, and the $18 Million Race:
             Closing the McCall Pattern Deal   132

Chapter 9   Piloting McCall for a 90-to-1 Gain   157

Chapter 10   The Biggest Deal of All: The Billion-Dollar
             LBO of Beatrice   187

Chapter 11   International Headaches and Domestic Roadblocks   218

Chapter 12   Bravura and Brinksmanship: Closing the
             Beatrice Acquisition   230

Chapter 13   Taming a Business Behemoth   251

Chapter 14   A Door to a New Universe   273

Chapter 15   Connoisseur, Philanthropist, Citizen of the World   283

Chapter 16   "I Am Not Afraid of Death"   293

Epilogue   308

Sources Interviewed   312

Index   315

Prologue

Strolling briskly along one of Manhattan's better known boulevards, 44-year-old Reginald Francis Lewis reared back and unleashed a quick right uppercut. A crisply executed left jab followed, but both punches struck only air, leaving eddies of August humidity in their wake.

Continuing down the Avenue of the Americas in his $2,000, dark blue Italian-made suit, his ruggedly handsome features tinged orange from the mercury street lights, Lewis threw punch after exuberant punch until he grew arm weary. All the while, he flashed a gap-tooth grin and emitted a booming belly laugh as a phalanx of well-dressed business partners accompanying him chuckled too, or looked on with bemused expressions.

Trailing about 50 feet behind with its parking lights on, Lewis's black Mercedes limousine shadowed the group. Inside the car, where the air conditioner was set at precisely 70 degrees and classical music played on the radio—per Lewis's instructions—the driver watched attentively for a casual wave of the hand indicating Lewis was tired of walking and ready to ride.

But on the night of August 6, 1987, Reginald Lewis was in the throes of such an invigorating adrenaline rush he could have walked all night and into the dawn. A successful corporate lawyer who remade himself into a financier and buyer of corporations, Lewis had bought the McCall Pattern Co. for $22.5 million, guided it to record earnings and recently sold it for $65 million, fetching a 90-to-1 return on his investment.

But even that improbable achievement was small potatoes compared with what Lewis had pulled off a few hours earlier: This audacious African-American born to a working-class family in Baltimore had just won the right to buy Beatrice International Foods, a global giant with 64 companies in 31 countries, for just under $1 billion.

That's why Lewis was happily jabbing his way down the Avenue of the Americas, in a most uncharacteristic public display of mirth and light-heartedness. He and his colleagues had just left the 50th Street offices of investment banker Morgan Stanley, where Lewis signed the papers associated with the Beatrice International auction. Now—foregoing his plush limousine—Lewis preferred to walk the six blocks from 50th Street to the Harvard Club, located at 44th Street.

A richly appointed bastion of Manhattan's old boy network, the Harvard Club invariably reminded Lewis of just how far he had come from his blue-collar youth in segregated Baltimore and just how far he intended to go.

Constructed of red brick, in the tradition of most of the buildings on Harvard's campus, the Harvard Club of New York City was a favorite Lewis haunt. He and his victorious entourage walked through the front door and into the lobby, toward the double French doors topped by a sign reading "Members Only." Lewis half walked, half floated through the double doors, past the over-stuffed couches and desks with Harvard Club stationery on them, and into the Grill Room, with its crimson-colored carpet, walls paneled with dark wood, and subdued lighting.

Lewis seldom went into the cavernous main dining room, where row after row of mounted animal heads grace the walls and chandeliers the size of small plants dangle from the ceiling, above endless rows of tables covered with fresh, white linen.

Passing the Grill Room's backgammon tables and fireplace, where a fire was usually lit in the wintertime, Lewis walked toward his favorite table. A uniformed waiter with a lilting Caribbean accent rushed up to greet Lewis with a mixture of formality and familiarity established over the course of a long-running relationship.

"Good evening, Mr. Lewis," the waiter said, smiling.

"How goes it, Archie?" Lewis replied, ebulliently grasping the surprised waiter's hand and patting him heartily on the back.

Lewis made a move toward his table; then, with surprising fluidness and grace for a man 5-foot-10 and about 20 pounds overweight, changed direction and made a beeline for the snack bar. Sitting on a cantilevered wooden table, as always, was a bowl of popcorn, one filled with pretzels, and another containing Ritz crackers. The fourth bowl had what looked to be a mountain of Cheese Whiz, with two gleaming silver knives sticking in it.

Grabbing a small white porcelain dish embossed with Harvard Club insignia, Lewis filled it with cheese and crackers, then headed to his table, where he ordered two bottles of Cristal champagne—at $120 a pop.

After several toasts, a third bottle of Cristal materialized, followed by a fourth and a fifth, bringing the total to one bottle for each of the five men at Lewis's table. Lewis cut the celebration short—there was still much work to be done. Winning an auction for Beatrice International was easy compared with the incredibly complex, time-consuming, and expensive effort it would take to close the deal.

Even so, winning the auction was a tremendously satisfying feat, made even sweeter by the fact that Lewis outbid several multinational companies, including Citicorp, that were aided by squads of accountants, lawyers, and financial advisers. Lewis had won by relying on moxie, financial and legal savvy, and the efforts of a two-man team consisting of himself and a recently hired business partner. In fact, when Lewis tendered his bid, a representative of one of the investment banking firms handling the auction called Lewis's office and said, "We have received from your group an offer to buy Beatrice International for $950 million. We have a small problem—nobody knows who the hell you are!"

The world knew who Lewis was by the time he succumbed to brain cancer in January 1993, at the relatively young age of 50. His net worth was estimated by *Forbes* at $400 million when he died, putting him on the magazine's 400 list of wealthiest Americans. In the last five years of his life, Lewis gave away more money than most people dream of earning in several lifetimes, and he generally did so without fanfare.

More than 2,000 people attended Lewis's funeral and memorial service, including Arthur Ashe, just before his own death. Opera diva Kathleen Battle sang "Amazing Grace" at the memorial service and

Lewis's family received words of condolence from Bill Clinton, Ronald Reagan, Colin Powell, and Bill Cosby, among others.

"Regardless of race, color, or creed, we are all dealt a hand to play in this game of life," Cosby wrote. "And believe me, Reg Lewis played the hell out of his hand!"

With his deep-set, piercing eyes, bushy moustache, seemingly perpetual scowl, and megawatt intensity, Lewis wasn't the most approachable of individuals. Either through expertise or influence, he commanded respect.

A romantic who once surprised his wife Loida by flying her on his private jet from Paris to Vienna just to hear a classical music concert, Lewis was a Francophile who spoke French fluently and maintained a Paris apartment in King Louis the XIV's historic Place Du Palais Bourbon. In Manhattan, Lewisesque standards of luxury called for a 15-room, 7-½ bath co-op purchased for $11.5 million from John DeLlorean. Weekend getaways were enjoyed on Long Island in a $4 million Georgian-style mansion.

Charming, irascible, and prone to mood swings, Lewis was as quirky an amalgam of pride, ego, and towering ambition as ever sauntered into a boardroom. Quick to unsheathe his razor-sharp tongue and intellect against adversaries, quaking employees, and even relatives, Lewis achieved one of the more spectacular corporate buyouts in an era of such mega-deals.

But not before he first overcame daunting obstacles and setbacks with a single-mindedness that should inspire not just entrepreneurs but anyone fighting against prohibitive odds, as Lewis did.

Lewis was proud to note that he was the only person ever admitted to Harvard Law School without having so much as submitted an application. But it wasn't a primrose path that Lewis walked—his acceptance into Harvard Law School came only after he had doggedly maneuvered himself into a position where charm and hard work enabled him to crash the gates.

So it was with most of the noteworthy accomplishments of Lewis's life. Nothing came easily or without enormous preparation and dedication on his part. A harbinger that Lewis was not one to be cowed or intimidated by barriers of any kind appeared when he was still a small boy.

I remember being in the bathtub, and my grandmother and grandfather were talking about some incident that had been unfair and was racial in nature. They were talking about work and accomplishing things and how racism was getting in the way of that. And they looked at me and said, "Well, maybe it will be different for him."

I couldn't have been more than about six years old.

One of them, I can't remember whether it was my grandfather or my grandmother, said to me, "Well, is it going to be any different for you?"

And as I was climbing out of the tub and they were putting a towel around me, I looked up and said, "Yeah, cause why should white guys have all the fun?"

This is Reginald Lewis's story.

1

A Kid from East Baltimore

Reginald Francis Lewis was born on December 7, 1942, in a neighborhood of East Baltimore that he liked to characterize as "semi-tough." The Baltimore of the 1940s and 1950s was a city of gentility, slow living, and racial segregation. No one had heard of Martin Luther King . . . or civil rights . . . or integration.

As in other Southern cities of the time, there were many things black people in Baltimore couldn't do. They couldn't try on clothes or shop at many downtown stores. They couldn't eat in certain restaurants or go to certain movie theaters.

East Baltimore was a city within a city. It was mostly made up of black migrants from the South who had come North in search of jobs at area steel mills such as Bethlehem Steel at Sparrow's Point. Lewis grew up in a world marked by block after block of red brick row houses, many of which had outhouses in their backyards. A city ordinance passed in the late 1940s finally outlawed outdoor toilets.

Tucked deep inside East Baltimore was Dallas Street, where Reginald Lewis spent his early years. More akin to an alley than a street because it was so narrow, Dallas Street was also unpaved. Each house had three or four white marble steps leading directly to the front door. The steps served as porches and outdoor chairs.

Although he didn't move to Dallas Street until he was five, Lewis would look back on it years later as a special place.

The street was more a collection of rough rocks and pebbles than anything else, unlike the smooth black asphalt of the streets in better neighborhoods. At 7, it didn't matter that City Hall paved the block just north and just south. That just gave the grown-ups something to talk about all the time. . . . 1022 North Dallas Street, the heart of the ghetto of East Baltimore, is the street where all my dreams got started.

Lewis was born to Clinton and Carolyn Cooper Lewis. Reginald was their only child and not long after his birth, Lewis's young mother took him to her parents's home in East Baltimore. Samuel and Savilla "Sue" Cooper lived at 1022 Dallas Street, in one of the ubiquitous brick row houses.

Carolyn's 6-year-old brother, James, gleefully awaited the arrival of his first nephew. "I can remember the day, the evening—it was starting to get dark—when they brought him home. My sister told me to go upstairs and sit down because I was real fidgety."

James did as he was told and a moment later, Carolyn appeared holding Reginald. "She handed him to me that day and said, 'This is your little brother.' See, I was the little brother and I didn't like being the little brother. That stood out in my mind, because I am no longer the little brother. I am now the big brother."

Carolyn's simple gesture earned Reginald the unwavering support of an uncle, cum older brother, who would fight for Reginald at the drop of a hat, support that would come in handy on the rough-and-tumble streets of East Baltimore. James was one of eight Cooper siblings, all older than Reginald, who played with, pampered, and nurtured the boy. He was also doted on by his grandparents and was the youngest child on his block, making young Reginald the unrivaled center of the universe not just at 1022 Dallas Street, but for the entire 1000 block. And of course, he was his parents's only child.

Reginald Lewis developed a strong sense of self-worth early on, in addition to an expectation that he would be catered to and get his way.

Clinton Lee Lewis, then 25, was a diminutive man with a café au lait complexion, wavy black hair, and high cheekbones. He held several jobs in succession, first as a civilian technician for the Army Signal Corps and later as the proprietor of a series of small businesses, including a radio repair shop and a restaurant. Shortly after the marriage, he left to join the Navy.

Lewis seldom mentioned his father, even to close friends. Business associates who made it their business to study Reginald Lewis drew blanks when it came to his father. No one knew for sure if he was dead or alive.

Lynwood Hart, a college roommate of Lewis's, recalls that, "Reggie saw his father as somebody who didn't have much of a dream. I don't know that he had a lot of respect, though I think he had a certain caring for his father. It was clear to me in the conversations we had about his dad that he thought his dad was an underachiever. One day after stopping by his father's restaurant in Baltimore, I said, 'You never talk about your father.' He said, 'Naw man—I don't know. He could do so much more with his life.'"

Clinton never remarried, and he passed away in 1983, living long enough to glimpse his son's success as a Wall Street lawyer.

Carolyn Cooper Lewis was a light-skinned beauty with expressive brown eyes. Just 17 at the time of Reginald's birth, she was to be a major influence in her son's life. Both as a child and later as a successful businessman, Lewis always exhibited a fierce protectiveness toward her. His aunt, Elaine Cole, noted that, "He loved and adored his mother. In his eyes, she could do no wrong."

Lewis was still a young boy when his mother left Clinton Lewis and moved into her parents's home on Dallas Street. The move into the Cooper household was a seminal experience for Lewis.

My mother left my father when I was 5 and arrived at grandma's house in the middle of the night with me under her arm. Everybody got out of bed. Grandmom and Grandpop, Aunts Charlotte, Beverly, Jean, and Elaine, Uncles James and Donald. Uncle Sam was away in college. Aunt Doris was married and Uncle Robert was in the Air Force. After my grandfather exploded about more mouths to feed, Grandmom asked one of my aunts to take me up to bed. As I went upstairs, I heard my mother say that we would not be a burden, we'd pay our way. That stuck.

It was a lesson that Reginald Lewis would carry with him all his life. Carolyn Lewis looks back on her decision to leave her husband, saying, "My husband and I never had bad feelings. But there are some people you just can't live with. He was into being the head of the entire Lewis clan and at that point, I could not see me fitting into that mold. It gave me no sense of my own identity."

Lewis remembers that "My mom was about 22, and I rarely saw her in the mornings because she was working two jobs—a waitress, and at night a clerk at a department store."

"I wanted for nothing," he later wrote.

Lewis's grandfather, Sam Cooper, held several jobs as well. At one point, he was a waiter at one of Baltimore's fanciest hotels, the Belvedere. At the same time, he waited on tables at the Suburban Club, a Jewish country club in suburban Baltimore, while also working private parties at posh homes.

Sam Cooper was an orderly man who liked everything to be just so at home and at work, a trait he passed on to his grandson. When he came home, the Cooper household had to be neat and clean or there would be hell to pay because Sam had a terrible temper. He never had trouble finding work, which was a good thing because he quit several jobs in fits of pique. His hair-trigger temper apparently had an effect on his grandson, whose own outbursts became legendary.

Sam Cooper would often bring home all kinds of delicious leftovers from work, including frogs' legs, which the children hated, lobster newburg, Smithfield ham, turkey, marvelous desserts, and even champagne, which the children were allowed to have in small portions. Reginald Lewis retained a fondness for quality champagne all his life.

Because of his work, Sam Cooper would not get home until long after the children had gone to bed. To make up for that, he would rise early to cook everyone a big breakfast of eggs, bacon, hot cakes, and hash-brown potatoes.

He would set the table with linen tablecloth and napkins, flatware, and glassware and then he would serve the children as though they were guests in a fine restaurant and he was their waiter.

Despite his initial grumbling, Sam Cooper adored his grandson. "The first time my mother and Carolyn walked in the house with that boy, tears came to daddy's eyes and from that point on, Reggie was daddy's baby," says James, one of Cooper's sons.

In fact, James remembers his father taking Lewis to the Belvedere Hotel, and, with a white towel draped over his left arm, escorting him to a dining room table and serving him lunch, which in Reginald's case usually consisted of a grilled cheese sandwich and tomato soup.

Sue Cooper was a warm, loving, deeply spiritual individual who was also a no-nonsense taskmaster. In addition to raising eight children of her own and two of her sisters's children, she cleaned other people's houses.

She made sure that each child had a job to do, with the youngest children doing the dusting and the older ones washing dishes, scrubbing floors, and helping with the ironing.

Next door to the Cooper house was a vacant lot that over time became filled with trash and broken glass. Sue and the children cleaned it up and planted flowers of all kinds. She set aside an open space in the middle of the lot where she and the children could have picnics and play.

Neither Sam nor Sue Cooper had gone beyond the eighth grade in school but, as one of their daughters put it, "Both had PhDs in common sense." Lewis learned a great deal from his grandparents—how to conduct himself with people from different backgrounds and races, including white people. He noticed that when his grandparents talked to whites, they did so with head erect and gaze unwavering. Sam Cooper emphasized that his children and grandson should always be courteous in their dealings with whites, but never servile.

"Be whatever the situation calls for and if you need to use them, use them. And after you've gotten what you want and where you want to go, then you proceed on," one of Sam's daughters, Lewis's Aunt Charlotte, recalls her father saying.

I feel very good about my base values, which I think is so important that we instill in our young people and children. On this note I think of my grandparents, even more than my mother. My mother was active, having a lot of other children and dealing with all that entails. But my grandparents, I think, had a wonderful facility for programming young people. And being able to convince you that you were someone special, that you had something to bring or something to contribute, too.

I carried that with me a long way. It's been extremely important to me.

Thanks to the Cooper family, I never had a fear of white people. And I think my grandmother always emphasized, "Don't be afraid of them. Be afraid of situations or be concerned in certain situations, but never fear any person—be they black or white." And she never showed any fear in terms of dealing with whites. And that was important, because that wasn't true with a lot of other people that I've known.

Sam Cooper had little tolerance for racism. Shortly after Lewis was born, he thumbed his nose at the firmly entrenched Jim Crow policies of Baltimore by marching into a downtown department store to buy his new grandson a blanket. When he felt like it, he would also "dare" to watch movies in segregated theaters, his self-assurance and fair complexion overcoming any indecision on the part of the cashier who might not be sure if he was white or black.

Despite some early childhood clashes with his grandfather, Reginald Lewis always looked up to Sam and Sue Cooper, who he always referred to as Grandpop and Grandmom. On his periodic visits to Baltimore, he would invariably make it a point to visit them. Years later, he would confide to friends that one of his proudest moments was when, as a successful tycoon, he was able to take his grandfather to lunch at the elegant Harvard Club in New York. Lewis truly valued the years he lived with the Coopers.

I behaved and had a knack for being a real boy but one who also respected his elders. Everybody in the Cooper family worked and went to school. We were sort of a first family of the block. My grandmother always had a helping hand for others, whether the need was advice or food.

The Coopers were also known as a tough family. If you fought one, you had to fight all, including the women. I remember several men getting their heads busted bloody for picking on one of the younger members of our clan. Sometimes injustices were done. Once when I was about 7, my best friend's brother, who was about 14, knocked me around for no reason. I told my uncle, who rounded up a couple of his henchmen to search out the culprit. Unable to find him, they grabbed his brother—my best friend—and kicked his ass instead. I didn't have a best friend for a few days, although I did speak out as he got slapped around. My uncles said the guilty brother would get the message. He did.

Early on, Lewis displayed a talent for sports. He was extraordinarily competitive, and it was important to him to get on the playing field, even if most of the time he was much younger and smaller than the other players.

Dallas Street also served as an athletic field, where all the boys played a brand of touch football that made tackle seem mild by comparison. We skinned our knees and elbows as a matter of course. For the big games, usually around the end of fall, we'd go to the park with makeshift helmets; some of us had them and some didn't. There were also second-hand shoulder pads and assorted equipment that left you feeling unbalanced until the first hit. All my friends were about 12 or 13 and sometimes in those games I would not get to play a lot. The boys were afraid I might get hurt, meaning they would have to answer to my uncles and aunts or even disappoint my grandmother, Mrs. Cooper.

On those occasions when the football in play happened to belong to Lewis and he was on the sidelines, the game was abruptly terminated. If neither team picked him, he would instantly snatch up his ball and leave, oblivious to the angry stares—and comments—of the other children.

By the time he was seven, Lewis's mother enrolled him in a nearby Catholic school.

I went to St. Francis Xavier, a Catholic elementary school about five blocks from Dallas Street. A couple of my younger aunts went there before me and my youngest uncle tried, but was thrown out on his ear for being too advanced. The Oblate Sisters were the teachers, and they were rough. My mother, who had gone to public school, always bragged about her son going to "parochial school."

As I think back on it, the place left a lot to be desired, but the discipline was good and the sports programs, though ragtag, were pretty good. The nuns would slap you around at the drop of a hat, sometimes for nothing. I really hated this, and let a few know it early with terrible tantrums when I was in the right. So they generally left me alone, especially since the priests liked me a lot because of my grandmother's work for the church and my sports ability. Science programs were virtually nonexistent at the school, but social studies were very strong. I was about a B or B+ student in later years, but did not feel real strong academically.

St. Francis Xavier was located on Central Avenue in East Baltimore, inside an imposing four-story brick building surrounded by a black wrought-iron fence. It had kindergarten through eighth grade. Before leaving for school, little Reginald Lewis would don a pair of blue pants, white shirt, blue tie, and thick-soled black-and-white leather shoes.

The Oblate Sisters of Providence ran the school and are an Afrocentric order founded in Baltimore in 1829 by Elizabeth Lange, a Haitian immigrant who courageously educated African-American children in her own home during a time when enslaved blacks were forbidden to read and write. The Sisters wore black and white habits with silver crucifixes dangling from their necks. They practiced what has come to be known as "tough love." Lewis's aunt, Elaine, recalls that "if you did the wrong thing, you got cracked on the hands with a ruler. You didn't fool around too much there—some of those nuns were pretty big."

The mischievous and strong-willed Lewis had several run-ins with the nuns. His lasting impression of Catholic schools was influenced by a put-down he received from a nun who told him that he would never amount to anything more than a carpenter. Years later, Lewis swore to his wife that their children would never set foot in a Catholic school.

Meanwhile, because of his mother's many jobs, Lewis wasn't seeing much of her. His aunt Elaine would often babysit him until his mother came home. "I was supposed to watch over him and that was it. He used to get mad, though, when his mother wasn't home. He used to say to himself, 'Yeah, she'll be home when the moon turns blue.'"

Carolyn Lewis was a working mother with a demanding schedule, but she always found time for her son and remained a major influence in his life. "I wanted him to look a certain way at all times. I was really hard on the poor child. When I came home from work, I always wanted him to look spiffy. The poor child used to get around three baths a day.

My mother would bathe him and he would get his clothes changed. So when five o'clock came and I came home, he would greet me. He'd look really great. He wanted dungarees so bad and I said no, you just can't have them. I think it was on his seventh or eighth birthday, my mother bought him a pair of jeans and he thought that was the greatest thing. I think my mother went up on a shrine when she bought him those jeans!"

One time, Lewis lost several buttons from his shirt while horsing around with a friend. Frantically searching for a quick fix, he ran to the home of a neighbor. "Miss Isabelle," Lewis implored, "Miss Isabelle, you're gonna have to sew these buttons on before my mother gets home. My mother is not going to like this." He was eventually rescued by his grandmother, who changed his shirt.

Lewis revered his mother and he wouldn't tolerate anyone bad-mouthing her. Dan Henson, a high school friend of Lewis's, recalls one day when he was playing what's known as "the dozens," a timeless game of oneupmanship played in the black community where insults were hurled back and forth between verbal combatants.

Lewis didn't play the dozens. But one day as he was heading home, Henson goaded a friend of his into taunting Lewis about his mother. "I put him up to talking about Reggie's mama, because I knew what was going to happen to him," Henson recounts. At first, Lewis kept on walking and ignored the insults. So Henson whispered to his friend, "Come on man, he didn't hear you. He didn't hear you."

Henson's friend obliged by shouting something like, "Your mama wears combat boots," whereupon Lewis turned around and hit him in the throat. "The guy went down and started crying," Henson recalls with a chuckle.

Lewis generally lived a happy, relatively care-free existence in East Baltimore. He was the center of attention and never lacked for playmates, affection or life's necessities. Best of all, he had no rivals for the woman he adored the most in life, his mother.

A NEW FAMILY

The last part of that equation was about to change dramatically re-ordering Reginald Lewis's universe. His mother had met Jean Fugett, a young soldier based at the Edgewood Arsenal, an Army installation north of Baltimore. Two years later, in February 1951, they were married.

His mother did her best to prepare Lewis. She had always told him, "Through thick and thin, it's the two of us. You can depend on the Lord, yourself, and me." She assured him that her marriage "would not diminish my love, because there's a certain love you have for a child and there's a certain love you have for a husband. It's like comparing apples and oranges. I was not asking him for instantaneous love for Butch (Jean Fugett's nickname), but for respect. And in time, see what it brings. I said, 'You're gaining—you're gaining your own room, you're gaining the friendship of another person. You haven't lost anything. You've gained a whole lot.'" Years later, Lewis would look back on the era when a new man entered his mother's life.

My mother remarried when I was about 9 and moved from Grandmom's to West Baltimore. My stepfather, Jean S. Fugett, Sr., was a terrific man who worked two jobs and also went to college to finish his degree. He taught me that sometimes what appears to be a complicated problem can have a simple solution. After they were married, he could tell for about a month that I was very intense and uneasy around him. Finally, one day we were alone and he asked, "What's the problem?" I said something like, "I don't know what to call you!" He said, "That's simple. Call me Butch, and don't worry so much." It was a terrific lesson and we got along great. There is no person I respect more than him.

Fugett remembers Lewis as a typical youngster. "He'd be out in the street playing catch with his uncles or other guys his age or a little older. He always believed in playing with people older than himself. He thought he improved himself faster that way."

Originally from Westchester, Pa., Fugett felt at ease around Carolyn's big clan. He left the Army after Carolyn told him that she was "not going to marry anybody who stays in the Army." He began working at the post office at night and going to school at Morgan State College in Baltimore during the day.

Carolyn Lewis made it clear that her son would always be a major priority in her life. "Butch knew that Reginald would be my main consideration, along with him, because there were certain things that were due to Reginald—there were certain things that I had placed on my drawing board before I met Butch. Reginald would have the best that I could afford: he would have a good education and he'd be able to go to college wherever he wanted to go. That's what I had worked toward when I met Butch. He had no problem with that."

The family left East Baltimore and moved to the West Side, which was more upscale. Fugett used the GI bill to buy a row house at 2802 Mosher Street.

Soon I had a younger brother named Jean Jr. Well, for me this was a big event. I felt a special responsibility toward him and began to plan his future right away. I was about 9 or 10. The other brothers and sisters came rapidly: next Anthony, then the twins, Joseph and Rosalyn, and finally Sharon. They were all about a year and a half apart. These were tough years for my mother. I am very proud that she did not have to worry about taking care of me. I could, and did, take care of myself.

Lewis's fierce pride and independence sometimes proved problematic. He and his mother possessed strong personalities and occasionally butted heads. "We had plenty of disagreements," Carolyn says. "My ideas and his ideas didn't always coincide on how we should do things. He had a strong will and so did I."

Fed up after one disagreement, a seething Lewis stalked to his room on the second floor of the Fugett home. One of the Fugett children rushed down to tell his mother that Lewis was packing a bag. She went upstairs and asked him what he was doing.

"Well, maybe this is not the place for me," he replied.

"That may be true, but let's think about it for a minute. Here, you have your own room and, I would say, a lot of freedom. If you went with your grandmother, you would not have your own room and no freedom. If you went with your father, you would have plenty of freedom, but no privacy. So where does it leave you to go? The only alternative I see is the Baltimore City Jail, where you have nothing. So those are your options. You decide what you want from me, decide what you want from yourself, then you'll decide where you want to live," Carolyn Fugett said. She then left the room and went back downstairs.

"I went to my kitchen window and looked out to my garden, because I loved my garden. I was very prayerful that I had said the right thing and left it on the altar of the Lord as to which way it was going to go," she remembers.

In time, Lewis came downstairs and said, "I'm going out for a while," and stepped out. "It was never discussed after that," his mother says.

Early on, Lewis seems to have decided he was on his own in life, perhaps feeling left out as the family increased and his mother had less time for him.

Years later, many of Lewis's classmates at school and his colleagues at work would view him as a loner. He took on a number of jobs to ensure that no one would ever have to worry about Reginald Lewis being a financial burden.

At 10 he got his first job selling the local black newspaper, the *Baltimore Afro-American*. Displaying unusual discipline and responsibility for someone so young, he increased the route from 10 customers to more than 100. Along with nasty dogs and bad weather, Lewis had to contend with deadbeat subscribers. The task of handling delinquent accounts fell not to him, but to someone more formidable—his mother.

"He was trained not to argue with people; he turned them over to me," she says. Carolyn Fugett still recalls how she shamed late payers into making good. "This is a job for him; it's not a recreation. It's a job. It's just like your job. When payday comes, don't you want your paycheck? That's the way it is for him. When he collects on Saturday and he figures out his paper bill, he should have a profit. He must show a profit every Saturday, so there will be an incentive for him to add on more papers, and that's why I'm asking you to pay on time."

If those early lessons in no-nonsense negotiating failed to sink in, Carolyn had yet another one in store for her son. She delivered it after Lewis attended summer camp, leaving the paper route in his mother's dependable hands.

While her son was gone, she diligently delivered the *Afro* on Tuesdays and Fridays, the days it came out—while pushing Jean Jr. in his baby carriage. A neighbor with a small child joined in and she and Carolyn pushed their carriages together while delivering newspapers around the sweltering streets of West Baltimore.

After a few weeks, Lewis's summer camp ended. He came home eagerly anticipating a windfall from his paper route. "You want to settle up?" he asked.

"What are we going to settle up?" his mother replied.

"The money!" Lewis replied.

His mother reminded him that she had done all the work while he was away and therefore the money was hers. "But that's not the way it's supposed to be. I'm gonna get me a lawyer. I'm gonna sue you!" her son told her.

Jean Fugett intervened and suggested that his wife give their son his paper route profits. She complied, but Lewis's lesson wasn't over yet.

"Now let me tell you something. It's good to start the way you're going to finish. Now you didn't explain to me that this was the procedure—we just agreed that I would sell the papers. So I believe I should keep the money, because I did the job. Is that right or wrong?" Carolyn Fugett told her son.

Lewis replied, "You're right."

"Set your terms up front," Carolyn told him.

Having successfully grown the *Afro* paper route, Lewis moved on to a new challenge. He began to deliver the *Baltimore News American*, which was more profitable but also more demanding, because it came out daily instead of two days a week. He sold the *Afro-American* route to his friend, Dan Henson.

"I was probably his first leveraged buyout," says Henson, who later went on to become a successful real estate developer and the housing commissioner for Baltimore. "If I remember correctly, $30 was the price. Of course $30 was like a million dollars to me at that time, and to him. Thirty dollars was probably a fair price; it just turned out to be more than I should have paid. I think $2.50 was what I was supposed to pay him every week. No interest. There were some weeks that I couldn't pay. He got mad and we'd yell at each other. He'd make it clear that a deal was a deal and that we shook hands on it. And we'd have to fight," Henson recalls.

Lewis, who was bigger than his friend, always got the better of those contests. "Reggie was pretty good and he was quick with his fists. He hit me in the stomach one time and I thought I would never recover. I could beat most of the kids in the neighborhood, but nobody messed with Reggie. Not unless you were crazy. And keep in mind, there's a real difference between a guy who can handle himself and you don't mess with him and a guy who's a bully. Reggie was not a bully," Henson says.

As the oldest child, Lewis liked to assume a certain mantle of authority around the Fugett household, acting at times like a surrogate parent. This, however, did not always sit well with his younger brothers and sisters.

Joseph Fugett remembers that when Lewis was asked to babysit, he would order his siblings upstairs to their rooms, then watch television by himself. Occasionally he would summon one of the detainees to fetch him a steak submarine sandwich, potato chips, and a milkshake from the neighborhood deli. Lewis's instructions were precise: the bread was to be grilled, not toasted; the mayonnaise was to be spread on only one side of the sandwich; the milkshake was to be made from strawberry syrup not sauce; and don't forget the potato chips!

Joseph and his sisters would get back at Lewis by occasionally stealing the chocolate chip cookies Lewis hoarded in a special place and counted as he ate.

"Reginald was treated very special," Carolyn Fugett agrees. "When I married Jean, Reggie had his own room. Regardless of how many children came, he didn't have to share his room. He had his own room and his own things and the rule of the house was that they didn't bother his things."

HIGH SCHOOL YEARS

In the ninth grade, I had to go to public school. I knew the choice of a high school was important and that I could not leave it to my mother alone. So I asked around. Actually going through the school selection process was probably the first independent research I ever did. I couldn't get into the Catholic high schools, because my test scores apparently were not strong enough. It was just as well.

On this matter, mother and son's recollections diverge. That he wasn't accepted into Catholic schools they agree. But Carolyn's rationale was different. "It was rare in his day for a Catholic high school to take a person of color in," his mother says. "We're talking about, uh, I wouldn't say racism, because I don't like to use that word. Because sometimes ignorance is more prevalent than racism, you know? I find that people are very frightened of the unknown. They don't know what to expect from Negroes, black folks, or whomever. So in that fear, they move to isolate them. And I think that's what I was facing as a parent with Reginald coming up, trying to get him into the best high school that he wanted to go to. He had to face rejection at an early age."

Carolyn Fugett put the best possible face on the situation, and told her son it was the Catholic school's loss. Still, the episode pained her. "It was very difficult to really put it in words, because you were trying to teach them the love of God and bring them up in Catholic surroundings. But see, man's way is not God's way and I told him that there will come a day that he can work toward those things. It was a no-win situation—we didn't labor over it."

Jean Fugett, who had come to the same conclusion, says he saw the teenager who had once been an altar boy drift away from the Catholic Church after being turned away from Catholic schools.

Lewis had a choice of at least three public high schools in West Baltimore that had black student populations. He chose Dunbar, an East Baltimore school named after African-American poet Paul Lawrence Dunbar. High school brought with it an exciting new phase in Lewis's life.

2

Lewis's "Demon Work Ethic": The High School Years

It's been said that your high school years tend to be some of the best of your life, and that you will never again be as free of commitments and worries.

Serious beyond his years and determined to succeed, Reginald Lewis immersed himself totally into high school, where he excelled in football, baseball, and basketball. He also began to exhibit a demon work ethic, toiling after school to earn extra spending money.

Overcrowded and with less modern facilities than its white counterparts, Dunbar nevertheless had a good reputation academically. A large percentage of its students went on to college and those who could not make the grade were "pushed out," in the words of Dr. Elzee Gladden, a former Dunbar principal.

The school had an all-black faculty that took pride in its profession. Dunbar teachers drummed into their students that in order to succeed, dedication and commitment to excellence were critical.

Dunbar also had a mystique about it in the 1950s that persists to this day because of its fabled athletic teams. It was a point of pride within the black community each time Dunbar walloped white high schools.

I chose Dunbar for its sports coach, the famous Bill "Sugar" Cain. Dunbar was great. The school was known for its great basketball team and for sports generally. What was not so well known was that the A course for each grade level was absolutely superb academically. I was accepted into the "in crowd" right away because of my ability in sports.

Athletics were a big part of Lewis's life at Dunbar and football was his first love. He and an old friend, Red Scott, tried out for the school's junior varsity football squad with Scott winning a starting guard position and Lewis becoming Dunbar's starting quarterback. Under his guidance, the team had a winning season the 1957–58 school year, although it didn't win a championship.

Lewis's physique filled out in high school, where he stood about 5-foot-10, weighed roughly 170 pounds, and had a well-developed upper body to complement athletic, well-muscled legs. In addition to his deliberate manner and coolness under pressure, his greatest asset in football was a powerful right arm. He could pass with finesse if need be, but preferred to fling stinging line drives to his receivers and backs.

Lewis's unrelenting drive and confidence made him a natural leader. In addition, he was good and he knew it.

In all modesty, I was a hell of a performer. I earned four varsity letters in baseball, three in football—where I was the starting quarterback from my sophomore year on, and two varsity letters in basketball. In football, I believed there were only two passers in Maryland worthy of mention—Johnny Unitas and me. I could put the ball on a dime from 40 yards. And when I played, I never doubted my ability and could look into the eyes of my teammates when the heat was really on and tell who could perform and who couldn't.

I also learned that the voice and the eyes in the huddle could make a real difference. When you said, "Okay, we're going in," you had to mean it and you had to deliver. I generally had the reputation that I came to play and that I was serious about the game.

There was one contest in particular that Lewis would always treasure. State scholastic officials had just relaxed a prohibition against black high schools playing against white high schools in contact sports.

Dunbar was scheduled to go up against Polytechnic Institute, a white high school from the West Side.

Many of Dunbar's players were pessimistic about the game, recalls Lewis's teammate, Clarence "Tiger" Davis. They expected to lose, but were determined to at least keep the score close, lest they embarrass themselves and the black community.

But not Reginald Lewis. He viewed Poly as just another opponent and reprimanded his teammates for having defeatist attitudes. Before the big contest, he told Coach Cain, "Coach, I play to win."

"Sometimes, Reggie would be so intense you'd think he was going to explode. He was so serious that when he smiled, he made everybody else laugh, you know what I mean?" Davis, now a Maryland state legislator recalls, laughing himself.

Lewis trained for the game with the same focus and preparation that he brought to everything in life. "He was a tremendous competitor, he was a take-charge type of guy," his teammate Scott says. "You couldn't joke at all in the huddle. He would say, 'Hey, no talking. Shut up—shut up!' We had a no-nonsense coach, Sugar Cain. And everybody in East Baltimore wanted us to win. It was serious to us, we wanted to win, we wanted to beat the predominantly white schools. We all practiced hard—we trained like we were Marines at Parris Island boot camp. The guys were really vicious in blocking, tackling, things like that. We had a tremendous team."

The hard work paid off with a stirring victory that bolstered Lewis's already considerable faith in himself. The local newspapers started calling him "Bullet Lewis."

I experienced my greatest highs in football, especially going up against bigger schools with better equipment and generally better programs. I led Dunbar to victory against Poly, a large white school for boys that was famous for its football team. The newspaper headline "Dunbar Upsets Poly in Rough Contest" was heady, heady stuff for a 15-year-old sophomore in his first start of the season.

Lewis was a leader off the field as well. "I had a problem once, right?" Davis says. "I was a father at 16 and it was getting to me. Reggie knew it was getting to me one time when I got kicked out of a football game for unnecessary roughness. I was Reggie's center and he didn't like that at all, because my job was to protect him. To be quite frank, I had suicide—everything—running through my head, right? Reggie was pissed off about it because he thought I was being weak and sentimental, I think."

Lewis confronted Davis off the field and challenged him: "Are you going to lay down or get up? This isn't the only time in life you're going to have a problem, so you may as well be a man about it now."

Putting his arms around Davis, Lewis said, "Hey Tiger, man, you're too important to the team."

"I really appreciated that and I'll never forget him for that. There was a lot of love in that, too," Davis recalls. "The reason you couldn't be mad at him for the things that he said was: One, he was right and: Two, there was no question about his trying to motivate me and get me up."

His teammates looked up to Lewis even though he was a tough taskmaster. On Mondays, he would have them run more laps than Coach Cain called for. Davis remembers Lewis exhorting the team, "Come on, let's get that weekend out of us."

Even the fact that he was from West Baltimore did not diminish the esteem in which Lewis was held. "We always thought that West Baltimoreans thought they were better than us," says east sider Davis. "They always acted grandiose in the presence of East Baltimoreans. But Reggie was not like that."

However, Lewis never did become one of the boys. The focused manchild remained aloof from most of the juvenile joking and cavorting the other players frequently engaged in. For example, the first-stringers had a ritual of buying miniatures of scotch or gin for 35 cents apiece before a game, then knocking them back with dispatch.

Lewis would stand off to one side observing. He never criticized, but never joined in, either.

Lewis never had much of a taste for alcohol as a young man, largely because he was an athlete, but also due to an incident that took place during a gathering at the Cooper house when he was five years old. "He loved soda," James Cooper recounts. "They were having a party one day and he and I were drinking the soda. But he couldn't distinguish between a drink of liquor and a drink of soda. My aunt drank 100 proof Granddad and left her cup and her chaser sitting out. I drank the chaser and he drank the Granddad. Never again did he drink any more liquor, until he was grown."

Lewis's athletic prowess wasn't confined to football. He was also a shortstop for Dunbar's baseball team. Once again, it was his commitment and drive to succeed that brought him notice on the playing field.

"He was a kid that if you didn't know him, you may have gotten the impression he was egotistical and in love with himself," says Dick Brown, Lewis's junior varsity baseball coach. "But it was his drive. He had one thing that I can always appreciate and that I always tried to instill into my athletes: That is, 'I am the best. I am the greatest.' That drive, that desire for excellence eventually made him the man he became. It was already in him at Dunbar.

"He was always on time, he was always doing something to improve himself in whatever he did. He was one of the persons who come along rarely. I realized that he was different back then, but I didn't expect him to go as far as he did."

Brown, who also taught math at Dunbar and retired from coaching baseball in 1991, knew Lewis longer than any of the teenager's other instructors, because Brown's daughter had been a classmate of Lewis's at St. Francis Xavier. Even though Lewis set exacting standards for himself and for his teammates, he could be tolerant of others when they made errors.

"He felt that if a guy pulled a boner, the guy felt bad enough as it was, so you didn't have to ride him. He would say, 'Don't worry about it, you did your best.' He'd try to find a nice way of getting on the kid's back without insulting the kid," Brown remembers.

Lewis fielded his shortstop position well. He displayed little emotion, even if calls went against him, and could hit for power. Tiger Davis remembers him studying pitchers and says Lewis would maul fastballs. Curveballs were another matter—they represented a mystery he never did unravel.

"In basketball, he was basically a bench-warmer, a last-minute substitute when a Dunbar victory appeared assured," says teammate Red Scott. They were both guards at a school often ranked the top prep basketball school in the nation. A number of Dunbar players have gone on to play in the National Basketball Association.

Even in a limited role, however, the Lewis drive was on display. "He was a ball hawk, I can tell you that," Scott says of Lewis's court style.

"He wanted the ball ALL the time. Not to pass it—to shoot it. And he really didn't have a good shot, but every time you'd look up he was calling for the ball."

"TRYING TO CONQUER THE WORLD, KID?"

While sports was a big part of Lewis's world in high school, so was work. Perhaps emulating his stepfather, who was moonlighting as a cab driver, working full-time in the post office job, taking classes at Morgan, and playing on the football team, Lewis took on an exceptionally heavy workload for someone in high school.

While in high school, I had jobs in my junior and senior years. During the week, I worked in a drugstore from six o'clock until ten o'clock following sports practice, which lasted from three o'clock until five o'clock. Then, maybe I'd have a late date from ten-thirty to midnight, and would be home by one o'clock. I would get about four hours of sleep, maybe an hour of study, a quick look at the sports and business pages and then I'd make a mad dash for school, which was across town.

At 16, I made a big decision. Instead of playing baseball during the summer six days a week, I took a full-time job at a country club where my grandfather worked as a captain. The pay was $50 a week—no tips permitted—but if you picked the right members to give that little extra effort to, they would find a way to "take care of you."

I learned a lot working there, both from the staff and the members. From the staff, the virtues of being a real pro. My grandfather, Captain Sam, took tremendous pride in his work and other waiters really respected him a lot. People who were really good did not have to take a lot of "shit." Not taking a lot of shit was the goal of every employee there.

The only sure way to avoid the bull from the bosses was to know your stuff and mind your own business. The more conscientious staff members always watched their drinking—alcoholism was a real problem. As an athlete, this was never even a slight temptation for me. I never smoked until my sophomore year of college.

From the members of the club, I learned that talk is cheap. I knew that already from my mother's family, the Coopers, but here among so-called rich people it became really clear. A lot of the club members talked a good game, but I could tell they were not on top of their game. It showed in how they treated the staff.

One incident I remember in particular was when a quite nice lady had a special party and I busted my gut to make the service great—not only my own, but that of other workers, too. I was 17 at the time. After the party, she pulled me aside when everyone had left. She did the talking and it went something like this: "Reggie, you know your skin is dark, so you have to work harder. One day, I am sure you'll make a good living." One part of her message was fine, but her style was patronizing. The other part of what she said implied inferiority. She then gave me $2.

I thanked her with a nod and probably a quick look that unsettled her a little but was in no way threatening. Almost immediately, I felt sort of an athletic surge go through my body, but remained controlled and thought to myself, "You poor soul, you don't know who stands before you. A good living! I plan to, and I will have more money than you will ever have, and I'll have the good sense to recognize superior performance and not embarrass myself by giving only a $2 tip."

In fact, my grandfather asked me what her tip was. I didn't answer and he said something like, "You're right, son, keep it to yourself. Whatever it was, it doesn't matter—you did a helluva job. If she tipped you at all, it's an accomplishment because word is she never tips and her status with the club is a little shaky. Always remember, your skill is what's important. Get that and build on it and sooner or later you'll have a big payday—count on it."

It came fast. I had a big party of businessmen that had cocktails, dinner, and then played poker. I stayed late and did a real number. I was the last person on the staff to leave—members with families left sooner. In fact, even the parking attendants had taken off. When I saw that, I raced to the lot and started bringing up the cars one after another. Guys were slapping all kinds of money in my hand and saying thanks. Finally, at about 3 A.M., the man who threw the party and who had told me to go home about three times that evening—and who was cold sober unlike the others—took me by the arm.

He looked me right in the eye and said, "Holy shit, kid, what are you trying to do, conquer the world?" There was a little moment that passed between the two of us as we looked each other in the eye, then he gave this little knowing smile, slapped a C note in my hand and said, "Helluva job, son." I knew he was right. I made about $500 that night, about 10 times my weekly salary.

My last year at the club ended when I was 18. The manager was disappointed that I didn't work there through college, but I decided I could make more money in a union job at a brewery. But from time to time I would work at the club during weekends until my sophomore year of college.

SETTING HIGH GOALS

The Suburban Club, a private Jewish club in Baltimore County just a stone's throw from the city line, led to one of the few enduring friendships of Lewis's life. Ellis Goodman, a working-class white kid from West Baltimore, was the same age as Lewis and also in need of spending money. The ambitious teenagers used to talk about their hopes and dreams for the future.

Goodman, who worked in the food supply room in the basement, had his sights set on becoming a U.S. senator. Lewis told Goodman, "I know that what I'd like to be is the richest black man in America." Nearly thirty years later, Goodman—by then a successful lawyer and real estate developer—and his wife Marcie met Lewis at the Harvard Club in Manhattan, one of Lewis's favorite haunts.

"He said to Marcie, 'You know, Ellis wanted to be a United States senator.' And we laughed and she said, 'What did you want to be?' He said, 'Well, I wanted to be the richest black man in America.' And we laughed, because that was in his thought process. He really was one of the consummate goal setters," Goodman recalls.

Back in their Suburban Club days, Goodman watched Lewis realize goals on a smaller scale. "He succeeded in getting what was a plum job," Goodman recalls. "And the plum was to be a waiter assigned to the women's cardroom. The reason that was a plum was because it put you in a position of being able to receive tips, whereas you didn't receive tips as a regular busboy or waiter in the dining room."

In the women's cardroom, there were no heavy trays to lug around. The most strenuous duty was having to carry coffee, tea, and sandwiches to the tables of women playing canasta.

"He knew how to take care of those women, and it was clearly an older, almost elderly group who were the card players at the Suburban Club. He had a sense of remembering their names—if somebody would pass by, invariably he knew their name and always addressed people by their names."

Goodman followed the stock market as a teenager and used to seek out a chef who was a stock market buff. Lewis sat in on many of those conversations, and would ask Goodman to explain things after the chef left the room. One topic never broached during Goodman's and Lewis's wide-ranging discussions was race. "It just never came up," says Goodman.

"He was really a mature fellow in high school," says William Smith, a member of Lewis's class voted least likely to succeed who later went on to become a dentist and Army colonel. "Reggie knew how to read a stock market sheet. I didn't even know what a stock market sheet was."

With his busy schedule, Lewis had become something of a phantom at home. "He was never there," Tony Fugett says. "He would always come in late, like after practice, because he played sports and he would always leave real early. So it wasn't like he was at the house a lot."

The brothers became extremely close later in life, but while Lewis was in high school they were "very, very distant. We just didn't have a lot in common and we didn't share much. He saw himself as a little man, . . . not a high school kid."

Lewis wasn't home much, agrees his eldest brother, Jean Fugett, Jr. "What I remember about Reg was that he was always working. He would come home from school, athletic practice, or work and then spend the rest of the evening on his homework," he says.

"Back then, this puzzled me. I didn't see the payoff for doing the homework at the time. Now, of course, I do," says Fugett, who went on to graduate cum laude from Amherst and then proceeded to get a law degree from George Washington University while playing football for the Washington Redskins.

"Reg was always focusing on the future. The next accomplishment. The next objective. It was as if he was always preparing himself for something," Fugett adds.

A schoolmate of Lewis's, Robert Bell, now a judge on the Maryland Court of Appeals, recalls how Lewis worked one job after another. Bell worked with Lewis a few times—he vividly remembers one minimum-wage gig he took at Lewis's urging that turned out to be "one of the worst experiences I've ever had." During a college football game at Memorial Stadium, Lewis arranged for Bell to get a job filling soda cups while Lewis hawked them to the crowd. Bell apparently failed to sign the required paperwork, however, resulting in a day's work with no pay.

Another of Lewis's money-making schemes had them pulling a float along a downtown boulevard in a Thanksgiving Day parade, labor for which Bell not only got paid but received a free box lunch.

Although these endeavors were rare for Bell, they were common-place for Lewis. His hectic schedule took its toll on his grades. He was ranked 118th out of 196 students when he graduated from Dunbar.

Academically, I spent time on history and the social sciences, but never caught up on the sciences. To this day, I feel inadequate in biology and physics. I didn't know where to start or even get help. I muddled through and hate to admit most of my lab experiments were copied word for word from other students. I would like to do physics over.

Fatigue from playing three sports, holding down several jobs, and studying would sometimes overcome Lewis in the classroom. His class-mates would catch him fast asleep behind his French book. "Reggie would be asleep big time," William Smith, one of his classmates, recalls with a chuckle. "He'd appear to be looking down at the book, but he had this remarkable ability to get back into things if he was called upon, as if nothing had ever happened. He shucked and jived his way through a lot of classes."

"Reggie was not a brilliant student in high school," Bell agrees. "He was a smart fella—everybody knew that. He was a much smarter person than his average or his grades reflected. He had all this stuff that he was doing and still managed to do reasonably well. I know he wasn't in the top 10 percent of the class, but he was not anywhere near the bottom of the class, either. His intelligence was reflected after he left high school."

Despite his many commitments, Lewis still found time to run for vice president of the student council in his senior year. Taking a cue from Jean Fugett, Sr., he and his running mate, Robert Bell, followed the cardinal axiom of modern politics: Get your name before the public as early and as extensively as possible. The boys plastered "Bell & Lewis" posters throughout the halls of Dunbar before the school year started. An easy victory followed.

At Dunbar, Lewis sailed through life with such equanimity, most of his schoolmates had the impression nothing could trigger his ire. He was a big man on campus, a bonafide sports triple threat. He never resorted to fisticuffs at school, where he was seen as mature beyond his years, "a man among kids," as classmate Richard McCoy puts it. Lewis also had a rakish, womanizing reputation that he didn't discourage.

Lewis had taken to putting waves in his hair, which he parted slightly left of center. He possessed piercing black eyes and an attractive smile that he rarely displayed, perhaps because he was self-conscious about the gap between his front teeth, a lifelong concern.

One amorous interlude got him into a perilous spot. He had to rely on a rescuer from days past, his uncle James, to extricate him. James Cooper, who was married and had a place of his own by then, received a tense telephone call from his nephew.

"I got some problems," Lewis told Cooper and asked him to meet him at an address in East Baltimore. Cooper took a friend named Billy and went over. He rapped on the front door and saw Lewis look out the window. "What's the matter?" Cooper asked him.

"I can't come out. That guy over there is going to get me," Lewis replied. Cooper finally convinced Lewis to come outside. At this point, a man about Cooper's age walked over to them and said, "I'm gonna shoot him."

"For what?" Cooper replied.

"Cause he was in there with my girl," the man said as he pulled out a .22 pistol.

Cooper himself had brought along a .25 automatic which he drew and placed against the man's head. "If you gotta shoot, shoot me," Cooper told him. Then, turning to his friend Billy and Lewis, he said, "Go get in the car and leave."

Neither Lewis nor Billy moved. Cooper and the man had their guns pointed at each other. "I told them to leave because I knew this fool wasn't going to shoot. I said, 'Leave!' so they got in the car and drove up the street," Cooper says.

After a few tense seconds, the man finally told Cooper, "Man, I don't want no trouble out of you."

"I don't want no trouble out of you," Cooper said. Both then put away their guns.

"I walked up the street, they picked me up, we left, and that was the end of that. I think that's the last time I came to Reggie's rescue. I think the guy was really out to frighten him, more than to hurt him. I never did see the girl," Cooper says.

Even as a teenager, Lewis was very image-conscious, a trait that he kept through the years. At Dunbar, he wore tweed jackets, tapered pants, loafers, and thin, British neckties, in keeping with a fad known as the "collegiate" style. In one of his class photos, Lewis is decked out in a white shirt and tie and appears dressed for the boardroom rather than the classroom.

"When Reggie came in and didn't have a tie on, he looked kind of odd," classmate Ralph Williams remembers. "I guess that was just an inkling of things to come."

At the other end of the fashion spectrum from the collegiates were the "slickers," who favored big, floppy hats, pleated baggy trousers, and pointed-toe shoes. Lewis never chose to follow this style of dress.

In keeping with a pledge he made not to be a financial burden on his family, Lewis clothed himself while at Dunbar. "Reginald was practical, he really saved his money," Carolyn Fugett says. "He wanted this pair of shoes and it just amazed me that the shoes were so expensive. And he said, 'Mom, it's my money and I think I can spend it anyway I want.' And I said, 'Fine.' But when I look back on it now, that pair of leather shoes carried him from the 11th grade through law school. He was a master at planning."

A SPORTS CAR FOR LEWIS

In the early 1960s, at a school filled with working-class black kids, it was unusual for anyone to have a car. Here again, Lewis was different, putting his hard-earned extra dollars to use.

High school was a lot of fun. The girls were also great. I dated quite a few upper-class girls and in my senior year bought my own convertible—an English car, a Hillman.

Lewis spotted the car as he was going home from school on the bus. He noticed that the roadster was parked in the same place every day. Finally, one day Lewis got off the bus, looked up the car's owner and asked him if the car was for sale. "Anything is for sale if the price is right," the owner said. Lewis negotiated a price of $600. There was one small problem though. Lewis couldn't afford to pay both the $600 as well as the insurance payments.

To get the Hillman, Lewis made a rare financial request of his parents. He would pay for the car if Jean Fugett, Sr. would handle the insurance for him. The arrangement strained the family budget, according to Carolyn Fugett. But Jean Fugett, impressed that Lewis had worked so hard and saved to buy a car, found ways to make the insurance payments. He accompanied Lewis to pick up the vehicle.

"Reg was particular about who he let ride in it," Fugett remembers. "He used to tell his friends, 'If you didn't walk with me, you're not going to ride with me.'"

Tony and Jean Fugett, Jr. were playing in front of 2802 Mosher Street when their big brother glided up behind the wheel of his beloved Hillman. The purchase caught them totally by surprise. "It was great, he kind of rolled around the corner with it," Tony Fugett says. "We saw it and we said, 'You know, we really would like to go for a ride.' And he said, 'Hey, no problem, you can go for a ride—as soon as you finish washing it.'"

Other than Lewis, just one other senior at school had a car and he was the son of a well-to-do doctor. What made Lewis's acquisition even more remarkable was that his car wasn't some utilitarian appliance. In keeping with his well-developed sense of style and taste, Lewis's car was a sports car, and an imported one at that.

For some of his classmates, Lewis's cream-colored English convertible confirmed suspicions that he was really a bourgeois, superior West Baltimorean after all. "He brought an air about him from West Baltimore," classmate Richard McCoy remembers. "When you come from West Baltimore to East Baltimore, East Baltimoreans expect a certain kind of individual to exist over here. Reggie was, ah—his presentation as far as demeanor was concerned was a little too classy. He came to Dunbar with a demeanor that was, 'I'm a little better than you folks, anyway.' He had a car—who else had a car? He dressed immaculately and in expensive clothing. Half of us didn't have shoes to go to our proms with."

"Even so, no one harbored animosity toward Lewis, at least not outwardly," McCoy says. He speculates that the Hillman got a lot of mileage on it as far as the ladies were concerned.

"Reggie was a ladies man, or tried to be in class, but outside of class I don't know if he really was one or not," says Ralph Williams, another classmate. "He was always talking to some woman. Reggie did have the gift of gab and he would always be striking up conversations with them. I don't know if he was trying to get dates or trying to have that reputation of being someone who could talk to the ladies. But he never did anything out of place and was always a gentleman, that's one thing I can say. He was not one to do anything in front of anyone to make himself look bad or say anything to a lady out of place."

There's little doubt that Lewis cut a dashing figure in his motorized chariot, which broke down frequently. So what if it was nine years old? It was every bit as effective as a Ferrari when it came to attracting women.

Schoolmate Paulette Bacote-McAlily had some dates with Lewis. "Reggie and I went out a couple of times," she says. "He was fresh, he was forward, meaning that during the 1950s and 1960s you just didn't come right out and say, 'Come and go out with me, I have a car.' You'd woo the girls a little bit, but not Reggie. He was straightforward."

She says Lewis would drive to his house on Mosher Street, where they would stop and see his parents. Then they would get a hamburger and a milkshake at Mardel's, a West Side hangout popular with black kids, and he would take her home.

Lewis's nemesis at school was Bertram Hill, the class clown. Because he had skipped a grade before attending Dunbar, Hill was the youngest and smallest member of Lewis's class. Highly intelligent and born on April Fool's day in 1944, Hill was an incorrigible practical joker who'd harass and tease the bigger, more mature Lewis all the time, like an irritating gnat buzzing around a bull elephant.

Hill forever secured his place in Class of '61 lore with a prank he pulled on Lewis in their history and social sciences class. Lewis was running late that day and was the last to arrive.

"Reggie was always so serious," says Hill, now a strapping 6-foot-4, 240-pound giant with a booming laugh. "Man, he was always so serious. I said, 'Well,' I'm gonna get a rise out of him.' So I put a little thumbtack in his chair. We had the kind of desk that held you in, okay? The desk and chair combination. Reggie hits this thumbtack—'Owwwwwwwwwwooooohhhh!' And when he hit the desk, the desk knocked him back down on the thumbtack and he hit it again. He got mad at me, he wanted to fight me that day. I can remember it just as if it happened yesterday. I laughed until I cried. It was just so comical the way he did that, because Reggie was very proper and very reserved and for him to lose his cool with a yell was something. I got put out of class for a while, because everyone turned around and pointed at me. They saw Reggie take a swipe at me and hit me upside the head—he grazed me. That's one of the few times that Reggie lost his cool, as a matter of fact, and that's because he was embarrassed. He laughed about it later."

Suave, sophisticated Lewis usually never stooped to juvenile tomfoolery. But Hill's attack couldn't go unanswered. During lunch one day, a famished Hill took out his lunch bag. He was all set to dig into the meat sandwich he'd prepared the night before, but "someone" had removed the meat from the sandwich and replaced it with liberal amounts of ketchup and mustard.

"Being poor and not having a lot of money at the time, I used to have to pack my lunch. And that's all I had for lunch that day, ketchup and mustard. Reggie did it. He told me later, about two weeks later, because Reggie was quiet. And he was just so cool. I never expected that he was the one that did it, because he very seldom played practical jokes on people," Hill says.

While Hill and Lewis were polar opposites in terms of their personalities, Hill was one of the few classmates that Lewis allowed to see behind his teenage facade. "He and I had a certain simpatico. I read him and I read some of his frustrations and some of his pains. And he liked me because I read it and didn't disclose it. He liked me because I would do things to make him laugh and he knew I picked on him to bring some joy and levity and get him away from so much seriousness. One day I said, 'You know what? You don't even have to worry about lying to these people about girls and stuff that you may have and may not have. I know better—you're working too hard first of all, so when do you have time for them, after midnight? You can't stay out late, 'cause your mother will kick your behind! Now when are you going to have time for all these chicks?'

"Reggie really didn't have time to entertain. Reggie was always working or doing school activities or something like that. He missed a lot of his childhood that way, to me. I guess despite my pranks, I was a sensitive kind of soul, too. And I saw sometimes sadness in his eyes," Hill says.

"Reggie was always focused on what he had to do. Like I said, he was very reserved and, to me, even a little troubled. Reggie had like a burning desire and it's something that I appreciated later on in my adult life. Because when you look at things from adolescence, you don't really appreciate or understand things like perseverance, dedication, and purpose. Reggie always had goals, unbeknownst to many of us at the time," Hill says.

For Reginald Lewis, the time eventually came to leave Dunbar and move on to the next challenge. A mysterious new venue—college—beckoned. Lewis was now a big fish in a small pond. How would he perform in a college setting? He would find out soon enough. It was the spring of 1961 and high school graduation was just around the corner.

After receiving their diplomas, the Class of '61 scattered, as graduating classes typically do. Practically everyone in Dunbar's advanced academic course went to college. In those days, black students had a much smaller scholastic universe to pick from than today.

Much of the Class of '61 wound up at Morgan State or Coppin State colleges—both of which are black Baltimore schools,—or at Salisbury State on Maryland's Eastern Shore, Bowie State, Howard University, 45 miles to the south in Washington, D.C., or Hampton Institute in Virginia. For black students to attend white colleges, particularly prestigious ones like Harvard, Stanford, or Yale, was exceedingly rare.

The hours spent on the football field paid off for Lewis by helping him overcome his mediocre grades. Lewis got a football scholarship to Virginia State College in Petersburg, Virginia. Lewis had no way of knowing that his plans to be a football star would be derailed at Virginia State, putting him on a path to greater glory and accomplishment than he ever could have conceived of at Dunbar.

3

"I'm Going to Be a Millionaire": Lewis at Virginia State

Established in 1883 and situated close to the banks of the Appomattox River, Virginia State is the country's oldest publicly funded black university. Once known as the Virginia Normal & Industrial Institute, the school's rolling, tree-dotted campus sits atop a former plantation in Ettrick, Virginia, just outside Petersburg.

The capital of the Confederacy—Richmond—is about 18 miles to the north. Back in 1883, most of Ettrick's residents were poor white laborers who toiled at water-powered mills that fed one of five rail lines converging on the Petersburg area. News that a black college had been set up in the middle of town triggered tremendous resentment among the locals, many of whom had little or no formal education. In addition, many residents were still smoldering from having lost the bloody, divisive Civil War that was ostensibly fought over slavery 18 years earlier.

Residual animosity toward Virginia State students was still percolating 78 years later when Reginald Lewis started attending college. Chesterfield Avenue, which runs past Virginia State's campus, served as a demarcation line of sorts. Students seeking to avoid trouble prudently skirted the residential areas on the other side of Chesterfield.

College campuses tend to be insular communities and Virginia State was no exception. The growing civil rights movement barely registered a blip on the radar screen of student consciousness. That would change somewhat before Lewis graduated, though.

Lewis stepped onto this stage in the fall of 1961. "He wanted to leave home and go out of town. We were in an atmosphere where you had to be extraordinarily accomplished for a white school to give you anything. So, Virginia State made him an offer," his mother, Carolyn, recalls.

Except for his stint at summer camp when his mother delivered his newspapers for him, Lewis had never really been away from Baltimore for any extended period of time. Parting was difficult for mother and son.

"I won't say I cried. I'm not a crying person, really. It was tough, it was tough because you were sending your best friend. He served so many positions in my life. We always disagreed but we were never disagreeable, because we were so much alike. His views and my views sometimes didn't intersect very well, but on the basic things we never had a problem," Carolyn Fugett says.

When his goodbyes to friends and family had been said, Lewis crammed his belongings into his tiny sports car and headed south down Interstate 95.

"HE COULD BE A VERY DIFFICULT PERSON"

Before coming to college, Lewis had had a room to himself. That wouldn't be the case at Virginia State, because freshmen were required to stay on campus and have a freshman roommate.

"He had a hard time with roommates," Lewis's mother recalls. "He had his own way of doing things and they had their way. Eventually, he moved off campus and got his own place. See, he was an exacting person and everybody didn't like him."

Lewis's first roommate was Lynwood Hart, a homeboy who lived about four blocks from Lewis in Baltimore and played football with opposing Edmondson High School. They knew each other well enough to have developed a nodding acquaintance, although Hart today vividly remembers knocking quarterback Lewis out of a high school football match.

That Lewis and Hart wound up being Virginia State roommates may seem an unlikely coincidence. But as Hart recounts it, their being

roommates resulted from Lewis's gift for controlling situations and using that skill to his advantage.

Virginia State had a policy of pairing football players in dormitory
rooms. Lewis, Hart, and the rest of the team were lined up so the
coaches could decide which players would room together. A coach
stood in front counting off "One and two, you're roommates, one and
two, you're roommates."

Lewis saw how the sequence was unfolding in terms of which boys
ahead of him were getting the same room. He then moved up a few
places, positioning himself in a way that he and Hart would become
roommates. "Reggie denies this happened, but he did it—I saw it,"
Hart says.

"Reggie was the kind of guy that was always thinking ahead of everybody else. And that caused him a lot of problems with people.
There's people who if they are honest will tell you that Reggie was not
the easiest person in the world to deal with. He was always ahead of
most people relative to what he thought about life and what he was
planning to do. He realized it was kind of good to have a receiver as a
roommate," Hart recalls.

Lewis and Hart grew very close during their time at Virginia State,
but only after Hart got beyond his roommate's prickly persona. Even
though they were both black kids from the same neighborhood and
fellow athletes and graduates of Baltimore City public schools, they
couldn't have been more dissimilar in temperament and personality.

Hart found out for himself that Lewis could be difficult to live
with. "Reggie sometimes could make you very angry. He had a way of
talking about things that if you didn't know him, you would view as
a personal put down. But it was more of a kind of shock treatment,"
Hart recalls.

Lewis was self-assured, articulate, and dogmatic when expressing his
views. Whenever he and Hart debated some issue—which was often—
Hart's logic would come under vigorous attack, "Don't you understand? Don't you see the shortcoming of that philosophy, of that belief
that you're holding? Don't you think you need to rethink that?" Lewis
would insist.

There were many times, Hart recalls, when he wanted to tell Lewis
in exasperation, "Who the hell are you?" However, Hart adds, "But it

was never an exchange on an emotional level, where we got into great disputes and stuff. He was constantly shocking you into thinking about things in a way that kids coming from where we came from didn't normally think.

"Reggie, there's no question that he could be a very difficult person. And he could be, uh, very hard on people if he felt that they weren't giving 110 percent. If you said, here's 100 percent of mankind, I think Reggie probably felt that maybe anywhere from 20 to 25 percent of those people needed to be kicked in the ass," Hart remembers.

Also on a football scholarship, Hart came to Virginia State with the intention of majoring in general trade, then becoming an industrial arts teacher. However, his conversations with Lewis led him to change his major to business administration. He now directs international systems engineering for AT&T.

"A lot of thought processes were engaged after having a discussion with Reggie. I mean, he pissed you off, quite frankly. But if you took time to think about what he was really saying, you began to see some benefit, some value, and some substance. The shock treatment that I got as a steady diet as his roommate helped focus me," Hart says today.

Lewis loved to deal in the currency of ideas. He was a well-informed, versatile conversationalist and a voracious reader.

"Reggie believed that you should spend some time trying to figure out what was going on around you," Hart says. "I kind of felt like— 'Who cares?' I mean, I can't influence anything! Why is it important for me to read a newspaper, or try to figure out what this author was saying in this book? I mean, it's a waste of time, because I was never going to use it.

"I think if there was stuff that annoyed me about him, he was always pressing those kinds of things. Like, 'Hey, did you see what was in the (Washington) *Post*, or the *Richmond Times Dispatch?*' Or, 'Check this article out!'" Hart recalls.

Lewis even proselytized when it came to his tastes in music. "He had a tape recorder, a Webcor tape recorder. I'll never forget that darn thing. And he would play music by MJQ (Modern Jazz Quartet), Ahmad Jamal, and other jazz greats. And I would say, 'I want to hear some hip-hop.' He would say, 'Well you know, hey man, get your head together. Listen to something that's got some value and some quality to it.' Now I have an appreciation for music in a way that I didn't have back then," Hart says.

Even as a college freshman, Lewis refused to view race as an impediment or a handicap. Equally important, he wanted to bring others around to his point of view. One day Lewis was in the room reading and Hart, who had a habit of walking around their dormitory room pretending to be a radio DJ and newscaster, was puttering around reading an imaginary news script. Lewis looked up in bafflement. "Why do you do that?" he asked.

"Because one day I want to be a newscaster. That's what I want to do," Hart responded.

"Well, if you want to be a newscaster, why don't you do it?"

"They don't have black newscasters around—there's nobody doing this," Hart replied in a tone that implied what he'd just said was common knowledge.

To Lewis's way of thinking, Hart's attitude was a harmful, self-defeating fallacy. Lewis's grandparents had programmed and schooled him extensively in that regard: "No skill or vocation is the white man's exclusive province." And here in his dormitory room, without a white person in sight, Hart was already placing limits on his potential, based on his color. "Look dammit, if you want to do something, you can do it," Lewis passionately informed Hart.

A couple of days later, around 2 o'clock in the morning, Hart was lying in bed when he heard a knock on the door. It was Lewis, with a young black man he'd met while working at a nearby bowling alley after classes. Lewis's acquaintance was Max Robinson, who later joined ABC News as the country's first full-time black anchorman on a national evening news program. At the time, Robinson was working for a radio station in Richmond.

Lewis walked over to his desk, pulled the chair out, placed it in front of Hart's bed and offered Robinson a seat. "Now, talk to this guy about being in radio," Lewis said. And that's what they did, staying up all night engrossed in conversation.

Thirty-three years later, Hart still marvels at Lewis's conviction and his willingness to act as a catalyst for another young black man's dream. "Here's a guy who's saying to me, 'Hey, you can do this,'" Hart says. "'And not only can you do it, but I'm going to show you somebody who's doing it.' That was the kind of guy that Reggie was."

LEWIS LOSES HIS SCHOLARSHIP

Virginia State's football season was rapidly approaching; it was time for Lewis and Hart to start earning their keep. The Trojans, as Virginia State's teams are called, began holding football drills not long after Lewis and Hart arrived on campus.

Team pictures from 1961 show Lewis wearing his No. 17 jersey and a stern game face. Freshman football players, or "white shirters" as they were called, had the unenviable task of playing on the scout team. Basically, they simulated the plays used by Virginia State's upcoming opponent, while the veteran Trojans practiced against them.

"It was brutal, believe me," Al Banks, another football player from Baltimore, recalls. "First of all, we were all freshmen and less skilled people. And for quarterbacks, that was very intimidating, because those guys would blow in there and they would take cheap shots. It was kind of dangerous—they would come blasting through there and take out the freshmen quarterbacks and anybody else they could. It was not a pleasant situation. Me and Reggie were definitely practice quarterbacks that got killed."

The pounding was taking its toll on Lewis's throwing shoulder, which was injured repeatedly during his freshman year. He wasn't able to throw the football with the velocity he'd had at Dunbar.

Hart saw that Lewis wasn't keen on enduring pain and didn't like to be hit hard. "On the scout team, they just beat the living crap out of you. We would come back to the dormitory and he would just sit there and he was in a great deal of pain—emotional pain, too—because we came there to be stars. I had a lot of compassion for him, a lot of empathy too, because I knew what this guy was capable of doing. I kept waiting for the day when he would break loose, but it dawned on me that it wasn't going to happen," Hart remembers.

Once the season started, Lewis had to endure the ignominy of being a third-string quarterback, at the very bottom of the depth chart. Lewis wasn't helped by the fact that he was only 5-foot-10; his field of vision was often obscured by hulking defensive linemen boring in on him.

"In terms of football, I always thought that I was much better than Reggie," says Hart, who is 6-foot-1. "He was short and didn't have the mobility and all those kinds of things. I never looked at Reggie as my competition."

Melvin Smith, a 6-foot-4 junior who was a starting tackle, recalls that Lewis was rarely inserted into games unless it was during the closing minutes. "I think he was good, he was just too short," Smith says of Lewis. "He did fine, but normally it was over when he got in."

Hart was a starting receiver by the time Lewis made his quarterback debut. Given to exhorting his teammates at Dunbar, Lewis saw no reason to alter his approach on the college level. "Reggie got in the game and we were winning it, but we weren't winning by a lot of points. He came running in and we had these grizzly seniors and juniors in there and Reggie pops in with his collegiate look and collegiate attitude. 'Okay, gang, this is what we're going to do.' We had this big ol' grizzly guy who weighed about 240 pounds, Ernest "Money" Turner, who was playing fullback. Money listened to this for about 15 seconds and he said, 'Hey, man, this ain't no gang you got out here, this is a football team. Let's get that straight,'" Hart recalls.

"And I looked at Reggie's eyes and, boy, it was like somebody had rolled a shade across his face. It was that barrier between the seasoned vets and the rookie," Hart says.

A crisis was brewing in Lewis's life, one that no amount of exhortation would change. His football performance wasn't up to par and teammates were beginning to whisper that his scholarship might be in jeopardy. Hurting physically, Lewis would either have to ignore the pain and elevate his level of play or drop football altogether. It would be a painful decision either way.

Homecoming week and its festivities are one of the highlights of campus life. One of the primary attractions—if not the main event—is the weekend football game. Reginald Lewis's family drove from Baltimore to cheer him on in the big game.

"I remember at homecoming questioning why he wasn't playing," says Tony Fugett. After the game, Fugett asked his father why Lewis rode the bench the entire game.

"Why didn't he play, why didn't he play?" the disappointed eight-year-old asked. "My father gave me some kind of smart-ass answer. He kind of snapped at me. Obviously, he didn't like the fact that Reggie wasn't playing."

Needless to say, Lewis was unhappy. The episode further deflated his psyche and eroded his self-esteem. He could see his football scholarship going down the drain. Demoralized and depressed, he placed a telephone call to someone who'd been there for him in the past—Uncle James. "When he went to Virginia State, his shoulder was hurt, but his feelings were hurt worse than his shoulder," James Cooper remembers.

"I was first-string at Dunbar and I'm third-string here. I'm quitting," Lewis told him.

"Are you quitting school or are you quitting the team?" Cooper asked.

"They can keep their fucking money, I'll go academic."

"You're right, quit the team, 'cause you went there for an education," Cooper recalls telling him.

Lewis began taking stock of his situation. With his collegiate athletic career and financial ticket to Virginia State beginning to crumble, he sought out his roommate for some heart-to-heart conversations.

"I remember when Reggie realized that he wasn't going to be a star on the football team," Lynwood Hart says. The two were sitting in the room when Lewis blurted out, "I don't think I'm going to be able to do very much with this football thing, because I'm having too much trouble with my shoulder."

"What the heck would you like to do if not play football?" Hart asked.

"You know what I'd like to do? I'd like to own my own business," Lewis answered.

Hart was incredulous. "You gotta be crazy—nobody does that," he told Lewis.

"You know, I'd like to pursue my law degree, but I'd really like to have my own business," Lewis said.

Lewis also called his mother. "Mom, I'm gonna leave the sports alone. But I'm gonna be the best academic student that I can be," he told her.

Lewis's mother promised to find tuition money somehow if her son lost his athletic scholarship.

With the clarity of hindsight, Lewis might never have become a successful financier had it not been for his shoulder injury.

For their part, Lewis's friends, Lynwood Hart and Al Banks, went on to become Trojan football standouts. Both say that Lewis never displayed any envy over their success. "Reggie would say after a game, 'Hey man, you really did well. You played a great game.' I can't ever remember him showing any signs of jealousy about it," Hart says. "That, to me, was a surprise if you want to know the truth."

"TO BECOME A LAWYER, ONE MUST WORK HARD"

Despite his initial agony, Lewis managed to divorce himself from his football playing days with his self-confidence intact. He had other challenges to take on and, seemingly, never looked back.

"He said one day, he was going to be a millionaire," classmate Edith Morton Smith says. "I said, 'Well, I'm going to marry a millionaire.' He accomplished his dream—I didn't," laughs Smith, now an assistant registrar at Virginia State. "He was a serious college student. Don't get me wrong, he wasn't a dweeb. He had himself a good time at parties."

I quit football after my freshman year and decided to get serious about my studies. The college years were wild. I crammed a lot of living into those four years. After a rotten freshman year, I really started to study. I got straight A's in economics and always went beyond the course. I starting reading the New York Times *and* The Wall Street Journal *every day. But I had fun, too.*

Lewis did have academic difficulties in his first semester. He received an incomplete grade in an orientation course where students were merely required to attend class. Al Banks says Lewis wouldn't go to the course, which baffles him to this day.

Lewis hit a snag in his second semester, too. Ironically, the man who one day would complete complex business transactions worth millions of dollars didn't master basic math and received a failing grade.

However, starting in his sophomore year, Lewis's grades improved markedly although math continued to be his nemesis. He failed it again during his junior year before finally scraping by with a D. Classmate Alan Colon, who would become Lewis's senior-year roommate, suggested that Lewis do every other math problem in the textbook as a way to bring up his math proficiency. Lewis followed the advice.

Years later Lewis established a $5,000 award for Virginia State seniors graduating with the highest cumulative average in math from their sophomore year on.

Despite his struggles with math, Lewis continued his habit of juggling employment and schoolwork.

I worked throughout college, first as the night manager of a bowling alley from 1 A.M. to 8 A.M. This didn't last more than a semester and a half.

My next job was great. I traveled to elementary schools and high schools throughout the state of Virginia as a salesman for a photographic service. I could make $500 a week on commissions, which was big money in 1963. I had an unbelievable sales record, with about 60 percent of my calls resulting in sales.

I learned some great lessons. The key was to make lots of calls and build on each successful sale. Some principal who I'd sold would call his friend in another county and the next sales call was a layup. I set my college schedule so that I would have no classes on Tuesday. I would leave Monday night for the territory, stay at a Holiday Inn—get up around 5 A.M., make calls and set goals for the day. I would make my first visit by 7 A.M. I would try to see one principal at 7 A.M., another around noon, then three more in the afternoon and one in the evening and leave before it was too dark. This was not easy because these were rural schools not close to each other. I also wanted to start back somewhat early since the South was not a place where a black man wanted to get stopped or stuck once the sun went down. Fortunately, I never had a problem and, at night especially, I always kept well within the speed limit with my sports car.

I would usually settle up the same night I arrived with the owner of the photographic service, who was always very fair with me and amazed at my success. He would pay me right away and ask if I wanted dinner or anything. He usually wanted to talk, but I would rush back to the dorm, work on my studies until the wee hours, catch a few hours of sleep and attend class. The owner offered me a partnership in his company when I was 20 years old and I gave his proposal a lot of thought. I figured I would really expand that business but the owner had had a heart attack and told me he really did not want a big expansion to neighboring states or to hire more people or build more production capacity. So I passed this up—no regrets because my grades were really beginning to improve. I was getting mostly A's and B's.

Already ambitious when he arrived at Virginia State, Lewis was becoming incredibly focused. He was starting to write daily schedules that listed his itinerary for a given day, then would try not to deviate from it. On one schedule written on a piece of cardboard, he wrote, "To become a lawyer, one must work hard."

"He always had a purpose," Melvin Smith, another classmate, says. "Where other guys were taking courses to get out of school, Reggie had a master plan in mind. When other guys were reading comics, he was reading *The Wall Street Journal.*"

Lynwood Hart, Lewis's roommate, saw how Lewis could stiffen his resolve and become unyielding and determined in the face of obstacles. One time, Hart and Lewis were headed back to school after a break. What began as a mundane journey from Baltimore to Petersburg evolved into an epic battle of man versus machine.

"I remember Reggie had a Hillman and I don't even remember what year it was, but it was old. The thing was falling apart. The fuse in the thing kept blowing out and it just kept going dead on us," Hart recounts.

Worried, he told Lewis, "Reggie, this thing is not going to make it, man."

"Naw, naw, I'm telling you this thing will make it. We'll make it, we'll get there," Lewis reassured him.

"All right, okay, let's do it," Hart agreed.

The two roommates left Baltimore about eleven o'clock in the morning to go back to Virginia State. They were hardly out of the city when Lewis's prized automobile went dead.

"In those days, there wasn't a lot between Virginia State and Baltimore—it was pretty desolate road until you got to Richmond," Hart says.

He told Lewis, "You know, this thing has a long way to go and we might not make it and might be stranded out there."

"No, we can do this thing, man. We can do this thing," Lewis replied. The two stopped by an old car repair shop and somehow started the Hillman. Forty miles later, the car again went dead. Lewis and Hart had several fuses which they kept popping into the car to keep it going. But the car kept stopping and the two would have to get out and push it until they made it to the next repair shop.

After a while, Hart had had enough. "This is crazy, man!" he told himself. But Lewis was undeterred.

"He took this as a personal thing. He was going to get that car to Virginia State that night if we had to push it," Hart says.

Each time the car died, the two would find a way to get it to a car repair shop. "You could feel the thing getting ready to die on us, and he would say, 'Oh shit, not again,'" Hart says.

"The first couple of times it happened, my view was, get it to the next point, then we get a bus. My view after about the third time was, if he's this committed, then I'm committed, too," says Hart.

The Hillman and its two tired passengers limped into Virginia State late that night. They made it to a parking lot, but not their dorm. "We couldn't get to the dorm—we got into a parking lot in the middle of campus and it stopped. And we stepped back and looked at it and said, 'Shit, we made it.' He literally made this a mission for the two of us, and I bought in. That was the first of a couple of times I can remember being influenced by this guy to go beyond where we were. I think it was that kind of tenacity on his part that made him special," Hart marvels.

As at Dunbar, Lewis was one of a handful of students with an automobile—when the Hillman was running, that is. However, it was far more than a status symbol. Since football players roomed together and Lewis was no longer on the team, he and Hart couldn't be roommates. Rather than get used to a new roommate, Lewis moved into a small off-campus apartment. Having a car was critical to supporting that arrangement.

But there's no denying the Hillman's utility extended beyond transportation. One of Lewis's Dunbar classmates, William Smith, used to travel to Virginia State periodically to visit his friend. Smith distinctly remembers that while Lewis was off campus, the aspiring attorney was dating one of his teachers.

"He'd come through campus driving pretty fast and we'd say, 'There goes Reggie!'" classmate Fredi Savage Eaton recalls. "When he came in the first year, you noticed him, you knew who he was. It was a small campus. He just had an air about him, I'll put it that way. He had his own way of dressing. He was kind of preppy and in the South, we were not into the preppy look at all. He was always a person who was very observant. You could always feel that he was aware of everything that was going on. There are some people that I went to school with that I don't remember. I remember Reggie, because he was always doing things that the rest of us weren't. He had jobs off campus that I think a lot of people didn't have."

During Lewis's senior year, his purity of purpose and focus became even greater with the demise of a dear companion. A crestfallen and "dramatic" Lewis telephoned home to report the Hillman was no more.

"That was his baby, that car, goodness gracious!" Carolyn Fugett says. "He called and said he'd had an accident and the first thing we said was, 'How are you?' Not how's the car—how are you? He said, 'I'm okay, but I think the car is beyond repair.' The first thing my husband and I said was, 'Do you want us to come down?'"

Lewis declined their offer. His prized possession was no more and the loss of the Hillman also made it difficult to hold on to his various jobs.

However, Lewis eventually replaced the Hillman with yet another English sports car—this time an Austin Healy.

Despite his heavy schedule, Lewis was aware there were other aspects to collegiate life.

I didn't have a steady girlfriend and dated a lot of different women. I didn't want to get too serious, because the idea of getting married right after school was not in my program. I really didn't want the responsibility of a wife before I had a real stake in life.

Melvin Smith recalls one away game where Lewis was really feeling his oats. "I tell you, we went on a football trip once and there are a couple of young ladies out in Bluefield, West Virginia, one at least, that will probably love him forever. You know how it is after a game with guys out of town. It happened to a lot of us that we, uh, had people fall in love with us for a moment."

Back at Virginia State, "you had to plan your little liaisons very carefully—if you got caught, the girl and you would be sent home. He was never sent home, so it looks like he was a planner even back then," Smith says.

Students at Virginia State were issued a list of rules and regulations known as the "blue book" because of its cover. Young men were allowed to depart and leave campus at their leisure, but female students had a long list of restrictions and curfews, the violation of which could lead to expulsion.

All women students had to sign out of their dormitories anytime they left campus and could not ride in cars while on Virginia State grounds. Couples discovered *in flagrante delicto* could kiss their college careers at Virginia State goodbye.

Although Lewis didn't broadcast it, he had platonic female friends on campus, too. One, Carolyn Powell, was something of a soulmate.

"He was the one person I could be very serious with. We had a lot to talk about that we didn't necessarily talk to our friends about. We would just talk about our backgrounds and about school and having no money and things that we wanted to do. I knew he wanted to be a lawyer. I knew he was very ambitious and had an entrepreneurial bent even back then. Mostly what I remember him talking about at that time was going into law and eventually he wanted to have his own business," Powell remembers.

Despite Lewis's many activities, he still found time to join a fraternity, Kappa Alpha Psi. The Kappas are one of the country's oldest black fraternities. Lewis stoically endured the Kappa initiation rites with one exception. Some of his fraternity brothers wanted to borrow his car but he managed to deflect this request by telling them that the insurance had been paid for by his stepfather and didn't cover anyone else.

Lewis would later donate money to the New York chapter of the fraternity, which established a scholarship foundation in his name after his death. The Kappas gathered one last time to bid farewell to Lewis at a private service at Riverside Church the evening before the official memorial service in New York. Among those who spoke were Reverend Calvin Butts, the pastor of New York's Abyssinian Church, businessman and former Manhattan politician Percy Sutton, and Arthur Ashe, who succumbed to his fatal illness two weeks later.

Among Virginia State's faculty, Lewis had developed a reputation as someone who thought nothing of asking professors to prove the validity of their theories. That wasn't a problem for Hanley Norment, a young professor with the department of history, geography, and political science who was popular with students.

When Norment arrived at Virginia State, a veteran professor pulled him aside with a word of advice about Reginald Lewis. "This man here, I want you to know, just wants to argue all the time," Norment chuckles.

"He had an inquiring mind. I think that's why we got along so well. I was open to challenges, and that was not generally the case at black colleges at that time. I think he tried to be tactful, but I don't think he succeeded. But I did not mind because I could take what he said and make a teaching point out of it," Norment says.

By his senior year, Lewis had moved back on campus and was living on the third floor of Puryear Hall. Because Norment was single, he lived there, too.

Lewis would often drop by for discussions and the two of them traveled to Richmond to watch the state legislature in action. The two were also active participants in a discussion group that used to meet in the snack shop at Foster Hall.

"Hanley Norment was an extremely popular instructor," says Lucious Edwards, a member of that discussion group and now Virginia State's archivist. "We would all get a cup of coffee and a couple of donuts and we would sit in one of the corners in Foster Hall and talk about a variety of things—politics, political systems, civil rights. Those were long conversations. We talked about student apathy to the civil rights movement at Virginia State," he says.

Lewis spent a fair amount of time chatting with his new roommate, Alan Colon. Lewis had matured since his freshman year and was willing to at least entertain Colon's viewpoints, rather than force-feed him a Lewisesque take on the world.

"We had some intellectual stimulation from newspapers and periodicals. We would read through those and comment on world affairs. He always had an agenda, a sense of purpose, and direction. You could discern a sense of destiny about Reggie that set him apart from his peers. He had little time to waste. He had a disarming, but not malicious sense of humor. Reggie could talk trash with anybody and get a kick out of it. He would make a statement and then bust out laughing at his own brilliance," Colon recalls.

Colon noticed that Lewis had an idiosyncratic habit of pulling at his moustache when he was thinking. He'd often be sitting at his desk in the dorm, thinking or studying and pulling at his moustache to such an extent that Colon would laugh.

Lewis made his bed every day and kept his side of the room free of personal touches like pictures or posters. Lewis often had so little money during his senior year that he would periodically pawn his electric shaver to generate a few extra dollars. He became such a regular that every time he walked in the door, the clerk would begin to count out the money. Lewis always redeemed the shaver after a few days.

"He had a hard side to him that showed itself in his being very blunt, with no bullshit attached," Colon says. "I remember talking to Reggie about the possibility of a young lady that I was with being pregnant. He said, 'Man, don't you fall for that bullshit, she's just jiving you.' About a week later, she came and told me that everything was all right. I said, 'Damn, Reggie was right about that, but why did he have to be so cold about it?'"

Colon remembers Lewis worrying about whether he had enough credits to graduate on time. In fact, Lewis took three summer classes before his senior year to ensure that he would be leaving in May 1965. He was really pumped by the time regular classes began. Academically, it was do-or-die time.

In his last semester, he earned three A's, three B's and a C, which oddly enough came in an individual sports course. These grades notwithstanding, one of the defining events of Lewis's life was just over the horizon.

A GLIMPSE OF HARVARD

I began to think about graduate school or law school or maybe, just maybe, a really great university like Harvard. At this point, it was really pretty much a dream, but who knows—keep punching and maybe.

In my senior year, lightning struck. Harvard Law School started a program to select a few black students to attend summer school at

Harvard, to introduce them to legal study in general. Participating colleges would select five students from their respective schools and Harvard Law School would select just one student from each school.

I was excited, I mean, really excited. Calm down, calm down, I told myself. Develop a plan. It wasn't easy knowing where to begin. First, I needed to get the literature on the program. My school only gave a summary of it, so I wrote to Harvard for specific details the same day I found out about the program. Harvard responded immediately, which really impressed me. My approach was to first make sure I was selected by Virginia State. That would not be easy. Many students had straight A's and I had had a rotten freshman year, which hurt my cumulative grade point average.

I needed to supplement my application—obtain letters of recommendation perhaps. I spoke to a couple of professors. I told them that this was my shot at the big time. I said I didn't want a letter that just said "he's a nice guy," but a real substantive letter setting out what I did well and what I did poorly. I gave them a biography, grades, everything.

Hanley Norment figured to be a natural ally in Lewis's quest. Not only were they friends, but Lewis had received A's in both classes he'd taken from Norment. Mindful of the rapidly approaching deadline for submitting Harvard program applications, Lewis barged into Norment's office.

"In the spring of 1965, a number of black colleges—I believe 32—were given an opportunity by Harvard to nominate some students to attend a summer program that Harvard had for minority youngsters. Virginia State was asked to send either four or five applications and Lewis rushed over to me when he found out about it. He was not one of those asked to prepare papers for that opportunity. So, he asked me if I could write a letter of recommendation for him," Norment recalls.

"I was pleased to do it and did it quickly. I knew there was some urgency. I met the time frame and personally walked it over to the president's office. The person who handled it was the assistant to the president at the time, a Mr. Dabney. I don't remember his first name. He took the letter and began to read it with a pained expression on his face. I said, 'My god, what's this all about?'"

A tall, light-skinned man who wore glasses and squinched his face readily, Mr. Dabney said, "Well Mr. Norment, I see that you've put a lot into this letter, but I want you to know that Mr. Lewis is not one of the students that we've selected. But since you've put a lot into this letter, we will send it on. But Mr. Lewis will be an add-on to our selections."

Lewis was ecstatic. Against the odds, he'd made it.

Well, I made the college list, fifth. The college recommended four people above me because their cumulative averages were higher. But I made the cut. OK!

The paperwork was sent off to Harvard, beginning an anxious waiting period for Lewis. He monitored his mail daily, looking for anything bearing a Harvard seal.

Then the letter came—I was going to Harvard for the summer. I later learned that Harvard discredited my freshman year and liked my straight A's in economics and the letter of recommendation. The night I got the letter, I told my roommate, Alan Colon, "Alan, come September I will be in the incoming class at Harvard Law." He said, "Reg, this is just for the summer. Don't set yourself up for a major disappointment." I said, "Alan, just watch—I'm going to Harvard."

The Harvard summer program opened a door on a new world for Lewis. Characteristically, he kicked the door open, instead of waiting to be ushered in.

4

No Application Needed: Breaking Down the Doors of Harvard Law

Reginald Lewis was beginning to make his move. As he'd told his professors at Virginia State, the summer program was his "shot at the big time" and he wasn't to be denied. First, however, he would have to overcome one more obstacle in his path.

GETTING INTO LAW SCHOOL

Unbeknownst to Lewis, his goal of becoming a Harvard Law School student was something the creators of the summer program had given considerable thought to and expressly forbidden. The program was the brainchild of Louis Loss, a law school professor who later got Lewis interested in corporate takeovers. Alarmed by the paucity of African-Americans in law schools and in the legal community in general, Loss and a few other law school professors—including Frank E.A. Sander—pressed Harvard to establish a program to acquaint black college students with legal study. Perhaps mindful that Harvard Law School's highest ranking full-time black faculty member was an assistant reference librarian named George Strait, the school went along with Loss's suggestion. The Rockefeller Foundation agreed to fund the program, which provided room and board along with a $500 stipend.

In addition to giving participants a taste of law school life, the summer program was designed to give them a boost in the law school application process. The entire project was a grand experiment never attempted at Harvard or anywhere else prior to 1965.

However, the decision to create the program brought with it a damning proviso from Lewis's standpoint: It was *not* to serve as an alternative admissions route for black students wishing to enter Harvard Law School.

For that reason, the law school asked participating black colleges to send third-year undergraduates. That way, students would return to their schools as seniors and enthusiastically spread the law school gospel around their respective campuses. They would also be a year removed from the elaborate screening mechanisms Harvard had in place for selecting law school applicants. Part of Virginia State's reluctance to send Lewis to the summer program may have stemmed from his being a senior.

As far as Lewis was concerned, the whole thing was an elaborate forum for showcasing his talents and attributes. Before arriving at Harvard, Lewis read everything he could get his hands on about the law, the better to capitalize on this once-in-a-lifetime opportunity.

Lewis borrowed several political philosophy books from Virginia State Professor Norment to bone up for the summer program. Determined to impress the instructors at Harvard, he'd turned down an offer from IBM to work in the company's office products division. He was taking a real risk, but he approached the summer with a sense of purpose and determination that characterized his entire career.

I needed a plan. An incredible calm came over me and the plan began to emerge. First, have a tremendous final year in college; second, know the objectives of the program; third, break your ass over the summer, eliminate all distractions—nothing except the objective. The program was held over two four-week semesters: during the first semester, say nothing about going to Harvard. First, prove that you can compete; for example, take a difficult course at Harvard College during the summer and do well. Second, do the job. Build upon your strengths. This was the brief and I've never executed better.

Lewis left Baltimore for Cambridge in the summer of 1965. Over the course of the next eight weeks, he followed his "brief" to the letter.

Lewis and his fellow participants tackled law school subjects such as civil procedure, torts, criminal law, and contracts. They also took at least one course at Harvard's regular summer program that was unrelated to legal education.

The highlight of the program was a mock trial where students took opposing sides. Lewis stood out. Almost thirty years later, Professor Sander still recalls being impressed by Lewis's self-assurance and argumentative skills.

"He rose to the occasion. When he did the mock court thing, we all thought, 'This guy is going to amount to something. He's got a real drive and energy and fight and insight.' He stood out among those students," Sander says.

"I was rated either No. 1 or 2 out of the 40 or 50 outstanding students who competed that summer," Lewis wrote.

As at Virginia State, his instructors were definitely aware of his presence, although this time their impressions were uniformly positive. It gave him the foundation he needed to move in for his closing argument: An appeal to be admitted to the law school.

Lewis met with Sander at a small, nondescript restaurant on Battle Street, not far from Harvard's campus. Also present was James McPherson, another summer program student who had already been admitted to the law school. McPherson would later become a Pulitzer Prize-winning author.

Lewis, dressed in his customary shirt and tie, walked into the restaurant and purposefully took his place at the lunch table where Sander and McPherson were waiting. He ordered chicken pot pie and, virtually ignoring his lunch and McPherson, launched into a forceful, eloquent argument outlining why Reginald Lewis should be admitted to Harvard Law School. For the next hour or so, Lewis masterfully ticked off his positive characteristics and delineated the myriad ways an association between Reginald Lewis and the law school would be mutually beneficial. His appeal was based primarily on reason and irrefutable logic and was devoid of wheedling or whining.

His argument flowed freely and naturally. As far as Lewis was concerned, he was dealing from a position of strength. Harvard *really did* need someone as unquestionably gifted and destined for great things as he. He had an unswerving, total commitment to the product he was selling—Reginald Lewis.

In spite of his intensity and the high stakes, Lewis was loose and relaxed, because he felt he had nothing to lose. The worst thing Sander could say was, "You're not going to be admitted," which was already the case.

There had never been a summer law program for minority students before 1965, so Lewis was the first and probably the last program participant with the chutzpa to argue that the program should be a launching pad for admission.

Sander listened attentively, giving no indication one way or the other of being swayed by the glib, confident, aspiring lawyer. After lunch, Lewis left the restaurant, disappointed at not having gotten an affirmative response on the spot. He loved to win, but could cope with his plans going awry—as long as he'd expended maximum effort.

He maintained this attitude throughout his life. In later years, when one of Lewis's two daughters would bring home an average grade from school, Lewis would simply ask, "Did you do your best?" If the answer was yes, the issue was closed as far as he was concerned. Up to a point, the former quarterback really did believe that winning or losing was secondary to how one played the game.

A funny thing happened during that summer. By the end of the program, I really didn't care whether I got in or not. I had done my best and I knew I could compete. I had given it my best shot. That was enough. IBM had offered me a job last spring in their office products division based in Trenton, New Jersey. I also had a shot at the PhD program at Michigan. So I had alternatives. But I had created a climate at Harvard for the decisionmakers to say my recruitment would be a real coup.

In this critical instance, Lewis's high expectations were not to be disappointed. His talk with Sander bore fruit. Before the program for minority students wound down, Lewis was contacted by Harvard Law School Dean of Admissions Louis Toepfler and asked to come to his office. With an attentive Lewis hanging on Toepfler's every word, the Admissions Dean said he'd heard that Lewis might have the tools to excel at the study of law. He asked him if he had ever considered attending a law school. His hopes rising, Lewis answered, yes indeed, he had.

Toepfler then brought the conversation to a close with a promise to contact several law schools on Lewis's behalf and to see if he could get him admitted to one of them.

Lewis left Toepfler's office in a daze. He wasn't quite sure what to make of the encounter. By now, anyone even remotely associated with Harvard Law School knew that Reginald Lewis wanted to become a part of the Harvard tradition. He'd made his position abundantly clear. Lewis was gratified that the Dean knew his name and had taken a personal interest in his situation, but was baffled by the Dean's rather strange offer.

There was a reason for Toepfler's interest in Lewis—the young black man had successfully cultivated several influential advocates among the law school's staff, including Frank Sander. Sander and several other summer program professors had buttonholed Toepfler to discuss the impressive Lewis. They told Toepfler, "This guy is really terrific—you ought to take a flier and take this guy into the law school, even though we've said we're not going to do this."

With the summer program over, Lewis packed up his belongings and boarded the train to Baltimore, not knowing if he would ever get back to Cambridge. It was a long ride and Lewis had plenty of time to reflect.

His whole future hung by a thread. As far as further academic pursuits were concerned, it was Harvard or bust. One of the first things he did after arriving at Mosher Street was to put in a call to Toepfler's office.

At a farewell banquet for all the participants in the summer program, Associate Dean Louis Toepfler told me that he would like me to call him at midweek. When I did, Toepfler's secretary asked if I would speak to her, since the Dean was not in. She had before her a letter she was in the process of typing to me. I said of course. The opening line was, "There will be a place for you in this fall's class, if you want it." Great news! Plus the school was making loans available and gave me a one-year grant from the Rockefeller Foundation.

With glistening eyes, Lewis hung up the phone and informed the Fugett household of his good fortune, triggering an instant celebration. "We were just screaming and hollering and carrying on," his mother recalls. "Here it is my son—MY SON—is going to Harvard."

After the euphoria abated somewhat, the economic reality of the situation began to set in. The family members started asking each other: How would Lewis pay day-to-day expenses like meals, books, and clothing? Members of the Fugett and Cooper families chipped in what they could, but it didn't go terribly far toward defraying Lewis's expenses.

But Lewis was nonchalant. As far as he was concerned, the big problem had already been solved. Harvard Law School had offered him a place in the Class of 1968. Things like expenses were just minor details to be ironed out later.

Being admitted to Harvard reaffirmed Lewis's sense of destiny and further solidified his view of his own uniqueness. By refusing to entertain thoughts of failure, or to even consider the outrageousness of his quest, Lewis had leapfrogged sizable obstacles blocking his path to Harvard Law School.

First he'd pushed his way onto the list of Virginia State students earmarked for the summer law program, then lobbied hard to get himself admitted to the law school. Now he was going to attend world-renowned Harvard Law School, one of the premier training grounds for the country's power elite. The established routine of taking the Law School Aptitude Test or filling out a law school application were for ordinary mortals who lacked the boldness to craft their own set of rules. Yes indeed, he wanted a place in the fall class! And money was the least of his worries as he left Baltimore for Cambridge.

SETTLING IN AT HARVARD

I arrived in Cambridge in September 1965 as a member of the Harvard Law School class of 1968. The first thing I had to do was go to the school and complete an application. That's right, an application. I'm told that I am the only person in the 148-year-history of Harvard Law who was ever admitted before he applied.

Lewis came to Harvard's campus unsure of how he would pay for his room and board. He walked into the law school dean's office with $50 in his pocket. Dean Toepfler met him and extended a hearty welcome.

"How was Lewis set for money?" Toepfler wanted to know. Proud to a fault and fiercely independent, Lewis responded, "I'm in good shape, I'm in good shape." Pressed by Toepfler to describe exactly what that meant, Lewis allowed that he had a few loose bills in his wallet that came to $50.

A bemused Toepfler told Lewis, "Now that you're at Harvard, we take care of our own." Toepfler informed Lewis that paperwork for an educational loan had already been processed and a check for living expenses had been drawn in Lewis's name. All that was needed was Lewis's signature.

With that simple gesture, Lewis was freed of having to juggle school and work, as he had done at Virginia State and at Dunbar High School. For the first time in his life, he enjoyed the luxury of being able to focus on only one job—that of being a full-time law student.

Harvard's generosity made a lasting impact on Lewis. He would later repay Harvard manyfold. In 1992, he gave Harvard Law School a $3 million gift—at the time the largest individual gift in the school's history. In gratitude, the Law School named its international law building The Reginald F. Lewis International Law Center, the first building on campus to be named after an African-American.

Because of the 11th-hour nature of Lewis's admission to Harvard Law School, all the dorms were full, so Lewis was unable to live on campus. He had no qualms about that, having lived off-campus two of the years he was at Virginia State. In fact, living off campus was preferable to Lewis, given his private, independent nature.

I found a room in a local rooming house for a few days while I looked for a place to live. Then I had a bit of luck—two students, John Hatch, a third-year law student, and Bill Robinson, a second-year student, had an apartment at 1751 Massachusetts Avenue that was a short walk from the school and they offered me the third bedroom. I was set.

THE LAW SCHOOL GRIND

I will never forget that first year of law school, or the other two for that matter. It was a brand new ballgame. Dean Griswold, who I later had for taxation, greeted the class of 1968 with the line, "I am the head of this menagerie of prima donnas."

Harvard really knows how to make its students feel they are truly the elite. Fortunately, I never got carried away with their attitude, which by and large was constructive because the students really worked hard and were an incredibly gifted group.

The place had the smell of competition all around, but there was also a fair amount of humor in a lot of the classes. Wit was greatly admired. My civil procedure class with Professor Chadborne was probably the funniest, yet most instructive educational experience I have ever had. Chad really made the class come alive.

For the most part, my section had some great teachers. The entire class of 535 students was broken into four sections of about 130 or so students. All the first-year classes were required and you really got to know the people in your section. I also made lasting friendships with some of the faculty members.

As Lewis noted, competition at the law school was fierce, so much so that some students went to the trouble of attending less prestigious law schools for a year to get a feel for the legal education routine. They then dropped out and enrolled in Harvard's first-year class, writing off an entire year of law school in the process. It was deemed worth the trouble just to get a leg up on the competition at Harvard Law School.

Law school is unique in that students are assessed almost completely on the basis of exam results. But only one exam is given in most courses—after classes are over. For first-year Harvard Law School students of Lewis's era, the one exam came at the end of a full year of course work. By the time you realized you had fared poorly in the cut-throat, sink-or-swim environment, you had already drowned.

Lewis was secretly terrified of not doing well at Harvard. He was studying diligently and was beginning to incorporate terms such as *res judicata* and *res ipsa loquitor* into his everyday speech.

All in all, I was really scared to death that first year and never really got my legs, so to speak. But I hung in there, passed all of my courses and at the end of the year received so-called Gentlemen's C's. My second and third years were much better and when I left, I had moved into the B category and wrote my third-year paper for Professor Louis Loss's securities regulation course and got an honors grade. My paper was titled "Defenses to Takeover Bids." I remember the first sentence especially well: "The corporate acquisition has become a useful vehicle by which corporations can grow and prosper."

Years later, Lewis would often refer to this paper as spurring his interest in corporate takeovers.

While Lewis was scared, he did not let his terror get the better of him. In the classroom, for example, his technique was straightforward and simple. Professors at Harvard generally utilized a teaching technique known as the Socratic method. They would randomly pick students and quiz them on legal issues, without any clear indication as to what was the correct answer or if there even was one.

In Lewis's class, 130 pairs of eyes would bore into the professor's victim, waiting for the slightest misstep. Then scores of hands would fly into the air, their owners dying to show off a better grasp of the issue in question than the student who had faltered.

There was one way to escape the Socratic method—students who hadn't plowed through the 100 or so pages of assigned reading material for each class could sit in the last row of seats. There was a tacit agreement that professors wouldn't call on students seated in the rear, a practice known as back-benching.

Lewis sat on the front row, practically daring professors to call on him. A few went out of their way to pick black students in an attempt to humiliate or embarrass them. That strategy invariably backfired if one of them ran a finger over their seating chart and called out, "Reginald Lewis!" His preparation was invariably thorough and he was not shy about articulating his points of view in a room full of attentive Ivy Leaguers.

Lewis wasn't a gunner, one of those students whose hands are always flailing in the air as they practically turn cartwheels to answer questions. But neither was Lewis a back-bencher—his self-pride would not allow that. Lewis refused to give any professor or student the smug satisfaction of secretly ascribing a poor performance on his part to the fact that Reginald Lewis was black.

To Lewis's roommates, Bill Robinson and John Hatch, he seemed to be cruising along with minimum exertion. So it was Lewis's entire life. Those on the periphery were often convinced he led a charmed, strife-free existence, but practically everything Lewis achieved was extracted through hard work and titanic struggle.

Though Hatch and Robinson were fellow black students and ahead of Lewis in law school, he never asked them questions about the law. Robinson recalls that Lewis seemed to be focused on some distant horizon only he could see and was remarkably free of worry. And Lewis tended to keep late hours and operated without difficulty on only four or five hours of sleep, a lifelong trait.

His apparent nonchalance stemmed from something he picked up in the Fugett household, which was a custom of making the difficult appear easy. Repetition, endless practice and solitary preparation weren't for public consumption. Never let 'em see you sweat, just let 'em see you excel with seeming ease.

A BLACK STUDENT AT HARVARD

Of the more than 500 freshman students in Lewis's class, at least 17 were black, the largest number admitted to Harvard Law School in one class up to that point. Like Lewis, most of his black compatriots had poor or blue-collar upbringings and had attended black southern colleges. From those backgrounds, they found themselves thrust into an environment that easily intimidated even wealthy white graduates of the country's most exclusive finishing schools and colleges.

The school itself was more than a little concerned about how the incoming black students of the Class of 1968 would hold up under the intellectual cut and thrust to which they would be subjected. In a well-meaning, if slightly patronizing gesture, the law school paired each new black student with a third-year student who would act as a mentor. The same precaution wasn't taken for first-year white students, a fact not lost on many of the new black students.

The school arranged for its highest ranking black employee, George Strait, the assistant reference librarian, to meet with the fledgling black lawyers. In his talk, Strait told them to work hard and to consider themselves privileged for having earned a chance to attend Harvard Law School.

Some of Lewis's fellow black law students were indeed awe-struck and terrified at the prospect of attending Harvard Law School and of competing with the best students in the country. Others in the group were feeling a tad cocky and even arrogant. They considered themselves a bright, elite subsection within an already elite segment of the scholastic universe. In public at least, Reginald Lewis fit into the latter category, says Richard Brown, one of the black students on campus.

As far as Lewis was concerned, he'd already proven to himself that he could excel in a law school setting by turning the special summer program on its ear. That all of the program participants were black and that most of his law school classmates were white made no difference to him.

Lewis conceded nothing to anyone. And he was moving beyond classifications based on race and ethnicity. Which is not to say Lewis wasn't proud of his roots. He and the other black students were a close-knit group, surrounded as they were by a sea of white faces and subjected daily to cultural shock on a major scale. Not everyone, including some students and faculty members, jumped for joy on discovering that the black students' ranks had grown to 17.

Most of them, including Lewis, often congregated at the "black" table in Harkness Commons, which housed the dining facility for graduate students. Lewis frequently socialized with Robinson and Hatch, his roommates, and with other black law students. They shared a common excitement, and sense of irony, about the challenge that lay ahead.

But Lewis was equally likely to be seen in the company of white friends he made at Harvard. He fell in with a study group made up of five white first-year law students. They spent hours reading, summarizing their conclusions, sharing notes, and discussing what had been taught in class. The same first-year curriculum was required of everyone: Criminal Law, Criminal Procedure, Contracts, Property I, Torts, and Development of Law & Legal Institutions.

Lewis moved easily between both black and white worlds, because he didn't view himself as constrained by artificial barriers founded on something as trite as pigmentation. If others chose to perceive him a certain way because of his skin, that was their problem.

Lewis and his classmates attended Harvard in the middle of the 1960s, a tumultuous time unprecedented in the country's history. Values were being turned upside down, and, intent as everyone was on their studies, they were not immune from being touched by a rising social consciousness.

Among the black students in Lewis's class, there was a pervasive sense that their unique status brought with it unique responsibilities. While most of their white counterparts had law firm ambitions, many of the black law students were interested in civil rights law or poverty law.

In one incident, black students confronted Harvard's administration over the lack of black construction workers involved with a campus building project. Harvard students black and white also participated in a series of civil rights demonstrations on campus.

Lewis supported such activities in spirit, but skeptically drew the line at physical participation. For him, marching around on campus holding a civil rights placard wasn't an effective way to wield influence. Philosophically, he believed in systemic change, rather than demonstrations and placard-bearing.

While he was at law school, Lewis's sense of racial pride was burgeoning. He had never had any identity problems—he was no white man hiding in a black man's skin. Black pride was on the rise around the country and the movement made an impression on Lewis, too.

During a break from classes one summer, Lewis returned to Baltimore with his hair puffed out in a luxuriant Afro, in keeping with the style among young blacks at the time. His uncle, James Cooper, had never seen an Afro before. In fact, he still wore the close-cropped haircut favored by most African-American males before the "Black is Beautiful" movement.

Cooper took a long look at Lewis's haircut and asked, "Man, what kind of nigger are you with all that hair on your head?" Cooper called Lewis "nigger," as a term of endearment, a practice common in the black community. This time, Lewis took umbrage.

"Don't say nigger in my presence again," he thundered at his dumbfounded uncle. "We are all black people!" As the two men sat on the curb in front of Lewis's house on Mosher Street, Lewis then lectured his older relative for a good 15 minutes on the error of his ways.

Lewis was exposed to racist comments during his last year at Harvard. In his third year, he had taken an apartment by himself in a working-class, Italian-American neighborhood seldom frequented by college students. When walking through the streets to and from school, Lewis would invariably be the target of ugly racial epithets.

Bill Slattery, a white classmate of Lewis's, remembers how Lewis would tell him about the incidents calmly and matter-of-factly, not showing any hint of the hurt and rage roiling away just below the surface.

"ROBINSON, LEWIS, AND HATCH"

In his first year at Harvard, Lewis lived at 1751 Massachusetts Avenue, in an upscale section of North Cambridge not far from Porter Square. John Hatch had rented the entire third floor.

When Hatch first met Lewis, he was struck by the fact that the newcomer had already taken to wearing twill pants, wide ties, and tweed jackets, an ersatz style favored by a segment of the student population that would now be called preppy. "Reg could be sort of like a chameleon sometimes. He was always sort of quietly watching for what was going on. He seemed to have sort of caught on to the tone of Harvard right away," Hatch says.

Living off campus provided Lewis a respite from the frenetic, pressure cooker atmosphere of law school. He kept his room as neat as a military barracks, prompting his other roommate, Bill Robinson, to tease Lewis that he couldn't be studying, because nothing in the room ever seemed to be disturbed.

The three bachelors took turns cooking and did their grocery shopping at Boston's open-air markets. As a joke, they would often answer their phone, "Robinson, Lewis, and Hatch," as though they were already a big-time law firm. Lewis spent an inordinate amount of time on the telephone, generating the lion's share of the phone bill, which he paid unhesitatingly.

Many of his conversations were with young ladies. As gutsy in his social relationships as he was in the classroom, Lewis would often pick up the phone and call a women's dorm at nearby Boston University, blurting out, "I want to talk to a swinger." In response, white coeds Lewis had never seen before would catch taxicabs to his apartment, share a lust-filled evening, then depart in the morning. They usually paid their own cab fare, too.

"Whatever he had, it was powerful," marvels shy James McPherson, who first met Lewis at the summer law program and later moved into the Massachusetts Avenue apartment. "It was some kind of magnetism or power or something that I couldn't comprehend."

There was a constant stream of attractive young women going in and out of Lewis's room, including a black coed from Simmons College who appeared without fail whenever Lewis summoned her.

For a brief period of time, Lewis saw an older black woman from the Roxbury section of Boston. She would cook for the young law student, bring him food, and spend the night. Lewis grew weary of her after a few months—she had limited potential in his eyes. She wasn't able to float effortlessly between the worlds of rich and poor, black and white like he did, nor did she offer much in the way of intellectual stimulation. One day Lewis informed the woman that her services would no longer be needed and insensitively gave her the boot while McPherson watched.

During his second year, Lewis incurred the wrath of the handful of black women attending the law school. One day, he invited a first-year black student to his apartment, ostensibly to tutor her. He started off by discussing contracts and property but wound up attempting to seduce her. Realizing she was prey and not a protegé, she abruptly left. Lewis was hot on her heels, following her down three flights of stairs and out the door, talking a blue streak the entire way.

Word about the abortive interlude spread among the other black female law students and they indignantly declared a moratorium on all black, male law students, condemning all for the alleged sins of one. When a classmate of Lewis's, Richard Brown, asked him about the episode, he smiled, weakly protesting his innocence.

One day at Harvard, Lewis was walking on campus when he encountered an old friend from his high school days. Overjoyed to see Lewis, his friend rushed to greet him. But instead of returning his warmth or even saying hello, an unsmiling Lewis posed a simple question, "What was your LSAT score?" An ironic query, considering that Lewis had never taken the Law School Aptitude Test himself. After making his LSAT demand, Lewis turned on his heel and strode away from his dumbfounded buddy. Proud and competitive, Lewis didn't like the idea of anyone stealing his thunder.

Lewis did have a compassionate side, although he was careful about who got to see it. John Hatch moved out of the Massachusetts Avenue apartment before the lease was up, to live with a woman Hatch had gotten pregnant. In response, Lewis was very solicitous and concerned. He assured Hatch that the young father was relieved of any rent obligations, even though four months still remained in the spring semester. "I think he was a very humane person," Hatch says of Lewis.

Contrast that with Lewis's treatment of James McPherson, who lived in the Massachusetts Avenue apartment during Lewis's second year of law school. McPherson had repeated run-ins with another roommate, Hiawatha Brown, and as a result had announced he was moving out with nine months still left on his lease.

"Well, by the way Jim, you're still under lease," Lewis tersely informed McPherson. "You can move but you're going to have to pay." Not surprisingly, McPherson—who worked three jobs to meet his commitment and pay another rent—has a different take on Lewis than Hatch. "I didn't really like Reggie that much," McPherson reflects.

Lewis perceived McPherson's predicament much differently than Hatch's. McPherson was running from an unpleasant situation, a mode of problem solving Lewis considered an anathema. So McPherson had to be forced to live up to his financial responsibilities.

The future business titan was already adept at making hard-nosed decisions driven by monetary considerations. The lesson he'd learned from his mother when he went away to camp and demanded the profits of his paper route was now thoroughly ingrained. Set your terms up front and stick with them.

Afterward, whenever he saw McPherson, Lewis acted as though nothing had ever happened. As far as he was concerned, nothing had. Their disagreement wasn't personal.

MAINTAINING A SHARP MIND

At Harvard Law School, as at Virginia State, Lewis frequently held forth over informal sessions where he and others discussed current events.

Although Harvard is known as very liberal, I sensed a real balance among the students. There were people on the left, right, and the center. The faculty was also pretty balanced. It seemed that regardless of the issue under discussion, you could always count on hearing several theories espousing an opposite point of view.

Reginald Lewis did few things in life that didn't fit into some larger scheme. Chewing over the events of the day helped keep the gild on Lewis's already golden tongue and kept his thought processes sharp. He knew that those skills, combined with a Harvard law degree, would make him a formidable package once he graduated. Plus, there was a part of him that was naturally curious about the world around him.

Every Friday he would scour the campus and rustle up five or six people whom Lewis deemed worthy of cultivating or worthy of his friendship. He would then accompany them to a restaurant on Harvard Square called the Wursthaus.

"He would ask if you were going to make it, with a look in his eye that he would be very disappointed if you weren't there," classmate Bill Slattery says. "He would pick the people that he wanted there and you would definitely talk about things that Reg wanted to talk about."

During these gatherings, Lewis did a lot of listening while others did most of the talking. But it was clear that it was his party and he was in control. He arranged the seating, as "Picasso did his cubes," according to Slattery. The topic of discussion was usually world events.

Wursthaus discussions were typically free of high-minded idealism or philosophical meanderings, for Lewis was nothing if not a pragmatist. Ideas were things that had utility and possessed value in an almost mercantile sense.

At Harvard, Lewis began contemplating a new avenue for achieving greatness. He talked to friends about pursuing a political career and entertained thoughts of going back to Maryland to get started. His reasoning was that Maryland represented a small political pond in which to make a splash. Perhaps a bid for city councilman or state legislator? Not Reginald Lewis—he wanted to run for U.S. Senate.

Although he never made good on his political aspirations, he continued to talk about running for office even after he became a successful lawyer and businessman. Back in his Harvard days, Lewis discussed his political yearnings only with his white law school classmates—he never uttered a word to his black colleagues, who are invariably surprised to learn Lewis had any interest in politics.

During Lewis's third year, he began working as a volunteer in a community legal assistance office with other Harvard law students. Most of Lewis's clients were blue-collar whites with whom he interacted with ease.

Every Thursday night after working at the legal assistance office, Lewis would join Bill Slattery, who was also working there, and walk to Slattery's apartment. Jill Slattery, a nurse, would then cook a meal of beef, mashed potatoes, and peas—the only food Jill ever cooked for Lewis and his sensitive stomach. Lewis would later tell friends that dining at the Slatterys was one of the few times at Harvard he enjoyed a good, home-cooked meal.

The three would usually drink an inexpensive bottle of wine along with their dinner. Against the backdrop of a huge map of Southeast Asia taped to the kitchen wall, the three frequently launched into spirited discussions of United States foreign policy in Vietnam.

Even during his days at Virginia State, Lewis was solidly against the Vietnam war. His objections were based on principle rather than fear of being drafted. When he registered for the draft after leaving Virginia State, the results of his physical examination showed that he was diabetic. His diabetes could be controlled through his diet, but Lewis was still classified 4F, meaning he was not fit for military service.

"MAY I TALK TO SAMMY DAVIS?"

Lewis's taste in music was relatively eclectic. He and roommate Bill Robinson both liked jazz and Lewis borrowed extensively from Robinson's jazz collection. For his part, Robinson preferred to steer clear of Lewis's records because Lewis liked many of the same older jazz artists that Robinson's father liked.

Lewis augmented his jazz collection with recordings by Frank Sinatra, whom Lewis played frequently. When the other third-floor residents of 1751 Massachusetts Avenue climbed the stairs and heard strains of "Strangers in the Night" wafting through the hallway, that meant Lewis was home. Lewis was fond of calling himself the black Sinatra. Not that he could sing, which he most assuredly could not, but because Lewis admired Sinatra's wealth, prestige, and rakish reputation.

Lewis actually had a close encounter with one of Sinatra's pals and fellow stars, Sammy Davis, Jr. On one of the rare evenings when Lewis was not studying or working, he was watching late-night television and saw Davis lamenting that he had never finished his education. A few months later, after learning that Davis was doing a concert at a Boston nightclub, Lewis tracked down the hotel where Davis was staying.

Lewis called the hotel and got through to Davis. Lewis told Davis that he had seen him on television talking about his lack of formal education and invited Davis to sit in on a Harvard law class.

Davis replied that he was flattered and would have taken Lewis up on the offer had it not been for a scheduling conflict. However, would the young law student be interested in two free tickets to Davis's show, as well as passes to go backstage and meet Davis afterward? That was just fine with Lewis.

Ask and you shall receive. It never occurred to Lewis not to call and chat with the internationally known Davis.

Lewis also wanted to meet Supreme Court Justice William Brennan when the jurist came to Harvard Law School as part of its 150th anniversary activities in 1967. So Lewis worked out a deal where he was able to pick Brennan up at Logan International Airport in Boston and serve as the Justice's driver and host at Cambridge. Obstacles, barriers, pitfalls—those were things for the timid and the negative to dwell on. Lewis preferred to boldly seize the day.

He had a tremendous talent for talking himself into situations or places where he wanted to be. Years later, when Lewis was a practicing attorney in Manhattan, his brother Jean Fugett, Jr. was a tight end with the Dallas Cowboys and the Cowboys came to New York to play the Jets at Shea Stadium. It was a bitterly cold, blustery day, and Lewis and his stepfather, Jean Fugett, Sr., sat in box seats exposed to the elements as they watched the game. Lewis, who had his collar turned up and no hat on, finally turned to his stepfather and said, "We gotta do better than this."

Lewis hopped out of his seat and pointed in the direction of the press box. "Just follow me and act like you know where you're going," Lewis advised. He walked up the stadium's concrete stairs, right past a policeman guarding the press box and marched inside as though he were William Randolph Hearst himself, with Jean, Sr. behind him. "Just act like you know where you're going." Words to live by for Reginald Lewis.

Lewis had always been this bold. When Jean Fugett got two tickets to the 1959 National Football League championship game between the Baltimore Colts and New York Giants—a contest called the greatest NFL game ever—Lewis was disappointed that his stepfather didn't invite him. Fugett had given his other ticket to a co-worker who agreed to provide transportation for the 200-mile drive to New York City, in return for a chance to see the game.

Lewis convinced his stepfather that he could weasel his way into soldout Yankee Stadium if Fugett would let him tag along. Sure enough, the teenager put his negotiating skills to use and got himself a seat on the 30-yard line—giving him a much better view than that Jean Fugett had in the end zone.

EUROPE ON HIS MIND

In the summer of 1966, following my first year of law school, I went to Europe for the first time. I took a Harvard charter from Boston to Paris and back for about $200. I was there for four weeks and the experience changed my life. The moment I saw Paris it was coup de foudre, or love at first sight. I still get goose bumps when I see Paris. I also spent time visiting Switzerland, Germany, Amsterdam, and Denmark before returning to Paris. Europe was crowded with students that summer and I had lots of interesting encounters.

Lewis's love of France had its origins in the stories his grandfather, Sam Cooper, frequently told. Cooper had been in the Army in World War I with an all-black division and he had fought in France. He spoke fondly about Paris and of how black U.S. servicemen were treated with dignity and respect by the French, in contrast to the behavior of some white Americans. Lewis became a lifelong Francophile.

While in Paris, Lewis befriended a young Scandinavian artist named Helge Strufe. In a stunt typical of the young and carefree, Strufe had run out of money in one of the Western Hemisphere's most expensive cities. Lewis, who was hardly flush with cash himself, lent Strufe some money and even let the artist spend a night in his hotel room.

When Lewis went to Amsterdam he looked up the grateful Strufe, who invited Lewis to stay at his apartment. Strufe had covered one wall of his dwelling with exquisite watercolors Lewis admired. Lewis arranged for some of Strufe's paintings to be shipped to Harvard, where they were displayed. Strufe also sold some of his works to Lewis at a discount. Later in life, Lewis would be the proud owner of a magnificent art collection worth millions of dollars but Strufe's paintings represented his first acquisition of works of art.

Prior to his first trip to the continent, Lewis was beginning to develop a cosmopolitan side and the journey to Europe further whet his appetite for the finer things in life.

GETTING A JOB

After my second year in law school, I landed a summer job with the law firm of Piper & Marbury in Baltimore. It was a terrific firm and a great summer. Mr. Marbury was a really big name in the law and, in Maryland generally. I also met a lawyer named Matt DeVito, who was a young partner. Matt took a special interest in me and we had some talks about the law, politics, and life in general.

Matt was disappointed when I did not come back to Baltimore after my third year; however, the lure of New York was irresistible. But more about that later.

Naturally, Lewis's job prospects after law school were a major concern. Once, he broached a job option that struck classmate Roger Lowenstein as "optimistically naive." He suggested to Lowenstein that they both move to New York City after graduation and start an interracial law firm. Lowenstein, who lived in the New York area, was intimidated by the thought of trying to tackle the Big Apple with no legal experience.

"He was from Baltimore and just felt that he could do pretty much whatever he wanted to or felt like," Lowenstein says incredulously. In the not too distant future, Lewis would establish his own law firm in New York City, and an interracial one at that!

By the time Lewis's last set of final exams rolled around in 1968, he was weary of the law school routine. He called his mother and complained to her that his exams were scheduled so close to each other that he couldn't study effectively. He wanted badly to do well in his last semester.

Characteristically, Lewis took action. He strode into the dean's office to ask if he could get his exam schedule changed. His request was denied, but Lewis was told that if it were any consolation, Harvard had yet to lose a third-year student.

By spring semester of the third year of law school, everyone was ready to get out into the real world. The events of the year were just extraordinary—Lyndon Johnson not running for President, Eugene McCarthy's army of college volunteers, the King and Kennedy assassinations. It was really too much.

During the fall semester of my final year, I and other law students got involved in third-year interviews, an annual ritual where legal recruiters come to campus looking for prospective employees. Piper & Marbury, the Baltimore law firm where I had worked after my second year, had yet to make me an offer. Although I knew Matt DeVito would be pushing hard for me within the firm, I decided it would be best to test the waters just in case.

The choicest jobs were considered to be those with large New York firms. I picked out a few that interested me and began interviewing. I went to most of these interviews feeling pretty relaxed. I felt that even if I didn't get a single offer, I could always return to Baltimore, work in the state attorney's office or the U.S. Attorney's office for a few years, then begin my own law practice. But the prospect of cutting my teeth in one of the "great firms" appealed to me.

One of the firms I signed up to interview with was Paul, Weiss, Rifkind, Wharton & Garrison. The decision turned out to be a good one. I met with Bill DeWind, one of the top partners in the firm, and we had a terrific interview. He was very relaxed, asked a lot of good questions and was not the least bit racist or condescending in his approach, which at that time was the exception rather than the rule. At the end of the interview, Bill described how his firm assessed applicants and said the next step was for me to come down to New York and visit with some of his partners and associates.

A number of my friends were more excited than I was about my having "made the cut," and thought Paul, Weiss was my kind of place. I decided to stay cool and see how things played out. The New York visit did go well. I met three associates who subsequently became partners: Alan Thomas, Mark Alcott, and Donald Moore. All three were down to earth and struck me as being very good.

In early December, Paul, Weiss made me an offer to come and work with them. I would either be in the corporate or litigation department—the firm would decide which—and I was to make about $10,000 per year. Only after I had a concrete offer in hand did I become excited. I called Deke Miller at Piper & Marbury and told him to remove my name from consideration at that firm. I got a call from Matt DeVito, who expressed disappointment and let me know he had been fighting for me. I felt a little down because I knew Matt had good judgment. Furthermore, Piper was a known quantity—as was Baltimore—and here I was opting for Paul, Weiss and New York, which were big unknowns. However, I liked the idea of New York and Paul, Weiss was definitely considered one of the hot firms.

I accepted the offer and headed for New York.

5

Building His Own
Law Practice: The
Years of Struggle

Reginald Lewis was brimming with excitement as he and his stepfather,
Jean Fugett, Sr., drove up the New Jersey Turnpike toward New York
City in the summer of 1968.

For him, as for so many others, Manhattan was the end of the rainbow. It was where he would meet his wife, raise a family, and build an
international business empire. He had no way of knowing that, at the
age of 25, his life was already half over.

He and Fugett entered the Holland Tunnel, cruised under the
Hudson River, exited into New York City and promptly got lost.

PAUL, WEISS

*Manhattan was a real scorcher during July and August of 1968. I
found an apartment, a five-floor walkup on 21st Street on the west
side of Manhattan. It had one bedroom and the rent was $150 a
month. I could afford a lot more, since Paul, Weiss raised salaries to
$15,000 in response to a move by rival Manhattan firm Cravath,
Swaine and Moore—I've always had a warm spot for Cravath as a
result. But the idea of saving as much as possible was irresistible. I*

did splurge on a stereo, about $1,500, and a few custom-made suits and shirts, items I'd always bought off the rack. I decided against a car because of the expense and inconvenience of parking.

I'll always remember my first day at Paul, Weiss. I recall catching the E train at 23rd and 8th, getting off at 50th and Madison and then the feeling of walking up Madison Avenue to the firm's office at 57th and Madison. The day was clear and sunny and everyone was in a hurry. The moment had arrived—it was time to get going.

One of the administrative people gave me some forms to complete and I met my deskmate, Mark Weinstein, who was starting the same day. He was kind enough to let me sit closest to the window without the slightest argument. Mark is now general counsel at Viacom and a good friend. Edward Korman was also beginning that same day and we have remained good friends. Ed today is a federal district court judge in New York.

The firm had decided to assign me to the corporate law department. Luckily for me, it was a very busy place and young lawyers were given a lot to do. Paul, Weiss had a reputation for being a "sweat shop," but I found that to be completely unfounded. No one ever insisted that you stay late. However, they did tend to hire people who were generally ambitious and were just used to working hard. I got the feeling the place was well run.

The relaxed, cool attitude I had my first day at Paul, Weiss disappeared quickly and I began to feel really uptight. I felt a lot of pressure to prove myself and it affected my performance somewhat, but I stuck it out and pretty soon began to get the lay of the land, so to speak.

A number of people at Paul, Weiss went out of their way to be helpful. Leonard Quigley, who I think is one of the best corporate lawyers around, was especially supportive. Alan Thomas, one of the really fine men of the bar, Morty Rochlin, Neale Albert, Sy Hertz, and Charles Dickey all really tried to get me to relax and ease up a little.

I developed many other friendships among the younger associates. Ted Parnall, Phillip Kissam, Gary Schonwald, Bill Levine, Robert Smith, Mike Luey, Peter Haje, and Al Youngwood were all young associates everyone said had a light around them. Youngwood was especially nice to me. We'd all go out to dinner around 8:30 P.M. and Al would sort of hold forth among the younger associates.

I did the usual work doled out to beginning associates: Setting up corporations, preparing joint venture agreements, securities law filings, some not-for-profit corporate work. I worked on a series of transactions involving small venture capital type deals that were particularly instructive, and on several initial public offerings (IPOs) which were then all the rage. Len Quigley was an especially good teacher and the way he attacked problems and moved projects along was really good. I still use many of the approaches he took to get at the root of a problem.

Paul, Weiss was one of the elite, blue-chip, New York law firms but, in contrast to some of the others, it was relatively "democratic," in the sense that it was more open to minorities of all stripes. On the average, the firm hired 20 to 30 associates fresh out of law school every year. Out of this group, maybe two or three would make partner.

Outwardly, Lewis was perceived by his peers as a bright, ebullient, outgoing individual. Mark Alcott, who interviewed Lewis, vividly remembers the Lewis of 1968. "He was much more mature than any of the other new candidates. Clearly ambitious. He had set for himself certain goals which he intended to meet. It was obvious that things had not been handed to him on a silver platter but, in spite of that, he had already achieved a lot."

Lewis was in the corporate law department, which included such luminaries as Arthur Goldberg, Lloyd Garrison, and Theodore Sorensen. This must have been heady stuff for a fresh law graduate, even one from Harvard. But Lewis longed to be on his own.

The Paul, Weiss experience was a very good one for me. My skills developed and matured enormously, but at the risk of offending my many friends there, it was not an especially happy time for me and I never really felt at home or able to relax. This was undoubtedly more a matter of sensing my own shortcomings than any attitude or action by the firm itself. So after a couple of years I was ready to leave and maybe try to do my own thing.

In the summer of 1970, I got a call from Fred Wallace, a Harvard Law School graduate, class of 1964. I was familiar with his name but didn't know him personally. Fred was working for Gene Callender at the New York Urban Coalition and had a mandate to create more housing for low- and moderate-income people. Fred wanted to recruit some lawyers in order to form a law firm to service this aspect of the coalition's programs. Fred's opening line was, "When are you going to leave that place and start doing something serious?"

We got together and the more I thought about it, the more I liked the idea of starting my own practice. Fred was offering a floor on income for a year or so and the coalition would pick up most of the overhead in exchange for getting a priority on its work. Not a bad deal.

When he found out about Lewis's desire to leave, Leonard Quigley pulled out all the stops in an attempt to convince him to stay. He'd found Lewis to be a quick study, dependable and mature, and a proficient attorney. "You haven't done every kind of merger deal, you haven't done every kind of public offering, you haven't done every kind of partnership agreement, so stick around and learn how before you go off and hang out your shingle," he told the young lawyer.

Lewis listened politely for a few minutes and then replied quietly, "Nope. I know what I need to know." He thought the world of Quigley, but Reginald Lewis was his own man and knew what was best for him. He could never settle for being a faceless Paul, Weiss drone no matter how well he was treated or compensated.

Colleagues at Paul, Weiss were surprised when Lewis informed them of this decision. To leave Paul, Weiss for another top law firm, Davis Polk maybe or Cravath, Swaine, was understandable. But to leave an established firm two years out of law school to start your own firm?

"It was definitely a bold move. It made me nervous," says Alcott. In fact, he cannot remember anyone else at Paul, Weiss who made a similar move. In hindsight, it is hard to imagine Reginald Lewis spending his career as a corporate lawyer at Paul, Weiss. Many in his Harvard class saw the firm and others like it as the pinnacle of success. But not Lewis.

In addition, something else had happened at Paul, Weiss that strengthened Lewis's resolve to leave. A partner at the firm implied that Lewis might not make partner; however, he told Lewis that the firm could get him a teaching position in Connecticut if a career in academia appealed to him.

Lewis took the news calmly but it reaffirmed the correctness of his decision to go out on his own.

STRIKING OUT ON HIS OWN

Building a successful law practice calls for something not taught in law school: The ability to hustle and self-promote. No one beats a path to an unheralded lawyer's door. The phone is usually quiet and when it does ring, chances are a bill collector is on the other end.

Lewis realized all this when he left Paul, Weiss in 1970. As always, he had a plan. He joined Wallace and a handful of other attorneys in starting a black-run law firm geared toward business matters affecting New York City's black community. The firm has the distinction of being one of the first black law firms on Wall Street—if not the first. Its name was Wallace, Murphy, Thorpe and Lewis, but in time only Lewis would remain.

The firm was located in Manhattan's financial district one block from the New York Stock Exchange, on the 19th floor of an office building at 30 Broad Street.

I met the three other people Wallace had recruited, Charles Laurence, Rita Murphy, and Josephine Thorpe. Rita and Jo were especially bright and savvy, although they didn't have a great deal of experience. Charlie Laurence was much older and had been a sole practitioner for many years in Brooklyn. Fred would also be a partner, but not share in any fees from coalition work. We took offices at 30 Broad Street.

Things worked pretty well and I brought a lot of value to the group. I spent my days on coalition work and in the evenings began meeting entrepreneurs and a lot of banking types. There was a ready market in black economic development work, essentially involving small business trying to raise capital. Nonprofits were also an active area. I began to develop some friendships and attract some clients.

I joined the Harvard Club and learned to listen to a lot of hopes and dreams. After a while, I became very good at separating the men from the boys, so to speak. I was also absolutely uncompromising about my fees. It's hard not to laugh about it now when I think about how I had to fight for real peanuts, but it's just part of the process.

In any case, the firm prospered. Rita and Jo decided to leave after about two years and Charlie Laurence became a judge. I'd had some nasty conversations with Rita and Jo before subsequently buying them

*out for about $30,000, which seemed like a fortune at the time. I also
assumed all of the firm's liabilities, which had been at the heart of the
dispute and, of course, drove me up a wall. However, wise counsel
from Amayla Kearse, whom I had retained, suggested that I pay them
off and move on.*

*I had already hired Charles Clarkson as an associate and hired
Diana Lee, who was then in her third year of law school at New
York University.*

*I was already working about 12 hours a day and for the next
year I must have kicked it up to about 18 hours a day during the
week and 6 to 8 hours on Saturdays and Sundays. As I think back
on it, it was probably driving everyone nuts, but we all had a good
time and felt we were making something happen.*

*Within a few years, the client list grew to include General Foods,
Equitable Life, Norton Simon, the Ford Foundation, and Aetna Life.
We developed real expertise with small business investment companies
and our practice was truly national. In fact, we did a couple of small
international deals, too.*

When Lewis was a child, his mother always told him: Mean what
you say and say what you mean. The advice hit home. When Reginald
Lewis told a client he was going to accomplish something, he delivered.
And he did so sans hyperbole and overblown predictions.

"THAT IS NOT ACCEPTABLE"

Lewis's drive and ego meant that there could only be one kingfish at
30 Broad Street. As he began to bring in more business, Lewis also
began to flex his muscles regarding decision making. Sparks would fly
when anyone dared to counter Lewis.

In 1972, the real estate work from the Urban Coalition began to
evaporate because of problems inside the Urban Coalition. This development played right into Lewis's hands. He was now the major revenue
earner in the firm, or rainmaker, as they say in legal circles.

At this point, a new side of Lewis began to emerge, that of the
tough, goal-oriented taskmaster. Lewis had a sense of urgency that
many of his employees didn't necessarily share. He would never tolerate

their viewing his law practice as a mere job. Everyone had to give maximum effort all the time. Anything less would prompt Lewis to dismissively utter one of his favorite phrases, "That is not acceptable."

Lewis's all-time favorite target was Charles Clarkson, a white attorney Lewis hired in 1972 right after Clarkson graduated from Brooklyn Law School. The tone for their long relationship was set during their first meeting. Lewis told Clarkson he wouldn't be able to pay that much; Clarkson replied he wasn't making anything at the moment, so whatever Lewis could pay would be a 100 percent raise.

"Everybody was afraid of Reg over the years and it got worse," Clarkson says. "He would treat the opposition with kid gloves and he would scream at everybody else on his side of the table. It was warfare all the time with Reg."

Lewis and Clarkson had an unusual relationship, to say the least. Another lawyer who worked briefly with Lewis says Lewis was constantly threatening to get rid of the retiring, gentle Clarkson for reasons Lewis wouldn't specify. But when Clarkson discovered he had a tumor on his spine, a malady that caused him to miss many months of work, Lewis told Clarkson not to worry about his job and to take as much time off as he needed to recuperate.

Clarkson had a knack for bringing out both the saintly Lewis and the bullying Lewis. Clarkson was employed by TLC Beatrice International as a consultant when Lewis died in 1993.

Diana Lee, a young law student Lewis hired from New York University, has less sulfuric memories of her days at 30 Broad Street. A Chinese-American, she got a job with Lewis in 1973 and worked with him until 1978, the year the law firm became known as Lewis & Clarkson.

Lewis was pro-black in outlook, but when it came to business he hired only people who could deliver, regardless of ethnic and racial background. In the early days, his law firm was a rainbow coalition as he, Clarkson, and Lee worked long hours crafting deals. In time, Clarkson and Lee came to do the bulk of the legal work while Lewis concentrated increasingly on business development.

Lee recalls that on Fridays, Lewis would occasionally treat her and Clarkson to dinner at Mary's, an Italian restaurant he loved in Greenwich Village. Lewis was also a tennis buff and began taking lessons at the Wall Street Racquet Club. Rather than go by himself, he dragged Lee along, too. Unlike Lewis, who already knew how to play the game somewhat, Lee was a novice and only lasted three lessons before throwing in the towel.

Lewis often used the tennis court the way some businessmen use the golf links to cultivate business contacts and hammer out deals. So he wasn't above mixing business and pleasure if he could accomplish both without hurting the business side of the equation.

Clarkson bore the brunt of Lewis's verbal tirades at 30 Broad Street because Clarkson tended to knuckle under meekly instead of standing up for himself, Lee says. She, on the other hand, had a tendency to yell right back at Lewis when she felt she was right, making Lee a less tempting target. Despite those occasional run-ins, "I actually thought he was very fair," Lee says. "He was very tough and he really drilled into us the skills of being a good lawyer. He gave us excellent training."

Lewis worked long hours all his life and set the pace for his employees, who both admired his stamina and resented the fact that they were expected to keep up with him. Robert Suggs practiced law with Lewis for half a year in 1976. "Most people give you a timetable to do something that has slippage in it. If you came back to Lewis in six months, there would be no slippage in his timetable," says Suggs. "He was very focused and if he had 12 things to do to get to the next point, he'd do them in sequence. A lot of people bullshit and are vague and their story changes every time they tell it. He wasn't bullshitting."

Lewis was keeping impossible hours to make his law practice successful. "I never thought that Reg was a family man: He preferred staying in the office," says Clarkson, Lewis's partner of more than 20 years. "He always spent a lot of time in the office. A lot of times I would think to myself, 'Gee, why isn't Reg going home? What the hell's he still in the office for?' and I hated it, because I felt like I had to stay in the office as long as Reg was there."

One day in 1976, Lewis left around midnight while associate lawyer Robert Suggs, who was working on a big financing transaction, left afterward around 3 A.M. After a few hours sleep and a quick shower, Suggs was back in the office at 7 A.M., while Lewis came in about 30 minutes later. When Lewis saw his young charge already at his desk and working, he smiled. "Had Suggs been in the office all night?" Lewis wanted to know.

When Suggs replied that he had gone home for a few hours, a look of disapproval and disappointment flashed across Lewis's face. The display was probably for effect as much as anything else. Lewis was a master psychologist whose attorneys struggled to win his approval and praise. He was able to get maximum motivational mileage out of something as simple as a smile or two-word phrases such as "Excellent work" and "Great result!"

But it was the stick, not the carrot, that Lewis resorted to most often when he wanted to light a fire under someone. Reginald Lewis could be extremely intimidating and intimidate was what he did on a regular basis. Even so, anyone thick-skinned enough not to be rattled by his loud voice or his sarcastic comments usually found something instructive in his remarks.

Every now and then, a reflective, almost wistful side of Lewis would emerge. As early as 1976, he talked of wishing he'd taken more time to smell the roses, instead of being so success-oriented. He made that comment to a number of people over the years, up until the time of his death. But when those moments of reflection evaporated, as they invariably did, Lewis would put his nose back to the grindstone and work as though possessed.

Lewis was a well-rounded man, and was aware that many of life's interesting, pleasurable experiences were passing him by. When one of his young lawyers mentioned having taken two years off to travel the world, a fascinated Lewis listened attentively to a blow-by-blow description of the adventure. The thrill of such a sojourn would have to be vicarious.

Lewis had a pronounced bias for substance over style. His law firm mirrored that. The decor at 30 Broad Street could best be described as utilitarian. The carpet was an unattractive orange and visitors sat on a plain black leather sofa.

The firm had four small offices, one for each attorney plus the odd additional lawyer who joined the practice periodically. There were also three secretarial bays and a conference room dominated by a large round table.

In areas where a direct correlation existed between money spent and money generated, however, Lewis went all out. His law offices had top of the line copier machines, which allowed him to turn around documents—the life's blood of any legal practice—faster. That let him be more profitable than if he'd invested in fancy furniture and ancient copier machines that broke down all the time.

Lewis's bread and butter in his law practice was an emerging market of big Minority Enterprise Small Business Investment Companies, known as MESBICS. Created by the Nixon Administration, MESBICS are basically venture capital firms formed by corporations or foundations. They operate under the aegis of the U.S. Small Business Administration.

For every dollar a MESBIC kicks into a minority-run company, the SBA matches that by investing or lending up to $3. This multiplier effect means that a MESBIC scraping together $1 million for a deal would have $4 million to pump into a business after the SBA's contribution.

Part of the SBA's loan is of a nonrecourse nature, meaning that if a company goes belly-up, its assets are liquidated to pay back the SBA. In time, Reginald Lewis became probably the top lawyer in New York City—and arguably the country—when it came to doing major MESBIC transactions.

Lewis's negotiating skills were legendary. He routinely out-negotiated far more experienced negotiators when aiming to protect his interests.

"You had to fight and squeeze whatever you got out of him, and negotiate and manipulate and play every game you could," says Suggs. "He was intensely competitive and he could not negotiate without trying to get as many marbles on his side of the table as he could get. He always drove the hardest bargain he could. He was looking long-term structurally and financially, but he wasn't looking long-term in his relationships with people that he felt he could just use and, when they left, replace."

Suggs left Lewis after receiving an offer representing a 60 percent raise over his $15,000 annual salary. Lewis offered to meet the pay increase for six months, to be followed by a review. But after having seen Lewis continually increase the timetable for making partner and seeing him balk on a promise to pay health care insurance, Suggs decided it was an opportune time to leave.

"IF WE DON'T GET IT, WE'RE NOT CLOSING"

Like all new attorneys growing a law practice, Lewis had to beat the wolf away from his door at times. Plus, clients were constantly devising ways of wriggling out of his fee schedule, which always flipped the switch on Lewis's volcanic temper.

So intent was Lewis on getting his practice up and running that he sometimes dipped into his personal savings account to meet payroll during his start-up days. At home, there were piles of returned checks stamped "insufficient funds." Around this time, the wife of one of Lewis's Harvard classmates was working in a doctor's office where Lewis was seen. At one point, while Lewis was being examined by the doctor, Marion Auspitz took Lewis's frayed shirt into another room and stitched the collar. When Lewis put his feet up on his desk, a Lewis trademark once he started running the show, there would be circles on the soles of his shoes where the leather was nearly worn through to his socks.

Lewis pushed hard to collect his fees. He knew he was good. Damned good and not to be hired on the cheap. He had no qualms with charging fees comparable to those of large white-run law firms.

In the typical MESBIC deal, the legal bill usually isn't discussed up front. And an entrepreneur putting up $25,000 and getting $2 million was usually so happy that lawyers' fees were the furthest thing from his or her mind. So, Lewis generally saved the best for last.

"I've seen some borrowers really wince when they saw his fee," says Howard Mackey, the head of Equico, a major Lewis client and the largest MESBIC in the country at the time. "Personally, I never blamed him—I mean the man's out there on his own and that's his work."

With his business savvy growing exponentially, Lewis came up with effective ways of making sure his fees got collected. He began to stipulate that clients had to pay his firm as a pre-condition to closing their financing transactions.

But there were still occasions when Lewis simply had to back down and reduce his bill after a client complained and the MESBIC involved didn't go to bat for Lewis. He found this particularly galling, because most of the borrowers were black and Lewis knew they wouldn't dream of trying to make a white law firm reduce a legal bill.

Every now and then, Lewis would butt heads with an entrepreneur as ego-driven and stubborn as he. One such instance was when he worked on a MESBIC deal making it possible for *Black Enterprise* founder Earl Graves to buy two radio stations.

Lewis demanded his fee at closing; Earl Graves said no—Lewis would be paid in 30 days. "That's unacceptable," Lewis replied flintily. "If we don't get it, we're not closing."

If Lewis wanted a test of wills, Graves was up to the task. Graves got on the phone to the chairman of Equitable Life, Equico's parent company, to complain about their intransigent attorney. However, only after Lewis received assurances from Equitable that he would be paid in a timely manner did he relent and close the deal.

Again, it was just business for Lewis. There were no hard feelings on his part. He'd gotten what he'd wanted, which was to be paid immediately for the hard work he put into Graves's transaction. Graves came away with a heightened respect for Reginald Lewis—in fact, he was one of the first people to tell Michael Milken to keep an eye out for a budding business superstar named Reginald Lewis.

Equico president Mackey figured Lewis wouldn't have the nerve to quibble with Mackey about money. Wrong. "I always found him to be kind of hard-boiled, and we spent some time arguing about fees. I got mad at him, because I put him in the position at Equico where he was doing all of our business. I figured the last thing he would want to do would be to argue with me, but he started in on me like anybody else. We worked it out, but that's the kind of guy Reg was," Mackey recalls.

Lewis didn't even cut relatives slack. When his uncle James Cooper bought a Baltimore bail bond business, he hired Lewis to represent him. Cooper flew to New York, where Lewis ironed out the final terms of the sale.

Cooper got his bill and blanched. He asked Lewis, "Are you sure?" Yes, Lewis replied, his hefty fee was correct. There had been no error.

"Either pay me all of the bill or pay me none of it." Lewis told his uncle calmly.

Cooper paid his bill.

LEARNING THE ART OF THE DEAL

After a few years, Lewis's law firm began to prosper. In time, it pretty much cornered the market in terms of representing MESBICs. But Lewis was deriving something from his MESBIC work that would be far more valuable in the long run than income: He was amassing an incredible body of knowledge about how to structure corporate acquisitions through the use of debt financing.

Lewis was retained as general counsel by the American Association of Minority Enterprise Small Business Investment Companies and was shuttling down to Washington on a regular basis, attending meetings related to MESBICS.

He was staying abreast of the latest developments in this field and was also building his network of contacts. He made it a point to devour every piece of MESBICS literature he could get his hands on.

In Washington, Lewis frequently ran into childhood friend Dan Henson (to whom he had sold his first paper route). Henson worked for the SBA and later the Minority Business Development Agency. In "the mid- to late-70s, Reggie was getting pretty sophisticated in terms of his knowledge of how to do deals. He was learning the art of the deal," Henson says.

With his overcoat draped over his shoulder and briefcase in hand, Lewis would stride into MESBIC meetings in Washington, make contacts, then dash out the door and head back to New York—sometimes after just an hour.

In 1970, the same year he left Paul, Weiss, Lewis encountered someone who became a major client, friend, and future business confidant rolled into one. Lee Archer had just retired from the Air Force and was put in charge of running General Food's MESBIC, which was known as Vanguard. A no-nonsense former fighter pilot, Archer had been scouting around for a lawyer familiar with the MESBIC industry. Though Lewis had only two years of experience then, he came highly recommended to Archer.

The young lawyer dropped by Archer's office, where the two men sized each other up. Lewis was impressive as usual.

"I decided he was just what I needed," Archer recalls. "He knew a heck of a lot about venture capital and he seemed to have the personality to sit on the board. He was smart, he was straight-forward and honest. He liked the kinds of things I liked, like plays and concerts."

Lewis was eventually named as legal adviser and member of the board of both Vanguard and a Specialized Small Business Investment Company formed by General Foods known as North Street Capital.

Lewis participated in an incredible 64 business deals funded by General Foods. Being on the board also meant Lewis got a piece of the action in some of the transactions, including a movie by the name of "River Niger," which was financed by $40 million in MES-BIC money. Lewis and Archer both owned the rights to the music in that movie.

When black-owned Johnson Publishing and another company made individual bids to take over *Essence* magazine, Lewis and Archer possessed just enough stock to hold the crucial swing votes to approve or kill the deal. Lewis believed that *Essence* was already well managed and in excellent hands, so he and Archer nixed the takeover attempt, even though they would have profited handsomely if they had sold their stock.

By helping block the *Essence* takeover, Lewis had thwarted the ambitions of the then-wealthiest black man in America, John Johnson, who owns Johnson Publications and publishes *Jet* and *Ebony* magazines. (Lewis would later supplant Johnson at the top of the *Black Enterprise* list of the 100 largest black-owned companies with his acquisition of Beatrice International.)

Lewis and Archer worked well together in that they were somewhat similar: Both were formal, rather reserved, and not given to wasting time when there was business to be taken care of. Occasionally the two would disagree. Nevertheless, Lewis later named Archer to the board of directors of both McCall Pattern and TLC Beatrice International.

Word of mouth about the quality of his legal work was starting to bring dividends for Lewis. In 1973, Lewis managed to snare the largest MESBIC of them all—Equico Capital Corp., a subsidiary of Equitable Life. Then-Equico president Mackey felt Lewis's work was head and shoulders better than that of Equico's own in-house lawyers. Mackey wound up funneling Lewis all of Equico's work.

"He was very thorough," Mackey remembers. "He was always what I call a businessman's lawyer. Some lawyers basically were so conservative they would spend most of their lives telling you what you could not do. Reg's attitude and approach to doing work was to figure out how to get done what it was you wanted to get done. And the quality of documents, in terms of making sure you were well protected and that you had proper covenants in your loan agreements, was good."

Lewis often went above and beyond the call when it came to helping his clients. Mackey had a car with Washington, D.C., license plates that New York City police loved to ticket for not having New York tags. When Mackey's citations reached a critical mass, Lewis agreed to accompany him to the city parking violations bureau, where Lewis successfully negotiated a 50 percent reduction in Mackey's large fine.

Years later, when Lewis tried to take Beatrice public in 1989, with Merrill Lynch as the primary underwriter, Lewis made the black investment firm Pryor, McClendon, Counts & Co. Inc. an underwriter as a favor to Mackey, who was employed there.

As had been the case since high school, Lewis still had an affinity for fine clothing, when he could afford it. One of his shopping excursions led him to a small, black-run clothing store in Manhattan named LeMans Haberdashers. Lewis was impressed by the cut of the clothing, which came primarily from Italy and France, and by the manner in which it was displayed.

The LeMans visit started an interesting business and personal relationship with the shop's three proprietors, including Kermit Morgan, that generated more than its share of laughs and heated discussions.

Lewis felt comfortable around Morgan, a fellow black entrepreneur fighting to make a living in the rough and tumble of New York City. Morgan found Lewis to be very funny, ambitious, and committed to helping other black businesspeople.

Lewis would always exhort Morgan to give back to the community by helping other black entrepreneurs who had the potential to excel, but hadn't been exposed to essential contacts or financing sources. Lewis envisioned a network of black entrepreneurs that would be able to prosper by sharing information and helping others avoid pitfalls.

Morgan recalls that as far back as the early 1970s, Lewis was setting aside time to share his business expertise with black businesspeople, free of charge. But he was doing it quietly and selectively. Nothing was more valuable to the discerning Lewis than his time: It couldn't be wasted on someone lacking a total commitment to achieving success.

If Lewis harbored expansion-oriented dreams for himself during his days as a lawyer, he also had them for some of his clients. Lewis was impressed with LeMans, which had two stores in Manhattan. But Lewis envisioned it becoming even grander. He and Morgan butted heads constantly over whether the business should expand beyond its two locations and beyond targeting black consumers.

"We argued all the time," Morgan laughs. "He wasn't right all the time, although he thought he was."

Using his contacts, Lewis enabled Morgan to open a third store in Columbia, Maryland, an affluent, largely white bedroom community between Baltimore and Washington. The store did poorly and eventually closed.

"I guess what we learned from Reggie was to think large, because he had more exposure than we to raising capital and he stressed thinking on an international level," Morgan says.

More than a decade before Lewis purchased Beatrice, the seeds of doing business on an international scale had already taken root. In 1974, Lewis helped LeMans get $500,000 for business expansion purposes, a transaction Lewis "put together rather simply, based on his contacts," according to Morgan.

Lewis was more than just another attorney who drafted contacts or reviewed leases. He was always prodding Morgan to accompany him to the Harvard Club, or to wine-tasting sessions, activities the down-to-earth Morgan hated. Lewis wanted to introduce Morgan to influential white businessmen who might prove valuable to both of them later on.

"But it just wasn't my style," Morgan says. "He meant well and he wanted to expose us to big money, he really did."

Their business relationship ended on an unhappy note. Morgan's version is that he and his two companions—while generally very impressed with Lewis's work—felt he was just a tad too nice when negotiating with LeMans's business opponents. More than once, Lewis was reminded that he was being paid to represent LeMans, not the other side.

Charles Clarkson questions Lewis being too "nice" while negotiating for a client. "That would have been out of character for Reg," Clarkson says. "He was always very zealous when it came to representing a client."

But it says something about Lewis that his friendship with Morgan survived even after their business relationship broke up.

"I PAY MORE IN TAXES THAN THESE GUYS MAKE IN SALARY"

Lewis's prestige was burgeoning; his income was rapidly growing. However, despite all this and his Harvard law degree, the fact that he was black meant he could be "put in his place" within a matter of seconds.

Once a casually dressed Lewis came to 30 Broad Street on a Saturday to do some work. Lewis nonchalantly nodded to the security guard as he strolled past his desk. The guard ordered him to stop and state his reason for being in the building.

Lewis was justifiably outraged. Sensing the challenge was really about race as much as anything, Lewis felt the blood rushing to his face. Hassling a person on his skin color made as much sense to him as discrimination based on shoe size or the shape of one's earlobes. Could anything be less germane to a person's intrinsic worth?

"Reg was very sensitive about that," Charles Clarkson says. "He had a sense that he was black all the time and people treated him a certain way and he was always on guard. It was a big part of his life."

Still angry hours after the incident, Lewis mailed off a strongly worded letter to the building manager. Lewis knew nothing would come of his complaint, but failing to vent the rage eating away at him would be unhealthy and to stay passive in the face of bigotry would be untrue to himself.

One night, Lewis was changing a tire on his Mercedes outside of his Manhattan brownstone. Two city policemen pulled up behind Lewis's car and ordered him to spread his legs and place both hands on the hood of his vehicle. Lewis protested that not only did he own the Mercedes, he owned the brownstone, too. After the cops were shown the registration for the car, they apologized and drove away. Lewis later told a friend that during the confrontation he couldn't help but think, "I pay more in taxes than these guys make in salary." Wisely, he did not articulate that observation.

When confronted with racism, Lewis's response was to meet it head on. If he felt a maitre d' placed him too close to the kitchen, or that a waiter delivered indifferent service, Lewis would buttonhole the manager and bring it to his or her attention. Once when a taxicab passed him by in Manhattan, Lewis set out on foot after the offending driver. Sprinting at top speed along a New York City sidewalk packed with people, Lewis edged close enough to the cab to write down its number on a scrap of paper. He folded it, put it in his wallet and dashed off an angry letter to the city taxicab commission the same day.

Lewis brought the same intolerance for bias to the workplace. "He never tolerated even a hint of condescension or bigotry in his personal or his business dealings," TLC Beatrice General Counsel Kevin Wright says.

"I will not tolerate racism anywhere, from anybody on any joke or anything," a deadly serious Lewis once told his brother, Tony Fugett. "I will stop the president of the United States if he makes an inappropriate statement and tell him that it is inappropriate right then, at that point in time. Period."

Lewis didn't care for discrimination in any of its ugly manifestations or guises, including homophobia. A month before he passed away, he and his family had scheduled a skiing trip in Vail, Colorado, and had put down a $16,000 deposit, when an antigay law was passed. Even though his youngest daughter, Christina, wanted to go skiing badly and Lewis had to forfeit $16,000, he canceled the vacation, rather than be a party to a discriminatory situation.

One sunny weekend morning in 1982, Lewis and a classmate from his Harvard days, Bill Slattery, were driving from Manhattan to a summer camp in Massachusetts. Lewis's daughter Leslie was a camper there, as was a daughter of Slattery's. Lewis was in the passenger seat of Slattery's car, which was new, and Slattery's son was in the back seat. As they rode along a heavily traveled Connecticut road at a 56 mph clip, they passed a state trooper parked under a tree. The trooper immediately pulled out and settled in directly behind Slattery's car.

After a cat-and-mouse routine that went on for three miles, the trooper finally turned on his siren and flashing lights. The lawman left his cruiser, made an exaggerated display of adjusting his gun holster and started walking toward Slattery's car. Lewis turned to Slattery and said, "See what it's like?" There was no sarcasm or anger in his voice, just a trace of resignation. The trooper wrote Slattery a ticket for speeding, a citation he and Lewis felt was unjust, and got back in his patrol car.

"There was no question in my mind or my son's mind or Reg's mind that if Reg hadn't been in that front seat, he wouldn't have stopped us," Slattery says.

Luckily neither of Lewis's daughters were with him, because he didn't want them exposed to racism, even though he knew it was inevitable. When Christina was still a little girl, he took her to see "The Nutcracker" at New York's Lincoln Center one Christmas, and she asked an innocent question about something taking place on stage. An elderly white woman behind Lewis remarked that Christina needed to be quiet and Lewis turned around and leveled the woman with an acidic retort and a withering stare. He felt badly about it afterward, but still believed the woman would have remained quiet had an inquisitive white child asked the question.

In a perfect world, Lewis would have preferred simply to be a human being. Not an African-American or black man, just a man. That's why he strongly resisted attempts to put him on a pedestal as a black role model. "I'm not going to carry my race on my shoulder," he once told a close confidante. "If I can be helpful to others, that's fine, but I'm not going to do my work because I am a role model for all African-Americans. That's bunk. I'm not responsible for anybody's life, I'm responsible for my life. And I'm responsible for realizing my own dreams."

"I'M YOUR LAWYER, FOLLOW ME"

To write Lewis off as someone preoccupied solely with making money would be grossly inaccurate. He was far too multifaceted for that, as his dealings with Benjamin Chavis demonstrate. Chavis is currently the Executive Director of the NAACP, but when he and Lewis met in 1971, he was a young civil rights activist.

Chavis was on the staff of the United Church of Christ's Commission for Racial Justice, which had offices in Manhattan. The commission was looking for a legal counsel and someone had mentioned Lewis, even though he was a corporate lawyer. "We wanted a sharp, African-American lawyer who was fearless and Reginald Lewis was recommended to us on that criteria," Chavis says.

He went over to 30 Broad Street to check out Lewis, who was equally curious about the commission and the range of civil rights activities it handled. The first thing Chavis noticed was that Lewis was sporting an Afro. Chavis was also pleasantly surprised to find that Lewis knew how to "dap," as the intricate handshakes many black men greeted each other with during the 1970s were called.

"In our first encounter, he made me understand in no uncertain terms that he was from Baltimore, he was from the community and he knew what hard times were and he knew the plight of the African-American community," Chavis remembers. "And even though he had become relatively successful, he had an undeniable urge in ensuring that the civil rights movement in the 1970s would be effective."

Lewis and Chavis were instant friends. Lewis constantly admonished Chavis, who frequently traveled to the South to confront segregated school districts, to "Be careful. Watch your back. Who's watching your back?"

In 1972, Chavis was one of the Wilmington 10, a well-known group of activists arrested while fighting school desegregation in Wilmington County, North Carolina. Their bond totaled $500,000. In New York, Lewis helped the Commission for Racial Justice raise the bond money for the defendants.

Lewis was not the trial attorney for the Commission for Racial Justice, but he was the backup attorney. On one occasion in December 1972 when the primary lawyer was occupied with another matter, Lewis unhesitatingly took a tour of the front lines in the fight for civil rights. Chavis's presence was demanded in a Wilmington County courtroom for a bail hearing and Lewis volunteered to accompany him. Another black attorney, Irv Joiner, went with him.

They boarded a Piedmont Airlines jetliner from New York City to North Carolina and settled in for the flight. Not knowing what to expect, Lewis felt a mixture of excitement and trepidation, although outwardly he showed no emotion. The men were fully aware that their lives might be in danger once they reached North Carolina and there wasn't much conversation among them on their way down South. As the plane glided in for a landing, Lewis looked out the window and saw scores of uniformed sheriff's deputies standing on the tarmac, holding loaded shotguns. "These people don't look too friendly," he said to no one in particular.

Everyone else on the jet saw the armed posse, too, and sensing that the three young black men wearing the Afros might be the focus of all the attention, they scurried off the plane and down the jetway ladder as soon as the wheels on the Piedmont Airline jet stopped rolling. The flight crew wasn't far behind, leaving Lewis, Chavis, and Joiner alone on a now deathly quiet aircraft.

Out the window, they saw a tall lawman about 6-foot-5 and wearing sunglasses emerge from the sea of uniforms outside the plane. From the way he carried himself, the deference displayed to him by the deputies and the slightly impatient pose he struck that contained a hint of malevolence, everyone on the plane knew he was the sheriff.

Lewis was very concerned by now, and his face showed it, but he wasn't about to be cowed. Reginald Lewis had a knack for digging deep within and rising to occasions. If ever there was a time to conjure up that ability, this was it. He stood up and moved to the aisle of the jetliner.

"I'm your lawyer, follow me," he instructed Chavis confidently. Lewis, Chavis, and Joiner slowly walked down the aisle of the plane, out the door and down the ladder, where the sheriff was waiting at the bottom of the stairs.

Lewis took his time going down the stairs, as did Chavis. As soon as they got to the tarmac, the sheriff reached around Lewis in an attempt to grab Chavis, pushing Lewis aside slightly. "Wait a minute! Don't touch him," Lewis told the sheriff forcefully. "I'm his lawyer. . . . Who are you?"

A look of incredulity registered on the sheriff's face. Dressed in full law-enforcement regalia, right down to his shiny silver badge and brimmed colored hat, he had expected Lewis to meekly step aside and surrender Chavis. The possibility that Lewis would resist and actually dare to challenge his authority hadn't entered the lawman's head. "I'm the sheriff," he said, thrown off balance momentarily.

"Well, let me see your identification," Lewis ordered. The sheriff compliantly did as he was told, reaching into his back pocket, fishing out his wallet and holding out his ID for Lewis. "I thought what Reggie did took a lot of guts," Chavis says. "It just disoriented the sheriff. From that moment on, Reggie was sort of in control of the situation."

Chavis was put into the back seat of a squad car accompanied by Lewis, who demanded that Chavis not be taken to jail but directly to a magistrate. His request was granted and Chavis was taken before a magistrate who posted a $100,000 bond that Chavis met, securing his release. Chavis told Lewis that he was going to stay in North Carolina and hold a rally that night.

"Hey man, come on now," Lewis said. "We got you out on bond— you need to leave Wilmington." But Chavis insisted on staying and asked two of his assistants to drive Lewis to the airport in Raleigh.

Lewis took out one of his business cards, scribbled something on the back and handed it to Chavis. "If you're going to stay, here's my phone number," he said. "Make sure you call me no later than midnight to say everything is all right, okay? Watch your back, man."

Lewis also challenged the state of North Carolina's policy of investing bond money. He succeeded in forcing the state to pay the interest on the bond to the Wilmington 10 defendants. Some members of the predominantly white United Church of Christ who had been opposed to the church posting bond for the Wilmington 10 dropped their opposition when they learned the church stood to benefit.

Reginald Lewis may not have walked picket lines, but there was little doubt where he stood when it came to the civil rights movement and its quest to have all U.S. citizens treated fairly and with dignity.

"In order to get in a position of economic parity, you've got to fight abject discrimination and Reggie understood that," Chavis says. He and Lewis remained close friends. In 1992, Lewis lobbied vigorously to have Chavis elected as head of the National Association for the Advancement of Colored People. Chavis won election to the post in 1993, not long after Lewis's death.

"He was a regular brother, he was unpretentious," Chavis says. "A lot of times people surround themselves in their wealth and become pretentious. Reggie wasn't like that. Reginald Lewis was the kind of friend where the friendship was not based on political expediency and it was not based on popularity, it was based on genuine respect."

"He was very interested in ensuring that young people, particularly African-American youth, be given a fair chance at life itself," Chavis says. In the final days before Lewis's death, Chavis served as his spiritual adviser.

NETWORKING IN THE BLACK BUSINESS COMMUNITY

Away from his office, Lewis had begun to hang out with a select group of young, black businessmen involved in the world of high finance. It was inevitable that they would encounter each other at some point, since the number of influential black businessmen in Manhattan in the early 1970s could be counted on one hand. One was Cleveland Christophe, an executive at Citibank who Lewis had met in 1970 when he did some legal work for Soul-Stop, a Harlem fast-food restaurant that Christophe owned.

Another member of Lewis's circle was Travis Bell, now deceased, whose Daniels & Bell investment house was the first minority-run member of the New York Stock Exchange. There were other members of the elite group, including Thomas Bourelly, a University of Chicago graduate whom Lewis helped buy a food company in 1975.

They used to gather periodically at one of two uptown jazz clubs or at each other's homes to discuss their hopes and dreams, as well as the horror stories that only young black men working in a white-dominated financial world could fully appreciate.

"We came to the scene when banks were talking about their urban divisions financing barber shops and barbecue pits, so it was important for us to get to another level," Bourelly says. "We talked a lot about our future, the things we could do, our responsibilities to our society and to our people. We used to share each other's contacts, which was quite important."

Lewis, Bell, and Bourelly also had a professional relationship, because Lewis was the attorney for Daniels & Bell, and Bourelly ran the firm's holding company. Lewis helped Daniels & Bell do a leveraged buyout for a chocolate company, one of the first LBOs ever pulled off by a black business.

Bourelly remembers that Lewis the lawyer was very smart, tough, and a stickler for details. "You didn't have to worry about being blindsided once Lewis had gone over a business agreement. He'd usually catch potentially harmful loopholes and put in clauses protecting against contingencies most businesspeople never thought about."

"Reginald Lewis was an open, generous friend who didn't brook people wasting his time and who abhorred mediocrity," Bourelly adds.

In any group made up of bright, aggressive individuals, disagreements are bound to occur and Lewis's group was no exception. They gravitated to each other for their collective betterment, but their internecine clashes sometimes got in the way of what they could accomplish.

Lewis had his share of disagreements too, but no more or fewer than anybody else. "When you got into an argument with Reg, you came out of it pretty bruised. The guy knew what he stood for and fought for his views and positions," Bourelly says. "When he became rich and powerful, he tended to be a little bit more self-righteous."

However, even after Lewis captured Beatrice, he never forgot his friends from his early days in New York. And he always returned their phone calls promptly, whether he was at 40,000 feet in his corporate jet or in Paris.

In 1975, when Bourelly bought Chicago-based, Allfresh Foods with $1 million in MESBIC financing, he did so with Reginald Lewis acting as the lawyer in the transaction. Because Lewis had worked so hard to make the deal a reality, Bourelly paid him his fee and gave him a 10 percent interest in the company.

Later, in recounting to a friend that Bourelly had given him a 10 percent stake, Lewis said, "You know why the man did that? Because the man is smart." Allfresh was later sold at a profit.

Christophe introduced Lewis to a young Chase Manhattan executive named Hughlyn Fierce. Christophe boasted to Lewis that Fierce had the authority on his own signature to make loans up to $500,000. Without batting an eyelash, Lewis asked for a $25,000 unsecured loan on the spot.

Fierce was taken aback and turned Lewis down. Not only could a bus run over Lewis five minutes later, Lewis had no proof he could repay a loan for $25,000. They were soon going at each other, oblivious to Christophe who stood by shaking his head and wondering why he had introduced them.

"What Reg had done was to fundamentally put me in the position of having to defend why I would not do it," Fierce recalls. "Reg thought it was absolutely incredible that I would not be willing to make him a $25,000 unsecured loan. This from a guy who has the temerity and gonads to open a Wall Street law firm, when other brothers I know just want to join a law firm!"

As 1979 approached, Lewis was ready to move out of 30 Broad Street. He had outgrown his small offices and needed more space. At one point, part of the floor Lewis was on was unoccupied, so he asked the landlord if it was possible to use some adjoining empty offices for storing documents. What started as storage space was quietly turned into working offices for Lewis's practice until the landlord caught on. Now, with his lease up, Lewis was looking to lease offices with a little more panache and class than his dowdy quarters at 30 Broad Street.

Lewis had grown immeasurably both as a lawyer and a businessman during his nine years there. Maintaining a viable law practice had been a real struggle the first six or so years. Each MESBIC only generated about three deals a year, so Lewis was constantly hustling to ensure a steady stream of business. When times had been hard, Lewis and his attorneys even resorted to handling home closings to keep money coming in. And Lewis alone brought in new business.

Lewis hadn't forgotten all the nights he'd spent beating the brush for clients while the other attorneys were comfortably ensconced in their homes, eating dinner. Nor had he forgotten the times he was forced to use his savings so everyone else would have a paycheck.

Years later, Lewis could still recall for associates the occasions he had missed holidays because of work. There were times when he would find himself at an airport trying desperately to catch a late night plane back to New York in order to spend Christmas at home with his family, a holiday he never missed.

Lewis wound up doing MESBIC transactions for 14 years. But he began to feel more and more that he was trapped in a legal ghetto. Looking back, his accomplishments were remarkable. When he joined Wallace, Murphy, Thorpe and Lewis in 1970, he was just a bright young lawyer with two years of experience and no clients. Within a few years, his work was so highly respected that he had some corporate clients that large law firms would have coveted. But it wasn't enough.

Even though transactions involving MESBICS were often worth millions of dollars, that made no difference—the deals were marked, "For Minorities Only," and therefore second class as far as Lewis was concerned.

"Reg always hated the idea of using race to get business," says Clarkson. "It really irked him a lot. He got visibly angry, particularly when companies talked about hiring him because he was a black attorney."

Besides, bigger things were brewing. In the late 1970s and 1980s, merger and acquisition fever took hold of corporate America. But instead of being at the table with the big boys, Lewis had his nose pressed against the window. His rightful place was to be shoulder-to-shoulder with the white attorneys doing the big transactions, not working with companies fighting for financial crumbs, relatively speaking.

I was feeling pretty good about my situation, but knew that the best this would produce was good income. The more I got involved in business acquisitions, the more I believed this was the area where I could make my mark. I began to search about for deals, while keeping the law firm intact to pay the bills, too.

Lewis was again restless and he began to look elsewhere for his next business conquest.

6

"Masterful" Man: Winning Loida Nicolas

The most important event that occurred during Reginald Lewis's years at Paul, Weiss had nothing to do with work. He had been somewhat of a ladies' man all through Dunbar High School, Virginia State, and Harvard, and he had never entertained the thought of a serious romantic relationship. Having resolutely set a goal for himself, he was convinced that he would travel faster without the baggage of longterm emotional commitments. He was determined to avoid marriage until he was 35, an age when he was sure he would be independently wealthy and established. He once said, "I didn't want the responsibility of a wife before I had a real stake in life."

But life takes some interesting turns at times and all of Lewis's plans were about to go out the window, as far as romance was concerned.

The day after his 26th birthday, Lewis was at his desk at Paul, Weiss, working hard and planning to stay late, as usual. His desk phone rang and Reynaldo Glover, one of his black Harvard Law School classmates, was on the line. Glover had chosen to pursue civil rights law and was working in Manhattan as national president of the Law Students Civil Rights Research Council.

"Want to go out on a blind date tonight?" Glover asked. "With whom?" Lewis wanted to know. "My administrative assistant, Loida Nicolas," Glover responded. "Her sister and I will complete the foursome." After a few seconds of thought, Lewis answered, "Perhaps another time; I'm quite busy right now."

"Oh, that's too bad," Glover responded. "She comes from the Philippines." Lewis's eyes lit up, because he'd never dated an Asian before. He told Glover that he would be joining him and the two young ladies after all.

Like Lewis, Loida Nicolas had recently graduated from law school at the University of the Philippines. A member of a relatively well-to-do family from the province of Sorsogon, Loida was in the United States with her mother on the first part of a round-the-world trip, a gift from her father for having just passed the Philippine bar examinations. Loida and her mother were to wait in New York until her sister Imelda finished her masters degree in art history at Columbia University. Then they would travel to Europe. Rather than remain idle for several months, Loida began to search newspaper want ads. The *Village Voice* had an ad from a civil rights organization looking for an administrative assistant. Loida decided to apply and was hired by Glover. When Glover began to date her sister, Glover suggested to Loida that she come along on a blind date.

Going out with this Reginald Lewis fellow she'd heard Glover frequently mention would just be part of her brief American adventure, an evening's diversion . . . nothing more.

The two men agreed to rendezvous with their dates at the Aberdeen Hotel, where the women were staying. Glover entered the hotel lobby first, followed by Lewis. As he marched toward the Nicolas sisters, Glover introduced Lewis to Loida who extended her hand, looked into his eyes with a friendly smile and said, "Hi, I'm Loida. I've heard so much about you."

Lewis was taken with Loida immediately. She was attractive, had a nice figure and a decidedly classy, demure persona. In addition, she hadn't known him 10 seconds and had already stroked his ego, the quickest way to his heart. Yes, this was definitely going to be an interesting evening.

As the foursome walked toward Glover's Ford Mustang, Lewis reached out to hold Loida's arm. Educated in strict Catholic schools and raised in a society where casual touching between an unfamiliar man and woman was taboo, Loida thought, "Hmmmm. Fresh!"

The group went to "West Boondocks," a soul-food restaurant, where Lewis and Loida engaged in a stimulating conversation that covered a wide range of topics. Loida displayed a quick, facile mind—this woman was no intellectual slouch! Lewis prided himself on being able to make snap judgments about people and his read of Loida Nicolas was that she had the potential to be something more than a meaningless one night stand.

At some point, their discussion touched on the issue of race, particularly about the triumphs and problems of the African-American community. Lest Loida feel compelled to talk about race because of Lewis's ethnicity, and perhaps to let her know he was open-minded about women of all backgrounds, he proclaimed, "I am international."

Loida still recalls that her date ordered champagne at the bar, which impressed her. After dinner, the foursome took in a Beatles movie, "The Yellow Submarine." While en route in the car, Lewis informed Loida that his birthday had been the previous day. "Don't I get a kiss?" Lewis asked impishly.

Blushing slightly and not sure what to make of this forward man, Loida gave Lewis a little peck on the cheek. "How sweet," he murmured with a smile.

Loida didn't hear from Lewis the next day or the day after that. She had been impressed by his presence, his intelligence, and his somewhat roguish air. So she was delighted when he called three days after their meeting and asked her out.

The always fastidious Lewis took greater pains than usual to make sure his apartment was neat before he set out on their second date. His strategy was simple: After dinner and a meeting of the minds, he would take her to his apartment for a meeting of a different sort. The ambiance at the restaurant was just right, the meal enjoyable, the conversation even more scintillating than the first one. The mood was being set for a memorable evening.

At the right moment, Lewis asked Loida with studied casualness if she would like to see his Dutch friend Helge Strufe's watercolor paintings he had at his apartment. Although she was relatively inexperienced in dealing with men, the invitation to his apartment set off warning signals in Loida's head. Against her better judgment, she said yes.

Lewis gave her a grand tour of his abode, which didn't take long since it was a tiny one-bedroom flat. Later, Lewis would recall his fascination with this Philippine woman deepening. He was starting to like everything about her—her poise, the way she wore her hair, her self-confidence, her perfume, the lyrical sound of her voice.

After more conversation, Lewis made his move. He drew closer to Loida and kissed her on the lips. Surprisingly, she didn't flinch or draw away. Lewis pushed forward. More kisses followed, each more passionate than the preceding one.

Emboldened, Lewis lifted Loida off her feet and began carrying her in the direction of his bedroom. As she realized what was happening, Loida became frightened and cried out in terror, "Oh, no! no! no!" Lewis put her down immediately but continued to hold her. Somewhat facetiously, he hastened to reassure her, "I just wanted to be close to you."

Lewis's forwardness had brought what started as a delightful evening to a grinding halt. Loida left the apartment with a chastened Lewis tagging along at her side. The silence in the cab that took them to Aberdeen was deafening. Lewis dropped her off and was on his way.

The incident did not amuse Loida. She dashed off a dismissive letter to Lewis, "I never want to see you again. I will only have intimate relations with the man who will be my husband. I will always remember you with fond memories."

In keeping with his personality, Lewis chose to accentuate the positive when he received Loida's missive. The last line of the letter wasn't so bad, was it? Lewis refolded the letter and placed it back in the envelope. He knew that sometimes, in order to get something you really want, you have to be willing to wait. This was one of those times.

Two weeks went by before Loida got another call from Lewis. Despite herself, she was intrigued by this bold man. Hadn't she told him in no uncertain terms not to bother her anymore? Maybe he hadn't received her "Dear John Letter," she rationalized.

Although she didn't know it, Loida's letter had only heightened Lewis's willingness to see her. If there was a prime attribute behind Lewis's impressive accomplishments, it was his pitbull tenacity. He was like one of those cartoon characters who gets steamrollered, incinerated, and blown to smithereens but keeps coming back for more. When Lewis stumbled or got knocked down in pursuit of a goal, he would brush himself off and start all over again as though nothing had happened. Friend and foe alike both marveled at this side of his personality.

Loida was getting her first glimpse of Lewis's dogged side. After a bit of small talk, Lewis asked Loida for another date. To her own surprise, she accepted.

Lewis wasn't about to repeat his previous faux pas with the graceful Loida. This time, he would take her to dinner and that would be it. Throughout their meal, Lewis kept the charm turned up full blast. The hard-driving, aggressive Lewis could be quite considerate, solicitous, and gracious when the mood hit him.

After dinner, Lewis and Loida strolled through the streets of Manhattan, walking leisurely despite the wintry chill. Finally, Loida broke down and asked the question that had been in the back of her mind the entire evening, "Didn't you receive my letter?"

"Yes," Lewis calmly answered, "I did."

Then why did he call her again, Loida wanted to know. "I will not do anything, Loida, that you don't want to do," he assured her. It would be totally up to her whether they would continue to see each other.

Their next date took place around Christmas and was particularly enchanting: They went to the Riverboat Restaurant at the Empire State Building. The skyline of Manhattan was sketched in lights around them. Count Basie's band was playing. As the young couple flitted around the dance floor, Loida gazed into Lewis's piercing eyes and bared her soul.

"Reggie, I don't think I should continue seeing you because I feel I am falling in love with you. I don't want to be heartbroken: Nothing can come out of this because I am going back to the Philippines." Holding Loida a little tighter, Lewis smiled. He loved her too and was ecstatic to hear her articulate similar feelings.

"Why do you say that?" he finally replied. "You don't know what will happen."

Lewis and Loida became inseparable. They took in Manhattan's bountiful entertainment and restaurant scene whenever time allowed. They were from different worlds in more ways than one and each helped broaden the other's outlook and experiences. Loida had never eaten lobster before Lewis introduced her to the delicacy. They became regulars at Max's Kansas City, where the lobster entree was $4.95. An avid theatergoer, Loida took Lewis to his first Broadway play, "The Man of La Mancha," and "The Impossible Dream" became something of a

Lewis theme song. Both of them loved the cinema and they were often found in one of the city's moviehouses. Loida even got Lewis to watch several Japanese movies directed by Akira Kurosawa and starring Toshiro Mifune.

Lewis and Loida spent a lot of time in his apartment, where she learned to cook his favorite dishes, and dutifully watched televised football games with Lewis. In April 1969, four months after they met, Lewis and Loida jetted off to St. Thomas, the Virgin Islands for a brief getaway. They stayed in an inexpensive hotel with a spectacular view of St. Thomas' pristine beaches and the beautiful, aquamarine Caribbean. Lewis loved the way Loida drew out his romantic side, and spent one memorable evening dancing in the moonlight with her to the tune of "This Girl's in Love with You." He had spent all his life up to now studiously avoiding commitments of any kind to the opposite sex. He was focused completely on his career. But here Lewis was, letting himself go.

The two were proof that opposites do attract. Loida's easy-going manner and serene air nicely countered Lewis's hard-charging, intense personality. He was from urban Baltimore, while she was born on the other side of the world in a provincial town in the Philippines. Whereas he could be blunt and astringent, she tended to be tactful and diplomatic.

But he knew all too well not to underestimate Loida and her quiet strength—his foiled seduction attempt had shown him Loida would not hesitate to stand up to him, if need be. Lewis couldn't get serious about a woman lacking the backbone to occasionally dig in her heels and tell him where to get off. As long as it happened infrequently, of course.

Years later, Lewis would confide in his friends that while Loida was friendly and had a relaxed manner on the outside, she was really as tough as steel. "Never underestimate her," he would say.

Lewis felt that Loida would be an ideal partner for him. As he told her innumerable times before they got married, "I'm going to marry a woman who will grow with me!"

One might expect that Lewis and his special lady cemented their fairytale romance with him proposing on bended knee in some romantic setting, engagement ring at the ready. In reality, the setting was far more prosaic—a noisy, smelly subway car in Manhattan. And it was

Loida Nicolas who popped the question in May 1969, albeit in a somewhat indirect way.

"We were sitting in the subway together and I remember asking him,
'Darling, do you want a big wedding or a small wedding?'" she recalls.

If Lewis hadn't been ready for a lasting commitment, he could easily
have turned her question into a joke. But of the scores of women he
had dated, none had excited him like Loida. He had found his soulmate and was ready to settle down.

"Ah, I think we should just have a small wedding and get married in
the chapel at New York University," Lewis responded decisively. "And
then we honeymoon in Paris and Venice."

Feigning a sudden realization of what he just said, he put his hand on
his head and said, "I have a headache." Loida laughed knowingly and
kissed him. There was no engagement ring and Lewis always regretted
not having one. He made up for it on their 20th wedding anniversary in
August 1989, by giving her a ring with a hefty five-carat diamond.

Loida's mother, Magdalena Nicolas, had met Lewis in early 1969, at
the Aberdeen Hotel. She was favorably impressed by him, particularly
by the fact that he took her daughter to a black tie dinner held by Paul,
Weiss, when he could have taken someone else.

Now it was time for Loida to meet the other important woman in
Lewis's life, Carolyn Fugett. Lewis and Loida traveled to Baltimore,
where Loida was warmly welcomed into the Fugett-Cooper clan.

Some of Lewis's relatives and friends were surprised to learn that he
was marrying someone from the Philippines instead of an African-
American woman. Such reservations invariably evaporated on meeting
Loida. Everyone was struck by her intelligence and grace and how well
she and Lewis seemed to co-exist, making race a non-issue.

One of Lewis's friends from childhood days, Dan Henson, had never
seen Lewis fall head over heels for anyone before. "The first time I saw
him really excited was when he told me about Loida," Henson relates.
"When I learned that she was Filipino and whatever, I said, 'What is
this shit?' But after half an hour of conversation with her, I realized
how perfect she was for Reggie. I couldn't imagine too many other
women putting up with him," Henson laughs.

For her part, Loida says her husband's racial background was never a
concern for her family, because her parents never classified people according to economic, social, or racial background.

At Paul, Weiss, Lewis was still putting in long hours, but where he had previously been working 10- to 14-hour days during the week, he started to lop off an hour here and there so he and Loida could have some time together. He never turned into a love-smitten, dreamy-eyed zombie, though—his burning ambition and unrelenting drive wouldn't allow that.

Loida, on the other hand, was beginning to think about the ramifications of the marriage they planned. It would mean that she would be living in the United States permanently and would rarely see her family. Loida felt as much devotion and love for her kin as Lewis did for his, and she also would miss her beloved homeland.

She rarely thought about these things in the intoxicating presence of Lewis, but was mulling over their plans more and more when she had time alone to think. Developing a major-league case of cold feet, she decided she couldn't go through with the wedding.

Lewis was deeply disappointed to hear of her decision. He was tempted to ask her to take some time and mull it over, but he knew that you couldn't dictate affairs of the heart. Plus his pride would never allow him to plead.

So in June 1969, after Loida's sister Imelda finished her studies at Columbia, the two of them caught a plane to California with the intention of leaving New York and Lewis behind forever. The women planned to visit some friends at Stanford University in Palo Alto, California, and then go on a brief Asian tour before returning home to the Philippines.

However, in the time it took to fly to the West Coast, Loida became heartsick and miserable. By the time the women reached California, Imelda noticed her sister was walking around with a blank expression as though in a daze. Imelda didn't say anything—she already knew what the problem was. "Everything was bleak and gray. I couldn't see any other colors," Loida recalls.

There was only one quick-fix antidote: A phone call back to the East, specifically to New York City. "Darling, I can't stand it anymore," Loida told Lewis after breaking down and calling her love, "I'm coming back."

"No, Loida, don't do that," a relieved Lewis advised his fiancee. "Go back to your parents, tell them we're getting married and then you can fly back here in two weeks. We'll get married at NYU, then we'll honeymoon in Paris and Venice."

The suggestion that Loida return to the Philippines was particularly magnanimous coming from Lewis who had a jealous and possessive side. Generally though, his attitude toward women was predicated on his high opinion of himself. If a woman didn't want him, it was her loss.

Loida already knew that in addition to his other qualities, he could be short-tempered, moody, and sarcastic. She knew that he could be very intense and that he could hold a grudge with the best of them.

She loved him because of his ambition, his sense of family, his take-charge attitude. "I wanted someone who would wear the pants in the family," she says. In many ways, Lewis reminded Loida of her father, who was also an entrepreneur.

Now certain that marrying Lewis was the right thing to do, Loida could relax and see a bit of the world before settling down. She and Imelda left California for the Philippines, by way of Taiwan and Korea. They had decided to take the long way home to give their parents time to digest the news about the marriage. Loida had written to her parents about her plans but she still was not sure that they would agree to the wedding.

Loida wrote to Lewis every day, but in the course of her whirlwind journey, she had forgotten about the two-week marriage deadline she and her fiance had set. Lewis was furious when Loida finally called from the Philippines.

"We were supposed to get married in two weeks!" he said icily, informing her that he had gone through the trouble of arranging to have their wedding held at NYU's chapel. Loida waited for the storm to blow over, apologized, and told Lewis she needed to spend some time with her family. And since she would be the one giving up her homeland, what did he think about a wedding in the Philippines? Her family had made this suggestion and she agreed, wanting Lewis to see her in her milieu.

Lewis was caught off guard by this request, "Let me think about it." One day, he happened to casually mention his situation to another Paul, Weiss attorney, Ed Korman.

"Look Reg, isn't it really kind of romantic?" Korman suggested. "You're flying 10,000 miles to claim your bride." Lewis called Loida and told her they would have a Philippine marriage.

Loida's father, Francisco J. Nicolas, was cut from the same cloth as Lewis. Having lost his father at 11, Nicolas had to fend for himself. At 21, he had to abandon his dream of becoming a lawyer because his fledgling lumber business was becoming very profitable. Nicolas's lumber company eventually became one of the Philippines's largest and best-known furniture manufacturers, NICFUR.

Francisco had great plans for his daughter, Loida. He saw her becoming a congresswoman, governor, or even senator. Those plans would be derailed however by her marriage. Naturally, he was quite curious about this African-American who was stealing his oldest daughter. Could Loida at least show him a picture?

She pulled out a picture of Lewis standing on the beach in St. Thomas, gazing intensely at the camera. Francisco Nicolas studied the man in the photograph for a few moments and smiled. He understood why his strong-willed, independent daughter had finally been swept off her feet.

Lewis flew into Manila a few days before the wedding. He was alone because none of his family members or friends could make the trip.

An archipelago of more than 7,000 islands, the Philippines was ruled by Spain for 400 years before becoming an American possession from 1900 to 1946, the year the country gained its independence. American influence was still very strong in the country in 1968, and today English is still widely spoken.

Loida came from a tightly-knit family of three brothers and one sister. The night before Lewis's wedding, Loida's male relatives, including her three brothers, threw a stag party for him at the house of an uncle, Pedro Manalac. Loida's kinfolk tried mightily to get Lewis drunk, but getting blitzed was not his style. Moreover, Lewis didn't want his future in-laws to see him three sheets to the wind. After all, he was representing the United States of America. He made it through the night with his sobriety—and dignity—intact.

Lewis and Loida were married on August 16, 1969, in a lavish ceremony that made the society pages of Philippine newspapers, including many of the country's top business and social elite. The country's then Vice President, Fernando Lopez, acted as one of the godfathers of the couple.

Lewis and Loida exchanged vows at the Paco Roman Catholic church, a romantic, Spanish-era structure in the heart of Manila that was surrounded by a beautiful garden. The most memorable gift was from Clinton Lewis, who paid to have a photographer film his son's wedding for the folks in the United States.

The Lewises began their weeklong honeymoon in Japan, where they enjoyed exploring Tokyo and Kyoto. But their next destination, Hawaii, left a sour taste in their mouths.

Loida Lewis, who had a tourist visa, was detained for 45 minutes by U.S. Customs officials after she told them she planned to live permanently in the United States with her husband. Producing her marriage certificate didn't expedite things either.

Ironically, if she had shown them her tourist visa and said she planned to go sightseeing, Loida Lewis would have breezed through. The absurdity of that situation made her decide on the spot to specialize in U.S. immigration law once she became eligible to practice law in New York.

After they'd cleared Customs and were traveling around Honolulu, Lewis felt that some of the white American tourists he encountered were looking at him in a manner that conveyed condescension and disapproval. Having just visited the Philippines and Japan where he could relax and just be a man—not a black man—Lewis was less tolerant than usual of American bigotry. Couldn't he simply enjoy his honeymoon without being subjected to racism? Furious, Lewis cut short their stay in Hawaii, with the couple leaving after only one day.

The Lewises stopped in San Francisco for a day before heading back to New York, to Lewis's tiny one-bedroom apartment at 333 W. 21st Street, in a section of Manhattan known as Chelsea.

Lewis loved Loida for her personality, spirituality, and intellect, plus her family's social status served to further stoke his ambition. He was determined to show his new wife an opulent, affluent lifestyle of his own making, even though the unassuming Loida never coveted material possessions or social status. In later press interviews and speeches, Lewis would often pay tribute to Loida, calling her "one of the least materialistic persons I know."

Loida Lewis believed in her husband and in marriage for better or for worse. In the early 1970s, when finances were tight and even her butcher wouldn't accept her checks, Lewis would grumble to his wife that she needed to do a better job of balancing the budget. But there wasn't too much Loida Lewis could do. After all, the family had to eat.

Not one to sit idly around the house, Loida Lewis got a job working with Manhattan Legal Services, a Johnson-era, publicly-funded law firm catering to low-income clients. When contrasting his job with Loida's, Lewis would joke, "Reg works for the rich and Loida works for the poor." She worked with Manhattan Legal Services from 1970 to 1973.

In 1972, Lewis earned a particularly large fee from one of his clients. The Lewises were expecting their first child and the fee enabled them to make a downpayment on a brownstone at 351 W. 22nd Street, also in the Chelsea section of Manhattan.

The following year, their first daughter, Leslie, was born. In preparation for the birth, the couple spent seven weeks learning the Lamaze method of natural childbirth. Lewis was in the delivery room when Leslie came into the world. A very proud father, he had also seen how difficult and potentially life-threatening the process of childbirth had been for his wife. Consequently, he was reluctant to put her through it again. It would be seven years before the Lewises had their second child, Christina, in 1980.

Lewis always firmly believed that his wife should be free to develop a separate career with her own interests and goals. "Some men believe in keeping their wives barefoot and pregnant; I'm not one of them," he often told her. From 1971 to 1979, she published a monthly magazine for the Filipino-American community that was financed by her husband.

Lewis was proud of his wife's achievements. After Loida passed the 1974 New York Bar examinations making her one of the first Asians to do so without attending a law school in the United States, she applied for a lawyer's position at the U.S. Immigration and Naturalization Service and was turned down. With Lewis's backing and his firm as her counsel, she sued INS alleging discriminatory hiring practices and won three years in back wages. During the three-years' hiatus, Lewis supported Loida's decision to practice law with Antonio Martinez, who ran a law office specializing in Hispanic immigration. In 1979, she was sworn in as a general attorney with the INS and, for eleven years, stayed on the job even after Lewis's success in the business world. She finally said goodbye to the service in 1990 in order to relocate to Paris with her husband and children.

Loida sums up her 24-year marriage as exhilarating. "I knew I would not meet another man like him again," Loida Lewis says of her late husband. "He was masterful."

7

"I Was Not Ready"

When he was the subject of glowing news stories after acquiring Beatrice International in 1987, Reginald Lewis would complain about how some of the media made it look as if he'd achieved his success quickly and effortlessly. "That's not true. I was no overnight success. It took 25 years of hard work to get to where I am. That's what everyone has missed," he would tell people.

His success had been achieved at great personal expense. His metamorphosis from unknown, struggling lawyer to celebrated, international financier was a lengthy, at times painful, affair. His initial attempts to purchase companies uniformly failed, not for lack of effort, but for a host of reasons that Lewis later crystallized into one.

"I was not ready," he concluded, characteristically coming down hard on himself.

These early failures resulted in numbing depression and stinging self-doubt the likes of which the supremely confident Lewis had never encountered.

As an attorney, Lewis participated in scores of deals where his legal expertise helped others acquire companies. Tired of operating based on the whims of MESBICs and borrowers, Lewis was ready to leave law practice behind and do corporate acquisitions himself.

One source of Lewis's disappointment with his law practice came in 1979 when new Ford Foundation head Franklin Thomas, who happened to be African-American, decided to cut off all business to Lewis's law firm. The Foundation had been one of the firm's largest clients and to lose this revenue for no clear reason frustrated Lewis.

Another setback suffered by Lewis had to do with Aetna Life and Casualty. Lewis & Clarkson had been doing legal work for the mortgage financing division of Aetna since 1979. The division had made it a practice to use minority firms whenever possible. In 1984, Aetna's legal division changed managers and the new regime demanded that Lewis & Clarkson go through the whole interview process from scratch, including submitting bios for all of Lewis's attorneys, as well as an explanation of the type of work they did. The demand enraged Lewis. He and Clarkson drove over to Aetna's offices with Lewis bellowing the entire time as a cringing Clarkson kept his mouth shut, silently wishing they would get to their destination quickly, so he could leave the car.

"Why the fuck do we have to prove ourselves over and over?" Lewis asked. "I've got to go to the other side of the table. This is not the way I want to spend the rest of my life."

THE FIRST ACQUISITION TARGET: PARKS SAUSAGE

Lewis's first opportunity to "go to the other side of the table" and become an acquirer and owner of a company came in 1975. The target was a black-owned firm in Baltimore named Parks Sausage. The company's founder, Henry Parks, was suffering from Parkinson's disease and ready to get out of the business.

An old friend once said that you have to kiss a lot of frogs before you meet one prince. This sums up the search for deal opportunities. When Henry Parks was said to be ready to sell Parks Sausage, of "More Parks Sausage, Mom" fame, I joined the fray. I lined up some local Baltimore support and talked to Chemical Bank and even got a letter out of them saying they would support my proposal. Parks Sausage was then traded publicly, but it was controlled by Henry Parks and his longtime partner, Willie Adams, who was a legend in the Baltimore community.

Ellis Goodman, Lewis's friend from his days at the Baltimore country club, had a connection to Parks: his father-in-law knew Henry Parks personally. Lewis asked Goodman to arrange a meeting.

I came down to Baltimore for the meetings and met Henry Parks privately first, then with Willy Adams at Ellis's office. I might as well have been the man from the moon. They just were not having any of it. I persisted nonetheless, explaining how I knew how to put the deal together, inviting them to stay involved, and saying all the things from deal-making 101.

The total value I proposed was about $3 million, which was a good premium to the then stock price. After several more visits and the bank letter, as well as other letters from my sources of financing, Willy Adams said, "Look, you're a sincere young man and I believe in helping our young people, so before I take another bid, I'll give you a shot at topping the other offer."

Well, I thought, that's progress. Wrong. Within a week, Lehman Brothers brought in another buyer, signed and announced the deal the same day at a price roughly the same as mine. When something like that happens to you and when you are inexperienced and let your ego run wild, you are crushed. You second-guess every decision you made, when rarely does any of that matter.

It's just a deal that got away. You move on. Easy to say now, but not then. I felt it for weeks. But I was later to learn it gets worse.

Lewis, who was 31 at the time, had made quite an impression on the Parks team.

"He was dapper," recalls Parks Chairman and CEO Ray Haysbert, who was a company vice president at the time. "And he had an air of confidence. I guess that stemmed from his education and prior experiences as a lawyer. And he dressed like a New Yorker—as I recall it, dark blues, and very white shirts with very stiff collars and I guess what passed for power ties."

But it wasn't enough to carry Lewis over the top, Haysbert muses. "As usually happens to young black people—black men—there was a credibility gap. They didn't believe he could back it up."

Lewis's mother, Carolyn Fugett, recalls that her son came to Baltimore with a check for $1 million in his briefcase when he was trying to close the Parks deal. It was all she could do to keep her composure upon seeing his immense disappointment over the failed transaction.

"It hurt him deeply," Mrs. Fugett says. "He foresaw that he could take that company and make it a giant among all companies. I think it impugned his ability."

Lewis managed a wan smile for the benefit of his mother, who wound up doing more talking than he did. She assured him that one day he would buy a business that would make Parks seem puny by comparison.

"I hope you're right, Ma," said Lewis, who had nothing else to say.

A NEW ACQUISITION PROSPECT: ALMET

Returning to New York, Lewis rededicated himself to the practice of law. But his desire to buy and run a company continued to burn unabated. Lewis was to take a second stab at the corporate takeover game, an experience that left the aspiring business mogul shattered and reeling.

The subsequent attempt took place in 1977, two years after Lewis's unsuccessful run at Parks Sausage. The opportunity materialized one day during a tennis match in Los Angeles, where Lewis had travelled for a business conference. During the game, Ricardo Olivarez, a close friend whom Lewis had met during one of his MESBIC deals and would later nominate to the boards of both McCall Pattern and Beatrice International, introduced him to a businessman named Paul Christian.

Paul, Rick, and I loved tennis and we got in a game during a break in the conference. Paul had heard about my ability to raise capital and asked me about the kinds of situations I was interested in. I said, low-tech, high cash flow, and good management. Paul, who was a finder (broker) and had a lot of contacts, responded with the proverbial "Do I have a deal for you." Ever eager, I said, "Let's hear it."

The company's name was Almet. Well, it was a fine company. Superb record of growth in an interesting industry—leisure furniture. Sales about $12 million, profits about $1 million; $3 million in cash on the balance sheet at year end, two plants. It was 40 percent owned by an outside investor who was ready to exit after 17 years in the deal, and 40 percent by the president of the company, a 61-year-old man named Bill Cammer.

Paul arranged for a meeting between myself and Bill Cammer. Almet's plant and offices were in Vernon, California, in an industrial park near downtown Los Angeles. What followed was a 1½-year courtship of Bill and his associates. To this day, I believe it was among my best work.

Detail-oriented Reginald Lewis left no stone unturned in his efforts to woo Cammer, marvels Charles Clarkson, who was also involved with the Almet deal. Not only did Lewis send birthday and wedding anniversary cards to Cammer, he even sent them to Cammer's wife, along with gifts and roses, Clarkson says. Lewis even went to the trouble of helping Cammer's daughter get a job.

Cammer was a chain-smoking, hard-working, driven man who has been described as "a lunatic." He later said he was favorably impressed by Lewis, who had a Harvard Law School pedigree and shared his ambitious plans for Almet's future with Cammer.

Almet was a medium-sized company with a profitable market niche. It made aluminum beach chairs and umbrellas. The key to buying Almet was Cammer, whom Lewis was counting on to manage the company as President and Chief Operating Officer.

Lewis painstakingly put the pieces of the puzzle together. As his acquisition vehicle, he set up a company called Republic Furniture and Leisure, Inc. whose initials just happened to be RFL. RFL, Inc. would purchase all the shares of Almet including those held by Cammer and other managers and Cammer would operate the company for RFL, Inc. with a fat employment agreement as his incentive.

Lewis convinced Chemical Bank to put up $5 million of the $7 million purchase price. He then went to several of his MESBIC clients, including Equico, and asked them to put up the rest of the money in subordinated debt. Six of them agreed. An actual contract of sale was signed by Cammer and the other shareholders. Chemical Bank transferred the $5 million to its branch in California where the closing would take place. Everything seemed to be going according to Lewis's plan.

The day of the closing arrived. Clarkson had flown to California while Lewis stayed in New York and dealt with the bankers. The final signing of documents was scheduled to take place at the offices of Almet's law firm.

Representing Lewis were Clarkson and Tom Lamia, Lewis's California counsel, of the firm Paul, Hastings, Janofsky and Walker. Also present in the room were representatives of Chemical Bank and the six MESBICs. On the other side of the table were Cammer and his lawyers.

Ah, but the story does not have a happy ending. In fact, it was a disaster—no deal.

We got to a definitive agreement after 1½ years of meetings. I put together a $7 million package consisting of $5 million in bank financing and $2 million of subordinated debt with warrants to own about 40 percent of the company. I was putting up about $200,000 together with my brother Jean Fugett, who was then a tight end with the Washington Redskins. To make a long story short, after two years of work—on the day of the closing—Bill decided to back out of the deal.

It was unbelievable. He simply wanted out and figured he would break the deal, contract or no contract. The fact is that I had to let it happen because if he did not want to continue after the sale to help run the business, then it was a very different deal.

The deal never closed because at the last minute, Cammer announced that he would not sign his employment agreement, which was one of the conditions of the acquisition. Worried, Clarkson and Lamia decided to call Lewis. Lamia briefed Lewis and then put him on speaker phone in the room.

That conversation remains etched in Clarkson's memory. Huddled around the phone on the West Coast were Clarkson, Lamia, the various representatives of the lenders, and Cammer and his lawyers. Lewis and his associates hovered around a speaker phone in Manhattan. Also listening in at another speaker phone were Chemical Bank executives at their office in New York.

Cammer puffed on one cigarette after another. Appearing quite nervous, he seemed to be shaking slightly during the conversation. He began by saying that the conditions for closing had not been met and therefore the deal couldn't close. He repeated to everyone that he would not work for Lewis and would not sign the employment agreement.

"And since he was really the pivotal operating person, the whole deal fell apart," Clarkson says.

Cammer did not stop there however. Clarkson was incredulous when he heard what Cammer said next. "I do not want to work for Reginald Lewis. I will not work for someone who has offered me money under the table," Cammer said.

Everyone involved in the acquisition attempt blinked disbelievingly. "Here we are taking notes at a conference call and this guy is, you know, saying things that any intelligent person in the world would know would be libelous—slander! He virtually called Reg a liar and a cheat," Clarkson says.

Lewis went ballistic. "How dare you impugn my integrity. You are a liar! I never ever offered you any money under the table. I will sue you for every dollar you have. You cannot attack my integrity and walk away unharmed," Lewis fumed.

"He expressed total outrage—that this was obviously a lie," Clarkson says. "When he got going, he could talk as well as anybody. The outrage poured through. I knew right then and there the entire deal was falling apart."

One and a half years of work by Lewis, as well as his dreams of owning a majority stake in Almet, were going up in smoke.

The night this happened, I came close to a breakdown. The walls began to close in around me, I began to hallucinate and lose my balance. Somehow I went to sleep. The next morning, around 6 A.M., I had slept for maybe two hours. I went down to see my bankers to try to hold the deal. A particular banker who had actually tried to break the bank's commitment met me and said, "Reg, this guy is going to give you problems." It was true and the first time this guy had come straight in the whole process, because at that point of course it was in his interest to do so. I went to my office and Diana Lee said, "Reg, we can't let this guy get away with this." I had kept Diana out of most of the action until the very end, so that we could keep the money coming into the firm. I said, "Diana, see what you can do; stir up the pot."

Diana got on the phone and got Tom Lamia, who was my counsel in California, to turn up the heat. Tom said he had already started preparing the legal papers against Cammer. For the next few days, we kicked and screamed and worked out a settlement which was reasonably attractive—some of my investors in kindness said they thought I had planned it that way. Nothing could be further from the truth.

Lewis threatened to sue Cammer for breach of contract and libel over his remarks over the speaker phone. Cammer's own legal counsel resigned the next day and Cammer later agreed to compensate Lewis for all of his expenses in the transaction and to pay him a break-up fee. In addition, Cammer paid Lewis a $250,000 settlement in exchange for dropping the libel suit.

Seventeen years later, Cammer claims that Lewis failed to come up with the cash needed to buy Almet by closing day and says he refused to grant Lewis an extension.

"Plus, there's the fact that he was going to have his half-brother, who was at that time playing for the Washington Redskins, be the head of the company. He was going to let me run it, but his half-brother was going to be in charge, so to speak," Cammer says.

A short time after rebuffing Lewis, Cammer sold Almet to a Baltimore company for about $11 million, instead of the $7 million Lewis offered him. He was subsequently sued by a former partner whom he had bought out prior to the sale. Loida Lewis recalls her husband saying when he read of the sale, "You see, I educated that son of a bitch!" Loida herself harbored thoughts about the Almet transaction. "It was personal. I did not tell him, but my own opinion was that Cammer would not want to work for an African-American. I never verbalized it to my husband," she says. Cammer denies that race was a factor.

As far as Lewis was concerned, the settlement he received was a small consolation.

I flat out got my butt kicked and the settlement just eased the pain a little. I took $10,000 and went to Puerto Rico on vacation. My family was in the Philippines, since I had sent them away a few weeks before the deal was due to close to avoid any distractions. During my vacation, I replayed the deal, but my mind was not working—I could not understand. The only conclusion I could reach was that even after finding the needle in the haystack, putting together great financing, courting a 61-year-old businessman, getting a definitive contract signed without a penny up front and more, much more, I STILL WAS NOT READY. My mind could go no further.

I took the vacation, returned to New York, and threw myself completely into my law practice. Six months later, I had my first $100,000 month from the practice of law, net to me. But in human terms, I wasn't there.

Lewis took part of the settlement and bought a vacation home in the exclusive Long Island community of East Hampton in a section known as Hampton Waters. Located on Springy Banks Road, the house had a relaxed, cozy feeling about it with huge floor-to-ceiling picture windows, a large outdoor deck surrounding the house, and a small, man-made bubbling spring. Groves of large trees shielded it from neighbors. This was where Lewis retired to lick his wounds.

Those close to Lewis—including his wife—had no inkling of the torment Almet was causing him. An intensely private man, Lewis allowed no one to witness the pain and despair raging just behind his elaborately constructed mask. He prided himself on being a man of his word and on being able to deliver. He felt he'd lost face before his financial backers—whom he thought would be reluctant to ever support him again—his business associates, friends, and even his wife.

On the surface, Lewis was upbeat and blasé. He even boasted to a friend, "Even when Reg loses he wins," a reference to the money he was paid by Cammer.

After the deal fell apart, Lewis began putting in 70-hour work weeks at 30 Broad Street.

With Lewis practically living at his law office in the wake of the Almet debacle, law partner Clarkson saw more of him than anyone. "I thought he took it pretty much in stride," Clarkson says. "And I knew him pretty well, but I never got the sense it was such a blow to him. He certainly hid it very well when he got back to the office. I was there with him every day—I never got the sense that it got to the point that it would cause a breakdown with him."

Lewis had resolved to deal with his Almet demons in private and he was his own toughest critic.

The only constant in my mind was "I WAS NOT READY." During that summer, I bought a vacation home in East Hampton which the family loved. It's a very nice house and in 1978 I spent a good part of the summer there. I began to take my daughter Leslie for long walks, or would watch her ride her bicycle on deserted roads near the house. One day, Leslie and I were out and she was on her bike and the thought came pounding in my head again, YOU ARE NOT READY.

But this time, on a somewhat cloudy day in East Hampton, an answer started to emerge. Leslie was getting too far ahead, and as I ran a little to catch up, the answer came roaring through, "WELL, IF YOU ARE NOT READY, ALL RIGHT. THEN GET READY— GET READY." As I approached my daughter, then five years old, I knew that what I was going through was a mental process of burying the hurt ego of the last few months. I decided to wipe it out of my mind for the moment: My five-year-old needed help turning her bicycle around.

I said, "Here Leslie, this is how you do it." When I told her that, I hadn't another thought in my head, and without thinking, I knew the healing process had begun.

I decided first to restore my own self-confidence. This had begun instinctively right after the blown deal by turning my attention back to the law. Next, why not take inventory? I decided to grade everyone involved in the deal, including myself. Part of this effort was to review the work of others who appeared to be successful. I then became a prospectus junkie and read all the deals which were publicly reported. It is amazing how much you can learn from public records about how people go about things.

After sifting through the ashes of the Almet deal, Lewis began studying successful corporate takeovers and subjecting himself to rigorous self-analysis. Like a dissipating fog, his languor and self-doubt lifted and a plan began to come into focus.

Slowly, oh so slowly, I felt a certain picture emerge. I had to guard against being too easy or too hard on myself and found that I did have the ability to get outside myself and remain neutral in my thinking. The hardest fact to come to grips with was that many of your strengths can indeed be weaknesses at different stages in the deal process. For example, in Almet, I was the finder of the deal, chief financial analyst, fundraiser, quasi-legal officer, and chief strategist. In short, I was going about it assbackwards.

For five years, I had gone about it all wrong, using an approach that could get me close, but not get the job done. A hard pill to swallow.

Another issue which emerged quite quickly was to take the emotion out of the equation to the fullest extent possible. These were business transactions, nothing more. Not jousts, tests of moral fiber, etc. Of course, passion is often important to get a project started, but once it gets going, the pendulum shifts very quickly to cold calculation from passion.

Another hard fact was that most of the people who were good at this were involved full time. Part-time deal-making is almost a contradiction in terms. Also, forget about the old boy network. What was driving transactions in today's market was fees. Fees to the banks, the investment bankers, the lawyers, the accountants, the deal-finders. Strong economic incentives were very much the order of the day.

I began to feel there was hope for me yet.

Armed with a new outlook and with his shattered psyche on the mend, Lewis was finished brooding. He soldiered on in his law practice but he would eventually return to the corporate acquisition fray with a vengeance.

99 WALL STREET

Some addresses, like 1600 Pennsylvania Avenue, say all that needs to be said. The address of Reginald Lewis's next law offices, 99 Wall Street, falls into that category. Lewis could have found cheaper offices, as his partner Charles Clarkson had suggested. But how could someone like Reginald Lewis resist a chance to work literally on Wall Street? The address fairly screams, "I've arrived, I am to be taken seriously and treated with respect!"

Lewis moved to 99 Wall Street in 1979, renting out the 16th floor. Visitors stepping from one of two elevators found themselves facing an attractive, polite receptionist seated behind a desk. Immediately behind her, on the wall, was the name Lewis & Clarkson in elegant, stylized silver letters.

Although Clarkson's name was in the firm's title, a lawyer who worked there joked that Lewis's name should have been capitalized and Clarkson's should have been in small letters. Even Clarkson acknowledges that he was a partner in name only, and to this day has no idea what kind of revenue Lewis & Clarkson generated.

"Reg was very, very non-informative in those areas," Clarkson allows. There was never any doubt about who controlled the law firm.

A glass entryway partitioned off the firm's lawyers and support staff, who always appeared to be working quietly, but at a frenetic pace. Inside the small reception area, the cheesy look of 30 Broad Street had been replaced by contemporary, understated furnishings and tasteful artwork. The ambiance was restrained and a little more corporate, but by no means lavish.

Lewis had purchased a gray tweed modular sofa in the shape of an "L" for his spacious corner office. A law library and conference room were opposite his office.

By this time, Lewis's clientele was mostly corporations, with a sprinkling of entrepreneurs also providing revenue. The days of existing hand-to-mouth and having to do an occasional new home closing in a pinch were becoming things of the past.

However, Lewis could still be tight-fisted with money. One December, Lewis and two other lawyers with firms at 99 Wall Street held a joint Christmas party. The expenses came to about $400. Lewis received a bill for a three-way split of the party expenses, about $133 per man. He hit the roof and called Peter Eikenberry, one of the other hosts of the party.

"He called me up and raised hell," Eikenberry remembers. Lewis forcefully argued that since only a few of his Lewis & Clarkson staffers had attended the party and Eikenberry had invited plenty of people, a three-way split was simply not equitable. Period. Lewis may have been a hot-shot corporate attorney on Wall Street, but $133 was still worth going to war over.

"I think he wanted his people to go out and negotiate for that last nickel every time," says Eikenberry, who also recalls that Lewis could be quite charming and amusing at times.

Even at this stage of his career, Lewis liked to cultivate an aura of inaccessibility. Ray LeFlore was a veteran black attorney who leased part of the 16th floor from Lewis. He would frequently invite Lewis to lunch on the spur of the moment, but Lewis would generally turn him down.

"Invariably, he'd always say when I did that, 'Gee, Ray, you know we haven't had lunch together for a good while. We really ought to go out together. How are you next week?'" LeFlore recalls.

At one point, Lewis and LeFlore talked about LeFlore's joining the law firm permanently. Even though LeFlore was comfortable with Lewis, whom he found to be a gentleman and a straight-shooter, the strong-willed men decided their friendship would be best preserved by not joining forces, so LeFlore left after one year to open his own office.

In 1981, two new faces appeared at Lewis & Clarkson: Kevin Wright, a black Harvard Law School graduate with five years of experience, and Laurie Nelson, a Jewish New York City native straight out of Brooklyn Law School. There was a definite Harvard-Brooklyn clique practicing law at Lewis & Clarkson, in keeping with the two name partners' respective alma maters.

Wright's father was one of Lewis's first major clients. Wright himself would in time become Lewis's trusted right-hand man, the so-called "Reg, Jr.", who stayed with Lewis until Lewis's death. Nelson, who had a habit of occasionally lording over support staffers, left after five years and remained a Lewis protege because her brashness reminded Lewis of himself.

The task of going to law schools and recruiting prospective lawyers fell to Wright and Nelson. Lewis would send his young recruiters out with explicit marching orders, "Look, when you go into those interviews, you are going to see a lot of drek. Get rid of it! I do not want to talk to anybody that you don't think can cut it. If you don't think they can cut it, I definitely won't think they can cut it. And I don't want any distinctions made between minority students and nonminority students, except that if you see a minority student who's really excellent, I want to talk to her or him."

Full-time lawyers and even summer interns had to be able to hit the ground running at Lewis & Clarkson, because Lewis made a habit of giving them tremendous responsibility right off the bat.

Clarkson was thrown into a multimillion dollar MESBIC closing his first day, while Nelson worked on a $30-million hotel loan transaction on her second day. Lewis didn't have the luxury of bringing a new lawyer along slowly like large firms did. So it wasn't just a matter of Lewis setting unrealistically high standards. He needed people who could, as he was fond of saying, "do the work."

"This guy basically made me what I am," says Nelson, who now practices real estate law with a large New York City law firm. "You're talking about a man that I idolized for years. Pretty much all of the practical skills that I have today, 12 years after I graduated from law school, I got directly from Reg Lewis."

When he was chairman of Beatrice International, Lewis insisted on implementing a summer intern program for young business and law students. For all his gruffness, he liked to spend time with his interns. He often sat around for hours, discussing the state of the world.

Orlan Johnson, a Howard University law student who interned at Lewis & Clarkson one summer, remembers one evening when Lewis lectured Johnson and two other black students who were going to business school about his concern that too many African-American entrepreneurs were looking to start businesses from scratch, rather than acquiring companies already up and running.

"I've never seen a black guy that was so driven to be successful in my life," Johnson says. "He was a hot-tempered guy and he wanted to get things done. He didn't like mistakes. 'How could you make this mistake? You're an attorney, you're supposed to be good, that's why you're here.' Whenever there was anything that Reg disagreed with or thought there was problem with, he would get loud."

As at 30 Broad Street, Lewis liked to interact with his employees away from the workplace. A favorite lunchtime hangout was Fraunces Tavern, a restaurant in the financial district. Lewis had a table at the restaurant and treated his lawyers to lunch there from time to time.

Shortly after Wright and Nelson joined the firm, he also took his entire office staff to Springy Banks, his summer house in East Hampton. Those not staying at the home were put up in a local hotel. Everyone enjoyed a weekend of partying and tennis, and catered meals were served in Lewis's backyard, including a Sunday brunch.

Around this time, Lewis was involved in a clash with New York City concerning the handling of some real estate he and his wife owned on 10th Avenue. The Lewises wanted to sell the property, which consisted of three apartment buildings. The city maintained that extensive repairs had to be made to the buildings and ordered Lewis to take care of them. Before he could act, the city started proceedings to take over the buildings, blocking their sale. The whole affair made Lewis apoplectic.

Sputtering, "These people are not according me due process," Lewis fought the lawsuit and it was resolved in his favor.

In the mid-1980s, Lewis had taken to smoking cigars. He picked up the trait while attending a Paris birthday party for a good friend from the Ivory Coast, Dominique Kanga. Lewis saw cigar smoking as very Parisian and *trés continentale.* He and Kanga had a smoking ritual they adhered to without fail when they were in a restaurant. First, a waiter would bring them a humidor from which they would select an expensive Cuban cigar they were partial to, in particular Monte Cristo No. 3. They would then hold the cigar next to an ear and roll it through their fingertips, the sound being an indication of whether the tobacco was brittle, and therefore, not fresh. Then the waiter would clip off one end of the cigar and a long match would be used to set that end aflame. A nice smooth draw on the first try signaled mission accomplished.

In his law office, Lewis had ashtrays on his desk, by the sofas and strategically placed at different corners of his office. Each ashtray would have a partially smoked cigar in it. Lewis had a habit of moving about his office while working on some matter, lighting a cigar and taking a few puffs on it, then moving on to another stogie parked in a different section of his office. Smoking was a pleasure to be enjoyed by the managing partner only, though. Other smokers and their smoking implements, be they pipes or cigarettes, were not welcome or tolerated.

In later years, Lewis would become so fond of Cuban cigars that his staff would go to all kinds of permutations to purchase them and fly them into the United States. One TLC Beatrice executive in Switzerland would even go to the trouble of smuggling several boxes of cigars by car over the border from Switzerland to France and then send the package by courier to Paris where it would be tucked into the luggage of yet another executive on his or her way to New York and a waiting Lewis.

By 1984, more new faces showed up at Lewis & Clarkson and the firm began to have a family flavor to it. Jean Fugett, Jr. started work as an associate. When not absorbing the fine points of corporate law from Clarkson, Fugett would huddle with Lewis in Lewis's office, deep in conversation. Young Joseph Fugett was also employed as a law librarian.

When it came to Jean, Lewis always felt a sense of ambivalence. On the one hand, he had always admired Jean's athletic ability and trusted him implicitly in a way he trusted no one else. Lewis also gave a lot of weight to Fugett's feedback on business and personal matters.

Fugett was an Amherst cum laude graduate who played pro football, first with the Dallas Cowboys and later with the Washington Redskins. While with the Redskins, he worked his way through law school at George Washington University and during the off-season worked as an intern with the *Washington Post,* earning several bylines in the process.

Even so, something about Jean always left Lewis feeling vaguely ambivalent. For one thing, he felt that being a tight end in the National Football League had been to his brother's detriment. Lewis believed that professional football had brought Jean too much of the good life too fast with too little hard work and dedication. Plus, how could anyone have a properly Calvinistic outlook when they only worked six or so months out of the year?

Whatever Lewis may have thought of his brother Jean, he turned to him again and again over the years. He picked Jean to run the Almet company with Cammer, had the deal gone through; he would later single Jean out to run a radio station in the Caribbean. Then on his deathbed, Lewis would turn to Jean to help run TLC Beatrice International Holdings, Inc.

LEWIS AND THE POLITICIANS

The enduring fascination Lewis had for politics continued at 99 Wall Street. One day he ushered Jesse Jackson into the law firm for a private conversation, causing some of his staffers to nearly fall out of their chairs in surprise.

In 1984, when Jackson made his first run for President, Lewis held a fund-raising dinner for him at Fraunces Tavern. He later invited Jackson to tour the McCall Pattern offices. Lewis would also host fund-raisers for a number of African-American politicians including former New York City Mayor David N. Dinkins, as well as another one held for Jackson during his Presidential campaign in 1988.

Among the other African-American politicians Lewis assisted were Virginia Governor Douglas Wilder, Los Angeles Mayor Tom Bradley,

North Carolina senatorial hopeful Harvey Gant in his losing bid against Senator Jesse Helms, New York Assemblyman Al Vann and two old friends of Lewis's, New York politicians Basil Patterson, a candidate for Lieutenant Governor of New York and a former deputy mayor of New York, and Percy Sutton, a former Manhattan Borough President.

When Dinkins was mayor he appointed Lewis to his Economic Advisory Council in 1989 and had nominated him to New York's powerful Municipal Assistance Corporation, which controlled a sizable chunk of the city's funding, when Lewis died in 1993.

Dinkins would occasionally visit the Lewises at their home in Long Island, where he and Lewis engaged in some spirited tennis duels. Dinkins has a rapier-sharp sense of humor and when it came to the strong-willed Lewis, he would often joke, "You know, one thing about Reg is, success has not changed him—he's always been an arrogant guy."

Lewis for his part liked to tell stories of the times when he acted as a speechwriter for Patterson early in his career. At one point in the 1970s, Dinkins and his law partner, Basil Patterson, offered Lewis a partnership in their law firm, an offer Lewis turned down. Dinkins later called this "the smartest move Reg ever made."

Laurie Nelson used to tell Lewis that politics seemed like a natural challenge for him to tackle next. Lewis would merely flash a gratified smile and say, "I don't know, I've thought about it. We've given it some thought."

Lewis did think about jumping into politics from time to time. He often mulled the pros and cons of taking on Democratic Senator Daniel Patrick Moynihan. He would later contemplate running against another New York Senator, Republican Al D'Amato.

Lewis's ambitions weren't confined to the Senate.

"If I got into the Senate, well, a few years of making speeches and who knows? Lightning could strike," Lewis would say. Indeed, David Dreyfuss, Lewis's video production guru, would later say with regret after Lewis's death, "There are some of us who thought he could have been President."

Lewis did make it to the White House, where he dined with Presidents Reagan and Bush during state dinners and business meetings.

Reginald Lewis (kneeling), with his cousins Doris Hill (left) and Connie Hill, and his grandfather Sam Cooper in the alley alongside 1022 North Dallas Street. From the day he first saw Reginald, his grandfather treated him as his own son.

Reginald F. Lewis, ten years old, posing in front of the West Baltimore apartment on Druid Hill Avenue where he lived for a short period after his mother married Jean S. Fugett. They later moved to 2802 Mosher Street.

Jean S. Fugett, Sr.; Carolyn E. Fugett; Jean S. Fugett, Jr.; and Reginald Lewis in their apartment on Druid Hill Avenue in 1952. Lewis took pride in and loved being a big brother, and would become a lifetime mentor to Jean, Jr.

In the food service business, waiting tables was probably the next best thing to being maître d'. It was a prestigious position for a teenager trying to earn extra cash. As this letter of recommendation attests, Reginald F. Lewis was taught by his grandfather to be the best.

THE SUBURBAN CLUB
OF BALTIMORE COUNTY
PIKESVILLE, MD.

Augsut 30, 1961

To Whom It May Concern:

During Reginald Lewis's period of employment here June 1959 to August 1961) I found him to be entirely dependable, completely trustworthy and very efficient. Based on these facts, I would strongly recommend him for any employment you have available particularly that of a waiter.

Kindest Regards,

Stephen Gaal
Maitre D'Hotel

Reginald F. Lewis received letters in basketball and football when he graduated from Baltimore's Dunbar High School in 1961. Because of his skills as a quarterback, the local newspaper referred to Lewis as "Bullet Lewis." *Photo credit:* Dunbar High School yearbook, *Golden Memoirs.*

Reginald F. Lewis poses with his father, Clinton L. Lewis, after his graduation from Harvard Law School in 1968. Clinton Lewis remained a friend of the Cooper and Fugett families after Carolyn remarried.

As a student at Virginia State College, Reginald F. Lewis knew what he wanted out of life. This rigid schedule he put together at the beginning of a semester reflects his discipline as a student. The caption at the bottom, "To be a good lawyer, one must study hard," served as a constant reminder of his ultimate goal.

MON.	TUES.	WED.	Thurs.	Fri.
6.30 Get Up	—	Get Up		—
7.00 Breakfast		Breakfast		
7.50 Math	Com. Health	Math	C. Health	8 Math
8.50 History	Study	History	9-11 Study	9 Hist.
9.50 ROTC		9-10 mis.	11-12 mis	10 mis.
10.50 German	Orientation	German	12 lunch	11 German
12.00 Lunch	—	Lunch	12:15 mis.	12 lunch
12.50 English	miscellaneous	English	1:15	1 English
2.00 Study	study	Study	1:15 Study	2 study
3.15 Library	library	Library	3.15	3.15
3.20 Football		3-5 ROTC	3.20 Football	3.20 F. Practice
7.00 Practice		5-7 F. Practice	7.00 Practice	7.00
7.30 Study		7.30 Recreation	7:15 Study	7.15 Study
9.00 Library		10 15	9:15	8.15
9:00 Recreation			9.15 Recreation	8 15 Recreation
10:15		10:30 Lights Out	10.15	10.00
10:30 Lights Out	—		10:30 Lights Out	10.15 Lights Out

To Be A Good Lawyer, One Must Study HARD.

Black Graduates See Opportunities,

(Continued from Page 1)

Though most of the alumni expressed an intention to continue to work within white society, many acknowledged that the goal of blacks should be to create institutions independent of whites, and a few expressed outright hostility to white institutions including the Law School. Yet all of them agreed that a Harvard Law degree conferred special status on black lawyers and placed them in a peculiar middle ground between the white establishment and the black community.

The predominant youth of the alumni group reflected the recent trend of increasing black enrollment at the Law School. Nine of the 11 alumni graduated from HLS within the past six years, when black enrollment had expanded to meet the demands of the civil rights movement of the 1960s.

The conference began with a morning panel discussion on "Nixon Administration Policies and

no effort to defend the national leadership, but rather justified their jobs as a valuable training experience for black attorneys. Patricia A. King '69, Deputy Director of the Office of Civil Rights in the Department of Health, Education and Welfare, urged blacks not to be "shortsighted." She said, "If we're going to set up our own institutions, we need to know what the hell we're doing." She named the Tax Division of the Justice Department, the National Labor Relations Board, and the Securities and Exchange Commission as good locations for "short-term experience" for black lawyers.

Frederick L. Brown '67, New England regional counsel for the Department of Housing and Urban Development, told his audience "your Harvard Law School education will be the single most impressive thing that happens to you." He said, "The best courses are the least interesting and stimulating ones. What you should avoid is becoming social workers."

Mark MacNeil

Afternoon panel participants (left to right): Richard Banks, Claude Pickens, BLSA Chairman John Daniels, 2L, Reginald Gilliam, Reginald Lewis, Weldon Rougeau, Clarence Ferguson, Robert Washington.

Their Effect on the Practice of Law." Massachusetts Secretary of Community Development Thomas I. Atkins '69, a former Boston City Councillor, described the two major effects of the Nixon Administration as being "the elimination of priorities-setting at the national level" and the "shifting of control of local priorities back to the local level" and away from the federal government, through revenue sharing. He urged black law students and lawyers to shift their attention to the functioning of state and local government, saying, "If you study the national government, you're preparing for the past."

Two current Nixon Administration officials made

Bishop C. Holifield '69, Deputy Director of the Florida A & M Business Development Corporation, an organization specializing in assisting minority business enterprises, strongly urged blacks to "set up our own institutions. And nothing is more important than establishment of black law firms." He said blacks must become independent of the "whims and caprices of the man in Washington."

In response to a question, Atkins scored the failure of black professionals to provide leadership for their community. He said, "In order to become leaders, the first thing black lawyers must do is get down in the street and take the same shit as their brothers." He noted, however, that there is

In the fall of 1973, Reginald F. Lewis (fifth from left) was invited back to Harvard to take part in a conference focusing on minority issues in higher education.

After a six-month courtship, Reginald F. Lewis flew to the Philippines to marry Loida. After the ceremony, bride and groom pass through a garden on their way to the reception. Lourdes Gardose, Loida's niece, is the train bearer. *Photo credit:* Wedding Philippines, Inc.

Loida M. Nicolas and Reginald F. Lewis during marriage ceremony at St. Pancratius' Chapel in Paco Park on August 16, 1969, Manila, Philippines. The wedding was held at seven A.M. The reception, which followed, was held at the Champagne Room in the Manila Hotel. *Photo credit:* Wedding Philippines, Inc.

Front row: Danilo A. Nicolas II, Callen Corleto, Asuncion Manalac, Roman Gardose.
Rear row: Magdalena M. Nicolas, Imelda M. Nicolas, Reginald F. Lewis, Francisco J. Nicolas, Francisco M. Nicolas, Jr., Jose M. Nicolas, Danilo M. Nicolas.

Thanksgiving, Baltimore, 1976. Reginald F. Lewis looked forward to his mother's cooking, especially for Thanksgiving or Christmas dinner every year. This photo was taken in the entrance foyer at 2802 Mosher Street. *Photo credit:* REJ & Associates Inc.

From left to right: (first row seated) Leslie N. Lewis, Sabrina E. Fugett, Pepper (the dog); (second row, seated) Jean S. Fugett, Sr., Lena C. Fugett, Carolyn E. Fugett, Joseph M. Fugett; (standing) Reginald F. Lewis, Loida Nicolas Lewis, Jean S. Fugett, Jr., Anne Payne Fugett, Anthony S. Fugett, Trittye C. Fugett, Sharon M. Fugett, Rosalyn T. Fugett.

Family reunion at Broadview, Amagansett, New York, Summer of 1991. Reginald with his wife, daughters, parents, brothers, sisters, brother-in-law, sisters-in-law, uncle, aunt, nieces, and nephews at their annual family reunion. *Photo credit:* Reed Photo, Inc.

Seated on floor (left to right): Marcus G. Fugett, Audie Fugett, Marissa Jennings, Elliott A. Wiley, Jr., Brandon Fugett, Reginald Fugett, Kahn Kanga, Kemi Kanga, Justin C. Wiley, Stephenie H. Fugett, Christina S. N. Lewis, Joseph Russell Fugett.
Seated (second row): Anthony S. Fugett, Lindsey N. Fugett, Leslie N. Lewis, Carlotta O. Fugett, Samuel J. Cooper, Jr., Jean S. Fugett, Sr., Carolyn E. Fugett, Jean S. Fugett, Jr., Sharon M. Fugett, Beverly A. Cooper, Trittye C. Fugett.
Standing (rear): Lena C. Fugett, Elliott A. Wiley, Sr., Rosalyn Fugett Wiley, Loida Nicolas Lewis, Reginald F. Lewis.

Arthur Ashe visited Reginald F. Lewis at his Manhattan office in 1991 to discuss support for the career development of promising young African-American tennis players. Ashe later delivered the eulogy for Lewis at a ceremony held by their fraternity, Kappa Alpha Psi. Ashe died two weeks later. *Photo credit:* Christie Jones.

CARIBBEAN BASIN BROADCASTING—THE SEARCH FOR ANOTHER DEAL

Meanwhile, the search for another deal went on unabated. Lewis couldn't get his hands on enough public offering prospectuses. His desk was piled high with them—they even littered the windowsills in his office.

Product, he would call the prospectuses. "I want to see more product," he would frequently tell investment bankers.

One of his lawyers came into the office at 6 A.M. one morning to find Lewis already at his desk, plowing through prospectuses. Dutiful student that he was, and still smarting from his failures to acquire Parks Sausage and Almet, Lewis would leave absolutely nothing to chance this time. He'd been telling Clarkson for years that he would reach the pinnacle of capitalistic success by buying companies.

"We had a lot of bull sessions," Clarkson says. "We'd sit there and talk for hours. Reg was a real dreamer. I always kept saying to myself, 'God, this guy dreams good!' They came true, though. He was very clear about the fact that there were businesses that he wanted to acquire and he wanted to basically take control over. He had a sense of what the future could be if he was able to get these things done."

Most people would have found the prospectuses incredibly tedious reading, but not Lewis. He read them closely, dreaming a little and learning a lot. Each prospectus was like a little history book that told Lewis about the officers of a company, their salaries, their strategic thinking—even about lawsuits filed against a company. Lewis ate all of this up and he liked nothing better than to take a set of prospectuses home to read.

In 1982, he found out that two radio stations in the U.S. Virgin Islands, WCRN-FM in St. Thomas and WSTX-AM in St. Croix, were up for sale. Because of his vacations in the Caribbean with his family, he was relatively familiar with the area and he immediately began to visualize a whole network of Caribbean radio stations that would eventually stretch to Latin America.

Lewis started by trying to get his financing into place. A friend of Lewis's, Frank Savage, tipped Lewis off to a Washington MESBIC, Broadcast Capital, Inc., that specialized in broadcasting loans for minorities. Savage was on its board, so Lewis figured getting a loan should be a "slam dunk," as he was fond of saying. He put together a detailed business plan and traveled to Washington to meet with the head of Broadcast Capital, John Oxendine.

Lewis took his brother, Jean Fugett, Jr., with him. Oxendine immediately had reservations about Lewis's proposed Virgin Islands venture.

"It was a bit difficult for us to do," Oxendine says. "It was kind of overseas and not easy to monitor. I think that at that time he was going to buy the stations and have Jean commute back and forth."

Oxendine was further troubled by the fact that Lewis wouldn't be a hands-on operator for two financially troubled broadcast properties. He was also concerned that Fugett, who had done some football color commentary for CBS Sports and was putting some money into the deal, had no background in radio management.

Oxendine promised Lewis he would submit Lewis's request to his board along with proposals for other applicants. However, that arrangement wasn't quite what Lewis had in mind. He insisted on being able to present his proposal himself, a request Oxendine turned down because it was against procedure.

Lewis acquiesced but, wanting to leave nothing to chance, he personally lobbied each of Broadcast Capital's board members. He showed up at the front door of one member who lived in Manhattan, Paul van Hook, and proceeded to make the case for his proposal.

"He was very, very aggressive, he really wanted the deal very badly and he did everything that he could to try to make it work," Oxendine recalls. "I mean, I had to go to a convention in New Orleans—he followed me to the convention to push his deal. I don't know if he had any business in New Orleans, but he certainly was there."

Oxendine was eating breakfast inside the restaurant of his hotel with a business associate, when who should walk in and start striding toward their table but Reginald Lewis.

"How's my proposal going?" Lewis asked. "Is there anything I can do?"

"Lewis was very articulate, very persistent, and very tenacious," Oxendine remembers.

On the day Oxendine was to go before his board, Lewis traveled down to Washington from Manhattan. He insisted that he be physically present in the conference room while the board met, against the wishes of Oxendine who requested that Lewis wait outside the room.

As he reviewed each proposal for the board, Oxendine generally had a few supportive words to say. But when he went over Lewis's loan application, Oxendine was silent. The board picked up on Oxendine's silence and voted to reject Lewis's business plan, with only Savage voting in favor. Lewis couldn't believe what had happened. Savage's help and Lewis's lobbying had been for naught. In protest, Savage resigned from Broadcast Capital's board the same day and he and a smoldering Lewis turned on their heels and headed north for New York.

Lewis continued to plumb his contacts to arrange for financing. His next stop was CVC Capital, a Manhattan MESBIC that specialized in lending money to minorities buying broadcast properties. It was run by Joerg Klebe.

"He was a very tough negotiator," Klebe says of Lewis. "He wanted things that we weren't prepared to give to him. We wanted personal guarantees and he was very reluctant to give that to us. But it didn't seem that he had any other source of financing, so we pretty much got what we wanted."

Although Klebe harbored some of the same reservations Oxendine had, he pushed the deal through. "Reg wasn't really an owner-operator, and that kind of deal isn't going to fly unless you're an owner-operator," Klebe says. "I think it was the first deal that Reg really did. I think the deal was more important than the operational side of the thing. Reggie was at no point prepared to manage and operate this station."

CVC agreed to make Lewis a loan for $150,000, provided that it was secured by the three apartment buildings Lewis and his wife owned on 10th Avenue and some Warner Communications stock Lewis owned.

Lewis also succeeded in tapping a Puerto Rican bank, Banco Popular, for a loan of $275,000. The loan was secured by a personal guarantee from Lewis and by his vacation home at Springy Banks. "I promise that you'll get every penny back," Lewis told the bank.

With his financing in place, Lewis went ahead with the purchase of the St. Thomas FM station in July 1982. A portion of the financing was used for the station's initial working capital.

The purchase of the St. Croix station did not push through, so the St. Thomas station became the first piece of what Lewis optimistically christened the Caribbean Basin Broadcasting network. The station was renamed WSTT-FM. Lewis appointed a board of directors for the company that included a number of friends, including Ricardo Olivarez, James Obi, a senior executive at Equitable Life Insurance, and an architect from St. Thomas, Robert De Jongh. Meetings were held at the elegant Harvard Club in Manhattan. Unfortunately for Lewis, things began to go awry with his broadcast property almost immediately.

The station operated out of a rat-infested trailer located in the mountainous area of the island, making its signal difficult for most listeners to receive. Its equipment was ramshackle at best and often on the blink. The station spent more time off the air than on, and building a profitable advertising base proved more difficult than the optimistic Lewis had predicted.

WSTT had a husband and wife team that acted as disc jockeys and sales staff. It soon became clear they weren't up to the task.

Lewis put his brother, Jean, in charge. Fugett actually moved to St. Thomas and at one point became an on-air personality. However, he was put in the middle of an impossible situation where revenue did not cover expenses. The station became a financial black hole for Lewis.

In July 1986, Lewis cut his losses and sold WSTT, putting an end to his dream for a Caribbean radio network. However, he would continue to explore the possibility of purchasing other radio stations.

Phyllis Schless, an investment banker with Bear, Stearns & Co., represented a client trying to unload six small stations experiencing financial difficulties. In early 1983, Schless was looking for a potential purchaser of the properties. Klebe put her in touch with Lewis, who was very interested in buying the stations, located in Florida, Ohio, and New York. Lewis moved expeditiously to solidify a deal.

"I was impressed with the fact that he seemed to be very knowledgeable, seemed to know what he was doing, and what he could do," Schless says. "I thought he would be a very good candidate to acquire these stations."

The transaction was worth about $3 million and Lewis had to come up with $1.5 million. However, the management company owning the stations was not particularly impressed with Lewis. It decided that

Lewis wasn't good for the remaining $1.5 million needed to purchase the stations, nor was he capable of successfully managing the stations if he ever obtained them. The deal collapsed in July 1983.

The ignominy of Caribbean Basin Broadcasting and Lewis's failed attempt to buy more radio stations would have discouraged most individuals, but just served to further whet Lewis's desire to buy and run a successful business.

In August 1983, Schless got a phone call from Lewis in her office. "I have an interesting little situation," he told Schless. "I'd like you to come over. Why don't we kick it around?"

Schless came by to see Lewis at 99 Wall Street. His "interesting little situation" was a company by the name of McCall Pattern Company, a 113-year-old maker of home sewing patterns with revenues of $51.9 million. Lewis had just tried and failed to pull off an acquisition valued at $3 million. His reaction was to go after another acquisition more than seven times bigger.

8

Drexel, the Bear, and the $18 Million Race: Closing the McCall Pattern Deal

The year that Reginald Lewis went after McCall, 1983, it seemed that every day brought news of yet another corporate takeover or leveraged buyout being consummated. The huge conglomerates built up in the 1950s and 1960s were now being dismantled and operations that did not fit in with a company's business emphasis were being unceremoniously sold off to the highest bidder.

Exciting things were happening on Wall Street and Lewis was itching to get into the game.

One day, Lewis chanced upon a *Fortune* magazine article that focused on The McCall Pattern Company, a designer, manufacturer, and marketer of home sewing patterns. McCall's parent company was Norton Simon Industries, a multibillion dollar conglomerate with its hands in everything from Avis rental cars to Hunt Wesson food products.

In 1983, Norton Simon was acquired in a hostile takeover by Esmark, Inc., another conglomerate that owned among other companies, Swift, a meat and poultry producer, and Playtex, a maker of women's undergarments. Esmark head Don Kelly was quoted in the

132

Fortune article as saying that McCall was one of several Norton Simon companies that didn't mesh with Esmark's long-range plans. When Lewis read that, his eyes lit up.

Lewis had represented Norton Simon in 1973 when it sold McCall's magazine to Capital Cities-ABC. From the due diligence he'd done in that transaction, Lewis had learned quite a bit about the pattern company's operations. Intrigued by the *Fortune* piece, he put in a call to Tom Lamia. Lamia had served as Lewis's lawyer in the abortive attempt six years earlier to buy Almet, the California furniture firm.

Lewis told Lamia he was giving some thought to taking a run at McCall and solicited Lamia's suggestions on how to get the ball rolling. Lewis liked some things about McCall that repelled other potential suitors. For one thing, fewer women were staying at home to sew and the home-sewing market had been declining at a rate of roughly 9 percent each year since 1976, when 171 million home sewing patterns were sold. And McCall, a wholly-owned subsidiary of Norton Simon, had no long-range expansion plans.

Consequently, Lewis could practically envision a giant "Discount" sign hanging around McCall. He would buy the firm on the cheap, light a fire under management, reduce expenses, and increase profitability. Then he'd sell it after a few years. McCall would be Lewis's toehold the realm of high finance.

On July 29, 1983, Lewis began his campaign in earnest. He created TLC Pattern, Inc. for the purpose of taking over McCall. He also created a Delaware-based holding company, TLC Group, Inc.

In June of 1983, Dave Mahoney, CEO of Norton Simon, announced a proposed management buyout of Norton Simon, Inc. My law firm had done some work for NSI in the past and had an excellent relationship with the company. My interest was not merely in the potential effect on my law practice, but also in whether one of the businesses under the NSI umbrella might be for sale if the buyout went through. I pulled out several years' worth of NSI annual reports and their 10k (an SEC document with detailed financial information on a corporation) and started poring over the various businesses. There were a number of potential acquisition possibilities.

Don Kelly of Esmark announced his interest in NSI and put in a bid superior to Dave Mahoney's. Anderson Clayton and KKR were *also nosing around. I studied Don's bid and concluded that it was a great deal for Don and for Esmark. The jewel of NSI was Hunt Wesson, but there were other valuable properties like Avis and Somerset Imports, which had Johnny Walker scotch, Glass Containers Co., and lots more. There was also $40 million to $50 million of holding company overhead that could be eliminated and good cash on the balance sheet. There was plenty of debt, but much of it was off-balance-sheet and related to Avis. Don Kelly was masterful in his approach, and in July he took NSI for Esmark.*

I remember calling Cam Trowbridge, longtime general counsel of NSI and a friend and a client, shortly after the deal was announced. We had lunch a few days later at the Boardroom, a luncheon club on Park Avenue, a favorite NSI watering hole. Cam, always pleasant, thanked me for offering my help during the hectic past few weeks and said that things had moved so fast that he hadn't had an opportunity to get me involved. I said I'd imagined as much and fully understood. I then made the faux pas of remarking that "I thought Esmark was not paying enough."

Cam gave me a benign look that suggested I was nuts. "Reg, they are paying a billion dollars. Before this deal, the market cap was about $600 million." I let the matter drop with something like, "Well, I always felt NSI was a great company even at that price."

We then turned to other topics. I told Cam that I needed a change from practicing law and was interested in buyouts. I asked him which management teams within NSI did he especially like, and so forth. Around dessert, I mentioned McCall Pattern Co. and sought his views about its management. Cam gave them high marks across the board but said the market for home sewing was going down and not likely to improve.

I asked him who I should call if a group I represented might be interested in taking a crack at buying it. Cam said the Esmark people would, of course, call the shots. But Bob Walter, who was Dave Mahoney's finance man, was staying around through the transition and would be a good place to start. Cam knew that I knew Bob and suggested I give Bob a call, and he said he would let Bob know of my interest. We parted in a warm and friendly manner, as usual.

I called Bob Walter that afternoon. Bob took the call right away and said that Cam had just called and mentioned my possible interest in McCall's. Bob said Esmark would probably want to sell it, and he would pass along our group's interest to the Esmark people. He also said McCall would report to Joel Smilow, who ran International Playtex for Esmark. Bob said he would get back to me.

A few weeks passed and I'd heard nothing. I called Bob a few times, but could not get through. During that two or three weeks, I gathered as much information as I could on McCall. I put together a small summary of financial data and, most important, read everything on Simplicity, which was a direct competitor of McCall's and a public company controlled by Charles Hurwitz, the Houston investor and deal man.

The more I looked into Simplicity and McCall, the more I liked the business. It had very high profit margins, value-added products, brand names, and excellent distribution—and it generated significant cash.

At the same time, I was also working on a deal involving six radio stations. It had been brought to me by Phyllis Schless, who was then at Bear, Stearns. Even though our radio deal didn't go through, I was very impressed with Phyllis's approach, which was to try and keep things on track. I showed Phyllis my assessment of the McCall situation, told her of my earlier conversations with Bob Walter, and said I thought it was time to go directly to Esmark. Would she arrange a meeting?

Phyllis put in a call to Joel Smilow who was the head of Esmark's Playtex division and responsible for McCall. Yes, they would entertain offers and were willing to meet. Within hours after the meeting had been set up, Bob Walter called and was beautifully candid. He said management was trying to put something together at McCall Pattern but they'd had enough time and that he had let Smilow know of my group's interest. I asked Bob if he would let the Esmark people know of my prior favorable dealings with NSI. Bob said he would, but not to worry about all that. He wished me luck and said, "Reg, they want to sell it." I quickly asked if he knew of any other interest in McCall, and Bob said, "I don't know of any. Most people don't like its prospects."

I gave Cam a call and asked him to tell me a little more about McCall's management. I also asked him to give McCall CEO Earle Angstadt a call and let Angstadt know I would like to meet.

Now, this was the team for the meeting with Smilow: There was Phyllis, of course, Tom Lamia and myself, and Doug Walter, a very bright tax lawyer from Chicago. I did not have a top finance man, but that would come later.

After studying McCall's financial situation, Lewis had determined that McCall was worth at least $18 million. Schless had advised him that because he was an unknown quantity and a novice at the acquisition game, in order to succeed his bid would have to be higher than any competitor's. In other words, he would have to pay a premium, the price of admission, as it were. Lewis agreed.

The role of investment bankers in this world generally, and in the business world specifically, is one of the great mysteries of the universe. The simple fact is that you don't hire investment banks, you hire people—or in some cases, a person. Because Phyllis Schless had labored for many years on Wall Street with one of the top investment banks in the country, Bear, Stearns, I wanted her thoughts about the price to pay for McCall.

Doug Walter, a tax lawyer, was important, too. I always respected Doug's ability to think through a problem. Actually, I utilized Doug's services as much for this as his tax skills, which are considerable. In chatting with Doug about McCall, I said, "Okay, we want to take this—let's discuss the key points." Doug asked about price, but I suggested we forget price for the moment, since that was simple. I was being a little cute, but I meant it.

Doug went along, but asked, "Okay, why?" I said, "Because No. 1, we will require a financing condition to our bid and, No. 2, we will offer whatever we can finance." Doug said, "So Reg, you want to be preemptive?" I liked that line and would use it often thereafter. TLC would be preemptive in its approach.

McCall was earning about $6 million in operating profit. This was a figure I would repeat often. The fact is, however, I never focused on earnings. Others like to hear it so I repeated it, but I kept my eyes glued on cash flow. When I worked through the numbers, over a 2½-year period NSI had pulled about $18 million in cash out of McCall. That, then, was my price—$18 million. In my heart I was ready to go higher.

Before meeting with Smilow, Lewis, Tom Lamia, and Doug Walter put their heads together and crafted a letter of intent that outlined the terms of their offer for McCall. They would offer Playtex $20 million in cash and $2.5 million in subordinated debt, a total of $22.5 million and $4.5 million more than Lewis' original price of $18 million.

The letter of intent for Smilow said the McCall offer was being made by the TLC Group, TLC being an acronym for The Lewis Company. Lewis had a proclivity for giving his acquisition vehicles and his companies personalized acronyms—recall the birth of Republic Furniture and Leisure, Inc. (RFL) in the failed Almet deal. In future years, Lewis would smilingly deflect queries from reporters curious to know what the TLC in TLC Beatrice stood for.

Lewis had more work to do before the Smilow meeting. After his failures with the radio stations and Almet, he decided to play things differently with McCall. Reluctantly, Lewis decided to rely on a little guile. Instead of presenting himself as the person looking to buy the company, Lewis claimed to represent a consortium of investors. He knew everyone on the other side of the table would automatically assume the members of the investor group were white. Because Lewis did not hold himself out as the potential acquirer of the McCall Pattern Co., he could at least rest assured that race was not a factor if he failed this time.

He discussed his strategy with his wife before going after McCall and she supported his idea. "Yes, darling, you've got to go with guile on this one," she told him. Lewis asked his friends who had been on the board of Caribbean Basin Broadcasting to invest in his bid. Only two, Sam Peabody and Rick Olivarez, could come up with money quickly enough to help finance his acquisition effort. Peabody and Olivarez contributed $10,000 and $5,000, respectively. Now Lewis could maintain, with a straight face, that he was representing an investor group.

Lewis rented a stretch limousine for the trip to meet with Smilow in Stamford, Connecticut. Lewis was excited and ebullient during the journey, confidently mapping out his future plans for McCall as though the purchase were a fait accompli. After Lewis and his team pulled into the parking lot of International Playtex headquarters, they were ushered inside and made to cool their heels for about an hour. Normally, Lewis would never have endured a 60-minute wait. But in this instance, he had little choice.

Playtex headquarters were in Stamford, Connecticut. I hired a limo and we all piled in for the one-hour trip. When we arrived, we met Smilow, who had Hercules Sotos—his longtime right hand— and Coleman, his longtime counsel with him.

I opened by thanking them for meeting with us and said I represented a group that was interested in McCall Pattern. Smilow said they were open to offers and that McCall was a good business that really did not fit with their plans. We agreed to exchange some information. They gave us McCall's business plan for 1983 and a good bit of other information. They said they would tell CEO Earle Angstadt of our interest and ask him to cooperate. The meeting went very well. Finally, I was talking to professional managers who did not want to fool around and posture. This deal felt right.

Smilow, Sotos, and Coleman received the TLC delegation in a huge conference room. Initially, Smilow was quite curt with Lewis. "What's this all about?" he asked brusquely. "I got this letter—who are you?" Lewis told Smilow that he and his team were the TLC Group referred to in the letter and that they wanted to buy McCall.

"Who are your investors?" Smilow demanded. Lewis cagily responded, "I can't say right now."

Smilow began looking around the room, fixing his gaze first on Lamia. "How about you, Tommy, are you an investor?" he asked. Receiving a noncommittal answer, Smilow turned to Doug Walter. "How about you, Doug, are you an investor?"

Lewis didn't want his people to say yes, but he didn't want them to say no, either. Smilow's pointed questioning made for some uncomfortable moments. But Lewis accomplished his initial goal of getting his foot in the door. Smilow ended the meeting by setting a deadline for Lewis to produce a commitment letter from a financial institution pledging to come up with most of the McCall purchase price.

Personal credibility is priceless in most fields of endeavor, but particularly so in high finance. Lewis had assembled a quality team, a fact not lost on Smilow.

"He came in with financial advisers who were credible," Smilow recalls. "He was very smart, gentlemanly, dignified, tough. The kind of person you like to deal with."

Herc Sotos liked what he saw of Lewis also. "He bowled us over," Sotos remembers. "He came in prepared, he came in attuned to events that were unfolding, he was able to get the financial support he needed from the banks and he was determined to do it. He said, 'Herc, I'm going to do this deal.'"

But it would take a lot more than favorable first impressions for Lewis to win McCall. To facilitate his quest, Lewis devised the following division of labor at Lewis & Clarkson: He and Kevin Wright were to devote all of their time to the McCall transaction, while Charles Clarkson and Laurie Nelson were to continue doing the legal work that paid the bills.

In the meantime, Lewis boned up on the sewing pattern business and on McCall. He may not have grasped the minutiae, but from a macroeconomic standpoint Lewis had an excellent sense of how the pattern industry operated. That's because he would sit down at his desk in his law office or in his den at home and study the business until he understood what made it tick.

An obsession of his was to "get behind the numbers" generated by a business. In the course of reading prospectuses, he would grab Kevin Wright or Charles Clarkson and say, "Here's a figure on the page. I want to understand why that number is there, what are the components that go into making up that number. What individual had to do A, B, C, and D to make it what it is? And why isn't it better?"

When not studying the pattern industry, Lewis was making sure his business advisers for McCall were earning their keep. He held a number of animated, late-night discussions with Phyllis Schless, Tom Lamia, and Doug Walter that lasted until the wee hours of the morning.

"The McCall transaction was a much more emotional transaction for him than anything that happened subsequently," Schless observes. "He was really deeply involved in it, not simply analytically, but emotionally. It was the first real big test of 'Could he do this?'"

Lewis also consulted a few other people outside his circle of advisers, freeing him of the burden of constantly having to appear the supremely confident leader. One person whose counsel Lewis sought during the McCall deal was Joerg Klebe, who was involved in Lewis's Caribbean radio deal.

"He showed up at my office every day to tell me about the progress and ask me, 'Should I do this or shouldn't I do this,'" Klebe says. "The deal kept changing and he was very uncertain about whether he should or should not do the deal. I said, look, this is a great opportunity for you. Go for it. I was prepared to give him a million dollars for the deal, except that he didn't want to sign for it personally."

McCALL—PUTTING IT TOGETHER

Lewis had other ideas about how to get the finances necessary to buy McCall. First though, he had to meet with McCall's management.

Let's forget price. This was a people deal and I had to get to know management.

Enter Earle Angstadt. Earle is right out of central casting for a CEO. Tall, blond, blue eyes, well-tailored, and in command of the social graces. He had been CEO of McCall's for 15 years and had survived when many division presidents at NSI could not.

When I called Earle and said I'd like to get together, the first thing he said in a rather crusty way was, "What are you going to do for management?" My response was, "Let's talk about that." We had our first of many meetings at the Harvard Club. He came dressed in a corporate blue Brooks Brothers suit, looking great. I was well prepared for the meeting. I knew his background and had a couple of people call him to let him know I didn't have horns.

I decided to sell him. I opened with my work in putting deals together. I knew how to buy this company. Would he run operations substantially as he had in the past? I needed his knowledge and experience. Of course I could find another manager, but if it ain't broke, why fix it? Earle and I both looked each other right in the eye and decided to continue taking small steps together. He had been told to cooperate.

Good relations with Earle enabled us to expand our team rapidly. I decided we would piggyback on the McCall organization, which was formidable.

Lewis's acquisition strategy called for recruiting the top manager of the target company. He intended to set the strategic direction for the company, while a professional manager ran day-to-day operations. That was why he needed Cammer in the Almet deal. To do McCall, he needed Earle Angstadt.

Angstadt and his management team would have to be highly motivated and effective for Lewis to extract maximum value from McCall. Angstadt vividly recalls his first impression of the earnest Lewis, who was smoking a cigar and wearing a ruffled suit and a blue shirt.

"He had all of his thoughts and proposals well organized," Angstadt recalls. "We related to each other very quickly in our first meeting. My first instinct was that this was the man with whom I wanted to make a deal."

Lewis peppered Angstadt with questions about the mechanics of the pattern business, which also left a favorable impression. After his face-to-face with Lewis, Angstadt lobbied International Playtex management on behalf of the fledgling financier.

With McCall's management seemingly on board, Lewis assembled the other key elements of his bid.

I also hired Price Waterhouse, which served as Simplicity's auditors and therefore knew the pattern business. My first choice was Deloitte, Haskins and Sells but that firm had a conflict because of its representation of NSI.

Although I had hired Bear, Stearns to raise the bank financing, I could not resist making some efforts myself to pull that together. Doug Walter introduced us to the people at First Chicago and a team from there tried to put together a group of banks. It would become a useful dry run. B. J. Chubet of Bear, Stearns and I went to New Jersey and made a similar effort with Midlantic and the leading New Jersey banks—no go. But it was a useful exercise nonetheless.

I felt I was stuck on the McCall deal and was not sure whether Bear was trying to scuttle the deal or not. I decided to give Bear a little competition.

I was a real prospectus junkie and was reading all kinds of prospectuses. I remembered looking at the Kinney Parking Lot deal. I was very interested because I had thought of buying that. Kinney had done a preferred stock deal with Drexel. When I read through that prospectus, I said, "Holy cow, if these guys could get a deal like this done, Drexel is an outfit we should be talking to." I decided to put the heat on Bear. I wasn't sure the firm was pulling out all the stops for us and even feared that if I was not able to meet my deadline, the Bear might step in and do the deal with management. I decided to light a fire under Bear.

I called in my close colleagues Charles Clarkson and Kevin Wright and brainstormed to determine who our contacts on the Street were that might be helpful. There were damn few. Our practice did not involve a lot of contact with investment bankers because the deals were generally small, about $1 million to $3 million, and did not often involve public companies.

I mentioned that this firm called Drexel seemed to be able to sell anything: Did we know anyone there? Charles said he thought that Jean Wong, a client of ours whom we had helped start a computer software company, had gone to work there. So I called up Jean Wong in California and said, "Jean, we got a letter of intent on McCall Pattern Company. We want to buy it." Jean got really excited. Before I could even give Jean the full picture, he said "Reg, we'll do it and I'll get right back to you." Jean called back the same day with a guy named Peter Ackerman on the line.

I outlined the deal and my plans. Ackerman focused on one thing, "Do you have an exclusive letter of intent?" I said yes. He repeated the question and I said yes again. He then asked if I would review the numbers again. I did so. Yes, we were buying it at about four times cash flow, but the business was in decline.

He said, "I know this situation very well, because we were working with Dave Mahoney on the leveraged buyout. I didn't even get my expenses. We can help you. What do you want?"

So I said, "Well, we want $18 million of debt. We'll take care of the rest."

"Well, where is the rest coming from?"

"I'll take care of the rest."

He said okay and asked if I was willing to give up some equity.

"Yeah, we're willing to give up some equity if we really get some value."

He repeated Jean's line—we can do it—and asked if I could come immediately to Los Angeles. I said no because of commitments here: Could he come to New York?

He said he expected to be in New York shortly anyway and we would get together. So Ackerman came to New York and came by to see me. I told him about Bear, but noted the arrangement was not exclusive. He said, "The first thing I want you to do is fire Bear, Stearns."

"Forget it, I won't do that."

Second, he wanted the brochure that Bear put together. I would not give it to him. I let him see it, but I would not give it to him. I said, "Look, I don't want to start my career on Wall Street by taking somebody else's work and giving it to you."

Then I said, "Here is the basic information on the company. If you can come up with $18 million, you can get some equity." He came back with a structure. He said, "You'll own 55 percent, we'll own 45 percent, and we'll raise all of the money." I said, "Okay, whoever gets to the finish line first, they get the deal. The first person to get me the bank financing has the deal. Period."

He said, "When we, Drexel, Burnham, Lambert sign on, we do the entire financing, not just the bank." "Well," I said, "the other piece is substantially in place. But we can talk about it."

Ackerman told me the first thing Drexel wanted me to do was get an extension. I told him no. "There's no extension. You have to buy my timetable."

And, of course, then he said, "You've got to come out and see Mike Milken—you've got to come out and see Mike." My reaction was, "Look, the deal is here in New York, it's not in Los Angeles." I wasn't that informed yet in terms of Mike and what he was doing, so I would not go to Los Angeles.

It was a good conversation. I immediately called Phyllis Schless at Bear. I told her I did not feel her firm was putting its full resources behind the project and that I wanted the firm to know that I was talking to Drexel. That really got them in gear. You would have thought from Phyllis's reaction that I said the Russians were about to invade the Bear's headquarters on Water Street.

"Reg, this is a mistake—we are working very hard here!" I said, "Phyllis, I want results and I don't have them. I am going with the first guy who can get me home." Phyllis said, "I'll get right back to you." I put the phone down and smiled and said to the boys, "Well, it's going to get interesting."

Bear—specifically Phyllis and B. J. Chubet—really started to turn on the juice. Phyllis called one afternoon and asked if I could go up and see Bankers Trust. I was tired but said yes.

Peter Offerman was at Bankers Trust with one of his colleagues, who seemed very interested in the McCall deal. Peter was moderately friendly and asked if I would summarize the deal and my plans. It was probably good that I was tired because I laid my rationale out for the deal in clear, crisp terms that focused on the cash flow, the reasons I liked McCall, and how I would approach it. I spoke for about 20 minutes. Peter was cool but very knowledgeable and seemed to like what he was hearing.

Believe it or not, I really didn't care about his reaction. I believed that one way or another I was going to do the deal. In hindsight, this probably gave him the impression that I felt I had a strong hand and had an attractive piece of business for the bank. The meeting concluded with Peter saying they had a good deal more work to do and asking whether they could visit the plant. I said sure.

B. J. set up a meeting a few days later with Acquisition Funding Corp., people who had done a lot of deals. Craig Harding was the vice president there and the chemistry was terrific. They wanted equity but would do the entire deal. Of course, the timing was mentioned again—could I get an extension? The answer was, "No."

Peter Ackerman and I spoke every day and it was the same thing—"Fire Bear, get an extension, and we'll do it. Just tell Bear to get out of the way—we'll even pay their expenses." This was a real turnoff, and although I kept Ackerman in the process, I decided that maybe our values were too different to do a deal together. But I liked him personally and respected his quick mind and his nothing-gets-in-my-way attitude.

Ackerman was difficult to deal with. He dredged up the worst instincts in me. He was also preoccupied with ethnic considerations. I had to pull him up on that about three or four times. "I don't talk about your Jewishness," I told him, "so don't you talk about my ethnicity. It's not relevant to anything that we're doing." So I put him completely on the defensive on that score. Got him so that he was afraid to make any comment.

Phyllis called and said Offerman wanted to visit McCall's production facility in Kansas and would have an answer upon his return.

Fine. Acquisition Funding had their lawyer do some work, and a deal structure was put in place. Fine. I was already formulating a structure where Joel (Smilow) would be asked to take back a lot more paper. I also called Allen & Company to see if they would play. This was a mistake, because it ended up generating a competitive bid.

We were almost at the deadline. Acquisition said yes, but it would be expensive and the timing still bothered them.

Offerman returned from Manhattan, Kansas, and called me around noon after he had met with "the Pope," which was our name for Bear's credit approval executive. Offerman said, "Eighteen million, and I believe you are buying one helluva company." I asked, "When do we sign?" and Peter said, "This evening." Peter then said, "Oh, Phyllis says the $2 million in subordinated debt may not be all spoken for—is that correct?" I said, "That's right. What do you have in mind?"

Offerman said, "Maybe we can go another million for 20 percent of the equity. Would you like me to talk to the Pope?"

I told him yes. He called back in about 15 minutes with $19 million. I called Phyllis and asked if Offerman was for real. "Yes, Reg, he is for real," she responded.

I would not allow myself more than five minutes to feel good— there was no time to feel good. Damn it—execute, think—sign their goddamned commitment tonight. Get the lawyers for Bankers Trust what they need. I called Charles and Tom Lamia and Doug Walter. Get this signed and do not sweat the details. Holy shit—execute, man, and forget about everything else!

That evening, at the office of Kaye, Scholer (a New York law firm), Bankers Trust delivered a written commitment for $19 million. It was unbelievable—the horse had talked.

Lewis was referring to a favorite story of his about a king who had sentenced his magician to death but then agreed to the magician's plea to delay the sentence for a year, during which time the magician promised he would make the king's horse talk. The magician reasoned that "Anything could happen in a year. The king may die. The horse may die. I may die. Or, the horse may talk."

Now I could cut Ackerman completely out of the deal. I didn't, by the way, tell him that we signed up with Bankers Trust. I just said,

"Well, you know, if you can't play on my timetable, we can't do any-thing." Ackerman then told Jean Wong, "He'll never get this deal closed." And so I called Jean and told him the deal was closed and that I would be happy to come out and brief them on the situation. "Really? Everybody around here said you'd never get it closed." I said, "Well, we got lucky." They didn't realize that the prior 15 years I had been closing an average of 20 deals a year that were as tough.

Peter Offerman of Bankers Trust Co. played a critical role in Lewis's pursuit of McCall and offers the following assessment of Lewis:

"He had a terrific strategic view of his business and a real view of how the financing would work in the context of the business plan he had. He kind of exuded the kind of personal qualities that anyone who's assessing people would check off as positive. Reg was one of the most finely tuned negotiators I've ever met." Offerman chuckles as he recalls that Lewis was wearing a shirt with a broken collar stay, causing one side of his collar to comically curl up in the air. Lewis, intent on driving his points home with Offerman, never even noticed.

Lewis had given Offerman a list of 10 people that Lewis had done business with over the years. Offerman called each of them, and they all praised Lewis's integrity and intellect. Finally, Bankers Trust ran Lewis up against the so-called "Five C's of credit": Character, Capacity of the business, Capacity of the person seeking the loan, Capital, and Collateral. Lewis checked out on all counts.

Tom Lamia was with Lewis when he got the letter from Bankers Trust pledging $19 million to buy McCall. He remembers that Lewis remained remarkably composed when he saw the missive for the first time. He was within arm's reach of his objective, but he wasn't there just yet.

"Now we're in the game in a serious way," he said, smiling.

Bankers Trust's multimillion dollar vote of confidence had taken a lot of pressure off. The next closest financing commitment was for $14 million. That didn't matter now, because Lewis and his team had most of the financing necessary for McCall in the bag.

In any corporate buyout, the first key hurdle is to arrive at an agreement on price. Lewis was well beyond that phase. But two critical steps still remained. Lewis still had to negotiate the terms and conditions of the transaction, which entails conducting due diligence and drafting a small mountain of documents and covenants. Only then would Lewis be able to move to the third and most critical phase: Getting the deal closed.

Large-scale closings usually take place inside law firms, where scores of lawyers and accountants go over documents related to the transaction. A closing agenda is followed, a process that can take weeks before it is completed. Then and only then are titles and funds transferred, completing the transaction.

Even though Lewis knew those steps lay ahead, he figured himself to be almost home free once Bankers Trust came up with a commitment letter promising to provide $19 million in financing. He still had to raise $1 million in investor equity, but he was confident of being able to scare up that kind of money.

The commitment letter needed to be modified before it could be submitted to Playtex, so Lewis put in a call to Kevin Wright and Charles Clarkson.

"Boys, we're getting ready to do this commitment letter for $19 million," he told them. "Do you guys want to get Tom Lamia involved in this, or do the two of you think that you can come and do it yourselves?" Wright and Clarkson said they were up to the challenge and caught a cab uptown to meet Lewis at Bankers Trust's offices.

Over the course of several hours, Lewis and his associates worked with Bankers Trust's attorneys to put the commitment letter in its final form. The date was November 19, 1983. The sun had long since set by the time Lewis, Clarkson, and Wright finished their duties and left the bank's offices.

The three were strolling down Park Avenue engrossed in conversation when Lewis, in a surge of jubilation, coltishly clicked his heels and descended joyfully to earth, startling his comrades with his light-hearted display.

The following morning, Lewis, Kevin Wright, Phyllis Schless and Doug Walter all piled into a limousine waiting for them in midtown. The vehicle navigated its way through Manhattan's sea of darting taxis, double-parked cars, and gridlocked intersections before cruising north, toward Connecticut. Spirits were high inside the limo. The general consensus was that McCall was snared and ready to be skinned.

After the group arrived at Playtex headquarters, Smilow met them and Lewis confidently whipped out his $19 million commitment letter and theatrically handed it to Smilow. Lewis then gave a brief description of the terms laid out in the letter.

Looking unimpressed, Smilow took the letter, read it briefly, and then turned to Lewis and said, "I'm sorry, but I can't sell you the business based on this statement. The deal would be too leveraged and that would be unfair to my employees."

Lewis looked at Smilow in astonishment. Lewis had pulled off a minor miracle to get Bankers Trust to commit $19 million to his first major deal, and here Smilow was telling him that the transaction would carry too much debt . . . ridiculous! Smilow was playing some kind of game, and everyone in the room knew it. His goal was to keep Lewis off balance so Smilow could shop Lewis's offer around in search of a better one. By now, Lewis was smoldering.

Straining to control his temper, Lewis informed Smilow in measured, yet forceful tones that they'd had a gentleman's agreement and that Lewis had abided by the terms of their pact. By rights, he ought to be able to cement his bid to buy McCall. Nothing new had been put on the table—why was Lewis's offer suddenly unacceptable?

Other members of Lewis's team also began to chime in with objections. At this point, Lewis and Smilow repaired into another room for a private discussion. Lewis was furious to think he had been a mere stalking horse, but he was mindful of the fact that Smilow controlled the business and Lewis's ability to take control of it.

Choosing his words with care, Lewis argued that Smilow should accept his deal. However, Smilow wouldn't budge, so Lewis and the TLC team left Playtex and climbed into their limo for a glum ride back to New York City.

"It was like coming back from a funeral," Kevin Wright says. "The ride back was tough—there was just a pervasive sadness in the car. It was the first time I ever heard Reg talk about something he was involved in being 'unfair.'"

They stopped at a restaurant along the way for a cup of coffee and a despondent post mortem. Lewis asked each member of his team why they thought Smilow had turned them away.

Lewis mulled over each response, saving Wright's for last. Wright had a two-fold answer: First, Smilow feared that McCall was going for too low a price. Second, Wright wondered whether race hadn't played a part. Years afterward, Lewis would harken back to Wright's response and remark that he'd hit the nail on the head when none of Lewis's high-priced advisers had; Smilow says he was only motivated by business.

Lewis was bitterly disappointed. From Wall Street came whispers of what Lewis had already suspected—Playtex was shopping McCall around in search of a higher offer. He even found out that an investment banker he'd approached early on was now quietly trying to buy McCall behind his back!

Lewis was in limbo, and the day-to-day uncertainty was grinding on him and his acquisition group.

One night, after working at 99 Wall Street until 1 A.M., Lewis and Wright were on their way out together. They had something of a late-night ritual where Lewis would drop Wright off at the World Trade Center to catch a commuter train to New Jersey.

As they waited for the elevator, Lewis looked Wright in the eye and asked, "Do you think we're going to get this done?" Wright answered unhesitatingly, "Yeah, Reg. I do."

Lewis smiled and replied, "I do, too." Wright's vote of confidence had been reassuring.

In the meantime, the calendar was inexorably moving forward. November gave way to December and still there was no word from Smilow. All the while the meter was running among Lewis's business advisers, lawyers, and accountants, who were accumulating fees by the bushelful as Smilow continued to beat the bushes for a more lucrative offer.

Acutely aware that the passage of time was costing him a small fortune, Lewis responded with an interesting gambit. He ushered Phyllis Schless, Doug Walter, and Tom Lamia into a conference room and laid a very big carrot on the table to encourage them to get the wheels turning on his transaction once again.

"I don't know what you guys can do that you aren't already doing," he said, "but I want to be sure you do it. So I'm going to double your fees on the deal if we get this thing closed in a reasonable time frame."

Bankers Trust was also eyeballing the calendar. Financial institutions pledging millions of dollars for corporate transactions can't sit by forever. Bankers Trust had their lawyers send Lewis a letter that essentially said, "You haven't done what you said you were going to do and Bankers Trust is no longer committed to providing you with $19 million."

Worried, Lewis began to approach other potential financial backers. Christmas was approaching and he could feel the deal slipping away. Lewis might wind up having to ante up hundreds of thousands of dollars in expenses with nothing to show for it. Each passing day solidified Lewis's and Wright's view that Lewis was being jerked around because he'd pulled off his end of the bargain too skillfully and stood to make too much money for himself if the transaction was consummated.

One evening, Lewis was working in the study of his home with the television on when Jesse Jackson appeared on the screen. Jackson was talking about running for President. Lewis would later relate to a close confidant that a single thought ran through his head, "If this man can run for president of the United States, I can buy the McCall Pattern Company."

CLOSING THE DEAL

By January 1984, it was clear to Smilow that Lewis held the most attractive offer. Smilow asked for a meeting, this time agreeing to come to Manhattan.

The meeting was held at the Yale Club, to which Smilow belonged. Years later, Smilow and Lewis would become good friends and even discussed the idea of combining Playtex and TLC Beatrice. But as the McCall deal was being finalized, Smilow was not Lewis's favorite person.

Smilow sought more advantageous terms than he'd originally requested: Now he demanded a 7.5 percent stake in TLC Pattern, Inc., the holding company Lewis had established to control McCall Pattern Co. Lewis was not pleased by Smilow's new demand, but he was anxious to close the McCall deal, so he acquiesced.

"You reach a stage where you almost have to close," Doug Walter explained. "You've got to make the last concession because you've got so much money invested in it that the only way you can get it back is to get the company. It doesn't give you a whole lot of leverage."

Bankers Trust said that it would stand by its commitment of $19 million, prompting relieved sighs all around.

The final terms of the agreement called for Lewis to pay a cash price of $20 million and give a note worth $2.5 million as well as the warrant for 7.5 percent of the new entity. The deal required McCall to have at least $1,855,000 in cash on its balance sheet by a specific date. Anything less than $1,855,000 would be subtracted from the purchase price; anything more would be added to the purchase price.

The McCall transaction was back on track but Lewis was still not at the finish line. From a logistics standpoint, a corporate buyout is one of the most complicated human endeavors imaginable. The point man, in this case Reginald Lewis, has to ride herd on scores of major and minor transactions and crises, any one of which could be a potential deal breaker. Equity has to be raised at the same time banks are being contacted about how much money they'll give and what their lending requirements are. Due diligence has to be conducted on the target company, which entails burrowing through mountains of records and making sure everything is in order. Armies of lawyers, accountants, and investment bankers are all working simultaneously at a fever pitch, sometimes at cross purposes due to miscommunication or petty rivalries.

Someone must act as a conductor to orchestrate the efforts of these hundreds of players into a smooth and efficient exercise. The role of maestro fell to Lewis. Everyone looked to him for their cues. He was stepping into a role unlike any he had played as an attorney, and he had to remain calm and upbeat when situations were particularly tense or bleak. Lewis rose to the challenge magnificently.

When Lewis was under intense pressure, his palms tended to sweat and they remained moist throughout the final stages of the McCall transaction. Otherwise, Lewis showed no outward signs of concern or worry. He had worked out this deal in his head many times, gauged the strengths and weaknesses of his team, and formulated a game plan for making an intricate and unwieldy transaction manageable. So when closing time came on the McCall deal, Lewis had his various players and their roles already assigned.

Tom Lamia was to be Lewis's quarterback. Lamia was responsible for handling negotiations, tax planning, and the drafting of documents during the course of the negotiation. Doug Walter would be a backup quarterback who would serve as a second pair of eyes for Lamia's work. Charles Clarkson was assigned the role of document control, keeping tabs on the blizzard of paperwork the deal was manufacturing and making sure that documents wound up in the right place at the right time. Laurie Nelson was responsible for intellectual property agreements, which govern things such as trademarks. Kevin Wright was to review all employment agreements for key McCall personnel.

Originally tasked with finding bank financing, Phyllis Schless served as a Lewis confidante who helped keep him focused on the big picture as the deal progressed. Lewis's role was that of field general and big kahuna.

"He didn't want any sloppy work," Lamia recalls. "He didn't want any confusion. He didn't want anybody stepping on his lines. He wanted to be the star of the occasion."

Lewis never lost sight of one simple fact throughout the complex buyout: He wanted the McCall Pattern Company. Period. He made full use of his ability to cut to the heart of a problem and to understand interpersonal relationships. Also, once Lewis staked out a position on some point, he never publicly wavered on it. He entertained plenty of second thoughts in private about the McCall deal and tended to agonize—even procrastinate—when it came to major decisions. But that process wasn't for public consumption.

His outward appearance of making a decision, focusing on it in the face of myriad distractions and not displaying any doubt would prove invaluable.

Toward the end of the transaction to acquire McCall, Lewis began to follow a pattern of behavior that first surfaced during the failed Almet transaction. Until he was reasonably certain the target firm was within his grasp, Lewis would unfailingly appear at every meeting, every negotiation, every brainstorming session. However, once it appeared that he would prevail, he kept a low profile until the actual closing. Lewis would give his troops their marching orders via the telephone in the meantime. Although not present physically, Lewis stayed on top of developments like a hawk and was intimately familiar with the smallest setback or bit of progress.

When obstacles were encountered, Lewis generally had a Plan B already at hand and waiting to be implemented. "He was very unusual in his ability, or desire, to keep his options open until the very last minute," Doug Walter says. "He was constantly keeping alternatives in front of him in order to sort of be able to rearrange them at the last minute."

As Lamia and Playtex's attorney negotiated the purchase agreement for McCall, Lamia reported back to Lewis by phone, walking Lewis through a 40-item checklist issue by issue. After conferring with Lewis, Lamia would then go back to the seller's lawyer and the issues were gradually narrowed until an agreement was at hand.

The process took about four days. In the course of negotiating one contract, Lamia made a concession on a confidentiality agreement that Lamia assumed he had the authority to make. When told of the concession, Lewis was livid. "You mean to tell me you would just take it upon yourself to do something like this without asking your client?" Lewis screamed at Lamia.

"Reg, either I have the authority to negotiate or I don't," Lamia countered. "This is the kind of thing I've got to have some discretion about." The explosion caught Lamia off guard, because it was the first time he had experienced the legendary Lewis temper directed at him.

In the meantime, Lewis had a pressing matter to deal with prior to closing: He needed $1 million in cash. He was very methodical in his approach. Who would be a logical person to hit up for that kind of money? A good place to start would be with McCall's top managers: Giving them an equity stake in the company would stimulate them to seek optimum results. Plus, who would be easier to sell on McCall than someone already intimately familiar with it? Lewis put the touch on Earle Angstadt and Angstadt's second in command, Bob Hermann.

"He had acquired cash elsewhere, but he was very anxious for my check," Angstadt says. "I put in about $110,000. My associate at McCall, Bob Hermann, put in $67,000. Reg was very anxious to get that money, because I think he was on the hook for it."

Lewis already had $15,000 from friends Sam Peabody and Ricardo Olivarez. He then turned to one of his MESBIC contacts, Equico Capital Corp., and came away with a loan of $500,000.

Finally, Lewis asked his banker, Robert Winters of the Morgan Bank, for a personal loan of $500,000 which Lewis promised to repay within a month. Such was Winters' faith in Lewis that the loan was made on an unsecured basis. Lewis now had more than he needed to close the deal, but kept that little piece of information to himself. And true to his word, Lewis repaid the Morgan loan in a month's time.

It was raining and snowing in Manhattan the Friday before the McCall transaction closed. Lewis, Kevin Wright, and Jean Fugett, Jr. had just come from Equico and they were standing at an intersection waiting for the light to change as a slate-colored sky drenched them with chilling precipitation. All three men were weary from working round-the-clock on the McCall closing. Looking at Wright and seeing that he was clearly fatigued, Lewis said, "You don't have to come in tomorrow, take Saturday off. Just come ready to deal on Monday."

Wright walked off toward a midtown destination where other closing matters awaited. Before he left, he gave Lewis a contact phone number. As Fugett waited, Lewis used a pay phone to call Clarkson back at Lewis & Clarkson.

"Wright is standing by if you need him," he told Clarkson. "Call him if you need something taken care of." Not long afterward, Clarkson summoned Wright to the law offices, but there was no work to do when Wright got there. When Lewis called again to check up on things, he was furious to learn that Wright was sitting by idly when there was plenty of work to do on the McCall deal.

"Why the hell did you call him up there if you don't have anything for him to do?" Lewis barked into the phone. "Why do you have him there when he could be doing something else?"

In the meantime, McCall's chief financial officer had come up with a balance sheet showing the company had less than $1,855,000 in cash on its books. According to the agreement between Lewis and Playtex, TLC Pattern Inc. was owed $627,000, the amount of the deficit. Esmark balked at paying the amount and the matter was sent to arbitration. Lewis won in arbitration a year later and as part of the settlement was allowed to repurchase the TLC Pattern, Inc. stock—7.5 percent—that Smilow had demanded. As a result, all of the common stock in TLC Pattern was controlled by Lewis.

On January 29, 1984, the date of the McCall closing, everyone wondered about the $1 million Lewis was supposed to bring to the party. It should have been taken as an article of faith that he would show up with it, but not everyone was so sure.

"Until the day we got to the closing, everybody thought that some white guy was the money man and he was going to appear at the last minute," Kevin Wright says.

Lewis arrived early at the offices of Kaye, Scholer, Fierman, Hays & Handler, a Manhattan law firm where the closing was to take place. After visiting the suite of offices reserved for the McCall closing, Lewis and Wright went downstairs to take care of some other matter.

Meanwhile, businessmen associated with the closing were starting to trickle into the closing offices upstairs. Where was Reginald Lewis? Surely he wasn't going to be late for the closing? Was he out somewhere making a desperate, last-ditch effort to round up the $1 million, or was he really just a front man all along?

When the check for $1 million arrived, it wasn't with a white businessman making a dramatic last-minute entrance, but in the hands of Reginald Lewis. He hadn't lied when he claimed to be representing investors trying to buy McCall; Lewis just hadn't bothered to say that he would be the principal owner. It is worth noting that he'd gotten a major deal done only after diverting attention away from himself—and his race.

As Lewis took his place at a conference table in one of Kaye, Scholer's offices, he got another vote of confidence from Peter Offerman, who'd made the $19 million in Bankers Trust money possible. "I already put $20 million in your bank account," Offerman coolly volunteered.

As the final touches to Lewis's deal were administered, one part of Kaye, Scholer was devoted to real estate closings for mortgages on McCall land and property. Banking people were in another room. In the conference room that served as the nerve center was Reginald F. Lewis, standing serene and dignified near a conference table. Comporting himself in the manner of a powerful captain of industry would be no problem—Lewis had always carried himself that way. He was flanked by a coterie of advisers seated at the table, including Tom Lamia, who periodically passed along documents that required Lewis's signature.

Like falling dominoes, the conditions for closing McCall were being satisfied one by one. Several hours had elapsed by the time the last document had been signed. The only thing left to do was wire the money to the bank. Afterward, Lewis and the scores of people working for him waited for the ceremonial confirmation of the wire transfer, which would signify that the deal was closed. When confirmation came, Lamia turned to Lewis and said, "We're now closed."

Reginald F. Lewis was now the chairman of the board of the McCall Pattern Company. He had managed to acquire the company for $22.5 million without putting up a cent of his own money.

Lewis approached Lamia and did something he had never done before: He hugged Lamia, an act out of character for Lewis who hated being touched by nonfamily members. Lewis then handed Lamia his fee, a check for $75,000.

Although there was no doubt McCall belonged to Lewis, he still wanted to see something indicating it was his. He turned to a beaming Kevin Wright and said, "Okay, Kevin, where's my stock certificate in TLC Pattern, Inc.?"

A look of dismay flashed across Wright's face. "Oh, shit!" he thought. In fact, Wright realized that no one had prepared Lewis's stock certificate, which would have been a big issue only if Lewis had been hit by a bus after leaving the closing. Still, Lewis wanted to see and hold that piece of paper, tangible evidence that he was attaining his true station in life. Wright scurried from the room and hastily had a stock certificate with Lewis's name on it prepared.

After all the I's are dotted and T's crossed in a corporate buyout, it's a tradition for the investment banking firm involved to throw a party in honor of the new purchaser. Bear, Stearns never held such a celebration for Reginald Lewis, to the consternation of Phyllis Schless. Chagrined, Schless and her husband took Lewis and his wife to dinner at The Four Seasons in Manhattan.

But all this was far from Lewis's mind as he fielded congratulations. After taking a few moments to bask in the glow of his accomplishment, Lewis took Wright, Tom Lamia, and Charles Clarkson to the Harvard Club for lunch. Champagne flowed like water. After 11 years of trying to conclude a major transaction, and after nine roller coaster months of hell, he had finally pulled it off.

9

Piloting McCall for a 90-to-One Gain

Established in 1870, McCall Pattern is one of the nation's oldest home sewing pattern companies. Its executive offices are located in Manhattan, New York City, while its production facilities are in Manhattan, Kansas. In 1984, the company had 580 employees.

At the time of Lewis's acquisition, McCall was making approximately 740 patterns for home sewing. Many of the patterns were based on drawings by such well-known designers as Willi Smith, Liz Claiborne, and Laura Ashley. Eighty-seven percent of its revenue came from the United States, with the rest coming in from Puerto Rico, the United Kingdom, Japan, Mexico, Canada, Australia, and other countries.

McCall was then the second-largest company in the home sewing pattern business with 29.7 percent of the market. Its major competitors were Simplicity Patterns with 39.4 percent of the market, Butterick with 19.1 percent of the market and Vogue with 4.7 percent of the market.

The company had revenues of $51.9 million with income of about $6 million.

This was the company that Reginald Lewis took over and by the time he sold McCall three years later in June 1987, Lewis had piloted the company to the two most profitable years in its history. Under him, McCall's income doubled in 1985 and 1986, years the company earned $12 and $14 million, respectively. And Lewis made himself a very wealthy man in the process. But within two years after he sold the company, he would be the subject of a major lawsuit. All this was still to come, as Lewis assumed the chairman's office at McCall's 230 Park Avenue headquarters in February 1984.

INTENSE MANAGEMENT STYLE

As intense and focused as Lewis was prior to buying McCall, he kicked up his intensity level a couple of notches and became even more driven. He acted as if every decision carried life and death ramifications.

Lewis ran McCall with a firm, yet innovative, hand. His style was an amalgam of Wall Street financial savvy, Harvard legal acumen and brassknuckle street toughness from East Baltimore.

"When he realized how people reacted when he turned up the heat a little bit, he used it," Kevin Wright says. "It was fun for me to watch this African-American intimidate these very senior, established Caucasian businessmen. His entire demeanor just changed and sometimes he was acting and sometimes he wasn't. He could generate incredible passion, angry passion. He would just tell you in no uncertain terms that your way was fucked up, that this was the way it was going to be done, he'd tell you why it had to be done this way and that's it. He'd give you a speech, an angry, passionate speech that could go a minute, two minutes, however long he felt he had to talk to get his point across."

"Reg was a powerful person even before he became rich," Tom Lamia remembers. "He could be bullying at times, he could be charming at times, and he could be bullying and charming in the same conversation. Reg could intimidate people rather easily. There were many people who wouldn't have dared to breathe a word of criticism around him. He had a dark side, a brooding side."

Ultimately though, Lewis was toughest on himself. Whatever his successes, he would invariably ask himself, "Why didn't I accomplish more?"

At home in his study, Lewis would indulge in a lifelong habit of rating his performance as well as those of his executives. Like a hard-to-please schoolmarm, Lewis would dole out A pluses, A's, B minuses, C pluses, and so on.

Nor was his personal life exempt from constant assessing and quantifying. He loved to talk about his tennis game and where it was at a given point in time, but Lewis couldn't resist the impulse to dispassionately analyze the components of his play, be it his net game, serve or return of service. He'd grade himself on his oft-used A to F scale.

Lewis would even rate novels or magazine pieces he was reading. His mind was constantly gauging, seeking ways to fine tune and perfect. It didn't matter that perfection was usually unattainable—the quest for perfection was its own reward.

Lewis was also constantly writing notes to himself, calculating the bottom line, scribbling out agendas and tasks to be accomplished during the day, a habit that first surfaced at Virginia State. Whenever Lewis would meet with Wright or Clarkson or members of McCall's management team, he would always take copious notes.

Lewis actually spent little time at McCall's plush executive offices on the entire 10th floor of 230 Park Avenue in Manhattan. He had a two-office suite created for him there, but his favorite lair was his law firm at 99 Wall Street. He would go to McCall's offices periodically to make his presence felt, however, and to put the executives on notice that the new owner was watching.

Lewis still tried his hand at practicing law from time to time, but those occasions had grown infrequent enough to become noteworthy.

"Every so often during the McCall days, Reg would expressly remind us that he was the client. I mean, he'd say it in those many words," remembers Laurie Nelson, one of Lewis & Clarkson's lawyers. "He'd say, 'Laurie, right now I am the senior partner of this law firm and I am your client. And when I ask you certain questions, you're going to report to me as the client first. When I am done listening as the client, I'll put on my senior partner hat. And then we can analyze the work.'

"Sometimes the demands he would make on people would seem unreasonable. The thing was, the demand was 300 percent of the expected result. So if you took the demand at face value, you'd go nuts. You needed to take the demand to mean, 'I want the best you can give me, only I want it twice as fast as you're capable of doing it,'" Nelson says.

Lewis's demanding attitude may have made him a difficult boss but it also enabled him to raise the level of everyone's game.

"One of his strongest traits or characteristics was his leadership ability," says Everett L. Grant, III, whom Lewis hired in 1985 from the Price Waterhouse accounting firm to be a TLC Group vice president. Lewis had the ability to make people "achieve more than they ever thought they could," Grant says.

Under Lewis's stewardship, McCall undertook a number of innovations that increased its profitability.

IMPROVING CASH FLOW

Under Norton Simon, McCall had focused on operating profits and market share. Because of the shrinking market for home sewing patterns, its former owners believed that operating profits and market share were critical to the company's survival.

However, under the Lewis regime, a new yardstick for measuring operations emerged: cash flow. Because of the highly leveraged nature of the acquisition, McCall had a sizable amount of debt to retire and thus Lewis devoted most of the company's efforts to conserving and generating cash. That meant many things would be done differently than in the past. For example, whereas bills had always been paid when they came in the door under Norton Simon, Lewis decreed that they would be paid within 30 days, freeing up accounts payable money for an additional month.

Under Lewis, McCall's assets were always operated with an eye toward generating additional cash. He came up with the idea of using idle presses not grinding out sewing patterns to make greeting cards. As a result, greeting cards became an important profit center for the company and eventually McCall began to export these cards to overseas markets.

Lewis also shelved McCall's pension plan and instituted a 401k program, freeing up an additional $648,000 in cash that was used to pay down debt.

Not all of Lewis's McCall innovations were financial in nature. He set out to change the home sewing pattern industry's less-than-glamorous image by having the company sign up celebrity licenses with, among others, Diahann Carroll, Shari Belafonte-Harper, and

Brooke Shields. All three appeared in publicity photos wearing McCall designs.

THE PRICE ISN'T RIGHT!

One day Lewis was in his office at 99 Wall Street when Earle Angstadt called up and asked to see Lewis right away. Lewis rushed to Angstadt's office to see what earth-shattering crisis was afoot. An executive with McCall for 14 years and 17 years Lewis's senior, Angstadt tossed two huge bound catalogues on his desk, where they landed with a resounding thud. The catalogues had "Patterns at 89 Cents" stamped on their covers and were from Butterick, one of McCall's main competitors.

"They're running a sale," Angstadt said plaintively. "The last time this happened, we lost a fortune. We've got to meet their price." The logic behind Angstadt's argument hadn't quite registered with Lewis.

"Why?" Lewis asked. "Why do we have to meet their price?" Lewis and Angstadt argued heatedly over pricing, with Lewis adamantly opposed to meeting Butterick's price and Angstadt all for it. Exasperated, Lewis decided to defer to Angstadt's years of experience in the pattern business.

"Okay," he said. "I tried to talk you out of it and I don't think it makes sense. But if you think this is the way to go, this is the first time I've been confronted with the issue. We'll go with your judgment."

The move to match Butterick's prices was a disaster. McCall lost $2 million during the course of the promotion. Lewis was livid. He gave McCall's executives hell and vowed never to compete on price again.

The next time the pattern industry became involved in a price war, Lewis stuck to his guns. "No, we will not go on sale with those discounts," he said without hesitation. "I want to show these people that we're not here to basically cannibalize the industry. I'm not going to meet their sales price—we might lose a little money or not make as much, but I'm not going to lose money every time I sell a pattern. The price of a pattern is such a small price, let's raise prices some more."

Instead of lowering its prices to meet the competition, McCall followed Lewis's suggestion and raised its prices. The move led to a double-digit increase in net sales and a small drop in market share. Lewis was more than willing to accept the tradeoff.

But then, I think the magic started to happen when I sold the organization on some key principles: The name of the game was to hold market share, not increase it at any expense. It was equally important to hold an increased price and moderate the level of increases, and to hold the line on expenses. The earnings started to pop.

Lewis's decision not to compete on the basis of price and to forsake market share for profit were key moves in increasing McCall's profitability. And the impetus came not from the company's seasoned executives but from his own instincts. It was a lesson he would always remember.

FIGHTING THE COMPETITION

When his competitors weren't sniping away from a pricing standpoint, they were trying to spirit away McCall personnel. In a period of five weeks, Simplicity lured away the McCall vice president in charge of design, the executive to whom the design chief reported, and then the VP in charge of promotions. Lewis didn't take kindly to the defections.

"He had a fit," Earle Angstadt says. "We said, 'Settle down, they'll be replaced by better people,' and they were within a period of about two and a half weeks."

It was a good overall organization. And I had high hopes. We had a crisis early on when we suffered some losses as a result of a price action. It was very clear to me that this was not something that we should do, that is, reduce our prices. But things chugged along. We had four or five vice presidents walk out. Bob Hermann, I remember, went out and found replacements. He called me and said, "Reg, you know we're going to have to pay a little bit more to get these people, but I think this is what we should do." And I just said one word, "Go! Pay what you have to, shore up this organization. Make sure it's tight." What's interesting is, they always appreciated that from me. That was one of the few times I dealt directly with

Bob rather than Earle, but to Earle's credit, he said, "This is so important, deal with Reg directly on this."

The chairman of McCall looked on with satisfaction as Bob Hermann filled two of the vacancies by stealing talented executives from Simplicity. Lewis briefly examined something that would bring the raiding to a close once and for all—he seriously considered acquiring Simplicity, the No. 1 company in the home sewing pattern industry. However, Lewis was advised that the Justice Department's antitrust experts would have a field day with any merger between the No. 1 and No. 2 businesses in a four-company industry, so talks with Simplicity were never initiated.

However, merger discussions did take place with Butterick and Vogue, which were both owned by American Can. With the market for home-sewing patterns steadily contracting, it made sense to try and eliminate some of the players from the field. However, Butterick and Vogue got cold feet and the talks never went anywhere.

FOCUSING ON SHAREHOLDER RETURN

Lewis had an uneasy relationship with many of his managers. One particular thorn in his side was Bob Hermann, McCall's number two manager. A six-year veteran of McCall's sewing pattern wars, Hermann crossed swords with Lewis regularly. They would go after each other during management committee meetings, arguing over such matters as product pricing and how aggressively McCall should go after customers. Hermann took the classic point of view that pricing promotions were a legitimate tool to increase market share while Lewis would argue that market share shouldn't supersede cash flow concerns.

"Plus, Bob, you really don't understand the economics of what's going on here, so this is the way it should be done," Lewis would tell him.

Lewis was "always there, trying to tell these managers what they needed to do to get this business running right," Charles Clarkson says. A veteran of McCall with a retailing background and today the company's president, Hermann didn't cotton to some upstart lawyer-financier telling him how the pattern business should be run, even if Lewis did own the corporation.

Lewis and Hermann would later face off in the lawsuit involving McCall. Ten years after Lewis's 1984 purchase of McCall, Hermann's only remark about Lewis for the record is "No comment."

Lewis viewed Hermann, Angstadt, and all of McCall's executives as critical to his plans, but there was always a certain tension in the relationship. Lewis and his managers essentially had different mindsets, with the managers focusing on running the company while Lewis was looking at the big picture and at maximizing shareholder return.

"He saw them as somebody you sort of had to have in order to get the thing operating. I mean, they were operating people and you had to have them, because he couldn't operate the company himself. But there was always a tension between him and the operating people," Clarkson says.

However, Lewis always respected Earle Angstadt, McCall's CEO. Later, when he was running Beatrice International, Lewis actually explored the idea of Angstadt's coming out of retirement to run the company. "I would be much further along if I had an Earle Angstadt," Lewis would say time and again.

He paid his operating executives generously, using money as an incentive to spur on his team. He would rigorously review the financial plan for the coming year, then peg bonuses to that plan.

"At the beginning of every year, management said, 'The plan's too aggressive, we're not going to be able to meet it, etc., etc.'" Everett Grant remembers. "Then, they'd meet it and they'd far exceed it." Under Lewis, McCall's executives earned maximum bonuses, something they hadn't received for a number of years before he bought McCall.

While Lewis was generally always on guard when interacting with the operating people, he would sometimes allow himself to relax a little. "He was fun to be with when business was set aside," Earle Angstadt says. "He and I spent a lot of hours on airplanes together. We enjoyed each other's company and we shared many confidences at 40,000 feet. I found him a very companionable, very pleasant individual. Reg and I didn't tell jokes to each other, but we had a good time."

There is no question that Lewis worked hard, but he also expected to be paid top dollar for his efforts. Lewis received various management and sponsor's fees as his salary for running McCall, a common practice followed by financiers in the 1980s.

"Reg played close to the line, no question about it," Tom Lamia says. "But he wouldn't do it recklessly. He'd get the best advice he could. Somebody unsophisticated might say, 'My god, you can't make money that easily unless you're stealing it, right?' Well, it all depends on how clever the plan is."

"Is it easy money if it takes an ingenious tax-planning stratagem to pull it off? Or a very high risk financial or tax strategy to pull it off? Some people would say that's easy money," Lamia adds.

"McCall was a means to an end for Reg," says Earle Angstadt, president and CEO of McCall under Lewis. "He didn't give a damn about the pattern business. He wanted to use it for one purpose and one purpose only, which was to make a lot of money quickly. He always couched it in terms of shareholder interest—well, about 86 percent of the shareholder interest was in his pocket. It became obvious fairly quickly. I'm not saying that's wrong as long as it didn't destroy people and didn't destroy the fabric of the company."

It should be noted that Angstadt himself, together with Bob Hermann, were among the shareholders enriched by Lewis. After the sale of the company in 1987, Angstadt retired from McCall a rich man.

PAYING DOWN DEBT

Lewis wanted a more permanent capital structure for McCall and had talked to a number of investment bankers about how to achieve that objective. Doing so would allow McCall to pay down some of its debt.

Lewis was told that to access public debt and public equity markets, McCall would have to have more than $5 million in equity on its balance sheet. So, Lewis began to explore various ways to raise equity above $5 million.

Selling the Manhattan, Kansas, facility to a third party, then leasing it would put millions on McCall's balance sheet. The problem was that a sale would lead to a significant capital gains tax, plus McCall would be subject to the whims of another entity. Lewis conceived of the idea of a sale-leaseback with himself as the other party. Why not sell the McCall plant to Reginald Lewis, then lease it back to the company? That's exactly what Lewis did on June 18, 1985.

The McCall plant was sold to newly created McCall Pattern Holdings for $2,426,000, the book value of the facility at the time of the transaction, which was slightly less than the orderly liquidation value. Lewis then had McCall lease the plant back from McCall Pattern Holdings under a 10-year lease, and had McCall issue $3 million in preferred stock to McCall Pattern Holdings, in return for the assumption by McCall Pattern Holdings of $5 million worth of debt that had belonged to McCall.

Finally, Lewis had McCall Pattern Holdings borrow an additional $1 million from Bankers Trust and pay $426,000 in cash to McCall. The result of all this financial engineering was that McCall's balance sheet was improved by $5.5 million. In addition, Lewis came away with a decade-long lease that paid him $1,152,000 a year along with an obligaton to repay a loan of $6 million to Bankers Trust. The sale-leaseback arrangement benefited both McCall and Lewis, but it would eventually come back to haunt him, playing an important part in a lawsuit against Lewis by the subsequent owners of McCall.

In 1985, however, Lewis could only see positives flowing from the sale-leaseback arrangement. "The main benefit to Reg accrued to him through his then about 82 percent ownership of McCall," Grant says. "Ultimately he did get to realize a significant appreciation on equity. The sale-leaseback strengthened McCall's balance sheet by removing $5.5 million of debt and increasing the amount of equity on its books through the preferred stock. It left the company stronger economically and this in turn enabled it to do the debt offering."

THE BOND DEAL

Lewis was only getting warmed up. Next on his agenda was a public bond offering for McCall. That would enable McCall to pay off the debt it owed Bankers Trust and then have enough left over to fund future acquisitions.

Lewis had another objective in mind, too: He wanted public markets to become familiar with the TLC name and with paper issued by TLC. To build the business empire that Lewis aspired to, having the ability to raise capital in the public markets was critical, because they're the most efficient way to raise capital.

The more he thought about it, the more enthusiastic Lewis became about a McCall bond offering. His first choice for an investment bank for the offering was Drexel, Burnham, Lambert.

Drexel said it could pull off an offering with no problem, but wasn't enthusiastic about raising more money than necessary to pay off McCall's Bankers Trust debt.

Drexel's marketing representative Jean Wong had stayed in touch with Lewis after the McCall acquisition. Wong pressed Lewis to attend Drexel's yearly bond conference in Beverly Hills, an event still relatively new and unhearlded. A couple of years later, the conference would become famous as the "Predators Ball" and an invitation to it would become as prized as a ticket to the Oscars. At this time though, Lewis was skeptical about its merits.

Jean Wong had nagged me to death to come out to L.A. to the Drexel Bond Conference, and of course at that time I did not realize that this was not the typical business conference. So Jean finally said, "Reg, Mike Milken asked me personally to please extend an invitation for you to come because we want this to be the premier conference between institutional investors and dealmakers like yourself. We regard you as one of the outstanding dealmakers in America today."

I guess this was enough for my ego, so I said, "Well, you never know. Why not?" And indeed, I like L.A. very much. I've been going there probably four times a year for the last 10 years, so I went out. I never regretted it. I remember vividly the first meeting with Milken. I had been meeting with Jean Wong, Bob Davidow, Bruce Brown, and a group of Drexel research people as I described the McCall transaction.

I noted earlier how I offered the deal to Drexel but Ackerman was really a little bit of an amateur because he didn't realize how experienced a deal person I was and gave me the ABCs of deal-making when I was already way past that. So as a result he didn't get the deal, and in fact he told people the deal would never get done. And of course it got done. Without Drexel. And more important, without Peter having any piece of it, which I'm sure killed him.

In any case, I'm sitting in this conference room and I'm going pretty good and all of a sudden, Milken walked in, moved to the head of the table and started listening. He's not an imposing person to look at. And what's funny is, until you get used to it, he has kind of a funny voice. Just a little squeaky and without a lot of resonance. But he is a great speaker and an unbelievable salesman. And I think not having a "Jesse Jackson-type" voice makes it better for him because he's always talking substance, so you end up listening to the substance. And he has a wonderful ability to take financial facts and weave them into a social scenario. He's probably one of the most effective speakers I've ever heard.

One funny thing was, I didn't realize that he had a toupee until somebody told me. First of all, I don't really get off on people's physical attributes. I take a lot of teasing because of my deep-set eyes. People always note that, or the space in my teeth or whatever. So I guess over the years I've always tried to look past people's physical characteristics.

I think the power of Michael's intellect surpasses any particular physical attribute. The way he was able to grasp very quickly what I was trying to do, and to give the impression that he understood precisely what I meant when I said that I'm driven by return on equity, and that I like cash flow characteristics and solid management.

Mike asked, "Why didn't you buy Simplicity?" I said, "I'm not interested in buying Simplicity at this point. Not until I've de-leveraged the company." Buying Simplicity would just buy a higher rate of decline. So the first thing you had to do was de-leverage.

Michael was actually right, except the timing was not good. My philosophy is, first, if you're using a lot of leverage, bring the capitalization into more normalized means before you start talking about another serious strategic play. In other words, digest a little bit of what you have and confirm your own judgment about the earning power of the assets before you start going off strategically. In any case, I remember I was in such a positive frame of mind that day, when in the middle of my talk, Milken got up and quietly walked out. And I just said to myself, "Well, Reg, I guess you've got some work to do."

Of course there are a million reasons as to why he could have walked out. But that was my first meeting with the great man. This would have been about the spring of 1984.

We wanted Drexel to do a high-yield bond deal that could be used to take out the Bankers Trust Company debt. That would also enable us to buy back the warrants that we gave to Bankers Trust, bringing in some of the equity again and maybe giving us a little bit of excess cash towards some other possibilities. One of the things that was always interesting to me, though, was that people thought the Drexel team was a little reckless, but I was always very impressed with their research. And their due diligence efforts were as good as any other firm that we had dealt with that was very careful in terms of analyzing companies. The point is, they weren't just wild men willing to do anything. The quality of their research was very good. Bruce Brown and Bob Davidow particularly were always calling on the phone, trying to find out what was going on. I think the way it worked is they would then feed their information back to Milken.

When I think about Milken, I have a vivid impression that he was very insightful. And he has an ability to be really interested in your business and what your company is all about. Something I felt we had in common was a desire to get behind the numbers. There are a lot of people who are very good at understanding the numbers and even extricating financial information from them, but to get behind the dynamic of what is producing the numbers is interesting. In fact, I almost think you're better off not being a finance person when it comes to doing that. I was glad I never went to business school, because it's one thing to be able to do a good quantitative analysis, which is important, but it's better to have a burning desire to get behind the numbers—what is driving this a particular way? And that's part financial but it's also understanding a culture of people. Ultimately, you will really generate significantly greater returns if you understand that.

I also appreciate bean counters and the way they understand a business. You need bean counters—I'm a very good bean counter myself. And I certainly have a lot of respect for them. Michael brought a lot of that to bear, along with enormous powers of concentration. So that if you had a half hour meeting with him, for that half hour he was totally and completely focused on your business.

His delivery style was also very good—he had a very good bedside manner. The best way to describe it is that during a lot of meetings with other firms on Wall Street, I could almost feel a banker's hands sliding toward my pocket. It's like, "Well, yes, that might be nice for the company," but he's primarily concerned about his commission even as I am speaking to him. But I never got that impression with Michael. That's something else I believe: Do the job and the fee takes care of itself. The two go hand in hand. I am sure some of my good friends on Wall Street will be a little resentful of me saying this—but I think it's fair. The culture tends to be, "How can we get the biggest fee for the least amount of work?" with the exception of people like B. J. Chubet, who is a dear friend, and Alan Schwartz, and John Sheehy, who spent a lot of time on the deals we worked on. And Michael did not give that impression. But Ackerman did give that impression—I found him a difficult person to do business with.

The next meeting I had with Michael, I took the initiative and called him up. I got Jean Wong and said, "Why don't I come out and give you a little briefing on our company?" This would have been about the spring of 1985. I flew out the evening before and got in around 11:30, 12 o'clock. The morning of the meeting I was with John Brennan, who was the chief financial officer of McCall at the time. Michael raced into the room, was running a few minutes late, and clearly didn't like the fact that he was late. He came in, sat down and started going over the deal. I vividly remember him standing up and saying, "Reg, why haven't you done it? You want to do a debt deal? What's so big about that? That's doable. Why haven't you done these things?"

I loved it. Here finally was a man as impatient as I was, and it was my company! Impatient about seeing progress in a business that was mine. After that meeting, I was sky high. The irony, of course, is that we did do the sale-leaseback without Drexel. And we did the bond deal without Drexel.

In any case, we got the bond deal off. Now, understanding that I'd done it with Bear, I still put Bruce Brown and his guys on the mailing list and sent them all of our public data so they could follow the story. I knew sooner or later I had to do business with Drexel if we were going to be in the marketplace. They were far and away the most dominant player and they were the only guys that I thought would spring for big bucks for the company. By the way, at that point my hot button was $100 million.

I remember sitting with Michael and saying, "Now Michael, this is another lead. Suppose we deliver great results from McCall and I came to you and I say, 'Mike, here is the situation. I need $100 million. What kind of reception do you think that will get?'" He said, "Reg, do the job and there's a lot more than a hundred there for you." This is a true story; he actually said, "There's a lot more than a hundred." And I believed him.

It didn't make much sense to Lewis to raise exactly enough money to pay off Bankers Trust, effectively replacing that debt with an identical one. He wanted an additional $10 million or so that could be used to grow his organization. So Drexel was scratched from the list. Ultimately, Lewis went with the firm that had helped him acquire McCall in the first place, and assigned the bond offering to Bear, Stearns & Co.

Lewis had Charles Clarkson and Kevin Wright handle the myriad issues and tasks associated with a public bond offering. Laurie Nelson and law intern Orlan Johnson were also put to work.

A lengthy prospectus detailing McCall's business operations and financial picture had to be assembled and filed with the Securities and Exchange Commission. From there, SEC approval would be necessary before Bear, Stearns' marketing force could use the prospectus to sell McCall bonds to institutions.

As the printing of the bond prospectus got under way, Wright, Nelson, and Johnson stayed at the printers shop from 8 P.M. until 7 A.M., proofreading the document. They were joined by representatives from Bear, Stearns and teams of paralegals, accountants, and professional proofreaders.

The drudgery of having to wait for a prospectus to be printed was offset by the fact that printers tend to pamper those associated with such printings. Grinding out thousands of copies of a multipage prospectus is a lucrative piece of business for printing companies. So an exquisitely prepared Italian buffet dinner was available, and Wright and Nelson finally started digging into it around 11 P.M. As they savored their meal, the last person they wanted to see come striding through the door was Reginald Lewis, so naturally that's who materialized.

He looked disapprovingly at his famished junior lawyers ravenously feeding their faces and demanded, "What are you guys doing?" Told that Wright and Nelson were eating dinner, an irritated Lewis posed another question, "You do realize that page 42 just came out at the print shop?" The chastened lawyers put down their plates and flitted off in the direction of the print shop.

Once Lewis had gone home for the night, a proofreading check turned up a major error in one of McCall's financial calculations. It was three o'clock in the morning—who would take on the responsibility of calling Lewis at home, waking him up, and telling him about the error? Since Johnson was only a summer intern, Wright and Nelson nominated him to make the telephone call to Lewis. Johnson slowly dialed the number, expecting to have his head handed to him when Lewis answered. Awakened from a deep sleep, Lewis was grateful to be made aware of the problem. He was instantly coherent and managed to craft a quick solution to the crisis.

The prospectus was eventually approved by the SEC, and Bear, Stearns sold $22 million worth of debentures, which are bonds not secured by specific collateral.

Lewis had walnut memo paper boxes made up for employees who played a key role in the bond offering. Each box had a copy of the cover of the prospectus on it and a brass plate inscribed with "From the $22 million, 7.8 percent subordinated debenture offering of The McCall Pattern Company."

Proceeds from the bond sale wiped out the debt from the Bankers Trust loan and put an additional $10 million on McCall's balance sheet.

"REG LEWIS WAS DRIVING THE SHOW"

Before McCall, Lewis was just another attorney, albeit one making a rather comfortable living. But the McCall acquisition had catapulted him into the ranks of the industrial elite. Now that Lewis was the millionaire owner of a large, profitable corporation, some of those around him began to perceive subtle, and not so subtle, changes in his personality.

"He got arrogant, I think, more so," a former Lewis & Clarkson employee says. "Reg's ego, it always seemed to me, got bigger and bigger as the years went on, as the successes mounted. Eventually, he felt there was nobody better financially than he. He felt he was the franchise. He actually used those words once—'I am the franchise.' He could do no wrong and he knew everything and no one else knew anything."

Another individual who declined to be named intimates that Lewis would frequently tell those in his inner circle, "'You don't know what you're talking about, you jackass!' He would say it in front of anybody. 'Asshole! You dumb son of a bitch!' That's why Reg was difficult to deal with. Being screamed at and insulted in front of other people was the worst."

Kevin Wright observes that after the McCall acquisition, Lewis bumped Charles Clarkson's compensation to a level that made Wright envious. He too observed a change in Lewis's demeanor after Lewis became the owner of McCall. "He knew he was at a new station in life and he expected to be treated in accordance with his station," Wright says. "And yes, there were people who had known him before, but they had to adjust or they had to go. You had to recognize that Reg Lewis was driving this show—he was going to do it his way. If you could accommodate that, fine. If not, 'Thank you very much for your contribution. I will always be your friend and if you need me, call me.'"

Tom Lamia, who remained Lewis's attorney on business matters beyond the McCall years before the two of them eventually had a falling out, found he had to make an adjustment to remain in the Lewis camp. "He could be very difficult," Lamia says of Lewis. "As he got older and more narcissistic than when I first met him, he became—frankly— sometimes hard to take."

On one occasion during the McCall days, a well-known black trial attorney came to Lewis's office at 99 Wall Street. The two of them sat in Lewis's office, shooting the breeze about being African-American males who used the legal system as a stepladder to success. Their conversation turned to the possibility of a joint business venture, then the subject of compensation came up.

"Well, you know Reg, once you're making a million a year everything else is just gravy," the swaggering trial lawyer boasted, quite taken with himself. "Well, no, I wouldn't say that," Lewis interjected. The pompous attorney was insistent. "Yeah, I know man, but once you got a million a year, come on!" Lewis, whose timing could be impeccable, paused a beat. He looked his compatriot in the eye and without a hint of a smile, uttered two ego-deflating words: "Trust me."

When it came to McCall, Lewis preserved his habit of fighting for the last nickel. At one point, the company became the target of a nuisance lawsuit seeking $20,000 in damages. Kevin Wright was acting as McCall's general counsel and he and McCall President Bob Hermann tried to fight the suit at first, then decided it wasn't worth the trouble. Settlement seemed the prudent path to take, so Wright and Hermann decided to give the plaintiffs $20,000 to disappear. Under their risk/benefit analysis, $20,000 was a minor sum to pay to stave off a potentially costly and time-consuming legal battle.

Afterward, Wright went back to 99 Wall Street to meet with Lewis. Charles Clarkson was in Lewis's office. "Kevin, anything going on with McCall," Lewis asked, glancing up briefly from some papers on his desk. "Yeah Reg, Hermann and I decided to settle this claim," Wright answered. He instantly had Lewis's undivided attention, because Lewis was loath to part with his hard-earned cash. "Okay, how much did you settle for?" Lewis asked. Wright replied the amount was $20,000. "Okay, how much was the claim?" Lewis wanted to know, starting to zero in. Storm warnings were waving inside Wright's head as he told Lewis the claim and settlement amount were identical.

"Come on, for Christ's sake!" Lewis bellowed. "Just to make them respect you, you demand SOMETHING. You don't just roll over." Lewis then launched into a full-scale dressing down of Wright when the young lawyer suddenly sprang from his chair, hurled a pencil across the office and stalked toward the door. Wright was on his way out and about to slam the door behind him, when he heard Lewis warn him in a calm voice, "Kevin, don't slam the door."

Wright closed the door gently and skulked next door to his office. The rush of anger that had emboldened him a moment earlier was quickly replaced by an acute sense of trepidation. After a few minutes that seemed like hours, Lewis knocked on the door to Wright's office and came in. "I'm thinking, 'Oh god, how do I play this now? Do I continue to stand for my rights, or do I capitulate?'" Wright remembers. He began to apologize, but Lewis cut him short.

"Kevin, for me to engender that kind of response in you, I must be doing something wrong," he said. And with that, Lewis formally apologized to Wright. The incident was quickly forgotten and the two men's special mentor-protege relationship continued forth undamaged.

If you were a buddy of Reginald Lewis's back in the days when he was poor, usually you'd made yourself a friend for life. "If he had come from a pompous point of view, that wouldn't have worked with us because that's not what keeps a friendship alive," says Ellis Goodman, who befriended Lewis when the two of them held down minimum-wage jobs in a Baltimore area country club. "He loved sharing his knowledge and having somebody around to enjoy it. I never found him in any way boastful, although he had plenty to be boastful about."

Lewis was the kind of wealthy relative anyone would love to have. He was generous with his family before he acquired McCall and became even more so afterward. He loved personally selecting gifts of clothes, jewelry, and fur coats for his wife and his mother. He lavished expensive gifts on everyone, particularly at Christmas time when he would load a car full of presents and then motor down Interstate 95 to Baltimore. Whenever he accompanied his relatives on an outing, Lewis would never allow them to pay for anything.

One time, Uncle James and the Internal Revenue Service were having a $75,000 dispute. Lewis insisted on taking care of it, an offer Uncle James gratefully declined. Another time, Lewis asked Uncle James if there was anything he could do for him. Uncle James was quiet a moment, then impishly asked Lewis to give him a million dollars, so Uncle James could enjoy the life of a millionaire, too.

"I ain't giving you shit," Lewis deadpanned. "I ain't giving you no million dollars. Earn it!"

If Lewis was magnanimous and big-hearted with his family, he didn't like them approaching him with hat in hand, jokingly or otherwise. He gave on his terms and when he felt the time was right.

HARNESSING THE PUBLIC MARKETS—THE McCALL IPO

By the fall of 1986, Lewis had grown fond of the pattern business. He felt that McCall had an infrastructure that compared quite favorably with organizations of much greater size. During the early phases of his McCall stewardship, Lewis's intention was to hold on to McCall and use it to acquire other companies. He decided that if a target business were related to McCall's operations, he would use McCall to capture it. If not, then TLC Group would acquire the target.

In the meantime, Lewis continued to search for a bigger acquisition. He was still an avid reader of prospectuses, leafing through them the way others might read a retail catalogue in search of interesting things to buy. He was constantly examining companies and brainstorming about what he could do with their proceeds after he got them. Although Lewis didn't possess an MBA, unlike many financiers, he had developed an excellent grasp of how to get the most out of a company financially. His understanding of finance was developed by examining transactions and this gave Lewis a utilitarian take on the subject.

By the summer of 1986, thanks in part to Lewis's efforts, McCall had a strong balance sheet and much improved earnings. Lewis was now ready to lead McCall into another arena. He decided to take the company public, thereby generating cash for his acquisition plans.

Lewis retained Bear, Stearns to handle the initial public offering, which aimed to put 2.2 million shares of the company on the American Stock Exchange. The estimated price range for a share of stock was $11 to $13, meaning that McCall stood to generate anywhere from $24.2 million to $28.6 million.

Two obstacles stood in the path of a successful McCall IPO. First, potential investors would probably be quite leery of a company whose line of business had been shrinking steadily over the last decade. Second, Lewis was also worried about the fact that Bear, Stearns had a backlog of deals to introduce to public equity markets that summer. Bear, Stearns would not get to the McCall offering until August when many investors would be on vacation.

Nevertheless, Lewis and his team embarked on a road show, the Wall Street equivalent of a Broadway road tour. Presentations about the company were held in different cities for the purpose of selling stock to investors. The group which included Lewis, Angstadt, and several Bear, Stearns executives headed first for Europe.

One day Lewis had just completed a meeting in Switzerland that had gone particularly well, leaving him feeling positive and upbeat. He pushed Bear to increase the price for McCall's stock from the planned $11 to $13 range to $14 a share.

Then Lewis got a phone call from New York that brought his mood crashing back to earth. Alan Schwartz of Bear, Stearns was on the phone and informed Lewis that, in part because of a negative *Wall Street*

Journal article on the IPO market, the market's bottom had fallen out. The McCall public offering was dead.

Within a few hours, Angstadt and a brooding Lewis were on a plane headed for New York. Alan Schwartz had a lot of explaining to do.

After Lewis arrived in Manhattan, a meeting was arranged with Schwartz. Joining Lewis were the top managers of McCall, Earle Angstadt, Bob Hermann, and chief financial officer Craig Woods. Exactly what was the problem with McCall's IPO, Lewis demanded to know? Schwartz began to outline the reasons why the McCall IPO would never fly, but that was the last thing Lewis wanted to hear after McCall had paid hundreds of thousands of dollars in advisory fees in order to go public.

When the window of opportunity starts to come down on the IPO market, Schwartz explained, it doesn't come down slowly. Bang! It just slams shut, and that's what happened to McCall's stock offering. A very angry Reginald Lewis listened skeptically. When Schwartz's explanation was over, Lewis started asking some pointed questions. He didn't totally buy Schwartz's view of what was happening and expressed an opinion that McCall's IPO might have gotten off the ground had Bear, Stearns not spent an inordinate amount of time working on the IPO of a clothing corporation, Leslie Fay. Lewis had a high degree of respect for Schwartz, but he was in no mood to hear Schwartz's rationalizations.

Schwartz suggested that the IPO might still be able to get off the ground if the price of McCall's stock was knocked down to $9 or $8 a share, but Lewis would have none of it. It was his price or nothing.

THE $19 MILLION RECAP

By now, Lewis was beginning to feel it was time to get out of the pattern business. He would like to have continued on as the owner of McCall, but it was becoming clear he wouldn't be able to access public equity markets. That in turn meant he wouldn't be able to use McCall as a vehicle for acquiring other companies, which in turn meant it had limited empire-building capability. So Lewis came up with a new plan to capture some return on his and his shareholders' investment in McCall before the tax laws changed at the end of 1986.

Lewis initiated negotiations with Bankers Trust that would lead to a change in McCall's financial structure through a recapitalization of the company. Under the plan, Bankers Trust would put a significant amount of money into the company, making it a 40 percent partner going forward, while Lewis and McCall's shareholders would receive a large cash payout.

The talks with Bankers Trust started toward the end of 1986. The negotiations dragged on almost up to New Year's day, with Lewis and Bankers Trust paying hefty fees to financial advisers associated with the recap.

Things appeared to be moving along smoothly until December 30, when Bankers Trust came up with a new and startling demand—in order to get the recap done Lewis would have to give Bankers Trust unfettered discretion with respect to the way McCall was to be run. Someone on the Bankers Trust team apparently felt that the fees Lewis had run up and the imminent arrival of unfriendly new tax regulations had placed Lewis in a position where he had to capitulate.

The bank had badly misread Lewis. "Okay, thanks," he told the bank's stunned executives who also had amassed considerable expenses up to that point. "I'm not interested," he said, and walked out.

This was an occasion where Lewis's penchant for always having a Plan B proved invaluable. He didn't have much time—one day, in fact—before 1987 and the new tax laws arrived. But he had a plan that might just work.

Lewis first declared a dividend of $3.6 million that was distributed to McCall's shareholders. Then he began repurchasing McCall subscription warrants—securities giving the holder an option to buy large amounts of common stock—that had been issued to Bankers Trust and Equico Capital Corp. Warrants essentially give a lender a chance to get in on the action if a firm starts to perform well, but at the same time don't expose a lender to downside risk if the company performs poorly and its stock goes down.

Bankers Trust and Equico were pleased to sell their McCall warrants to TLC Group: Each organization realized a handsome profit based on the increase in McCall's worth under Lewis and a corresponding bump in the value of the warrants.

Lewis had TLC Group, not McCall, repurchase the warrants for an aggregate price of $3.1 million. Had McCall bought the warrants back, the move would have significantly depleted the cash on McCall's balance sheet. That would have wiped out the positives accomplished in the sale-leaseback and the bond sale. Plus it would have set back the improvement in McCall's earnings Lewis had worked so hard to achieve.

Only after he had sheltered McCall's equity did he have McCall then purchase the warrants from TLC Group for $15.4 million, $12.3 million more than Equico and Bankers Trust had sold them for. The price was based on a valuation of the company of $70 to $90 million by First Boston as well as potential buyers. Lewis then divided the $15.4 million among himself, Earle Angstadt, Bob Hermann, Ricardo Olivarez, and Sam Peabody. Because Lewis owned 100 percent of TLC Group, he didn't have to share the money with his associates, who owned shares in McCall, not TLC Group. But for Lewis, it was a point of honor to share the profits of his labors with those who supported him when he was trying to buy McCall. Lewis genuinely viewed the other men as his partners, even Hermann. By now, the McCall shareholders had reaped a total of $19 million from the company—the $15.4 million from the warrant repurchase plus the $3.6 million dividend.

The chairman of McCall agreed to purchase the shares of his fellow shareholders. based on a company valuation of $55 million, with the understanding that if he sold the company for more, he would pay them the difference. In addition to rewarding those who had put their faith in him, Lewis had another objective in mind: He wanted the word to get out that if you did business with TLC, you were treated fairly and you got a superb return on your investment.

TIME TO CASH OUT

Buying back the shares from his fellow shareholders brought Lewis's stake in McCall from 81.7 percent to about 88 percent. Despite his affection for the firm, Lewis realized that the only remaining way to realize a truly significant return on his investment was to sell the pattern company.

"He clearly wanted to cash out," Kevin Wright says. "If you're a buyout group, you don't fall in love with any business. When you've made enough, you cash out and let somebody else take the risks inherent with that business. So, toward the end of 1986, Reg was verbalizing that he felt it was time to go home on this one."

Along the way, we pursued a lot of different alternatives in terms of raising the equity. We did a sale-leaseback transaction. We also paid out our bank debt in less than 18 months. We brought in some equity at a reasonable price, but also gave our investors a tremendous return in an 18-month period. We pursued an acquisition of the Butterick Company. We pursued an acquisition of the Simplicity Company. We tried to take the company public. We talked about a recapitalization with Bankers Trust. None of those things worked—well, the sale-leaseback worked, but some of the other things didn't work.

I was reading Tom Wolfe's The Right Stuff *at the time and felt almost like a jet pilot: I've tried A. I've tried B. I've tried C. Well damn, maybe I should die like a man or something. In any case, business turned up and by December of 1986, two years after the deal, we had $23 million in cash on our balance sheet. That was about $20 million up from what we had when we acquired the company. And we had increased earnings from $6.5 million of operating to roughly $13 million or $14 million. The rest of fiscal year 1987 looked pretty good, also.*

At that point, Earle Angstadt came down to my office and we had kind of an interesting meeting. He said, "Reg, I just may not be able to be with you for the next few years." He wanted to spend more time with his lovely wife, among other things. I said, "Okay, Earle, then in that case it's time to go." From there we did a $19-million recapitalization that resulted in impressive shareholder return in December of 1986.

All these factors pushed Lewis in the direction of a sale. He decided that an auction would be the best way to sell McCall and retained First Boston to handle the auction. He then got together with McCall's executives to prepare an offering document. It was completed in January 1987, and sent to about 80 prospective buyers.

Lewis was leaving McCall a revitalized company. He had strengthened its balance sheet and led it to the two most profitable years in its history.

"Reg comes in and extracts the highest profit margins they've ever had," notes Howard Mackey, a client from Lewis's attorney days. "I always wondered how he managed to do that from a law firm at 99 Wall Street. That is some testament to the way he managed things and managed people."

The auction ended in June 1987 when a British textile manufacturer, the John Crowther Group, bought McCall for $65 million, nearly three times what Lewis paid for the firm three years earlier.

I signed the contract with Trevor Barker of Crowther to sell McCall for $65 million, right on the heels of our recapitalization for $19 million. I sold to the bidder we thought was best for the Company—a publicly-held British concern—at a price of roughly $63 million, plus $2 million for our expenses.

TLC had also managed to keep the real estate, which was easily worth another $6 million to $10 million and we'd also gotten some other dividends, so all in all that was about $90 million on our original investment of $1 million, and it was all in cash. And not only that, we felt that we were leaving the Company in excellent shape because the new buyer was putting up $30 million and had some plans for what he wanted to do with it. I was feeling pretty good.

The name of the game is return on investment. After three and a half years, an investor in a "TLC deal" could surely smile with justifiable satisfaction. The closing was consummated on June 30, 1987. We signed the contract about June 15th. Rather than try to take Crowther up from $65 million, I said, "Okay, close in two weeks." I traded cash for speed and we got it done very fast.

When Lewis told one of McCall's directors, Lee Archer, about the price that had been paid for McCall, Archer actually laughed out loud. "What idiot would pay us $65 million for a company when it's in the record that we only paid $22.5 million," Archer asked incredulously. Lewis just smiled broadly.

On June 30, 1987, Lewis was seated in a conference room with Earle Angstadt and about 20 other people when the voice of a female vice president at Bankers Trust came over the speaker phone, "The funds have been irrevocably transferred." Angstadt sprang to his feet, uttered "Good night, gentlemen," and bid Lewis and McCall adieu. Lewis had made Angstadt a wealthy man.

"As far as his business acumen is concerned, if I had had his financial smarts, I would have taken over the company without him," Angstadt says. "But I didn't. I was never a student of the things he mastered."

An elated Lewis and his closest associates went to the Harvard Club where a party was held in his honor. Just the mention of the name "McCall" was enough to make the jubilant Lewis break into a wide grin, but in a couple of years his sale of the sewing-pattern manufacturer would spawn a litigious nightmare that would keep a perpetual scowl on Lewis's chiseled face.

Lewis would emerge victorious from the litigation but the experience would not leave him unscarred. He would always look back on McCall and his 90-to-1 gain as his "best work." Soon this feat would be much publicized—a development that benefited Lewis greatly in the long run.

RIDING HERD ON THE MEDIA: THE ART OF SPIN CONTROL

The financial media have the power to move markets, create fortunes, and make or break careers. Less than a year had passed since the abortive McCall IPO, and Lewis remembered well the cooling effect that a *Wall Street Journal* article had exerted not just on McCall but on the entire IPO market. Lewis read the financial press avidly and respected its influence, but he was no fan of the media, per se. Prior to acquiring Beatrice, Lewis had been content to operate in relative obscurity because he didn't need the press to accomplish his objectives, nor did he feel any burning desire to be in the spotlight. And frankly, he wondered about the motives of the Fourth Estate.

Lewis's wariness of the press became even more pronounced after the sale of McCall. Not long afterward, Lewis was in the study of his home reading newspapers very early one morning. As he was flipping through *The New York Times*, a piece about the new McCall president and CEO, Bob Hermann, caught Lewis's eye. The headline read, "McCall Pattern's Head Pleased by New Owner." The story opened by saying, "The McCall Pattern Company has been through several leadership changes that were not all good for its business. But being sold to its new owner, a British company called the John Crowther Group, 'is probably the best thing that ever happened to us,' said Robert L. Hermann."

Already Lewis's trademark furrow was working its way across his brow. Here was Hermann trying to steal his thunder, and doing so in a newspaper distributed around the globe. Lewis didn't know exactly how, but he intended to steal his thunder back.

This was the same Hermann who, in Lewis's view, wanted to take McCall down a discount-pricing path that wouldn't have generated the same spectacular financial results McCall enjoyed under Lewis's leadership.

But on another level there was something else about the *Times* article that bothered Lewis: Namely, the history of this country is replete with instances where noteworthy accomplishments by African-Americans have been glossed over, modified, or totally ignored by whites. Lewis was determined not to let Hermann do the same thing to him.

By now Lewis's rugged features had scrunched into a full-blown scowl. He folded the newspaper with irritation, strode out of his study, and awakened his wife to show her the offending article.

"Goddamn that Hermann," he exclaimed. "You see? They're rewriting history already. They're just going to overlook the fact that McCall prospered under my leadership!" This injustice would have to be rectified immediately. Lewis looked at the story again to locate the reporter's byline. Finding the offending scribe to be one Daniel F. Cuff, Lewis called directory assistance. There couldn't be more than one or two Daniel Cuffs in the phone book. Lewis got a number and punched it into his phone.

Members of the press like to perceive themselves as totally objective and free of biases, but ultimately USA *Today*, *The New York Times* and *ABC News* are all comprised of individuals harboring the same kinds of prejudices and pet peeves as anybody else. Not surprisingly, awakening a reporter at 6 A.M. is not a good way to ensure totally fair and objective coverage in the future. Any ill will that might result from calling Daniel Cuff early in the morning was the least of Reginald Lewis's concerns.

Loida Lewis got involved in her husband's spin-control project later that day. A *Wall Street Journal* reporter she knew recommended someone who might be able to assist Reginald Lewis—one Rene S. Meily.

Meily, who uses the name "Butch," was working at his desk at Burson-Marsteller, one of the country's top public relations agencies, when the phone rang in his Manhattan office. Loida Lewis was on the line, telling Meily that her husband had a public relations problem. She briefly outlined the matter with The New York Times and Daniel Cuff. Could Meily help out?

Meily got to work immediately, arranging a one-on-one interview between Lewis and Cuff, whom he knew. Lewis and Meily were to meet in the lobby of The New York Times that same day, then go upstairs to see Cuff. Meily was already in the lobby when Lewis arrived, wearing a dark, tailored business suit. After a handshake and a brief exchange of pleasantries, Lewis got right down to business. He talked about the upcoming interview and asked if Meily had any advice on how Lewis should handle himself. "Be yourself. You seem to know what's going on and how to handle yourself," Meily replied. "Stick with that."

When they met with Cuff, Lewis was at his most charming. The early morning phone call that day was most unlike Lewis, he assured Cuff. Nor had Lewis meant to unsettle Cuff or offend him in any way. Once finished smoothing Cuff's feathers, Lewis segued into a masterful capsulization of his ownership of McCall and how the deal had benefited his shareholders so handsomely. The interview with Cuff went well, although Lewis didn't think so. He said as much to Meily in no uncertain terms after they'd gotten into Lewis's chauffeur-driven car in front of the Times' entrance on West 43rd Street. "He was so nervous that he was really going at me in the car. I don't even remember over what, but I think he was upset over a couple of things," Meily says. "That was the first time I saw his temper."

A low-key, mild-mannered man with a knack for understatement, Meily notes that the episode in the car "may have set the tone for our relationship." Meily would later become the public relations person for TLC Beatrice and was the frequent target of vociferous verbal attacks from Lewis. Other TLC Beatrice executives welcomed Meily's arrival when an angry Lewis was venting his displeasure over some matter, because Meily would stoically endure the storm until the energy had been spent. "You don't take the temper stuff too seriously, you handle it well," Lewis later told Meily. "You're almost like a lightning rod sometimes for me."

However, Lewis also recognized that Meily excelled at the business of spin control. A few days after The New York Times interview, Cuff authored an article that described Lewis's stewardship of McCall in glowing terms. The piece noted that "Mr. Lewis, 44, is an intense lawyer who is likely to call an associate at 6 A.M. to deal with a problem." The headline for the story was "90-to-1 Return for Investor," which was the primary message Lewis wanted to get out. Lewis was justifiably proud after that article hit the newsstands. "He was ecstatic," Meily remembers. "He was quite sensitive to every nuance. He read and reread that article to see how it was slanted and if it was slanted. He was quite sensitive to how he was perceived."

Lewis was so delighted that he worked out a retainer arrangement with Meily's employers that made it possible for Meily to do public relations work for Lewis on a regular basis.

The 90-to-1 piece, which also included a picture of Lewis, represented the first time he used the media to do his bidding. There were several occasions when he and his team took copies of the article with them as they met with executives and financiers who could help them purchase and operate Beatrice. While Lewis remained wary of the media, he saw they could be a useful tool if manipulated properly.

About a week after the *Times* piece, Lewis received a congratulatory letter at 99 Wall Street from one of his high school classmates, William Smith. An Army dentist stationed in New Jersey, Smith wrote in part, "Accomplishments such as yours serve to fuel the aspirations and dreams of your people. Now that the mantle of leadership has once again been thrust upon you, it should be comforting to know that others are elated to have you wear it. Keep on achieving, my Brother."

Lewis, who was busy plotting his strategy for acquiring Beatrice at the time, took time to respond:

July 27, 1987

Colonel William Smith, Jr.
Headquarters US Army Dental Activity
Mills Dental Clinic
Fort Dix, New Jersey 08640

Dear Smitty:

Thank you very much for your letter. I appreciate very much your comments about the McCall deal. It has been a wonderful transaction for a lot of people, and I would like to share it with the world; however,

I continue to believe quite strongly that maintaining a low profile is the best strategy for achieving good results. I say this for a couple of reasons.

First, a critical element, I believe, of success in the investment area is to have a focused point of view—an anchor of beliefs and concepts which, while flexible, is unshakable. Rarely can these concepts and beliefs be communicated accurately through the media. When one reads these articles in the newspapers, they rarely convey the true message, and this tends to both distract from the primary mission and miscommunicate that mission to one's team. Second, we still live in a world where envy and jealousy are the normal state of affairs.

At the same time, some publicity is inevitable and is worthwhile to the extent it encourages friends like you to convey heartfelt and warm feelings.

Warm personal regards.

Sincerely,

Reginald F. Lewis

Lewis talked frequently to Carolyn Powell—a classmate from Virginia State and also a close friend who happened to live and work in New York—about the media. "Reg did not like to deal with the media, because Reg wanted to be considered a businessman and he didn't want a lot of fanfare," she says. "We used to say that if you're doing it, you don't have to talk about it. The limelight was not important to him—he wanted to do well. It's like, 'I can do this, a black man can do this, and I don't have to be like some of the black folks that have to shout about it to the rooftops. Let's just do business.'"

Consequently, TLC Beatrice wasn't exactly media friendly under Lewis. Requests for information were cordially received, but seldom granted expeditiously, if at all. And interviews with the chairman were exceedingly rare. Lewis granted just a few requests, usually after numerous inquiries. Which is not to say that Lewis didn't enjoy acclaim and kudos, because he did. Lewis just never blew his own horn in the press, with the exception of "90-to-1." And that might never have taken place had Lewis not first seen a story that he felt belittled his achievements.

10

The Biggest Deal of All: The Billion-Dollar LBO of Beatrice

In June 1987, Reginald Lewis had just successfully completed the biggest deal of his life and he was looking forward to some well-deserved rest. Yet even as he was rushing pell-mell toward the finish line on the sale of the McCall Pattern Company, he would come upon another company and another deal, one that would make McCall look tiny by comparison.

Two weeks before the McCall deal closed, John Sheehy of Bear, Stearns called and asked to have lunch. We met at the Harvard Club and we laughed about how astute our equity buyers were to pass up McCall at a third of what I was now selling it for. It was a good lunch, pretty laid back by our standards. There were a lot of laughs about all the capital market screwings and the countless, and I mean countless, scenarios I had considered in an effort to get value out of the McCall assets and cash flow.

John then mentioned that Kohlberg, Kravis and Roberts was selling Beatrice International through an auction conducted by Morgan Stanley and Salomon Bros. Was I interested? At that point, not really. I felt very tired.

The last six months had been a real killer and I felt very guilty about neglecting my family. John, knowing my hot buttons pretty well by now, said something like, "Reg, this thing has business and assets all over the place. You've told us of your strong desire to go international and your desire to be diverse, well, this might be it." I said, okay, I'll have a look: Do you have the selling brochure? John said, "It'll be at your office this afternoon." I told him to send it to the house instead, since I was going back downtown.

John told me an outfit in Canada, Onex, was interested in Beatrice's Canadian property. His company was interested in Australia and Asia and he thought he might put together a group to buy those pieces, along with an Australian named Solomon Lew, a real estate player and entrepreneur in Sydney.

We broke up and I went window shopping, which was depressing because I didn't see a single thing with the right combination of beauty, elegance, and value to turn me on. I got home around seven, early for me, had dinner, watched some TV and spent a little time with the kids. John's package had arrived, but I did not open it. I went to bed around midnight.

I awakened about 4 A.M. and went into my upstairs study. I opened the writeup on Beatrice International and read the whole thing quite fast. My initial reaction was, "Forget this, life is too short!" But I remembered how quickly I had dismissed some other potential winners and decided to be more neutral for the moment.

I asked myself, "What's interesting about this company and what isn't? How would I manage it? Who's the competition? What price will this thing fetch? What is the quality of management? Are there hidden assets?" The selling book itself was pretty complete. I decided to list all the things I did not like about the situation and then see if those "dislikes" could actually be disguised benefits.

High on my list of drawbacks was that the sale would be an auction. This meant the buyer would definitely pay a full price—not good. But it also meant that the market would be "heated" as a result of Morgan Stanley and Salomon's work to stir up interest. If a buyer planned to sell significant pieces, then an auction had some advantages.

Next, there was no real synergy among the various companies. This was an advantage if I planned to sell the parts, because what was not sold would be stand-alone business. The idea that the TLC Group would be doing a "billion-dollar deal," when in fact asset presales would immediately reduce the price before any capital was at risk—and just maybe sell at higher prices than would be paid to KKR—had great appeal to me. Such a deal could accelerate my plan by five years, I reasoned. And the businesses were all outside of the United States, which was definitely going to see a recession or a slowdown.

I spent about two hours weighing the pros and cons. By 6 A.M., I had decided that TLC would bid, win, and close Beatrice International. There was much work to be done.

REELING IN THE BIG ONE

As complicated as the effort to acquire McCall had been, it would be dwarfed by that necessary for Beatrice. Now that Lewis had gotten himself invited to the bidding process, he would have to determine a price for Beatrice. The other bidders for Beatrice, including Citibank, had armies of financial experts devoted just to the task of arriving at a price. Incredibly, the TLC Group was comprised of only a few people initially—Lewis, Cleveland Christophe, an old friend and newly hired business partner, and Everett Grant.

On June 15, 1987, Lewis walked into 99 Wall Street, entered his office and checked with his personal secretary, Diedre Wilson, to see if any important telephone calls needed to be returned. Lewis then walked into Christophe's office and closed the door behind him. He took the deal book and placed it on Christophe's desk.

"This probably doesn't make any sense at all, but why don't you take a look at it overnight and let's discuss it in the morning," Lewis instructed his partner. Lewis already knew that he wanted to buy Beatrice, but he needed Christophe's financial analysis. Christophe went home and stayed up all night going through the Beatrice book, which detailed Beatrice's far-ranging companies. Christophe began constructing financial models of Beatrice and its operations, to see what a reasonable offering price might be. He calculated it to be $950 million, which is what TLC Group bid for Beatrice the following week.

Ever since the early 1970s, Reginald Lewis and Cleve Christophe had chewed the fat about the two of them joining forces and going into the leveraged buyout business. When Christophe decided to leave his high-ranking post with Citicorp's overseas operations in March 1987, Lewis was determined to pull his old buddy into TLC Group. Among other things, Christophe was one of the few people Lewis trusted implicitly, plus Christophe's business skills might prove useful going forward.

The men enjoyed each other's company to the extent that their dinners were typically marathon sessions lasting five hours or more. They had closed many a restaurant while talking about business and about their dreams. When closing time interrupted their reverie, they would merely re-establish it in a nearby bar or eatery. Lewis and Christophe were remarkably similar—articulate to the point of glibness, supremely confident, highly intelligent, somewhat elitist, fiercely independent, and vainglorious. Given their similarities, it wouldn't have been surprising if their personalities had repelled rather than attracted.

To launch his courtship of Christophe, Lewis had chosen a setting that served as home turf—the Harvard Club. With its wood paneling and overstuffed furniture, the establishment fairly reeks of prestige, power, and affluence. Every time Lewis walked into the club, it almost palpably reaffirmed his standing in top-level society. Lewis, who warmly embraced everything the Harvard Club represented, had taken Christophe to dinner there in March 1987.

The men had chatted with an ease that comes naturally to friends of long standing, their facile minds touching a broad range of topics over a short period of time. On that occasion, however, Lewis viewed their small talk as an appetizer for the conversational main course. When they had finished eating and were both feeling relaxed and sanguine, Lewis broached what was really on his mind.

"Cleve, we've always talked about being in a position of doing something together," Lewis ventured. "You know me, you know my personality, you know my organization. I love this business that I'm in—I see a tremendous wealth of opportunity. I think we need to sit down now, given your decision to leave Citicorp, and seriously talk about putting the plan together the way we've always discussed." Lewis paused a moment, letting the gravity of his words sink in before continuing.

"The two of us could be infinitely more powerful than either of us could be individually. I need a partner and I want you to consider being that partner." Lewis's piercing gaze briefly took in Christophe's face, reading the other man's expression for the slightest hint of enthusiasm or reluctance. "I've got a small infrastructure, I know what you can do and you know what I can do, and we know what each other's strengths and weaknesses are. And I believe in your integrity."

Lewis knew Christophe well enough to know that a snap answer to such a major proposition would not be forthcoming, so Lewis wasn't surprised when Christophe asked for more time to mull over the open-ended offer to form a partnership. Lewis was a man who could sometimes agonize over decisions major and not so major, but he felt at ease with himself after getting home later that night. A partnership between the two men was something he could live with. It brought a degree of closure to his and Christophe's relationship that felt right.

Lewis felt that Christophe would make a good partner because he could analyze the financials of a situation quickly. Publicly, Lewis held himself out to be totally self-assured and confident, someone who knew precisely how to acquire Beatrice and run it effectively. Privately, he was sometimes prone to tremendous indecision and uncertainty. Lewis was not a timid man and cut a broad swath once he'd chosen a course of action. And after he'd committed to something, his word was his bond. However, selecting a course of action could be a tortuous process for him. Lewis preferred to carefully weigh and analyze his options before making a move. And that didn't apply just to major decisions, but sometimes to seemingly simple ones.

The result of all that thinking and re-thinking of positions was perceived as procrastination.

At one point in the deliberations over how to bid on the Beatrice transaction, Lewis looked at Christophe and posed a question about some issue. Without pausing a beat, Christophe rattled off an answer.

"Goddamit, you piss me off," Lewis barked at his startled partner. "I've never seen anybody who can take half information and come to a decision faster than you can." Lewis paused momentarily, a hint of a smile playing at the corners of his lips.

"I'm going to be honest—that's not really a criticism," he said quietly. "I've been reading recently and some of those readings in the *Harvard Business Review* suggest that great leaders have the ability to reach decisions more readily than others without having a full fact file. I guess what I'm really expressing is a bit of envy. Maybe it's my legal training, but I always feel that I need to agonize over things before I can come to a conclusion."

For the most part, Lewis and Christophe were on the same wavelength: they were both tough-minded businessmen trying to push through a precedent-setting deal in a world dominated by white males. The historical ramifications of what they were attempting weren't lost on either man. "We'll show 'em," Lewis told Christophe once. "The SOBs will be quaking in their boots." Lewis had no doubt that he and Christophe made a formidable team.

But life had taught Lewis to take nothing for granted, not even that a partnership offer extended to one's best friend would be accepted. The move appeared perfectly logical to Christophe and he was leaning toward accepting the offer. But Lewis left nothing to chance, and over the course of the next month, he used lunches, dinners, and persuasive telephone calls to soften up Christophe.

"You ought to do it, as contrasted with being out there alone," Lewis said during one meeting, using a tack aimed at Christophe's sense of logic. "You will immediately have a foundation and we can build the upside. You bring a tremendous strength to what I am doing and I'm very excited about the prospects. I've reached out to several key operatives and it's unanimous—everybody would be delighted. I can commit to you now. You do not have to commit to me until later."

Christophe joined TLC Group on June 18, 1987, with the title of senior vice president, a six-figure salary, and a guaranteed bonus. Plus, he was to have an equity stake in each acquisition of TLC Group—at the discretion of the chairman.

During the initial phases of the Beatrice acquisition, Christophe was Lewis's right hand man, much the same role Tom Lamia had played during the purchase of McCall. Christophe had replaced Lamia because Lamia had failed to come through when Lewis needed him. In addition to being talented, anyone who was a key Lewis operative was periodically subjected to loyalty litmus tests. Anyone who flunked ran a serious risk of being placed "in the doghouse" or in "deep freeze," two favorite Lewis terms for people he was on the outs with. Extreme cryogenics had been applied to Lewis's relationship with Tom Lamia when the wheels first started turning on the Beatrice deal.

In the early part of June 1987, Lewis had telephoned Lamia in Washington and asked if Lamia could be in Chicago the next day. Lamia declined, citing scheduled meetings with clients. "He always called me the night before and was always pissed when I couldn't be somewhere he wanted," Lamia says. About a week later, Lewis called Lamia again, ask-ing him to be in Beverly Hills the next day for talks with Drexel. Lamia begged off again because of previous commitments. "I think he was re-ally upset at that point," Lamia remembers. "I was not a team player or something."

Lewis made a mental note to himself that Lamia would watch the Beatrice acquisition unfold from the sidelines. Lamia was benched, rel-egated to the most frigid of deep freezes. Lamia's knowledge of Beatrice would have to come from a newspaper or from television, because he was now persona non grata. Period. In place of Lamia, Lewis chose his former law firm, Paul, Weiss, to provide him with legal counsel.

Whereas Lamia had twice flunked Lewis's loyalty tests, another member of Lewis's acquisition team from the McCall days, Phyllis Schless, passed with flying colors. Around the same time that Lamia got his second call from Lewis, Schless was in Cape Cod on the second day of a much-needed vacation when the telephone rang at 8 in the morning. It was Lewis. "I didn't mean to disturb you, but I need you down here by one o'clock for a meeting," Lewis intoned. Schless cut short her vacation and was on the next flight to Manhattan. "The short notice is just part of the game," she says philosophically. "Things are moving very quickly and you need stuff done in those transactions."

On the 24th of June, Salomon Bros. vice president Graham Cun-ningham picked up the telephone and called the offices of TLC Group at 99 Wall Street. Salomon was handling the sale of Beatrice for KKR. "We have received from your group an offer to buy Beatrice Inter-national for $950 million," Cunningham said. "We have a small problem—nobody knows who the hell you are!"

Cunningham came over half an hour later to meet with Lewis and Christophe. Cunningham was brought up to speed on the TLC Group and what it had accomplished: specifically, Lewis's acquisition and sale of McCall. The 90-to-1 *New York Times* article was already proving to be worth its weight in gold: Lewis used it to help further Cunning-ham's education.

I went to the office and had the Beatrice material duplicated. I called Carl Brody, (a former Norton Simon executive who Lewis called the "best tax man in New York") and asked for some prelim-inary work on taxes. John Sheehy came down to the office and we kicked around a bunch of his ideas. Bids were due shortly, actually within days. And there was to be no on-site due diligence. I reasoned we had to analyze and bid as if it were a tender offer. This was an important insight.

We called Bankers Trust and Pete Offerman said, "Reg, for this one you have to talk to my boss directly," and he set up a meeting. Bankers Trust Company was working with another bidder—for $500,000 they would set up another team. No thanks. We talked to Equitable, but with the wrong people and got pablum. No matter. The card I intended to play was Milken, but not right away. John kept bugging me, "Reg, have you called Mike?"

"No, John, not yet. When? Not now. Let's do the work first, TLC style. Do the work." It was a good message to my troops. In July 1987, we bid $950 million. I had a feeling we were high bidder. Why? Because Dick Beattie had said, "Reg, you're low, way low." At 19 times very suspect earnings, you could not be "way low." Anyway, now the question was not just more work, but just as important, credibility. My troops asked, "How are we going to get this done?" Get what done, the bid or close the deal? The two things were different. For the bid, we needed to show the capacity to raise $1 billion. To close, we would need less—one half to one third of that amount, if we stuck to our strategy.

Now for the first problem, which was an easy one. We needed credibility and no person has more credibility than Mike Milken.

Lewis had spoken to Milken on the day the sale of McCall had been announced in the press.

I had actually engineered the call to Milken a little bit. I think I called Bruce Brown—then a key research guy at Drexel and close to Mike—after the deal had been announced in the newspaper. I can't remember whether that was before or after the 90-to-1 story in the New York Times. I had made it my business to stay in touch with Bruce. He congratulated me: "Reg, great deal on McCall. Wow, run it through again—how much did you make?" I played it real warm, but I was also a little matter of fact. "Yes, Bruce, the returns are handsome, a lot of effort went into producing them, a lot of work, believe me."

"I know, Reg, I know. Michael was just saying the same thing at our morning meeting." I said to Bruce, "By the way, say hello to Michael." He said, "Say hello to him yourself," and he went off the line for a second and yelled out at the trading floor, "Mike, I've got Reg Lewis on line three." The word came back, "See if you can get him to hold for a minute." Bruce came back on the line and said, "If you could hold on for a minute, Michael wants to say hi." And I said, "Sure."

This call was critical at this point because TLC Group had decided to go for Beatrice International, and my people were bugging me to death about, "Aren't you going to go out and see Milken?" I wanted to wait and get him to invite me out without knowing about the Beatrice International deal. My theory on that was, let's let the full glory of the McCall pop sink in before I hit him with Beatrice International.

So Michael came on the phone in his usual style and said, "Great job, Reg—could you take me through this again? How much did you put up and what are you getting?" And I took him through it quickly.

"I bought McCall Pattern in February, 1984 for twenty-two five— nineteen million from the bank, two point five from the seller, and I put up a million dollars in equity. Recapped in December 1986 for nineteen and got sixty-five million on the sale. And we're keeping the real estate, which is probably worth another six to ten. So we make it to be about ninety million all on a million."

"That's great, Reg, just great. And how much do you own?"

"Eighty-one point seven percent."

"And who's the buyer?"

"A British public company with sound plans for McCall."

"Great. When will it close?"

"It's closed, Michael."

"Great! Well Reg, you've done one helluva job. Do you think you could come out and visit with me?"

"Well, Mike, I don't have anything pending right now."

"That doesn't matter. Why don't you just come out. Let's talk. Maybe we'll figure out how to give you a bigger bat to swing with."

"Well, that's what I was interested in, Michael."

"Well, you made $75 million." He then talked a little bit about taxes.

I said, "Well Mike, you've got to pay your taxes."

"Did you consider a tax-free deal?"

"I wanted the cash."

"Well, maybe we can figure out the next time how to hold on to a little more of your wealth. But I think, Reg, that it's now time for you to get serious. How about Wednesday, 9 A.M.?"

"Okay, Mike, I'll be there."

When I hung up the phone, I said, "Get serious?!" I called my wife, and I said, "Get this, I just talked to Milken. And do you know what he said? When I told him I just made $75 million, he said, 'Well, Reg, now it's time to get SERIOUS.' Can you believe it?—I just made $75 million in cash and he says it's time to get serious. Unbelievable—what's unbelievable is I don't think he was kidding. Holy shit, this guy is unreal."

I didn't know at the time, of course, that in 1987 Mike made $550 million in salary and bonuses.

I can't put my finger on exactly when Milken realized what I had done with McCall, but I think it was a series of things. Drexel had said, "One, you'll never get this deal done (McCall Pattern)." We got the deal done. "Two, you won't get a sale-leaseback done on that basis." We got the sale-leaseback done. "Three, the high yield bond market will never accept an issue from McCall." We got a high yield issue done. "Four, the business is dying—you'll be lucky if you could hold earnings." We doubled earnings. Five, we did a recap in December of 1986 that resulted in $19 million on a $1 million common base.

I think certainly by then, by the time of the recap, Michael was convinced that I was doing something very right. I think he was favorably disposed toward me then, and I think I did a good job of convincing some of the people around him that I was really driving the McCall strategic thrust and that the deal was going to be successful. And Jean Wong and Bruce Brown and Bob Davidow of Drexel were people I stayed in touch with. They sent me a lot of prospectuses of other deals that were getting done and so forth.

And Jean, in particular—at various internal meetings that Drexel had—would bring up our name and Michael would say, "Yeah, how is the situation doing?" or whatever. That's the impression I got. But

*of course the big change came as we continued to talk throughout
that process and I'd send him material and so forth. We had occasional meetings and I told him what we were trying to do and what
the result was, and we doubled the earnings from $6 million, $7 million, up to $13 million–$14 million. And he was very, very interested
in that. Very intrigued by it.*

*And then, of course, the big payday on the sale was the crowning
glory, so to speak.*

"Reg was a person with a legal background who understood capital
structure and finance and could run a business," Milken said. "It's like
playing a piano—it sounds one way if you can play with your right
hand, but it sounds totally different if you can play with both hands at
the same time. Very few people have the ability to play the right side,
which is the financial side, and the left side, which is operating those
assets. Reg came to the table, with the sale of McCall, proving that he
could play the piano with both hands. So I said, 'Hey Reg, let's get
ready. It's time to take the show to Broadway.'"

*A number of the guys on the Drexel team played instrumental roles
in the Beatrice acquisition, but ultimately that's because of Mike
Milken. I was very impressed with the quality of their personalities—
Jean Wong, Bruce Brown, Bob Davidow, Joe Hutch. And later on,
Leon Black, of course. And Dean Kehler. And then I got to know
Drexel Chairman Fred Joseph. One of the things that I learned is that
even if there's one fundamental decision maker, the climate around
that decision maker is extremely important. And so I tried to create a
good impression on the people surrounding Michael. That's perfectly
natural, because he was going to call the shots.*

*I definitely had to stay close to Mike. I am convinced that no one
else, within Drexel—including Fred Joseph—would have backed us
up in the way that they did in the Beatrice International deal without Milken. It took Michael's insight to stay the course with us, even
if things got tough. And that I'm absolutely convinced of.*

*What people really didn't understand about the deal is that
Michael really didn't commit to a billion dollars, even though that's
what Drexel pledged to do. We got a written commitment because*

Henry Kravis (KKR) insisted on it. What Michael really did was he gave us credibility. Kravis wasn't even going to let us in the auction unless he knew that we had backing.

Michael tells a great story about this. He was visiting Kravis and Henry said, "Michael, on this Reg Lewis—I know he's made a lot of money on the McCall deal, but he has no credibility with me on a billion-dollar deal." And Milken said, "Well Henry, he's got credibility with me." I love that story.

The fact is, if our basic plan on Beatrice International didn't work, the most Drexel would have had to raise was $500 million. Essentially, the plan was simple. We would bid the entire deal, but between contract and closing we would take advantage of the fact that there had been an auction. Not only for the whole company, but for different pieces of the company. And we would effectuate sales during the period of contract closing, while we had nothing at risk. We would then use those proceeds to reduce our debt, effectively selling assets at a higher multiple than we were buying them. That would enable us to reduce our leverage, making what looked like a $1 billion deal really a $400 million or $500 million deal. Then we would focus on a core group of operations, which we would then refinance and grow.

That was the plan, which I was somewhat concerned somebody might latch on to and run with. Beatrice CEO Don Kelly had basically made the decision, "Okay, we should exit the international food business." I think primarily because he was very concerned about all the minority interests that were in Beatrice International. So Beatrice owned 85 percent of this, 75 percent of that, 60 percent of this. They didn't always have 100 percent. And some of the minority partners were a real pain in the butt, as I later learned. Many of them were great partners and I've gotten along with all of them very well.

But Don made a decision that the best way to get value was not to break it up but to sell the whole thing. Even though I think KKR had toyed around with the idea of maybe breaking it up, Don wanted to sell it as a package.

The first time I mentioned Beatrice International to Milken was after the telephone conversation we'd had on the McCall deal. I went out to L.A. for a meeting. Michael went on for about an hour talking about his vision of the world and why didn't he and I set up a company called Turnarounds of America. "But Michael," I said, "McCall was not a turnaround."

"Well, it doesn't matter. We can perceive it as a turnaround." To his credit, at the end of an hour he turned to me and said, "Reg, is there anything I've missed, is there anything you want to say to me?"

I said, "Michael, yesterday we bid $950 million to KKR for Beatrice International Foods. Beatrice International has $2.5 billion in sales, $145 million of operating income, and 64 companies in 31 countries. Our plan is simple: Bid the whole thing and simultaneously, with our acquisition, we sell Canada for $200 million, we sell Australia for $75 million, we sell Latin America, maybe for $100 million. So now we've pared away about $400 million, and we've still got a company with $2 billion in sales and over $100 million of operating capital. But now we've only paid $550 million to $600 million.

Then we decide what we are going to retain, what we are going to keep and go from there. And we've lined up Onex, a buyout group up in Toronto led by Gerry Schwartz, to buy Canada. We've got Solomon Lew, an Australian businessman who's very interested in the Australian operations. And we think the Latin American division is attractive and will sell easily."

Michael said, "How the hell do you know Solomon Lew?" And I just said, "We know everybody," somewhat distracted by his question. And then he said, "I don't know the specifics of this deal, but I'll get somebody in here who does." Then he turned around and walked out. I could see him whispering in a very excited fashion to a colleague. And all of a sudden Ackerman came in and sat at the head of the table.

After the meeting, I got on a plane and went back to New York. A day or so later, Michael called me and said, "Has Peter Ackerman been in to see you? He's in New York—has he been by to see you about this deal?" Up until that point, Drexel hadn't done anything. Within half an hour, Ackerman was in my office with a Drexel executive named Dean Kehler. They came back and said, "We think you've got the best bid." So then we started organizing the due diligence effort.

Milken recalls this meeting too. He found himself growing more and more enthusiastic about the thought of a Lewis-Beatrice alliance.

"From that point on, all of our interaction convinced me that he was the right person for this transaction," Milken says. "I think it began a love affair of a different order between myself and Reg. My feeling was that he knew Beatrice better than I knew Beatrice. In fact, he knew it better than the people who ran it. It was complicated, it was diverse."

I put together the due diligence effort. I got corporate lawyer Matt Nimitz of Paul, Weiss involved, in addition to Bob Schumer, one of the outstanding young corporate lawyers with the firm. We got the Deloitte accounting firm involved. We got the tax people involved. We put together a big delegation to go out to Beatrice's headquarters in Chicago and hear the Beatrice story.

I gave one of my great speeches on this occasion. We had been listening to Beatrice's presentation when Bill Mowry, who was the president and chief operating officer of Beatrice at the time, said we would like for each prospective buyer to come up and say a few words about their approach.

I remember opening my remarks by saying that "I have to sit through a lot of presentations, but the presentation that we've just heard was one of the finest that I've ever heard." I wanted to thank them personally, because I knew what is involved in putting these kinds of things together. "There is an enormous amount of effort, and Bill, you and your team have really done an outstanding job."

And then I gave them a little talk about TLC Group and our work on the McCall situation and how we handled that. All the Beatrice people had the 90-to-1 story from the New York Times in their folders. I emphasized that we believe in working closely with the operating managers and let them make virtually all of the operating decisions. After the presentation, Bill Mowry and I met privately in the Beatrice suite at the Drake Hotel with Cleve Christophe and Geoff Murphy, Beatrice's chief financial officer. And Cleve and I sat down and said, "We're in this thing to go all the way."

Bill was a good man and started spreading the word around that "TLC is in this to win." We were the proverbial long shot and we were the last people permitted to bid. We were sixth in line and starting to give up.

THE THRILL OF THE CHASE

By the summer of 1987, Lewis was locked into an incredibly grueling schedule. From late June until the early part of August, he would come into his 99 Wall Street office around 8:30 A.M. and work on things related to the Beatrice bid until around 3 in the morning. On the weekends he took something of a break, getting into his office around 9 A.M. and leaving around 11 P.M.. This wasn't just a matter of discipline, which Lewis had in abundance. Just being able to pursue the Beatrice deal was a reward in and of itself.

"Reg enjoyed the competition, he enjoyed the struggle," former Beatrice executive Everett Grant says. "Since his enjoyment came from competition, and he was able to compete so much and so successfully, I think he did enjoy himself quite a bit, more than most people can conceive."

Lewis also derived pleasure from the fact no one expected a black man to be going after a two-billion dollar, international food company. He had paid his dues and had played the game by the rules and, miraculously, found they hadn't been changed in mid-game. Nor did he expect them to, because a central tenet of his was that hard work and dedication invariably take a person where he or she wants to go. Lewis had traveled a road bumpier than that traversed by his white compatriots, but despite that, he'd made it to his destination anyway.

One thing Lewis didn't like about the Beatrice chase, though, was the fact he couldn't tell people he held near and dear. He desperately wanted them to know what he was up to, but you never know when a loose lip could sink a deal still in its nascent stages. There may have even been an element of superstition in Lewis's reluctance, as if to talk about an unconsummated deal would result in jinxing it. His solution was to let folks know that something major was afoot, without getting into specific details. One of the first people he told of Beatrice in a very roundabout manner was his mother.

"He called and said, 'Mom, I'm entering into something that's so mind-boggling that I'm not going to tell you'." Carolyn Fugett felt her son had underestimated her ability to understand, but she knew not to press the issue. "I wish you the best and I'll put it on the altar," she told her son.

"That's what I need," Lewis told his mother. He hung up the phone, smiling. At age 44 the desire to gain his mom's approval and the pleasure he got from being able to do so was as strong as ever. By the same token, most big brothers like to be admired by their younger brothers—even into adulthood. Tony Fugett, an executive with IBM at the time, also received a cryptic heads-up about Lewis's newest venture.

"Tony, I think I got a real big one here," Lewis said conspiratorially. "A real big one. Keep your fingers crossed, because I think it's going to work for all of us." Lewis's voice conveyed a mixture of confidence, excitement, and a touch of hesitancy, as though weighing the possibility of saying more. "You don't know who's going to run their mouth and who's not when you're talking about stakes like that," Fugett says. "You don't take chances. He was a very conservative, cautious kind of person and he didn't want me running around IBM going, 'Oh, guess what?!' Not that I would have, but he didn't want to take that chance."

About to explode from having to keep his secret, Lewis called Ellis Goodman, his boyhood friend who was a lawyer and real estate developer in Baltimore. Following a brief exchange of niceties, Lewis tantalized Goodman as he'd done with his family members. "I'm working on a deal that's so big, I can't believe it myself," Lewis said into the phone. "You'd laugh if I told you. I don't want to say anything now, because I don't know where I'm headed with it. But I'm telling you, it's so big I can't believe it."

While Lewis felt he had to play it coy even with his mother, he could lay all his cards on the table with his wife, Loida. He talked frequently about Beatrice, which was starting to become an all-consuming passion. "He was very excited," says Loida Lewis, who would become TLC Beatrice's chairman after her husband's death six years later. "His eyes were brilliant and he was talking about what he was going to do with Beatrice and who would run it." Lewis's short list of potential CEOs included Earle Angstadt, who had been Lewis's CEO at McCall; Jim Ferguson, the former CEO of General Foods; and Dave Mahoney, the former CEO of Norton Simon Industries.

A TAXING PROBLEM

Coming up with a tax structure that would allow Reginald Lewis to buy Beatrice was the toughest nut to crack in the entire acquisition.

The tax considerations were incredibly complex, causing Drexel to get antsy about whether Beatrice could handle its debt service if Drexel came up with the money to buy the company. Drexel's commitment to Lewis was starting to waver, a situation he would definitely have to rectify if the deal were to go through.

At the risk of oversimplifying things, the money to buy Beatrice was going to be borrowed in the United States by the top-tier holding company, TLC Beatrice International Holdings, Inc. And the interest on the debt had to be paid in U.S. dollars.

But Beatrice's income was flowing in from 64 companies that were located in foreign countries—31 of them before Lewis started selling off assets. That meant the income was generated in foreign currencies. The question of the hour was: How do you get the income into the United States and into U.S. currency in order to pay off the debt? There were some intricate financial hurdles to be surmounted. Pesos earned in Spain, for example, would have to be converted into U.S. dollars, yet the cost of doing so would have to be kept at manageable levels and enough expenses would have to be tax-deductible to make the whole thing feasible.

When money is generated by overseas operating units, some of it disappears through foreign taxes and various charges, not to mention foreign exchange controls. And if those transactions collectively siphon away too much money, there might not be enough left to put toward the interest payments on Beatrice's debt.

It bears repeating that the Beatrice acquisition was the largest offshore leveraged buyout ever pulled off when Lewis did it in 1987. So there were no precedents or guideposts for Lewis and his people, vis-a-vis the tax structure.

None of that made any difference to Drexel, which had committed to raise $1 billion. Its only question was: How does Beatrice repay the debt on this loan?

Lewis would have to assuage Drexel's fears in order to keep the deal on track. He and Christophe arranged to fly out to meet with the Drexel people on July 30, 1987. Two days before the trip, Christophe started running financial models on his personal computer at home. What slowly began to emerge was a table showing what the Beatrice deal would look like if there were a 100 percent tax deduction of all appropriate expenses associated with the transaction, with a special emphasis on interest expense. The table, which went in 5 percent increments from 100 percent deductibility down to 50 percent, examined the numbers in terms of all critical coverages, including financial covenant considerations and operating projections.

At 99 Wall Street the morning before their Drexel meeting, Lewis and Christophe went over the tax deductibility table, deciding which was the best way to present the analysis and methodology contained in it. They decided against walking into the meeting and triumphantly throwing the computer model on the conference table. Instead they would let Peter Ackerman articulate all of Drexel's fears and misgivings, allowing Lewis to set the stage. Then he and Christophe would pull out the model and walk Drexel through it.

Lewis and Christophe actually wrote a script that anticipated what the Drexel people would say, how Lewis would respond and the best juncture for introducing the financial model.

When they got to Drexel's offices in Beverly Hills, Michael Milken, Dean Kehler, Peter Ackerman, and John Moriarty—a Drexel vice president in the corporate finance area—waited with grim expressions. "I just don't know if we're going to get there on this deal," Ackerman said once the meeting started. "You guys have not been able to come up with answers on this tax structure."

Ackerman went on for about five minutes before Lewis took center stage, reciting to perfection the lines he and Christophe had painstakingly crafted.

"You know, Peter, I can understand why you have those concerns," Lewis said reassuringly. "I mean, we too are concerned about how all of this will work out. But you know that's why we have the finest minds working on this problem and we think we're just about there. But clearly it's in our interest, just as it's in your interest, to know that what we're doing is well founded.

"So Peter, you would expect us to have been proactive in how we approach this.

"Do you think it might be useful if we ask ourselves the question: 'Well, what if we achieve different levels of deductibility? What are the financial implications of that, what are the implications in terms of coverages and what are the implications in terms of deal returns?' Would it be useful to construct something that allows us to measure those things?"

"And suppose we then separately go to our tax advisers and ask them where they are in the process, then pose this question: 'Given that you've got all these moving pieces in all these different areas and given where you are, what level of comfort do you have that at the end of the day you will be able to achieve a certain level of deductibility? How comfortable would you be that you can, say, get 95 percent deductibility?'

"Or suppose we ratcheted that down and said, 'Okay, given all of these pieces, how comfortable are you that you can get 75 percent deductibility?' And suppose I said that we were 90 percent probable that we'd be able to achieve that. Would something like that prove useful?"

Ackerman took a second to ponder the scenario Lewis laid out. "Yeah, I think that would be damn useful," he said. "Can we do something like that?"

Lewis paused for effect. "Well Peter, we've been thinking about this and Cleve has some thoughts that perhaps he could share with you," Lewis said, handing things off to Christophe in a well-choreographed move. Christophe then began passing copies of the computer model around the table.

The Drexel team was comforted by what they saw and heard, notwithstanding the fact that Lewis's tax advisers still hadn't categorically said how the tax structure would play out.

Having restored Drexel's confidence and enthusiasm, Lewis flew back to New York. A bevy of smaller crises awaited his immediate attention.

It bears repeating that Michael Milken's role was to add credibility, because Henry Kravis was conducting the auction of Beatrice through Salomon and Morgan Stanley and they didn't even want to let us in to bid. It was kind of funny to me that I had Christophe and Sheehy meet with Morgan Stanley and Salomon and presumably those guys were checking out our bonafides. I was in California at the time. I remember saying over the telephone, "Well, tell Henry Kravis that we have as much bonafides to do this deal as he did when he bought Beatrice in the first place."

But in any case, I got Michael on board. Mike delegated the thing to Ackerman, but he stayed involved and kept his foot up Ackerman's butt. Ackerman then started to get kind of excited when he heard my basic strategy, which was to bid the deal at the perimeter, then immediately sell off some businesses. Mike was *comfortable that Ackerman could raise $500 million of high-yield securities. Although he naturally said, "We'll raise anything you need," I once asked Mike confidentially, "What are you comfortable doing?" He told me $500 million.*

That let me know that I had to sell at least $400 million of assets and get a bank piece for $200 million to $250 million. That's because even though he said $500 million, I discounted what he said to a certain extent. But I did think that as long as Mike stayed involved that he would be able to do it. While I needed Drexel, I think the ability to hold on to control of that deal would have been very tough if they had been forced to raise more money.

With the commitment for $1 billion in place, the next issue was to get Drexel to understand that I was going to control the deal. And that was a tough, grinding battle that we finally came to terms on after the time had elapsed to bid. In fact, I just stopped the clock and said, "I will not participate in this deal unless I control it, pure and simple. No ifs, no ands and no buts." And they thought I was bluffing—of course I was not. And I think it was mostly Peter who wanted control. I don't think it was Mike.

Michael had to sit down with Peter in a very dramatic meeting at one point and tell him, "Peter, what we're doing is backing Reg. That's what we're doing here." And he just cut him off.

After some hard bargaining, Lewis did agree to allow a Drexel entity to purchase a 26 percent share in the deal's equity for a token amount because they had after all arranged for a significant portion of the transaction's financing. Drexel, and Michael Milken in particular, had also enhanced Lewis's credibility at a critical time during the bidding by committing up to $1 billion of the firm's capital, if necessary, to finance the transaction.

In addition however, Lewis gave up the equity because he believed that there was a commitment on Drexel's part to assist TLC Beatrice going forward in terms of raising money for future acquisitions and refinancing the debt. In this expectation, he would be bitterly disappointed. Drexel did not fulfill any of these promises. Although the firm would raise billions of dollars for acquisitions by Henry Kravis, Ron Perelman, and other dealmakers, it never raised another cent for Lewis after the close of the Beatrice transaction.

On December 21, 1971, Reginald F. Lewis flew with Benjamin F. Chavis from New York City to Wilmington, NC. Chavis was turning himself in to authorities, after being arrested while fighting school desegregation and then charged with accessory after the fact of murder for counseling and advising a suspect in a murder case. Lewis was his attorney and general counsel for the New York-based Commission for Racial Justice. *Photo credit:* Wilmington Morning Star.

Pictured (left to right): Lt. H. G. Grohman of the New Hanover County Sheriff's Dept., immediately behind Grohman is Detective W. C. Brown of the Wilmington Policy Department, Benjamin F. Chavis, and Reginald F. Lewis.

Reginald F. Lewis with his law partner Charles C. Clarkson and Lewis's wife, Loida, during a birthday party for Lewis held in his Paris apartment (Dec. 7, 1988). *Photo credit:* Studio de France.

Left: Reginald Lewis consciously put together a board of directors with African-Americans in the majority. Here, he listens intently to colleagues during a recess in the April 1990 TLC Beatrice International Board Meeting in Paris held at the Hotel de Crillon.

From left to right: Samuel Peabody, Reginald F. Lewis, Lee A. Archer, Jr., and James E. Obi.

Right: Reginald F. Lewis with Earle K. Angstadt, the Chief Executive Officer of McCall Pattern, following the sale of McCall. This picture was taken at the Harvard Club, Lewis's favorite haunt (1987).

Reginald Lewis being presented with an award in October 1987 by then Los Angeles Mayor Tom Bradley (right) with financier Michael Milken (left) looking on. Lewis had just finished addressing a minority youth conference in Los Angeles at which Milken was also a speaker.

Reginald Lewis receives an award from the New York Urban Coalition, a socially active, high profile group of New York City business, labor, and community leaders, on December 8, 1992. The event was the last time Lewis appeared in public prior to his death in January 1993. Among the recipients and participants shown in the photo are (from left to right): former New York City Mayor John Lindsay, Lewis, David Rockefeller, Andrew Heiskell, former Chairman & CEO of Time, Inc., then New York City Mayor David Dinkins, Walter Shipley, president of Chemical Bank, Robert Allen, chairman of AT&T, and Arthur H. Barnes, then President of The Urban Coalition.

A beaming Reginald Lewis presents his French partners Jean (center-left) and Jacques (center-right) Baud with a red Corvette ZR1 in early 1990 at the front of Paris's famed Crillon Hotel in the Place de la Concorde as a reward for exceeding the plan for the year. The Corvette ZR1 was so rare that Lewis's staff had to search out New York area dealerships for the car and then bid for it to ensure delivery to France, which in itself turned out to be no easy task. Jacque Baud got the Corvette while his brother, Jean Baud, received a Cadillac convertible from Lewis. Looking on (left) is Daniel Jux, president of TLC Beatrice France.

Reginald F. Lewis exits his first corporate jet, a Challenger, to meet with Vincent P. O'Sullivan (right), Chairman of Tayto, Ltd., and TLC Holdings, Inc. Tayto products dominate the snack food industry in Ireland (1990). *Photo credit:* Foto Estudio Angel, S.E.L.

CEOs of the top 400 businesses in the United States were invited to the White House in 1991 for a luncheon meeting. Reginald F. Lewis, shown here with President George Bush, was the only African American present. *Photo credit:* White House Photo.

During Jesse Jackson's run for U.S. president, Lewis (left) held a fund-raiser at the Harvard Club in 1988, raising over six figures for the Jackson campaign.

On April 23, 1993, The Reginald F. Lewis International Law Center became the first building named in honor of an African American by Harvard. Lewis made a three-million-dollar gift to the Law School in 1992, the largest from a single individual in Harvard's 175-year history. *Photo credit:* Bradford Herzog & Martha Stewart. Pictured left to right: Dean Robert C. Clark, Christina S. N. Lewis, Loida Nicolas Lewis, Leslie N. Lewis.

Loida N. Lewis and Reginald F. Lewis on the grounds of the summer home in Amagansett, New York during their 20th Wedding Anniversary celebration, August 16, 1989. Loida surprised him by hiring an airplane to circle overhead with a banner that read: "Reg! Loving you always. Loida." *Photo credit:* Chong Monalac-Capati.

Reginald F. Lewis, in 1987, reviewing the operations of Savoy, the largest chocolate maker in Venezuela. Lewis wound up selling Savoy, a part of his strategy to reduce debt from the Beatrice purchase. *Photo credit:* Foto Estudio Angel, S.E.L.

(Left): William Mowry, President of Beatrice International when Lewis made the Beatrice acquisition. Others in the photo are employees at Savoy.

Reginald Lewis and his wife, Loida, share a happy moment at their Paris apartment in 1990. The photo was taken by their daughter Leslie. A charcoal rendering of the photo hangs in Loida's office at TLC Beatrice International Holdings in New York City.

Reginald F. Lewis is on top of the world as he poses in the outer reception area of the TLC Beatrice International offices at 9 West 57th Street high above the streets of midtown Manhattan with the Empire State Building in the background. *Photo credit:* Gregory Heisler.

In fact, not only had the Drexelites been given common stock but, unlike the rest of the original investors in the deal, they had been given the privilege of purchasing this potentially lucrative stock without having to purchase any preferred stock, which essentially was a loan to the company with limited upside. In the end, Lewis regretted giving up the equity and he worked diligently until his final days to take Drexel and its minions out of the deal completely.

Now, in terms of the bid process itself, I pretty much felt that the price was around $950 million. We bid $950 million to be preemptive. But I was nervous about it. I was nervous because a lot of the operating units had sizable minority stakeholders, meaning you couldn't automatically bring the cash back into the United States. If the market for assets fell, then I would be stuck with a high-cost debt structure in a business that was generating all this cash out of the country.

We explored a number of different alternative financing structures, but none of them could be implemented under the time constraints we had for putting the entire deal together. Essentially, the strategy that evolved was very simple: We would bid $950 million or so and between the time of signing the contract and closing the deal, we would sell off at least three businesses for an aggregate price of $400 million. Then immediately after the closing, we would decide which businesses we wanted to keep and which businesses we wanted to sell. By then we would have a lot more information about them, because I would have had a chance to get out into the field and find out what was going on.

The aim was to retain a core group of businesses that had some synergies and would improve operating results even as we reduced expenses. That was basically the operating strategy, and it was a sound strategy, because we were in effect piggy-backing on the auction work that Morgan Stanley and Salomon had already done. They had effectively heated up the market for sales of pieces of the business. So while the fact that there was an auction was a negative from the standpoint that you knew you were going to pay a high price, it was a positive from the standpoint that the market for the various assets was going to be well heated. And that's the way we looked at it.

Next came the actual bid. That was taken care of in a fairly straightforward manner with a one-page letter. The structure of the financing was simple, also. Regarding our original goal of $250 million to $300 million in bank debt, we wanted a commitment for more than that because—I can say it now—we were considering cutting Drexel out of the deal if the control issues got crazy. So if the bank had agreed to put up an amount equivalent to the $450 million to $400 million we were getting from the asset sale, then theoretically we wouldn't need any high-yield debt.

But I decided against that strategy because: One, Mike had done an outstanding job; Two, I thought that Peter who was driving my costs up and was giving me a lot of aggravation—ultimately would follow Mike's lead on the major points. There's also the fact that there was an alliance between KKR and Drexel. I mean Drexel was KKR's lead banker for all of its major deals. And I knew that if I had cut Drexel out of the deal, there would be tremendous pressure on KKR not to do the deal with me. And I didn't want that.

In any case, I thought Ackerman could be handled. He was more of a distraction on a personal basis than anything else.

So now I delegated the due diligence effort to Paul, Weiss and Deloitte Haskins and Sells, with Cleve Christophe coordinating. Their job was to go in and review the numbers. Then I assigned the tax analysis to Arthur Kalish, a talented Paul, Weiss attorney who did some brilliant work in that regard. I limited myself to overall coordination and the asset sales, which I did with Charles Clarkson and Tom Lamia primarily. I kept Drexel completely out of the asset disposition strategy. I didn't want them involved at all.

Our bid went in. Word came out that KKR was going with somebody else. Ackerman even called and said, "Well, we got close." I said, "Peter, I don't even want to hear that. Call people—let's create a climate where we can get it done." There was about a 48-hour period where we really turned up the juice and placed a number of phone calls to key decision makers at Beatrice and KKR. To this day, I think KKR knew we were going to have the highest bid and was going to go with us all along, but they created doubt in our minds so that we effectively topped our own bid and increased it to $985 million. But that ultimately took it.

We signed a definitive agreement on August 6, 1987.

Reginald Lewis had done it. He'd managed to pull off a deal so large he could hardly believe it himself. Not only that, but the Beatrice acquisition was the largest offshore leveraged buyout that had been accomplished up to that point. Lewis had worked incredibly hard and very diligently for this moment, and it was every bit as sweet as he fantasized it would be.

A tidal wave of thoughts and emotions cascaded over Lewis, suffusing him with a glow no narcotic could ever come close to replicating. He could sense Grandpa and Grandma Cooper were somewhere beaming to themselves over his improbable accomplishment. Why should white guys have all the fun, indeed!

The smiling faces of his colleagues flashed before his eyes as though in a dream sequence and he saw hands thrusting toward him to pump his. Everything had an air of unreality about. People who thought Lewis never had any fun should get to know the euphoria that accompanies buying a billion-dollar company. And the thrill and the tremendous surge of accomplishment and pride were magnified three-fold for Lewis, because he had overcome obstacles and impediments that white financiers would never encounter and might not surmount if they did.

Lewis had a secret code that he shared with his wife whenever he accomplished something particularly noteworthy: He would sing the tune, "Raindrops Keep Falling on My Head." Lewis picked up the phone on his desk and, praying the line wouldn't be busy, dialed the villa in the South of France where his family was on vacation and waiting for him to join them. When Loida Lewis picked up, Lewis simply said, "Raindrops, Loida, raindrops."

"Darling, you did it!" Loida Lewis exclaimed excitedly.

Next, Lewis made a call to the other important woman in his life. "Mom, I did it," he said. "I accomplished what I thought I could not accomplish. I have bought almost a billion-dollar company." Carolyn Fugett says she really wasn't surprised by the call. "I didn't jump up and down and scream and carry on and all that kind of stuff," she says. "I have always, from the first day he came into this world, perceived greatness for Reg and each time that it happened, it just reassured my faith in him. I was elated and thrilled and what have you, but I can't truly say that I was overwhelmed."

After the euphoria at 99 Wall Street subsided somewhat, Lewis had to go to Morgan Stanley's offices on 50th Street to review some documents and sign them. When that task was taken care of, Lewis, Kevin Wright, Everett Grant, Cleve Christophe, and Tom Lamia walked out of a conference room and into a hallway. They strode around a corner, toward a bank of elevators. A smiling Lewis asked, "Is anybody looking?" After everyone had answered in the negative, Lewis jumped straight up and clicked his heels, reprising the feat he'd pulled off after getting a funding guarantee for McCall.

They left the building and walked toward the Harvard Club, with Lewis exuberantly throwing punches at the air. Once they'd reached their destination, Lewis ordered several bottles of the best champagne available, which he and his crew made short work of. As the champagne disappeared, Wright, Grant, Christophe, and Lamia each offered testimonials of sorts to the growing legend of Reginald Lewis. Christophe was first and had surprisingly little to say, but no one really noticed. The center of attention was Reginald Lewis. Smiling broadly and laughing readily when he entered the Harvard Club, Lewis was beginning to grow quiet and pensive as the evening progressed. The size of the task that lay ahead was sobering indeed. All the tension, hard work, and long hours that it took to win the bid for Beatrice were nothing compared to what would be necessary to close the deal for this globe-spanning empire, and Lewis knew it.

With that in mind, Lewis brought the curtain down on the Harvard Club celebration. There was still much to be done, he informed his colleagues. Feeling light-headed from champagne as well as his incredible victory, Lewis walked out of the Harvard Club and into the sweltering night air of Manhattan. The blare of car horns, the galaxy of twinkling neon signs, and even the smell of auto exhaust all seemed to register with a previously unexperienced clarity and vividness. Reginald Lewis's senses were on edge the night of August 6, 1987. He stepped into his car, breathed deeply of cool air-conditioned air laced with the scent of leather and told his driver to head toward Lewis's brownstone on 22nd Street.

It was premature to devote too much time to celebrating. It was time to devise a strategy for controlling the news media, so that news of the Beatrice bid would be released in the manner Lewis desired. As the sight and sounds of Manhattan glided silently past Lewis's window, he thought about ways to manage the press, rather than leaving them to their own devices.

MEDIA BLITZ

His brownstone rolled into view and Lewis's car stopped. He waited for his driver to get out and walk around to Lewis's side of the car and open the door. Lewis popped out, bid his driver a cheerful "good night," and went bounding two steps at a time up the stairs to his front door. The energy and sense of excitement he felt was incredible—having won the Beatrice bid made him feel like a frisky 20-year-old.

Once inside he went upstairs to his study and dialed Butch Meily's home telephone number.

"Butch, I need you to come over and work on a press release," Lewis said, his voice crackling with excitement. "I've just closed the deal to acquire Beatrice."

Meily dropped what he was doing and caught a cab to Lewis's house. "He was grinning from ear to ear and he was on the phone the whole time and he had this champagne he was drinking," Meily recalls. "He was laughing all the time and he was just really very, very happy, very pleased. He was in shirt sleeves, with his sleeves rolled up. He was half boozed up and just really happy."

Between phone calls, Lewis gave Meily the details of the acquisition and Meily started drafting a press release. Lewis asked what was the best way to break the news. The strategy Meily came up with solidified his standing with Lewis and paved the way for him to eventually become Beatrice's spokesperson.

Lewis wanted the focus of the Beatrice acquisition to be on him, not KKR or Henry Kravis or even Beatrice. And the focus was to be on the business aspects of the deal, not his background. "This is a success story due to the transaction, not because of my race," he told Meily. "Iacocca is not cast as an Italian-American businessman and Icahn is not a Jewish-American. Why should I be an African-American?"

Another concern of Lewis's was that Meily's employer, Burson-Marsteller, might put a spin on the story that made Beatrice the central focus. "Reg kept complaining that we had this corporate bias and he wasn't going to get any of his fair share of the publicity," Meily says. Lewis and the public relations people at Beatrice agreed that news of his acquisition would be released on Monday, August 10, 1987.

Meily suggested that Lewis also give the story to a select few news organizations, provided they would agree to hold the story over the weekend and run it Monday. Lewis liked that plan of action. He would have more control that way, instead of seeing his story haphazardly dissected and interpreted during a media feeding frenzy. So he and Meily decided to give the story to a handful of reporters—the *New York Times*, *The Wall Street Journal*, and *Financial Times*—the following day, which was Friday. The scribes would have to agree to sit on their exclusive for two days.

The next morning, Friday at 7 A.M., Lewis caught a flight from Manhattan to Chicago to address the top executives of Beatrice. Kevin Wright flew out to Chicago with him.

As the two men rode to LaGuardia Airport for their flight, past Flushing Bay and Shea Stadium, Lewis reflected that this might be one of the last times he would have to deal with a commercial flight. Beatrice had a corporate jet fleet and Lewis had tried unsuccessfully to have one of the aircraft included in his deal. Forever rushing, Lewis hated the lines and queues that typically form in busy airports. When confronted with a long line at an airport, theater, or ballpark, Lewis dealt with them by traveling along "Route 99." When he asked his family members, "Shall we do a Route 99?" what he really meant was, "Let's go to the head of the line." Lewis had the moxie to pretend to know the person at or near the front of the line. Sometimes, he wouldn't even bother with that charade.

In the near future, Lewis promised himself, he would pull a permanent Route 99 on queues near airport x-ray machines and metal detectors, distancing himself from the jostling and bumping that takes place near reservation counters, elbow-to-elbow flights on crowded jetliners and waits for in-flight service, by buying his own airplane.

Once he and Wright boarded their plane and settled into their seats in first class, Lewis looked out the window as the ground began to slowly recede away from the jet, taking New York City and the scene of his greatest business triumph with it. Flying seemed a most appropriate activity to be engaged in, given that his mood was still somewhere in the clouds.

Once the airliner reached cruising altitude and the seatbelt sign turned off, Lewis reached into his briefcase and took out a Beatrice annual report. Time to brush up on Beatrice one more time before talking to the company's top brass. After a moment or two, a thought raced through Lewis's head. He looked up from his annual report and turned

to face Kevin Wright. "All right, Kevin, what do you think my alternatives are in this deal? What do you think my strategy should be?"

"Well, Reg, I think you've got a lot of options."

Lewis shot Wright a look as though the younger man had lost his
mind. "No I don't," he replied. "I've got to sell assets and pay down
the acquisition debt." With that, Lewis turned back to his annual
report.

The meeting in Chicago went exceptionally well, with Lewis effectively allaying concerns that massive change and upheaval were in the
offing. It was a happy, but weary, Reginald Lewis who flew back to
New York.

The following day, Saturday, he went to 99 Wall Street to take care
of some minor business matters. Then Lewis had his driver take him to
Kennedy International Airport for his Concorde flight. The interview
with the *Financial Times* reporter was conducted in the back seat of
Lewis's car as Lewis rushed to the airport. The reporter who talked to
Lewis, James Buchan, was impressed by the fact Lewis didn't appear
to be under any stress or strain even though he was sure the Concorde
was about to take off without him. The interview went well and Lewis
dashed from the back seat of his chauffeur-driven car, into the airport
and through customs, then off to France.

The interviews with the *New York Times* and *The Wall Street Journal*
took place by phone while Lewis was in Castellaras in the South of
France where he and his family had a villa that came with an absolutely masterful chef and had a balcony offering a breathtaking view of
the French countryside.

The three exclusive interviews given by Lewis all ran on Monday,
kicking off a firestorm of interest in this mystery financier and his
background. Financial reporters across the country were hearing the
same question from their editors: "Why did we miss this story?" In their
frantic push to play catch up, some even managed to get the phone
number of Lewis's mother in Baltimore.

"The news media were sickening, really sickening," Carolyn Fugett
says, sounding suspiciously like her son. "The media always like to
find something wrong. They wanted to know if somebody was behind
him—it's very hard for people to realize that he had this ability to
think and to accomplish. 'Could it be true that this man did this on
his own? Could it be true that he could think this well? Could it be

true that he came from the ghetto?' He didn't come from the ghetto, he came from my home."

Beatrice was upset over all the news coverage Lewis got, feeling that he had broken his agreement to release the news on Monday. Christophe assured them that TLC had done exactly as they had agreed: The three exclusive stories focusing on Lewis were all released on Monday, weren't they? Anyway, Meily had tried to call Beatrice's PR people on Friday, but they were working a half-day schedule that summer and were out of the office. Christophe called Lewis in France wanting to know if the deal might be in jeopardy because of the publicity, a notion Lewis scoffed at.

"With McCall, basically we tried to do that deal in secret until we knew that it was going to be a success," Kevin Wright says. "Here, Reg had gone the other way and decided to shape the news rather than have it shaped for him."

At least one black man was furious to learn of the acquisition and of the prominence it bestowed upon Reginald Lewis and that was John Johnson, the owner of Chicago-based Johnson Publishing Co. Prior to Lewis's McCall acquisition, Johnson had run the largest African-American-owned enterprise in the United States and had become accustomed to his annual perch atop *Black Enterprise* magazine's list of major African-American-owned companies. But now, with revenues just surpassing $200 million annually, Johnson was a very distant second on the list to Beatrice, which had $2.5 billion in revenue in 1987.

Johnson viewed Meily and Burson-Marsteller as media manipulators who had conspired to demote him, and he made several sulfuric phone calls to Burson's offices accusing the firm of being part of an evil cabal out to get him. "I'm like a woman scorned," Johnson ranted at one of Meily's assistants on one occasion, reducing the young woman to tears. "He complained to Reg about us and Reg kept asking me about it," Meily says. "Reg several times tried to make peace with him. Our goal wasn't being No. 1 on the *Black Enterprise* list—our target was the mainstream financial community."

Johnson's pique seems to have lingered. To this day, his magazine, *Ebony*, has never mentioned Reginald Lewis.

Elated when he left the United States, Lewis became subdued and introspective after reaching the South of France. He was experiencing a palpable letdown following a prolonged and very pleasurable emotional rush. During the seven days he was in the French villa, Lewis was quiet and contemplative around his wife and children when he wasn't playing tennis or reading. Part of his downswing was undoubtedly due to exhaustion, but Lewis also went through a similar phase after winning the right to purchase McCall.

While I was in the South of France, all hell broke loose in the United States. I remember calling Dick Beattie, who was KKR's long-time counsel, and he said, "You're the talk of the town, Reg." Time magazine reached me in the South of France. The guy was a real jerk, so I hung up on him. Wouldn't talk to Fortune *because all they wanted to do was focus on the racial aspects of this, which were totally irrelevant to anything we were doing. But it was generating a lot of excitement.*

Butch Meily had received a green light to give reporters from certain national publications Lewis's phone number in the South of France. After having reached Lewis, who had just consummated one of the most noteworthy business deals of the year, the first question the writer from *Time* magazine asked was, "What's it like growing up in the ghetto?" Not only was the question preposterous and totally inappropriate, it was a stereotype that had no relevance to Lewis.

Lewis looked at the telephone receiver in disbelief. "What the fuck!" he bellowed, slamming the phone down. "I'm not going to have this," he growled inside his rented chateau. "This is not a minority deal or an affirmative action deal. This is a business deal and it required a great deal of effort and it's beyond color."

People have spent a lot of time trying to locate the wellspring of Lewis's unstinting drive and determination to succeed. Basically, every time he faced a snub he knew was based on race, it added another log to the flames of his fierce ambition. Every unanswered phone call, every naysayer, every pundit questioning whether Lewis was really just a front for a white man motivated him even more.

Although Lewis was far too complex to ascribe his powerful drive just to one factor, his reaction to racism was unquestionably a major component in his incredible journey to the boardroom of Beatrice.

Lewis possessed a powerful antenna for detecting slights centering on pigmentation. To nonblack readers it may seem that Lewis was a hypersensitive black man with a chip on his shoulder, constantly in search of insults real or imagined. However black males who have been shadowed by store clerks or wondered if only black males are into narcotics and commit heinous crimes—judging from television and newspaper coverage—can empathize with Lewis's take on the world.

The simple fact is that even after Lewis's incredible journey from the streets of East Baltimore to the pinnacle of business success, many whites simply did not want to believe he was genuinely responsible. And that rankled Lewis and made him even more defensive, sensitive, and more motivated to achieve.

"People that know I had a long and close relationship with Reg would say stupid things to me," says business associate Tom Lamia, who is white. "'Well, he didn't really do it. He's a token. Somebody must have handed it to him.' The assumption is he couldn't do it on his own, which is a lot of bullshit. He did it on his own and it's hard for people to believe that."

Time assigned another writer to the story who had the common sense to ask business questions. The piece that ran noted "the TLC chairman feels uncomfortable with being portrayed as a pinstripe Jackie Robinson. Says Lewis, 'It is wrong to focus on being the first black to do something.'"

The article continued, "Though Lewis may want to be thought of as just another tycoon, he is also an inspirational symbol—the first black businessman to gain full access to the giant pools of capital on Wall Street."

Feeling somewhat rested after a few days in the South of France, the next major thing on Lewis's agenda was discussions with a Canadian buyout group, Onex, that was interested in Beatrice's Canada division.

I came back to the United States and tried to tie the deal down with Onex. I sort of delegated that to Cleve Christophe. John Sheehy introduced Onex to us. Our first major screw-up was that I had bid the deal after asking Cleve Christophe what kind of cash did the Canadian business have. He said $10 million. It turned out they had $40 million. So I had to get involved personally with the Onex people and we split the $30-million difference on the cash. And we kept 20 percent. But it was my first realization that my team was not as disciplined as it should have been. And it was also the beginning, I think, of sort of a mini-falling out with Christophe. At that point,

I relegated him to purely administrative type stuff, which he did admirably. But in terms of all the major policy decisions, he was out at that point, because as far as I was concerned, he had cost me $15 million.

Christophe, who kept several spiral ring notebooks of notes from his days with Reginald Lewis and TLC Beatrice, doesn't dispute that he was associated with a major miscalculation on the Canadian assets. He claims the miscalculation occurred because Lewis was rushing to do the Canadian transaction quickly without first conducting adequate due diligence.

Whatever transpired, it's doubtful that anyone other than a very, very close friend of Lewis's could have remained in his employ after being linked to a transaction that lost Reginald Lewis millions of dollars.

"Reg had always introduced me as his partner," Christophe recalls. "That changed after about three months." There could only be one boss in an organization headed by Reginald Lewis, as Christophe was to painfully discover. That reality led to the spectacular disintegration of a friendship that had been nurtured and fortified over 17 years.

Because of the Onex deal, the once tight relationship between Lewis and Christophe was coming apart at the seams, but Lewis had far more pressing matters to deal with than the disintegration of an old friendship.

He was moving rapidly to get the Beatrice deal closed. A contract to sell the Canadian assets for $235 million was put together in August 1987, the same month Lewis won the bid for Beatrice. A contract to sell the company's operating unit in Australia for $105 million was also put together that month. Thus far, Lewis's strategy of selling assets to help decrease the actual amount of money he would need to buy Beatrice appeared to be working brilliantly.

Lewis would be called on to jet around the world to conduct due diligence at various Beatrice operating units. The constant grind of flights and international negotiating sessions was made somewhat easier by the fact that Lewis temporarily had Beatrice's corporate jet at his disposal. But it was still an incredible physical grind that wore down his travel companions and, to a lesser degree, Lewis too.

But first came the task of finding a new quarterback to take care of the nuts and bolts of the complicated transaction, following the unceremonious benching of Christophe.

11

International Headaches and Domestic Roadblocks

In order to come up with the financing for Lewis to purchase Beatrice, Drexel, Burnham, Lambert had to create a private placement memorandum that would be given to potential investors. The aim of the memorandum, which had to be finished by the end of August 1987, was to sell $340 million in preferred stock as well as debt notes.

The private placement was about three weeks late getting to Drexel, a fact that was driving Lewis up a wall. Did he have to manage every phase of this deal to make sure that things got done right? He was a perfectionist who wanted things done correctly, but at times it seemed he was the only one who felt that way. So it was a supremely irritated Lewis who read the riot act to his staff at 99 Wall Street. The memorandum was due three weeks before and it was critical to getting the Beatrice deal done! Whatever the problem was, Lewis wanted them to fix it and fix it *fast*. Lewis laid down an edict that the memorandum had to be finished in 24 hours.

Satisfied that he'd addressed the issue and assuming it was in good hands, Lewis was out-of-pocket the next two days. But decisions still had to be made on how the book should be put together and what information about Beatrice and TLC should be included. Christophe figured that since he was Lewis's partner, he'd make the call. "I had been up for 48 hours trying to get this book out, so Drexel could get started, in effect," Christophe says. "Reg disappeared on me for those 48 hours and there were some critical decisions that had to be made, and I made them."

After two days without sleep, Christophe went to his home in Connecticut and went directly to bed at 2 o'clock in the morning. At 4 o'clock, the phone beside his bed was ringing.

"Who in the hell do you think you are?" Lewis's voice boomed across the telephone line.

"You know goddamn well who I am," Christophe answered sleepily.

"Where do you get off making these decisions?" Lewis demanded. "Who gave you the authority to make these decisions? Who in the hell do you think you are?"

"Because they had to be made and you were no place around," Christophe shot back in a loud, abrupt voice. There was a momentary silence on the other end.

"Who in the hell are you yelling at?" Lewis screamed.

"The same crazy son-of-a-bitch that's yelling at me," Christophe screamed back.

Then and there, Lewis decided to appoint a new quarterback to direct the complicated Beatrice transaction.

Four hours after his heated Sunday morning conversation, Lewis placed a phone call to Maine, to the lawyer who had helped shepherd through the McCall deal for Lewis—Tom Lamia. It was time to take Lamia, who was in Maine on vacation, out of deep freeze.

"I'm having some problems with my team and I want you to do what you did before, which is be my quarterback," Lewis said. Lamia shelved the rest of his vacation and left Maine that night for New York. The following morning Lewis came into 99 Wall Street around 7:30 A.M. He ignored Christophe, who was already at work, went into his office and slammed the door. Lamia arrived about an hour later and the two of them could be seen engrossed in animated conversation.

Sometime later, Lewis's secretary, Deidra Wilson, called Christophe, Kevin Wright, and Charles Clarkson into Lewis's office for a meeting. Lamia was already present.

"We've really come a long way," Lewis said once everyone was present. As was his custom, Lewis was wearing his suit jacket and his shirt was buttoned all the way to the top. Rather than loosen his tie,

Lewis preferred to leave it tightly knotted. His sleeves were down, too, with his gold cufflinks in place and fastened. "This is tough duty, this is emotionally demanding duty," Lewis continued, speaking deliberately. "I've had some time this weekend to kind of reflect on how we're proceeding. I'm quite frankly getting a little concerned that some of us may be working too hard. And for that reason, I think maybe we need to make a few changes."

Lewis paused momentarily to let his words sink in.

"One of the changes that I'm going to make is, Cleve, I want you to step back from some of the things that you're handling. I really think that you are getting overextended. And I'm going to ask Tom to pick up responsibility for putting together the bank syndicate." The meeting was handled in vintage Reginald Lewis style. He had an objective to pursue and intended to keep his eye on the ball, no matter what. He tried to patch things over with Christophe later, but not until the Beatrice transaction had closed. Lewis had an amazing ability to filter out distractions and maintain a clear picture of what he wanted to accomplish, keeping his priorities well-defined.

Christophe made up his mind that after the Beatrice transaction was closed, he was history. "We were like the atom," Christophe says of himself and Lewis. "When we came apart, we came apart."

INTERNATIONAL TROUBLE SHOOTER

With sales contracts agreed upon for Beatrice's units in Canada and Australia, and the work on the Drexel private placement memorandum now finished, the Beatrice deal was getting back on track. There remained a problem in Spain with the Ballve family, which co-owned a Beatrice meat packing facility there. Pedro Ballve was essentially claiming that Lewis's purchase of Beatrice violated an agreement that Ballve had signed with the company. The upshot of Ballve's argument was that he should be able to buy 100 percent of the company, and at a price lower than the $90 million Lewis was demanding.

The next thing was there was an extensive negotiation with Pedro Ballve and he ended up paying my price of $90 million. And there was an extensive negotiation with Cadbury Schweppes out of

Australia, where they ended up paying us $105 million. We really were right on target. All these were done by September of 1987, because we were hoping to close the deal in October.

Before he was able to close the deal with Ballve, Lewis had to have a face-to-face meeting with him. Since France and Italy were also problem spots, Lewis went to Spain, France, Italy, and Brussels over the course of a whirlwind, four-day trip. Lewis flew to Europe in one of Beatrice's jets, the first time he'd ever been in a corporate aircraft. He was accompanied by Bill Mowry, the president of Beatrice; Tom Lamia; and Butch Meily. The trip over was a pleasant one and their plane landed in Paris at 2 o'clock in the morning.

In addition to his formidable intellect and determination, one of the things that made Lewis so successful was incredible stamina. Meily and Lamia were dog tired, but Lewis insisted on holding a meeting in the lobby of the Intercontinental Hotel in Paris as soon as they arrived.

From Paris they flew directly to Barcelona, where they were supposed to meet with Pedro Ballve in a fancy Spanish restaurant. The Beatrice executive for southern Europe greeted them at Barcelona's airport. They piled into his car for the trip into the city, but got lost because the manager couldn't find the restaurant. Lewis was disgusted by the sorry display—the manager had plenty of time to find out where the restaurant was located, rather than waste Lewis's time looking for it now. Lewis prided himself on his thorough preparation. If this executive couldn't even find a restaurant on his home turf, how could Lewis trust him to look out for the best interests of Beatrice in southern Europe? Lewis made a mental note that afternoon to fire the man after the Beatrice acquisition closed.

The initial talk with Ballve was cordial, but inconclusive. Butch Meily was so fatigued that he kept drifting to sleep in the middle of the dinner. Several times he awoke to find the other dinner participants looking at him with bemused expressions, including Lewis.

Ballve later flew to New York in September and met with Lewis at the Harvard Club, where they arrived at an agreement for Beatrice to sell its Spanish meat packing facility to Ballve for $90 million. Lewis had simply used the calendar as an ally to wear down Ballve: As the deadline to close the deal drew nearer and nearer, it became obvious to Ballve that Lewis might sell the company to somebody else. Ballve's father had founded Campofrio and it was his dream to buy it back for the family.

After Lewis left Barcelona, the next stop on his itinerary was Verona, Italy, for a visit with the most nettlesome shareholder of all, Teofilo Sanson, who owned 30 percent of a Beatrice ice cream company in Italy, Gelati Sanson. Sanson took the extraordinary step of filing a lawsuit against Beatrice in an Italian court, which froze the shares in Gelati Sanson owned by Beatrice until the matter could be resolved.

"I never saw Reg treated so poorly as in Verona," Lamia says. "Signor Sanson was and is a character." Sanson is a populist who is a tough businessman and who had built his business from scratch. Two young, elegant women, who happened to be Sanson's daughters, acted as interpreters.

Lewis's goal was simply to arrive at a mutually beneficial agreement with Sanson. What transpired was a very tense, uncomfortable meeting for all involved.

Throughout most of the dinner, Sanson gave Lewis the cold shoulder and had little to say. When he did utter something, his comments were usually brusque to the point of being rude. Sanson's daughters appeared quite uncomfortable at having to translate the remarks of their crusty, irascible father into English.

The gist of Sanson's position was that Lewis was a leveraged buyout artist who was going to pledge all of Beatrice's assets to get the financing to buy the company. Therefore, the company would no longer enjoy the financial strength it had, meaning Sanson wouldn't have the same capital expenditure budget he'd enjoyed in the past.

Naturally Lewis didn't take kindly to Sanson's behavior, but he remained calm and charming and kept his eye firmly fixed on the overall objective. He was out to close a deal for all of Beatrice's international operations, not get into a test of wills with the minority owner of one operating unit. He felt he could afford to take the high road and let Sanson be the one who came off as churlish and obstreperous.

Lewis requested a tour of Beatrice's plant in Verona, a request Sanson rejected out of hand. He would not have Lewis and his people trooping through the plant, needlessly scaring workers into thinking a management change was imminent. Lewis found himself in the position of not being able to see an operating unit of a company he was in the process of buying. He had to do an end run around Sanson's intransigence.

Falling back on his formidable powers of persuasion, Lewis talked Sanson into letting him see the Verona plant before leaving Italy. However, Sanson stipulated that Lewis would have to go by himself, leaving behind Meily, Lamia, and the Beatrice executives also present at the dinner. That night, workers at the ice cream facility were probably baffled by the presence of a lone black man taking a leisurely stroll around their plant like some curious sightseer.

An arrangement was later worked out with Sanson that accomplished Lewis's objectives and that Beatrice officials would rather not make public, lest they make waves anew with Signor Sanson.

From Italy, Lewis, Lamia, and Meily flew on to Brussels, for a meeting with the heads of all the Beatrice companies in Europe. The three men shaved, showered, and were on their way to the meeting by 7 A.M. By now, Lamia and Meily were dragging from sheer exhaustion. "It was like I had been run over by a truck," Lamia remembers. "Reg seemed fine. He looked great and had on this new Italian suit. It was a beautiful suit."

Lewis spoke to the Beatrice executives and as usual was quite impressive. That was followed by a trip to Beatrice's bottling plant in Brussels. In the meantime, a major potential problem brewing back in the United States had been brought to Lewis's attention. The tax structure of the Beatrice deal was incredibly intricate and was starting to worry Lewis's team.

With that issue weighing on his mind, Lewis invited Meily up to his room in the Brussels hotel they were staying, in order to rehash the events of the day. Having given a flawless speech to the different operating managers of Beatrice's European companies at an evening cocktail, now Lewis was starting to feel out of sorts. His head was pounding, and Lewis missed his family, a sacrifice his line of work often called for and that Lewis detested. He'd give anything to be able to kiss his girls goodnight, then let Loida massage his temples.

SUCCESS IS THE BEST REVENGE

Feeling better after the terrible headache he'd suffered the previous night, but still feeling under pressure because of the Beatrice transaction, Lewis got up early to prepare for a flight from Brussels to Paris to meet with the Baud family, Beatrice's local partner. From Paris, Lewis would fly back to the United States and deal with the growing crisis over the tax structure of the Beatrice deal.

Tom Lamia, Butch Meily, and Bill Mowry boarded the Beatrice corporate jet with Lewis for the Paris flight. His headache may have been gone, but Lewis was still tightly wound from the pressure and anxiety caused by the transaction. Meily didn't know Lewis well enough at that point to read the mercurial man's moods, and innocuously asked whether Lewis had arranged for transportation from Orly Airport into downtown Paris.

"Why in the hell are you asking me that question?" Lewis yelled, startling his travel companions. "Don't you believe that I have transportation waiting for me there? It's none of your damn business, anyway."

Meily, who no longer had any work to do for Lewis, merely wanted a ride into Paris from the airport. Loida Lewis was waiting at the airport and a preoccupied Lewis had only a word or two of greeting for her before everyone got into a waiting limousine sent by a Parisian friend of the Lewises, Dominique Kanga.

Before he left Paris for the United States, Lewis had a cordial but inconclusive talk with the Baud family, whose Paris-based grocery distribution business Lewis considered important to the success of TLC Beatrice.

Lewis would be back to Paris many times before the deal closed on the December 1 deadline—not because of the Baud family, but because of difficulty in winning French government approval to take over Beatrice's assets in France.

Meanwhile, back in the United States a battalion of due diligence accountants and lawyers had to be assembled to assault Beatrice's Chicago headquarters, unlike the preliminary initial effort. Most of the financial documents and agreements that would give Lewis an accurate financial picture of Beatrice International were located in a document room in Chicago. Cleve Christophe was put in charge of assembling a group of lawyers and accountants to handle the due diligence responsibilities.

Poring over box after box of documents isn't particularly glamorous or exciting, but it's critical and absolutely essential work. It can reveal unexpected problems with the assets being purchased. Lewis wanted the work to be done and he wanted a full complement of people to do it. He also wanted people who would create the right aura, who would convey a sense of professionalism. The due diligence mission would be the first time many Beatrice executives encountered anyone associated with Reginald Lewis.

However, his frugal side didn't want to pay a lot of money for a due diligence effort. So three days before the second wave was to hit Chicago, Lewis's team still wasn't assembled. "Why don't we overwhelm them with our strength—why don't you hire a whole bunch of actors?" Lewis said to Christophe one day, tongue firmly in cheek.

The due diligence effort did turn up previously unrevealed problems with Beatrice, specifically that extensive litigation had been filed against some operating units.

"Henry Kravis knows that the fair thing to do is give me a $10 million reduction in the price," Lewis told his wife one day as they were being driven home in Manhattan. "I'm telling Kravis, 'If you don't give me this discount—which is the only fair thing to do—I'll walk away from the deal.'"

Loida Lewis thought about that briefly, then offered this advice, "Darling, you have to pay a premium. You're going through the door for the first time on this one, so to speak. This is your first transaction of this magnitude."

But that wasn't what Lewis wanted to hear at the moment. "Why do you say that?" he barked. "You don't know anything! You don't know whether I can close this deal or not!"

"I don't know the deal, darling," Loida Lewis replied, "but I know you. You will do it."

Her husband was quiet after that.

Years afterward, Loida Lewis would ask rhetorically, "Would Henry Kravis run after him and say, 'No, no, no, please don't walk away—we'll do it at a reduced price?'"

"Success is the best revenge," Loida Lewis says.

BATTLING THE BEAR: THE STOCK MARKET SCARE OF 1987

If Lewis or his acquisition team had any illusions about their ability to control the events shaping and guiding the Beatrice deal, that conceit was blown away on October 16, 1987, a Friday. The Dow Jones industrial average sank 108 points that day, triggering concern on Wall Street and worldwide.

But the stock market wasn't finished. It went through an even wilder gyration the following Monday, October 19, as the Dow sank a terrifying 508 additional points. Privately, Lewis was as concerned as anyone else—if not more so—because he stood to lose millions of dollars if the economic climate suddenly destabilized. But he could not afford to be viewed as nervous or panicky in front of his acquisition team, because those emotions might spread like wildfire. So an outwardly confident Lewis continued to push ahead, giving no hint he believed the Beatrice deal would do anything but close on time.

By this time the transaction had picked up so much momentum that it seemed to have a life of its own that nothing could disrupt or throw off course.

In one important regard Lewis viewed the stock market drop as fortuitous. Now he could play hardball with Henry Kravis and demand that the price for Beatrice International be reduced. "King Henry," as Lewis was fond of calling Kravis, would simply have to come down on the price or Lewis would pick up his marbles and leave. A few weeks earlier he had backed down on seeking a cut in price because of undisclosed litigation Beatrice was involved with.

This time, Lewis fully intended to state his case before Kravis. The stock market crash called for at least a $25 million to $50 million reduction in Beatrice's price, and that's what Lewis intended to ask for. The Dow had fallen more than 500 points; enormous amounts of value had been wiped out. The request seemed perfectly logical from a business standpoint.

A meeting was set with Kravis at his KKR offices. Tom Lamia, Cleve Christophe, and Everett Grant were in the limousine that took Lewis from 99 Wall Street to see Kravis.

"If he doesn't do it, I'm walking," Lewis said to no one in particular. "I'm not in this for my health—I'll take my lumps and walk." Lewis and his business partners got out of the limousine at 9 West 57th Street, the site of KKR's offices. One day the headquarters of TLC Beatrice International Holdings, Inc. would be located in the same building—several floors above Kravis's.

Lewis was ushered into a meeting room at KKR. Also present were Leon Black and Dean Kehler of Drexel. Kravis was the last to arrive. In a calm and thoughtful manner, Lewis began telling Kravis that he was charging too much for Beatrice in light of the stock market stumble.

Therefore, "an appropriate adjustment would be in order," namely a price reduction of roughly $35 million, Lewis said.

In an equally calm and thoughtful manner, Kravis adopted a hardline approach. "Drexel has given us a letter in which they said they will get this done," Kravis said. "We expect them to get this done." Then Kravis asked Lewis if they could continue their conversation in Kravis's office.

"We appreciate your views on the matter," Kravis said quietly after closing the door to his office. "We've done our analysis and we don't quite get there the same way you do. We've really come a long way on this and we'd really like to see you consummate this deal. We're pulling for you."

"King Henry" had spoken: The price was to remain unchanged.

With the situation unchanged from when Lewis came over to see Kravis, he left. Lewis was ticked off and felt that he was being mistreated, not to mention that KKR and Kravis weren't doing the proper thing. Lewis gave some more thought about whether to actually pull out, as he had been privately threatening to do, but decided against it.

"I would have expected them to reduce the price by $25 million at the very least—that's what we were talking about to keep the deal together," Tom Lamia says. "But no, they didn't budge one inch."

Ultimately, the price reduction issue wasn't a dealbreaker from Lewis's point of view. He should have been granted his price cut, but Lewis knew that he would lose the deal if he insisted.

His meeting with Kravis took place on Thanksgiving weekend. The deadline for closing the deal—December 1—was fast approaching.

With the tension mounting exponentially with each passing day, Lewis was spending a fair amount of his time at 99 Wall Street inside his office with the door closed. "He was calm under pressure and thought well under pressure," Tom Lamia recalls. "He didn't let the little things get in the way and he was able to focus on the right things."

Away from the office, Lewis was dealing with the tension by popping movies into his VCR, or by going to classical music concerts. His favorite movie during the Beatrice negotiations was "Chato's Land," a Western featuring Charles Bronson as a half-breed being hunted down by a posse for killing a drunken man. Bronson gunned down each of the twelve posse members one by one—perhaps Lewis saw the movie as a metaphor for what he was going through in trying to get the Beatrice deal done.

GALLIC ROADBLOCK

The Beatrice transaction could have closed as early as late October 1987. The holdup was due to a problem Lewis was having with France, where his European headquarters would be based and where most of his operations would be located.

Lewis had to find a way to get the interest on the acquisition debt deductible in France, because a lot of the income to be generated in France was taxable there. So it was critical that Lewis be able to set up a French holding company, which would be the borrower and would pay the interest. In addition, the holding company had to be able to upstream income from the French operating companies, use that money to pay interest and have those interest payments deductible for French income tax purposes.

The only problem was, the French government had to give its approval, and the French weren't cooperating. The lack of cooperation was partially a function of chauvinism, because one of the unsuccessful bidders in the auction for Beatrice's international foods business had been Bon Grain, a French company.

For a time, Lewis practically lived at the Crillon Hotel in Paris as he waited for the French to act. Lewis's last day for gaining approval from the French was November 30, or he would have to scuttle the entire Beatrice transaction.

We had a big legal issue with the structure because we needed approval in France from its Ministry of Finance. Everybody thought it was going to be simple, but it got complicated. I had to make several trips to France to meet with its Finance Minister (Edouard Balladur, now Prime Minister of France). I was really shuttling for a while. Finally, I got to see the Minister's first deputy, Charles Dequase, and I looked him dead in the eye and said, "This delay is costing me $6 million." He was shocked, of course—that was about 30 million French francs. The next day we got the approval.

The green light from the French government came on November 28, just two days before the deadline.

The approval didn't come a moment too soon. The pace of the entire Beatrice deal had slowed down while everyone cooled their heels waiting for a final determination from the French. Also, putting the divestiture sales on hold for nearly a month had started to cause problems, too.

The senior management at Cadbury Schweppes, for example, had come to the conclusion they were paying Lewis too much for the Australian operations. So Lewis was told that up until December 1 Cadbury Schweppes would pay the agreed upon price. After that, all bets were off.

"There could not have been any greater pressure in any deal Reg ever did," Tom Lamia says of the French negotiations. "I think it was only when he got French government approval that he saw that the Beatrice deal was going to be done."

In the meantime, we also had to do a multicity road show to finalize the debt offering. We went to Los Angeles, Chicago, Boston, Minneapolis, New York, and Philadelphia to sell the debt notes, which struck me as kind of odd, since I think Peter Ackerman had once told me that he had sold the damn debt in a phone booth, between Columbia Savings, First Executive, and a few others. Most of the debt was taken by that, but they still wanted to do the road show, which I think was probably for some sort of after-market in the debt paper.

The lead bank basically was good but was a little bit of a pain in the ass. They were trying to insist that they had control over what I would sell and what I would keep. Christophe said they weren't going to change. I told them that we weren't going to do a deal. I just said, "Absolutely not!" They wanted to list all the assets that we had and select from it. Under no circumstance would I agree to that, and they finally caved in on that point. There were a number of other points that they didn't cave in on that hurt us— we should have been able to take out some of the higher cost debt before we paid them off entirely. But by and large they hung in: banks can be banks. In any case, that basically concluded the financing. When we got the French approval, everything was in place.

12

Bravura and Brinksmanship: Closing the Beatrice Acquisition

November 29, 1987 was a Sunday, the day before the Beatrice closing was scheduled to commence. Lewis, Tom Lamia, Cleve Christophe, and Everett Grant met at 99 Wall Street for a final preclosing briefing.

Lewis conducted a lengthy review to make sure everything was proceeding as planned on the Beatrice acquisition. He wanted to make sure that his team had everything in order, specifically regarding what was to take place during the closing, as well as the postclosing strategies they would pursue. "The real work will begin once the deal has closed," Lewis repeatedly informed his bundled up lieutenants. Something was wrong with the heating system at 99 Wall Street that weekend, putting a distinct chill in the air inside Lewis & Clarkson.

Meanwhile, activity related to the Beatrice closing was also underway that Sunday at the closing site, the offices of the Paul, Weiss law firm at 1285 Avenue of the Americas. Lawyers were busily going through the conference rooms where the closing was to take place and laying out tons of documents in accordance to the activity scheduled to take place in that particular room.

The goal was to make sure that all of the documents were in place so there wouldn't be any surprises when the closing got underway the following two days.

CLOSING BEATRICE: DAY ONE

The closing of the Beatrice transaction was a draining, grueling affair that officially started November 30, lasted two days, and was played out in the Manhattan offices of the Paul, Weiss law firm. There were plots, subplots, things that came together smoothly, and things that had to be glued together by roughly 180 lawyers, accountants, financial advisers, and corporate executives working in concert to get the deal closed.

In a figurative sense as well as in a literal sense, the whole process was akin to a byzantine maze: The different teams working on the Beatrice closing were spread out over the 23rd floor of Paul, Weiss, as well as floors 24, 25, 26, 27, and 28. On various floors and in separate conference rooms were the banking team, the equity team, the subordinated debt team, and the divestiture team.

Due to the fact that Lewis was selling three of Beatrice's units—those in Canada, Australia, and the meat packing firm in Spain—the divestiture team was further subdivided into three units, each with its own conference room and concentrating totally on one piece of an immense puzzle.

Of the various conference rooms, the one set aside for the bank people was the biggest, because their transactions generated the most paper.

There was also a conference room designated for the acquisition team, which was concerned with the purchase of the shares of the various companies being bought and sold, including Beatrice.

Because each party had its own high-powered legal counsel, attorneys from a number of prestigious Manhattan law firms were also involved.

Through a process of transactional natural selection, each conference room broke down into cells of people working on a different aspect of the particular transaction closing in that room. For example, there were people working on a legal opinion seated together at one end of the table going over some documents.

Others would be on telephones dealing with some condition to their closing, and there were periodic conference calls with people who weren't present but who were responsible for advising a client on an issue.

So in each conference room there were typically four or five little meetings taking place at any given time, with the sound of several voices going at once creating a hum in the air.

Most of the people in the rooms were white men, wearing white or blue dress shirts, ties loosened in many instances, shirt sleeves rolled up. Monograms adorned many of the shirt cuffs not rolled up. It was a safe bet that the guys with the suspenders were investment bankers, since they tend to be partial to that fashion accoutrement. And each room had many Italian suits costing $1,000 and flashy pairs of $500 shoes.

Practically no one smoked in the conference rooms and when someone did light up, it was usually a very expensive, very large, odiferous cigar.

Down in the basement of the building, copy machines were running nonstop, as were secretaries hauling documents up and down the elevators on their way to and from floors 23 through 28. To say there was a sense of urgency in the air would be overstating things slightly—a sense of purposefulness would be more accurate. Millions of dollars were at stake.

On the second floor, typists worked around the clock to churn out documents, because as the lawyers and accountants and businesspeople moved closer to closing, they invariably found it necessary to draft additional agreements to flesh out the structures of various deals.

The best way to generate a mental snapshot of something as unwieldy and complex as the TLC Beatrice closing is to view it as a series of hundreds of mini-closings. When every one of those smaller transactions was completed and the banks were finished wiring their funds, only then would the overall deal "close." To get the smaller deals closed, thousands of conditions had to be met to the satisfaction of parties on both sides of the transactions.

Thousands of documents also had to be in place and ready to be signed, which is why a pre-closing team had located the majority of the germane documents and laid them out in the appropriate closing room. To mention just a few, there were certificates of good standing, certificates of incorporation, certificates from state taxing authorities, employment agreements, and corporate contracts. In addition, the various parties typically had opinions of counsel regarding certain legal facts and conclusions.

A tiering of funding events had to take place in a certain order, or else the deal would disintegrate. There were closing activities geared toward bank financing, divestitures, and tax planning.

Canadian bankers were present to represent Onex, which had to turn over its funding in order to acquire Beatrice's Canadian operations. Australian bankers were at Paul, Weiss to handle matters associated with the Australian asset sale, Spanish financial advisers were present, and so on.

From the first hour of the closing until the last, many of the banks that were funding various pieces of the Beatrice transaction started exerting pressure to get the deal closed quickly. Each bank had earmarked several million dollars to fund various pieces of the Beatrice deal. Several million dollars sitting around idle for even one day represents a significant loss, because that money could be generating interest and making more money. So bank representatives were concerned about the cutoff points at which they could invest their idle fund balances, and were threatening to pull their money out and invest it overnight if their part of the transaction failed to close on the first day.

If even one bank had broken ranks and followed through on their threats, the closing would have been derailed.

Lewis never went to the Paul, Weiss offices on November 30, the first day of the closing. Instead he divided his time between his brownstone on 22nd Street and his office at 99 Wall Street. Lewis was busy working out postclosing strategies for Beatrice, specifically future divestitures he planned to pursue in order to take care of debt service. Periodically he would pick up the phone and quiz Tom Lamia on the progress of the closing, mirroring the roles they played when Lewis acquired McCall.

Being away from the transactional maelstrom at Paul, Weiss freed Lewis to keep his eye focused on the big picture, instead of getting caught up with the niggling issues and details that were being spun off at a furious pace.

If any matter called for Lewis's immediate attention, Lamia knew where to reach him. That was Lamia and Christophe's job.

The fact that TLC Beatrice International was a holding company was causing problems for some of the banks. TLC Beatrice had no assets per se, just shares of stock that it owned in its subsidiaries. But the banks wanted collateral and the only meaningful collateral would be pledges of the shares of stocks in companies scattered around the world after some of the operating units were sold off.

So Kevin Wright had to get lawyers located around the globe, as well as bank lawyers and Beatrice lawyers to agree on what was necessary to give a bank an effective pledge in scores of different sovereignties with different laws. Arriving at a satisfying answer "was a nightmare," Wright says. Because of all the collateral packages involved, the bank deal was the last part of the closing to coalesce.

By the end of November 30, most of the transaction documents had been signed, and the deal was more than 50 percent closed. Everyone, including Lewis, went home with the knowledge that barring some unforeseen, truly extraordinary circumstance, the wire transfer should be able to take place the following day.

A SKIRMISH, FALSE ALARM, PAY DIRT!

On the morning of December 1, Lewis's do-or-die date to get the Beatrice transaction done, one major piece of unfinished business remained that—to Lewis's way of thinking—was worth about $10 million or so. Rush-hour traffic was in full swing as Lewis's limousine glided through the streets of Manhattan, toward 9 W. 57th Street and the offices of Henry Kravis around 8 o'clock in the morning.

Lewis felt that the Italian litigation that had been filed October 30 and effectively tied up Beatrice's shares of Gelati Sanson, the Italian ice cream division, was a significant legal problem that hadn't been disclosed during the due diligence process. Consequently, Lewis felt he was entitled to a price reduction of $10 million, and felt Kravis was morally bound to grant it.

In fact, KKR had been resisting the reduction, which upset Lewis to no end. As he had done right after the stock market earthquake in October, Lewis planned to meet one-on-one with Kravis in an attempt to ratchet down the price of Beatrice's international operations.

But Kravis was cognizant that the Beatrice transaction was a high-profile deal and that Lewis was fully committed to getting it done. Plus

Lewis was on the hook for several million dollars in closing costs, so with or without a price adjustment, the odds were that Lewis would go through with the deal.

So Kravis again stuck to his guns, insisting that the agreed-upon price be adhered to. And as before, Lewis capitulated, feeling that discretion was the better part of valor.

"Plus or minus 5 percent on a deal isn't going to make it or break it, so there's nothing to be gained by breaking a deal over a less-than-5 percent issue," Lewis told Everett Grant afterward. Which isn't to say that he was happy with what had transpired at Kravis's office, but Lewis wasn't about to let a $10 million difference of opinion scuttle a transaction worth $1 billion.

After leaving Kravis's office, Lewis hopped back into his limousine and directed the driver to take him to Paul, Weiss. It was about 9:00 A.M. On the way to Paul, Weiss, Lewis placed a call on the car phone to get a progress report from Tom Lamia.

Once at Paul, Weiss, Lewis rode the elevator up to the 23rd floor to meet with Lamia and Christophe. Then he briefly walked through several conference rooms to get a sense of how the closing process was progressing.

Once that was ascertained and Lewis felt comfortable with what he was seeing and hearing, he ensconced himself in an out-of-the-way conference room where few people knew where he was, except for Lamia, whom he insisted stay in the room, too. "That made my job much more difficult, because I had to tend to Reg as well as tend to everything else that was going on," Lamia remembers. "But that's the way Reg wanted it, so that's what I was going to do."

On two occasions, Lewis went outside the building and took a stroll around the block, his limousine crawling through the busy streets of New York City about 30 feet behind Lewis, should he suddenly decide to forego his walk. Accustomed to being in control, Lewis hated having to wait around for someone else to dictate his fate to him.

Lamia went with Lewis both times and they talked about Lewis's post-acquisition plans for Beatrice.

Invigorated after his second walk, Lewis was feeling his oats and ready to rejoin his long-running battle with Drexel over his transaction fee. Once he was back in the building, the sound of his raised voice could soon be heard emanating from a corner office as he gave hell to representatives of Drexel, primarily Dean Kehler. Lewis's objective was to get a $7.6 million transaction fee. Drexel's objective was to thwart Lewis. Both sides had been going around and around on the issue for months and with the closing now actually under way, Lewis began pressing his arguments in earnest. Invoking the names of buyout kings Henry Kravis and Ted Forstmann, Lewis threatened to walk away from the deal if he couldn't get what he wanted.

In light of his make-or-break 5 percent rule, Lewis's threat to sink the entire transaction over $7.6 million was probably a bluff. Then again, given that Lewis could be unpredictable, he may have been dead serious.

"I gotta be paid," Lewis bellowed. "Henry Kravis gets paid for his work, Ted Forstmann gets paid for his work. What am I, chicken liver? I gotta be paid for my goddamn work!"

Prior to closing there had been a number of occasions when Tom Lamia and Cleve Christophe had gone to Drexel to hash over the fee issue. At one point, Lewis, Christophe, Lamia, and Leon Black and Dean Kehler came over to 99 Wall Street, where a shouting contest over the fees ensued.

"It was really brinkmanship on Reg's part, right down to the final hour," Christophe says.

Drexel argued that there was an important distinction between what Lewis wanted to do and the princely transaction fees routinely reaped by Kravis and financier Ted Forstmann. Lewis was going to gain control of a billion-dollar company and have almost half of the equity interest after putting up only $15 million of his own money, Drexel said. But when the KKRs and Forstmann Littles came to the table and wound up taking home large deal fees, they had also put substantially greater dollars into play.

But it incensed Lewis that the $7.6 million he was seeking was a mere fraction of what Kravis and Forstmann were making in transaction fees during the 1980s. In the end, Lewis and Drexel arrived at a compromise: Lewis didn't get his cash fee, but he got a considerable amount of Class C preferred stock that he was able to transfer to liquid assets some years later.

But the agreement on Lewis's fee didn't occur until the deal closed. And the deal didn't close until recurring snafus with the bank piece of the transaction was solved. The first indication of a problem initially appeared to be a pleasant surprise.

Two lawyers from Paul, Weiss approached Lewis around 5 P.M. and informed him that the bank closing section of the Beatrice transaction was finished, meaning the entire deal had closed.

There were celebratory handshakes and Paul, Weiss even received a check from Lewis to cover the law firm's legal fee for nearly $2 million.

The only problem was, the deal hadn't closed. There had been a miscommunication between the people working on the bank financing part of the deal and those working with divestitures. As a result, one of the banks involved, Manufacturer's Hanover, was not going to transfer its money until it was satisfied that all of the conditions necessary for the bank closing had been met.

Someone had to wade in the middle of the gigantic mess, put on a detective's hat and find out what the problem was. Since Lamia was running the show, that unenviable task fell to him.

He found out that Manufacturer's law firm simply hadn't read through all of the securities documents that had been prepared in order to perfect Manufacturer's lien. That meant there were hundreds of financing statements and security agreements that would have to be scrutinized on the spot.

Everyone had been under the impression that Manufacturer's law firm had already checked the documents when in fact it hadn't. So Lewis had little choice except to wait for the lawyers to read all of the documents, a herculean task that lasted six hours and went right up to 11 P.M., giving Lewis one hour to spare on the deadline to close the Beatrice transaction or watch it fall apart. The agreement to sell the international food company was only binding on KKR up to midnight!

Lewis was understandably furious at having been told the deal was closed when it wasn't, and at seeing his deadline nearly broken because work that should have been done wasn't, but his fury was mitigated by the realization that the complicated transaction was all but finished. Once Lewis was aware the wire transfer had been confirmed, there were slaps on the back and kind words in the conference room where Lewis and Lamia were. Then Lewis got on a speaker phone and made a speech in which he thanked everyone for their hard work and dedication. He also went to the various closing rooms and personally thanked some of the people working on the closing for their hard work.

"Reg did not like people touching him," Kevin Wright says. "We were walking down Sixth Avenue after leaving the Paul, Weiss offices where we'd signed the contract to buy TLC Beatrice International Foods. I put my arm around his waist and just patted him on the back and he did the same to me, and that was very special. You didn't see that often with Reg."

Just as he had done after closing the McCall transaction and after he had won the bid for Beatrice, Lewis accompanied a small group of his closest advisers to the Harvard Club for celebratory drinks.

Lewis would have to meet a whole new set of requirements that went with being the chairman and CEO of a billion-dollar, multinational company. He was now on an international playing field, which would call for a new level of sophistication on his part. Also, there was much work to do in terms of refinancings and selling off assets.

"He saw a need to rise to the occasion and meet the new challenges that he had inherited, which he did," Everett Grant says.

Going forward, Lewis's strategy was basically to sell off certain operating units and leave himself with a residual core of assets focused on doing business in Europe.

Lewis's tab for investment banking fees, bank fees, and related costs came to $53.5 million.

After the closing, I took a couple of days and I went to Europe. I put together a package of assets for $350 million and offered it to Nestlé and an outfit called Bon Grain, which had been the losing bidder. I offered them a package, which they should have taken because it consisted of the Latin American division and the ice cream division and one or two other small pieces.

Now the idea was to sell that for $350 million, which would have taken out all of our high yield debt right away, before the interest rates kicked in. We would have still been left with a big distribution business of close to $2 billion. But they were smart. They decided they didn't want to do it.

Well now, those businesses would cost a lot more money, $140 million for Latin America alone. But that didn't work, so then I came back and took the family for a short vacation down to St. Thomas. Bill Mowry was able to get the Beatrice plane for me, so that was the *first time I took the family on a private aircraft. St. Thomas was very relaxing. I needed the break.*

When I came back I immediately went to Europe again, spent some time in Chicago and began selling assets like crazy. I started working on my Latin America deal. I ended up getting a huge price, $140 million and $11 million of that came to me personally because of the way the deal had to be structured. So of the $15 million I personally invested, I was able to get $11 million back within about six months. And within nine months, we paid the bank back its entire $260 million in bank financing.

Then we sold a British candy company called Callard & Bowser that had great returns, something like $36 million, to Sir Hector Laing and Bob Clark of United Biscuits. We then started selling the Asian businesses, had extensive negotiations with the Chinese and extensive negotiations with the Japanese, as well as with Singapore and Malaysia. The sale of the Latin American assets was done with Venezuelans (Organizacion Polar). Then we sold our poultry operations to the Brits (Hillsdown Holdings).

Lewis thought the Latin American assets had tremendous potential and wasn't keen on selling them. But due to the difficulty of getting cash out of Latin America and his own need for cash, Lewis pulled the trigger on that deal, a move he regretted afterward. In any event, the Latin American sale brought Beatrice's debt down to comfortable levels.

"There were quite a few discussions about the pros and cons of selling Latin America, although fundamentally Reg always knew that it would have to go," says Everett Grant, who was responsible for structuring the divestiture in such a way that it generated $11.3 million for Lewis. He'd used $200,000 of his own money and $1.8 million borrowed from Beatrice to acquire a 25 percent interest in Beatrice's Latin American division for $2 million. Based on his original investment of $200,000, Lewis reaped an impressive 57 to 1 return on that one deal alone.

Lewis had also planned to hold on to the S.E.S. hypermarket chain in northeastern France and was looking into the possibility of a public debt offering for S.E.S. However, the chain didn't have sufficient cash flow to justify that move and it put a lot of debt on the balance sheet, so Lewis eventually sold it to the Bouriez family of France's Cora-Revillon business group.

Not long after the Beatrice deal closed, the company's general counsel in Chicago resigned, to Lewis's delight. "My god, more manna from heaven has fallen into our lap," he exclaimed to Kevin Wright. "Kevin, you've got to get out to Chicago and fill the vacuum."

Wright, who had a wife in medical school and was taking care of a four-year-old son at the time, demurred, saying his responsibilities compelled him to stay in New York.

"Well, you've got to be two places at once, then," Lewis said, only half joking. But Wright held fast, putting his family over Lewis and TLC Beatrice. "Clearly, that was one of the aspects in which I failed in his eyes, by not figuring out a way to get out to Chicago and become indispensable to the operating management of Beatrice International," Wright says.

"YOU HAVE THE MAKINGS OF AN ENTREPRENEUR!"

With TLC Beatrice secured, in January of 1988 Lewis began directing some of his energies toward a matter of a more personal nature: His frayed relationship with Cleve Christophe. He gave Christophe a bonus of $300,000 in early January, an amount Christophe terms an insulting "pittance" although it was double Christophe's annual salary. Chaffing over their previous run-ins over the Drexel private placement memorandum and the mixup that resulted in Lewis losing $15 million on the Onex deal—as well as the worldwide acclaim Lewis was getting and the fact that he never mentioned Christophe's name—Christophe had made up his mind to leave.

The two men had a talk at 99 Wall Street, where Lewis was still doing most of his business. When Christophe told Lewis he was leaving, that prompted an hour-long conversation. Among other things, Lewis told Christophe that they'd come a long way together and had accomplished quite a bit. Lewis admitted that he had shortcomings, but assured his friend that he was working on addressing them. In the meantime, Christophe's patience and forbearance would be greatly appreciated. Lewis argued he should be given the opportunity to come the distance. But when Christophe still insisted on leaving, Lewis abruptly changed his tack.

He accused his colleague of being too naive to understand what the deal-making process was all about, as well as the emotional strains it can produce. It all had to do with Christophe's immaturity, basically, as well as his inability to understand that Rome wasn't built in a day.

"Well, if you're hellbent on committing economic suicide, when do you want to leave?" Lewis asked heatedly.

"I don't want to do anything that's disruptive," Christophe answered. "There are still a number of things that need to be done and I am part of that transition. So, I'm prepared to stick around for a reasonable period of time in order to withdraw in an orderly fashion."

"Don't do me any favors," Lewis responded. "Make it easy on yourself."

"Fine," Christophe answered brusquely. "Two weeks."

"Okay, get the fuck out of here in two weeks, then," Lewis snarled.

About two hours later, Lewis's secretary, Deidra Wilson, summoned Christophe back into Lewis's office. Lewis's demeanor was as though the earlier conversation had never taken place.

"Cleve, we've got this problem over in France with S.E.S.," Lewis said. It seemed that one of the managers had sold some Beatrice property that he was not authorized to sell. "This is a mess and I'm concerned about the banks," Lewis said affably. "You're good at this stuff—would you go over to France and see if you can get to the bottom of it? You and Tom Lamia?"

"When do you want me to go?" Christophe asked noncommittally.

"I've already got you booked on a flight three hours from now," Lewis answered.

Christophe was gone for two weeks. After he returned, another week went by without Lewis making any mention of Christophe's desire to quit. Christophe decided to make another visit to Lewis's office.

"Reg, what I told you back in January is still valid," he told Lewis. "And more than two weeks have passed."

"Oh, I thought you had forgotten about that," Lewis said.

"No."

Lewis walked over to the door of his office, closed it and then took a seat on his couch, rather than behind his desk.

"Cleve, I really wish you would reconsider," he said. "You mean the world to me. I know what we can do, but I guess at the end of the day you've got to make your own mind up. If you are that intent, then what's the timing?"

Christophe repeated his desire to allow for an orderly transition. The two men agreed that Christophe would leave at the end of April.

Prior to that deadline, Lewis took Christophe on a number of lunches and dinners where they had engaging conversations and even managed to share a few laughs. But things just weren't the same—the old magic, the level of comfort and camaraderie that made their relationship so special in the past was missing.

Each time they would meet, Lewis would get around to asking Christophe whether he had changed his mind, and each time the answer was no. At one dinner, Lewis even said, "You're right about the screaming and stuff. I shouldn't be doing that with anyone."

In November 1987, Lewis bought a mind-boggling mansion known as Broadview on Long Island. On Christophe's penultimate day at TLC Beatrice, Lewis invited Christophe to Broadview.

"Hey Cleve, tomorrow I'm going to be taking a helicopter out to the island to meet with a tennis contractor to have a tennis court put in. You've never seen Broadview, why don't you fly out with me?"

"Reg, I'd love to, but I can't," Christophe said. "I'm going to be packing, because tomorrow is going to be my last day."

"Are you serious?" Lewis said.

"Yeah."

"Look, are you going uptown to take the train to Connecticut," Lewis wanted to know. "Why don't you ride up with me? My chauffeur is downstairs—I'll give you a ride to the train station, because I probably won't see you tomorrow."

Christophe took Lewis up on his offer and they took the elevator together to the ground floor and walked to the front of 99 Wall Street, where Lewis's limo awaited. After his passengers were aboard, the driver headed toward Franklin D. Roosevelt Drive, which runs alongside the East River in Manhattan. On the opposite bank of the river the drab shoreline of Queens started coming into view. Lewis's chauffeur took an entrance ramp for the FDR north.

In the few minutes it took to get to the station for Christophe's commuter train, Lewis was going to try to wear his friend down one more time.

"Would you please, please reconsider?" Lewis asked plaintively.

"No," said Christophe, who was probably secretly enjoying the test of wills. When he glanced over at Lewis, he saw a familiar flash of fire in Lewis's eyes.

"You know, this is the most juvenile, irrational set of economic analysis I've ever seen," Lewis said in a booming voice. "You are committing economic suicide. I'm embarrassed for you in the way in which you're allowing your emotions to push you into these amateurish judgments. Do you really know what I think?"

"Reg, I know what I think—I don't give a fuck what you think!"

The anger drifted from Lewis's eyes when he heard Christophe's words. "You don't give a fuck what I think," he said, repeating the words slowly.

With that, Lewis started smiling broadly and thrust his hand across the seat and grabbed Christophe's. "I love it," he said. "You have the makings of an entrepreneur yet."

Lewis's limo pulled into the train station and Christophe got out and caught his train to Connecticut. The two men wouldn't speak to each other for another two years and when they did, it was by telephone and after a call initiated by Lewis. Although Christophe took a job with a MESBIC just five blocks from 99 Wall Street, Lewis and Christophe never spoke face-to-face again after that encounter in Lewis's limo.

The next time that Christophe, who is also the godfather of Lewis's oldest daughter, Leslie, saw his former partner was at Lewis's funeral in Baltimore in January 1993. "I told Loida at the funeral, I love the man—there's no question about that," Christophe says. "I cherish the memories. There is nothing that transpired in the later stages of our relationship that will ever detract from the joy that I shared with him through most of our relationship."

"Reg tried hard to keep Cleve in the organization," Beatrice spokesman Butch Meily says. "I think Reg was friends with him, but he also saw a little rivalry there. He would always ask me if I knew what Cleve was up to, or if I'd heard anything about Cleve. He was always curious. Sometimes he'd start to make a phone call to him, then he'd stop. He would always look back on that relationship with regret that it had broken off."

But in a 1992 *Wall Street Journal* article, Lewis was quoted as saying that Christophe overestimated "what the market was for what he brought to the table."

BROADVIEW

To rejuvenate himself from the rigors of life in Manhattan, Lewis often traveled 100 miles east on the weekends, trading in the city that never sleeps for the idyllic ambiance of East Hampton, Long Island, located on Long Island Sound.

Back in the days when Lewis was running McCall, he and his brother, Tony Fugett, used to get together in East Hampton from time to time. A playground for East Coast blue bloods and scions of old money, East Hampton is filled with summer homes that eclipse most people's everyday homes. Lewis, an African-American with blue-collar Baltimore roots, felt perfectly at ease in such rarified company.

Since 1978, he had owned a three-bedroom weekend home that was located in a section of East Hampton called Hampton Waters. The house had served its purpose well, but Lewis had grander plans in mind. He loved nothing more than to take a leisurely ride in his convertible Mercedes two-seater, accompanied by Fugett, as the two of them ogled the imposing mansions and sprawling estates of East Hampton.

"I'm going to be in this neighborhood," he would tell Fugett when they encountered a particularly lavish home. "One day, we're going to be here."

In the fall of 1987, the same time he was working to close his acquisition of TLC Beatrice, Lewis began making good on his pledge to move to one of Long Island's most exclusive addresses. He and his family had outgrown their East Hampton home, which was even more cramped when Lewis entertained. So the Lewises asked their real estate broker to show them some larger homes in the tonier sections of town.

They did quite a bit of house hunting, but none of the dwellings they viewed possessed the right mix of style and uniqueness to satisfy the discerning Lewis. Then his real estate broker enthusiastically suggested that the Lewises look at a home that wasn't in East Hampton per se, but was so spectacular that it merited a look.

The broker took Lewis and his family to a section of the Hamptons called Amagansett and led them to a 25-room, Georgian-style mansion on 5.5 acres of land that went by the name of Broadview. Described in a realty prospectus as an estate that "would make even Gatsby envious," to get to Broadview one had to turn off Old Stone Highway and drive along a private road that wound its way through about a mile and a half of pastoral meadows and woods. The mansion itself was built near huge cliffs that offered a spectacular view of Gardiners Bay. Lewis and his wife were overwhelmed by the majesty of the place and Leslie and Christina fell in love with Broadview at first sight.

"I didn't want it because it was too huge for me—it was intimidating," Loida Lewis recalls of that first encounter. "But Reg, I think, saw himself in it."

Lewis visited Broadview about 15 more times after that initial visit, wanting to make damn sure he didn't experience $4 million worth of buyer's remorse if he bought Broadview, then had second thoughts. During the last of his many return trips, Lewis began pointing to locations where different pieces of his art collection would look good inside the massive house. They closed on Broadview in November 1987.

Lewis and his family extracted maximum enjoyment from the awe-inspiring abode. Lewis invited his boyhood friend from Baltimore, Ellis Goodman, to see Broadview and showed it off with obvious glee.

"This is right out of the Great Gatsby," Goodman said in awe.

"Well, of course it is," Lewis replied, chuckling.

Goodman remembers that Lewis took tremendous pride in the art collection he'd assembled at Broadview. Someone whose love for art began in an art history appreciation class taken at Virginia State, Lewis became a familiar figure in Manhattan auction houses and art galleries, from which he purchased African-American, French Impressionist, and Surrealist paintings to display at Broadview.

Despite buying the estate, Lewis opted to keep his smaller house in East Hampton because there were too many pleasant family memories associated with the dwelling to sell it.

The tennis court that Lewis had built at Broadview was put to good use. The Lewises hired a butler, Lucien Stoutt, who knew exactly how his boss wanted things to be arranged prior to a match: Lewis's routine called for his Prince tennis racquet to be resting against the backs of one of the courtside chairs. Two cans of Penn tennis balls had to be beside the racquet, with the seals on the cans unbroken. An opened can was an indication that the balls inside might not be fresh, an unacceptable condition for Lewis.

The umbrella for the courtside table needed to be in place and opened. Underneath the table was always a cooler containing water, ginger ale, and Lewis's beloved Diet Coke. Across the back of each chair would be one white towel for each of the combatants. Only then would Lewis be ready for war, which was often waged with Tony Fugett, one or two chosen friends, or a local tennis pro who was paid to come play for an hour.

In all honesty, Lewis—who was 45 in early 1988—was almost as interested in fighting the battle of the bulge as in fighting his opponent. "He always used to complain that his stomach was a little too big and he liked to move around on the tennis court," Stoutt remembers. Lewis hated to lose, but on those occasions when he was on the short end of the score, Lewis dealt with losing graciously.

While Lewis never put on airs for anyone, Broadview was one place he could totally relax. "This is a man who can afford to go to any restaurant and for lunch sometimes he would have Wise lightly salted potato chips and champagne," Stoutt recalls of Lewis's eating habits. The bubbly stuff was fetched from an amply stocked Broadview wine cellar.

Lewis's tastes in food and drink were surprisingly proletarian when he wasn't entertaining. At Broadview, the Lewises had a cook working for them, Dalma Walker, who made cheeseburgers and barbecue dishes to perfection. However, on occasion, Lewis would be just as happy munching on his potato chips, microwave popcorn, or fried chicken that he had Stoutt buy from a local deli.

On those infrequent occasions when Walker was not working and Tony Fugett happened to be visiting, Fugett and Lewis would putter around the kitchen and whip up pork chops, baked beans, and vegetables. Then a grinning Lewis would get on the phone and place a long-distance call to his mother. "Guess what me and Tony just did," he would chuckle. The tickled siblings would then have Stoutt serve them their meal.

At dinnertime, Lewis would run the show, right down to determining who sat where at the table. He and Stoutt had a code worked out that made Stoutt appear to be clairvoyant.

The reason Stoutt appeared magically to clear the table at the exact moment everyone was finished eating was because Lewis had an electronic switch placed under the carpet near the head of the table. When Lewis pushed the switch with his foot, it rang a bell in the kitchen that summoned Stoutt.

When Lewis was alone and Stoutt appeared, a finger pointed at a wine glass meant bring more wine—a nod of the head meant take away all the dishes. "Not only in business, but when he was dining, he still had control," Stoutt marvels.

Lewis threw his first Broadview bash on May 30, 1988, when he rented a bus to transport members of the Fugett and Cooper family from Baltimore.

Not long afterward, the Lewis family moved to Paris, where Lewis set up operations, since the bulk of TLC Beatrice's business was done in France. Lewis leased an opulent 18th-century Left Bank apartment in King Louis the XIV's historic Place du Palais Bourbon, a literal stone's throw from the French parliament building.

But Broadview retained a special place in Lewis's heart and he visited it whenever he could during one of his trips to the United States.

While the Lewises were in Paris, Stoutt had his run of Broadview. But what should have been a cushy, hassle-free assignment turned into a nightmare on the morning of November 6, 1991. Lewis had expressly instructed his butler to sleep in Broadview the night before, but Stoutt had helped his fiancee move to a new apartment on November 5 and stayed over at her place.

The following day a woman taking an early morning stroll two miles from Broadview noticed an unusual orange glow flickering against the morning sky and called 911. East Hampton Town Fire Marshall David Disunno was the first official at the scene. Flames were visible in each of Broadview's front windows as the grand old mansion burned furiously.

Stoutt's beeper went off at 6:30 A.M. It was the East Hampton Town Police wanting to make sure he was okay because Broadview was going up in flames! By the time Stoutt raced to his place of employment, the fire had destroyed the middle section of the splendid mansion and was methodically devouring the remaining ends. About 50 firefighters were spraying water on the conflagration, but little could be saved, with the exception of an attached three-car garage containing Lewis's Mercedes convertible and a Mercedes sedan.

Also, a small unburned section of the room where Lewis kept his pool table and library yielded an unexpected treasure: The family photo albums. The photographs were none the worse for wear, except they had to be treated to remove a sooty film.

At roughly noon Paris time, Loida Lewis was advised by Estela Ila-gan, the housekeeper, that Broadview and its multimillion dollar art collection were going up in smoke. "We started calling Lucien because we thought maybe Lucien had died in the fire," Loida Lewis says of the horrifying moments after she and her husband learned of Broadview's destruction. "We didn't know what to say. Could it be that somebody evil wanted to destroy it because of racism?"

Lewis flew back to New York immediately. It was a tortuous flight given that he knew for certain that a magical place in his life was no more. As he flew over the Atlantic, Lewis pondered whether some ne-farious person or persons had caused his misfortune intentionally.

Stoutt absolutely dreaded having to come face-to-face with his boss. Lewis exploded when he heard Stoutt had defied his directions and hadn't stayed overnight in the house.

"You fucked up," Lewis told Stoutt, each clipped word a scathing indictment that cut Stoutt to the core.

"Mr. Lewis, I know I did," he answered contritely. After asking Stoutt where he had been, Lewis really didn't have that much to say. No amount of talking in the world would restore his prized house or its artwork, or undo Stoutt's actions.

Stoutt was eventually forgiven and still works for the Lewis family today. But on that day in November 1991—when the embers of Broadview were still warm—Stoutt would have been well advised to give his seething employer very wide berth.

Not quite sure if the town officials in Amagansett could get to the bottom of why his glorious home had been destroyed, Lewis called a powerful government official he trusted implicitly—New York City Mayor David Dinkins. Could Dinkins arrange for someone to come to his Long Island mansion to sift through the embers of a fire that looked suspiciously like arson, Lewis wanted to know?

Dinkins got on the phone to Police Commissioner Lee Brown who arranged for two city police arson investigators to drive 100 miles to the eastern tip of Long Island. But when they got to the fire scene, they held themselves out as a lawyer and an insurance adjuster work-ing for Lewis.

Long Island police ran a check of the license on the duo's vehicle, which looked suspiciously like an undercover cop car. A check showed that the car was registered to the New York City Police

Department. When the "lawyer and insurance man" were confronted a second time, they admitted that they worked for the city. One of them, Lt. Phil Pulaski, headed the city arson and explosion investigation squad.

The New York media had a field day raking Dinkins over the coals for sending city personnel to probe a buddy's misfortune all the way out on the eastern tip of Long Island.

Loida Lewis was upset with the coverage of the fire by the media. "I feel that the whole thing was politically-inspired. The media were using the incident to get at the Mayor. Reg and I were and are New Yorkers. We had lived in the city for years. We voted there and Reg had paid millions in taxes. He asked the city to take a look at the fire and advise him as to who he should hire in terms of a top-notch arson expert. It's just as if an American living in Timbuktu is mugged. The first thing you'd do would be to turn to the local American embassy and ask for their help," she says.

Lewis himself was outraged at a tasteless *Fortune* article on the fire that had a picture showing the destroyed mansion. From Paris, he personally called the writer of the article, the managing editor and the publisher of the magazine to complain.

Lewis met with Tony and Joseph Fugett and several TLC executives regarding Broadview, but what could they possibly do? So Lewis got back on a plane and returned to France. He and his wife held each other tight for a long time in silence, as they realized that their beloved Broadview, the scene of so many happy memories, had been reduced to rubble.

"Reg loved that place," Everett Grant says. "I think he was happiest when he was out there. That's why when it burned down it was a great tragedy. You could see the pleasure that he took from the place."

Suffolk County arson investigators, private investigators hired by Lewis, and agents from the federal Bureau of Alcohol, Tobacco and Firearms—sent by President Bush's White House at Lewis's request—combed through the wreckage of Broadview, as did mechanical engineers who checked what remained of the heating and electrical systems. Authorities never came up with an official cause for the fire, although an arson investigator Lewis hired determined that it started in the electrical system near the bar that in turn ignited the boiler room in the basement.

But a year would pass before Lewis was made aware of that finding. Around the same time as the Broadview fire, he'd had his Bentley stolen from a garage on 23rd Street in Manhattan, and someone had removed a concrete lion that formerly graced the front of Lewis's brownstone on 22nd Street. Lewis was positive that the three occurrences involving his property were related.

He hired Ed Gregg, a former captain with the New York City Department of Corrections who ran the protective custody unit, to be his family's bodyguard and chauffeur whenever they were in New York. Twenty-four-hour-a-day security was instituted at Lewis's Chelsea townhouse and maintained until the family moved out.

The week of Thanksgiving, Lewis took an ad out in the local East Hampton paper thanking the fire department for its help. He also sent individual turkeys to the local firemen who helped during the fire.

13

Taming a Business Behemoth

For those who thought Lewis had depleted his bag of tricks when he bought TLC Beatrice, Lewis had another one: He showed them he was one hell of an operator, too. Lewis had done it once with McCall, but that was akin to navigating a yacht, whereas Beatrice was more like the Queen Elizabeth II. This time, Lewis was strutting his stuff on an international stage. From his point of view, though, nothing really had changed. A billion-dollar company could be guided by the same principles that worked with a $51.9-million firm like McCall. You just had to do your homework, work hard, and have good managers working for you.

Lewis's divestiture sales had transformed TLC Beatrice International Holdings, Inc. into an international food company whose operations are principally in Europe and are divided into two segments: food distribution and grocery products.

TLC Beatrice is the largest wholesale distributor of food and grocery products to supermarkets in the Paris metropolitan area, primarily through 418 stores operating under the Franprix name. TLC Beatrice franchises 383 of the stores and owns 35. The company also distributes food and grocery products in and around Paris through 95 stores operating under the LeaderPrice name. Of these, 49 are owned by TLC Beatrice and 46 are franchises.

TLC Beatrice's grocery products segment is a major marketer and manufacturer of ice cream in Europe. These products are marketed under well-known local brand names: Premier in Denmark; Artic in France and Belgium; Artigel in Germany; Sanson in Italy; Kalise in the Canary Islands; and La Menorquina in Spain and Portugal. TLC Beatrice is the No. 1 maker of potato chips and snacks in Ireland, under the Tayto and King brand names, among others. Finally, TLC Beatrice's grocery products segment operates soft drink bottling plants located in the Netherlands, Belgium, and Thailand.

When Lewis began divesting himself of TLC Beatrice's operating units in Australia, Latin America, and other international locations, many observers viewed him as a shrewd, callous LBO specialist who would break TLC Beatrice into small pieces, sell them, and enrich himself in the process. Sure Lewis had run McCall, the pundits said, but now he was at the helm of a billion-dollar, multinational firm with far-flung operations.

That Lewis knew little about the food distribution and manufacturing business was no handicap from his point of view. Lewis just took a deep breath and immersed himself in the challenge of running his new business. As at McCall, it was important that management share the Chairman's vision. So Lewis took to the air, visiting his far-flung operating units regularly. Local managers were probably surprised by their omnipresent new boss and his boundless curiosity about their phase of his business.

For one thing, TLC Beatrice would be much more decentralized than McCall had been, giving more autonomy to local managers. The flip side of that was Lewis set higher performance standards than most of his managers were accustomed to.

Lewis taught himself the food business just like he taught himself the home sewing pattern business. The really significant difference this time was that he was spending incredible amounts of time on travel.

It started right after he moved his family to Paris in 1988. On Wednesday, October 12, 1988, Lewis left his apartment at 7:15 A.M. and was on a private jet headed out of Le Bourget Airport by 8 A.M. By 9:30 A.M., Lewis was in Esbjerg, Denmark to meet with a manufacturing manager of one of his operating units, and to take a tour of the plant.

He left Denmark at 11:30 A.M. for a 12:15 ETA in Dortmund, West Germany to meet with some local managers there and to tour another of TLC Beatrice's plants. At 2:15 P.M., Lewis was back on the jet, where he had lunch as he flew to Paris. This was not an unusual itinerary. In seven hours, Lewis had been to three countries before returning to Paris. Granted, European countries are close to one another, but even continual short-distance commuter hops in the United States take their toll after a while.

On December 6, 1988 at 7 A.M. Paris time, Lewis flew to Zurich to pick up two business associates. After a 10-minute stop in Zurich, Lewis jetted back to France, where he touched down at Strasbourg Airport at 8:30 A.M. in order to tour the headquarters and warehouse of the SES supermarket chain, a TLC Beatrice business in northeastern France that Lewis eventually sold.

At 2:30 P.M., Lewis flew back to Zurich to drop off his passengers, then flew into Paris at 4 P.M. After a half hour layover to refuel, there was a flight back to Strasbourg to pick up TLC Beatrice President Bill Mowry and TLC France executive Daniel Jux. The men flew to Heathrow Airport in London where Lewis attended a business meeting before flying back to Paris at 7:45 P.M.

The return flight marked the end of a grueling 13½ hour day that saw Lewis make 15 takeoffs and landings in the course of hopscotching between three countries.

The following day, Lewis's 46th birthday, he departed from Paris at 8:30 A.M. headed toward Brussels Airport, in order to visit a unit of TLC Beatrice's Artic ice cream division. At 1:15 P.M., the Chairman and CEO of TLC Beatrice was leaving Brussels Airport on the flight path that would take him to Dublin Airport, so he could visit the Tayto potato chip company in Ireland.

Lewis was back in Le Bourget Airport in Paris by 5:15 P.M. Taking it relatively easy on his birthday, Lewis had only worked a 10-hour day.

In spite of the frequent travel and long hours, Lewis loved living in Paris. He felt more comfortable there than in the United States.

In Europe, the major difference is there is less overt hostility that's purely based on color. As you know, you can be insulted anywhere, but I've always been treated very well in Europe. Here in this country, there is a certain conspiratorial desire—regardless of what you do, how much you earn, you're still black. And that's meant to demean.

But it only demeans you if you allow it to. You encounter a little bit of racism in individuals from time to time, but you have to be careful because some of that can be self-generated. Sometimes, a guy may just be a jerk. Or maybe he doesn't like the tie that I have on, or maybe he doesn't like my suit. Or he may just be jealous that I'm worth a few hundred million dollars. It could be anything.

Regarding American bigotry, the legacy of slavery would certainly have to be a major factor. And I still get angry about that. It is a fact that a mediocre white kid has a lot better shot than a mediocre black kid. And there's this hypocrisy within our culture that somehow African-Americans have not achieved as much because somehow it's our own fault. I mean, it's such a vicious lie.

In fact, Lewis felt the media regularly gave short shrift to the African-American community, and not just on business issues.

Some writers have tried to put a twist on some of the noteworthy things that African-Americans do, or else they don't quite want to acknowledge them. They have a limited number of people they have a big vested interest in. Probably even a notion of white superiority. You can chronicle the achievements of African-Americans in so many different areas whenever the barriers have been broken. Look at the arts, certainly in athletics—even in business. And this has happened over significant periods of time.

I remember a few years ago when a kid who was African-American, and part Filipino, won one of the Olympic fencing championships. Well, that couldn't get any kind of really significant play. At one time here in New York City, the No. 1 chess player, a kid of African ancestry who was 12-years-old, was the national champion and received little if any publicity.

The media are truly not interested in promoting those types of stories.

Lewis once told Beatrice's public relations person, Butch Meily, "Every African-American male who's worth anything has a sense of anger built up in him against society." And Lewis used to chide Meily, who was born in the Philippines, about being far too idealistic regarding the state of race relations in the United States. "He often accused me of not understanding America and how deep the racism is here," Meily recalls.

Of all the barriers faced by African-Americans, the most insidious are based on perceptions grounded in misinformation and myth, Lewis believed. Basically, he saw society as having pulled the wool over the eyes of African-Americans by creating a mystique about how difficult it is to achieve and attain affluence. Lewis was on a one-man crusade to obliterate that myth and prove it a lie.

After he reached his goals, there was no chance of Lewis being co-opted by his wealth, station in life, or material possessions. Those things never blunted his sharply honed sense of outrage. "For all my money, if my car breaks down in the wrong place, I'd still have a problem on my hands," Lewis said. He was always more comfortable in France—and Europe in general—than in his native land. But that didn't mean Lewis didn't love the United States, warts and all. He used to wave the flag enthusiastically in France and would defend the United States in the face of Gallic criticism. While the United States was unquestionably not inclusive or egalitarian enough for Lewis, it was still home—and he flew back and forth between Paris and New York often.

THE INAUGURATION OF AIR LEWIS

Given the strain that the repeated trips were putting on Lewis's schedule and his body, Lewis felt it made perfect sense for TLC Beatrice to have a corporate jet. However, he was also aware of the tremendous expense associated with operating a jet, not to mention the danger that Lewis might be perceived as having gone "Hollywood." That last issue was a serious consideration, because above all else, Reginald Lewis wanted to be known as a dedicated businessman, not a showboater or someone fixated on the trappings of wealth.

Lewis decided the best solution was to lease an airplane from the Canadair aviation company in Canada. Kevin Wright was made Lewis's liaison for the project, and given responsibility for overseeing it. Lewis entered into a program where he would be able to lease a twin-engine jet for two years, then could walk away from it without any obligation if he so desired. The lease cost more than $100,000 a month.

Under the program, the plane's interior and its avionics package would be built according to Lewis's specifications. "As with everything else, Reg did not want to be overcharged," Wright remembers. So, a consultant was hired to ride herd over the project with Wright. Even with a consultant involved, Lewis was not pleased with the final price of his multimillion dollar aircraft when it was finished. "It was a huge expense—it was clearly something that was going to be his baby," Wright says.

For several reasons, delivery of the plane had to be taken in Delaware rather than New York or New Jersey. Kevin Wright took care of that duty. Lewis didn't see his new possession until later. When the two-year lease on the aircraft expired, Lewis exercised his option to buy it.

Lewis absolutely loved his airplane. He viewed it as his reward for his hard work and dedication over the years. Powerful and sleek, Lewis's corporate jet was unlike the Gulfstreams or Lears or even French Falcons that typically graced the hangars of so many of America's multinationals. Instead, it was a Challenger, built according to the owner's specifications at the Canadian Bombardier factory in Montreal. Everything about it was chosen by Lewis with the same painstaking care that he devoted to every other aspect of his life. From the Dallas Cowboy gray with the red and blue stripe that colored its outside to its light blue interior and blond mahogany wood panelling inside. And the plane's call letters were splashed almost defiantly on its tail—601-RL for the initials of its owner, Reginald Lewis.

Covering the plane's entire rear wall was an original painting by the noted African-American artist, Ed Clark. This painting had been commissioned by Lewis from Clark, who was his friend, specifically for the plane's interior. Entitled "Infinity," it was a kaleidoscope of dark and light blue colors that suggested many things to many people—a towering wave cresting on a beach perhaps, or a dark lunar landscape. The painting was just what Lewis wanted because it conveyed a feeling of airy openness and boundless space. Perfect for the long, lonely, trans-Atlantic flights from New York to Paris and back that Lewis took at least twice a month, commuting from his U.S. corporate headquarters to his vast economic empire spread across western Europe, the 20 or so food companies that made up the heart of TLC Beatrice International.

Butch Meily recalls accompanying Lewis on one of these flights. A tall, svelte African-American stewardess named Pamela Gunter silently served them a rare French red wine, vintage 1972. Puffing on his beloved Monte Cristo No. 3 Cuban cigar, with headphones on as he listened to Vivaldi's "Four Seasons," Lewis had a wool blanket with the initials of his company, TLC, draped around him. Sitting in his favorite chair where no one else was allowed to sit, Reginald F. Lewis looked for all the world like the master of everything he surveyed.

"Do you realize how far we've come?" he said to Meily as the thick, oddly pleasing aroma of cigar smoke wafted through the cabin. "Oh, you don't know. You weren't there during the early days," he quickly added.

Lewis pulled out a yellow legal pad, a habit from his days as a lawyer, together with his black and gold Mont Blanc pen and his favorite HP calculator and ran through some quick calculations just as he had done a hundred times before. "Ireland, $150 million. France, $600 million. Italy $100 million . . ." On and on he went, tripping lightly from country to country as he totalled up the net worth of each chunk of his Beatrice holdings. His eyes danced with pure delight as he shouted out the total.

"I love this plane." he then said to no one in particular.

"It's the ultimate perk." Meily answered.

"Yes." Lewis nodded. "That it is."

"Feel like a movie?" he asked. "Put on 'American in Paris,'" he instructed Meily without waiting for an answer.

Lewis and his plane had been up and down eight times in the last eight hours, hopskotching from city to city all across Europe. Meily, who was more than ten years younger, was exhausted and nauseous from the many takeoffs and landings, but Lewis seemed to be bursting with energy.

The cabin lights dimmed. Lewis twirled his seat to face the video monitor and on came Gene Kelly dancing through the streets of Paris. Lewis watched silently for a moment, fiddling with his headphones. He was grinning, seemingly transfixed by the images on the screen. Lewis loved movies, especially old movies, and he often mused about someday buying one of the big Hollywood studios.

The stewardess prepared his bed, then cleared out the dishes, and left the cabin. All of a sudden, Lewis burst into song, startling Meily, as Lewis sang along with Gene Kelly.

Lewis loudly warbled the lyrics, glancing gleefully around him.

A few minutes before landing, Lewis headed for the lavatory. He was fastidious about his personal appearance and he never left the plane or appeared anywhere in public unless he was dressed to the T.

He put on a dark suit, brushed his teeth, and splashed himself with cologne from the medicine cabinet. Finally, he put on dark glasses, patted his vest pocket to make sure he had his passport and wallet, and then walked slowly back to his seat, tugging at the window shutters to open them.

"How do I look?" he barked out.

"Good," Meily said.

"Good? We're not shooting for good. We're shooting for great. What's the matter with you?" he chided Meily in good humor.

Outside, it was dark but in a few minutes, the lights of Paris became visible below them. The sharply etched figure of the Eiffel Tower loomed over everything. The Challenger silently emerged from the night sky and onto the string of lights that marked the runway at Le Bourget Airport. It was a smooth landing, as it almost always was with Lewis's chief pilot, Captain Brendan Flannery, at the controls. This is where Lindbergh landed on his historic flight so many years ago, Meily thought when they landed at Le Bourget. Then he prayed that he would not have to accompany the indefatigable Lewis to the office that night.

The plane taxied to a stop. A black Mercedes emerged out-of-the-shadows and rolled to a stop on the tarmac at the precise spot where the ramp was being swung into place against the plane's door. Out jumped Lewis's French driver, the ever-dependable Patrick Lelong, neatly dressed in a suit and tie.

"Bon soir, Monsieur," he said with a slight bow to Lewis who was the first one out of the plane.

"Bon soir, bon soir," Lewis said with a smile and handed him his briefcase which as always was chockful of reports and company prospectuses. "Tout va bien?"

"Oui, monsieur. Tout va bien," Patrick replied.

He opened the door for Lewis who took his customary seat in the back of the car on the passenger side. Butch Meily slid in on the other side and Patrick ran to start the car, guiding it out of the airport past a pair of French gendarmes who saluted Lewis. Lewis returned their salutes with a friendly wave, even as he grabbed the carphone and automatically dialed the number for his New York office. It was nine o'clock at night Paris time but only 3:00 P.M. in New York. Lewis could still check in with his New York staff.

"You ready to go to work?" he said to Meily, who although he felt like anything but work, nodded slowly and replied, "Of course." Lewis smiled.

Lewis enjoyed traveling in the Canadair jet, but his employees did not. "Flying with Reg was something most employees tried to avoid," says Kevin Wright, echoing a sentiment other TLC Beatrice employees have voiced. "You're pretty confined and if he's flying with you to Europe and he's mad at you, there's nowhere to run."

Nevertheless, Canadair Challenger 601 allowed Lewis to become a more efficient and effective Chairman and CEO. The various asset sales Lewis conducted, in addition to the traveling he was doing to keep tabs on his operations and motivate local management, was having a positive effect on TLC Beatrice's 1989 financial figures.

We were much smaller and had the debt generated by the acquisition well under control. At the end of 1989, the net debt was down from $1 billion. At that point, the idea of going public really appealed to me. That would have enabled us to take out the preferred stock and also give me a security that I could use to make other acquisitions. John Sheehy suggested Merrill Lynch. We had a big discussion with some people there. The president of Merrill said they were behind us all the way. But when the going got a little bit tough, they just couldn't do the job.

In the meantime, I got hit with a bullshit lawsuit associated with McCall Pattern that mystified me. So we pulled the deal in 1989. I sort of decided to step back, focus all of my energies on operations and continued to sell off a few small things.

A PATTERN OF LITIGATION: DISPROVING A LIE

On December 9, 1988, McCall Pattern, Inc. filed for bankruptcy protection under Chapter 11 of the U.S. Bankruptcy Code, an event that would prove to be a source of frustration and anger for Lewis. Even though he had sold McCall to the John Crowther Group—a British textile manufacturer based in Leeds, England—in June 1987, the bankruptcy would result in Lewis being made a defendant in lawsuits alleging he was somehow linked to McCall's weak financial situation a year and a half after he sold the company.

Crowther, the new owner of McCall, borrowed from Shearson Lehman $35 million of the $65 million purchase price they paid Lewis. McCall later issued $35 million in debt notes to Travelers Insurance Co., and used the money from the debt offering to pay off Shearson. Not long afterward, the John Crowther Group was acquired in a hostile takeover by Coloroll, a British conglomerate.

Coloroll decided it didn't want McCall and tried to sell it but failed.

When McCall began to have trouble making its debt payment to Travelers, Coloroll decided to sever its ties to McCall and have it file for bankruptcy.

In September 1989, the creditors of McCall filed a lawsuit on behalf of the company in U.S. District Court for the Southern District of New York. Several defendants were named, including Lewis and Shearson Lehman. Accusing Lewis of fraudulent conveyance, the suit was basically a desperate attempt by McCall's creditors to somehow blame Lewis for McCall's financial woes.

"He was an easy target and he was somebody who had the financial wherewithal to respond to a judgment, so it was a blackmail kind of thing," says Mark Alcott, an attorney who worked with Lewis during his Paul, Weiss days and who Lewis picked to assist him in the lawsuits. "I think he certainly felt that he was being unfairly attacked and the reason he was being unfairly attacked was because he was successful. The court dismissed the case and it was a great vindication for him."

Lewis achieved his business successes by playing by the established rules. He was a hard-charger and he maximized the earnings potential of his assets whenever possible, but Lewis was honest and he was principled. So being accused of unethical behavior was more than Lewis could stomach. He viewed the litigation as an unfair attempt to sully his reputation. For Lewis, far more was at stake than driving home legal issues or determining guilt or innocence. "Reg said that before he would settle that case, he would die or go bankrupt," says Lee Archer, a board member with McCall and TLC Beatrice under Lewis.

In addition, the depositions associated with the lawsuit were infringing on Lewis's precious time during a period when he was attempting to shepherd TLC Beatrice through an initial public offering. Further-more, Lewis was having to pay lawyers to defend him. All of those things displeased him mightily.

"He would holler and he would cuss," Mark Alcott says. "But there was this looming intelligence about it—it was not ranting and raving. He was making points even in his anger that were important points, valid points. I would find myself in the odd position of having some-one chew me out and I would be taking notes."

Ultimately Judge Morris E. Lasker dismissed the suit in Lewis's fa-vor. The plaintiff "lamely admits it cannot figure out whether any of these parties is responsible, but seeks to keep them in the case in order to make that determination," Lasker wrote on July 3, 1991. "The Federal Rules (of Civil Procedure) do not permit such pre-emptive tactics."

Lewis was in the Canary Islands tending to TLC Beatrice business there when the decision was handed down. He placed a happy call to Alcott's home when he learned of the news. But his pleasure would be short-lived, because another McCall lawsuit would come down the pike shortly.

Suit No. 2 was named *The Travelers Insurance Co. and The Travelers Indemnity Co. v. Reginald F. Lewis.* It too was filed in U.S. District Court in the Southern District of New York and was heard by Judge Morris Lasker.

In essence, Travelers alleged that while Lewis ran McCall he put in place a method of financial reporting that didn't jibe with what Travel-ers was led to believe was being used. Had Travelers known the true pic-ture, it would never have issued $35 million in debt notes to McCall and its new British owners, Travelers said in court papers.

Travelers claimed that even after Lewis left McCall, he continued to exert influence over CEO Bob Hermann to the point that Lewis's financial reporting system was still secretly being used after Lewis was gone—a preposterous assertion given the prickly relationship Lewis had with Hermann.

But Hermann appeared to back up Travelers' assertion in the law-suit, claiming that Lewis had told him to never reveal the financial re-porting method in question to anyone. Lewis responded by filing a libel suit on November 7, 1990: *Reginald F. Lewis v. The Travelers Insurance Co., The Travelers Indemnity Co. and Robert Lewis Hermann.*

The libel suit was also heard by Judge Lasker, who by that time probably was more familiar with McCall and the home sewing pattern business than some of McCall's own employees.

"We were at war—that was the mindset," Kevin Wright says. "It was one of the toughest periods during my 12-plus years with him. He would react with more vehemence on issues in the litigation than on almost anything else I can remember. At the end of the day, Reg Lewis the defendant didn't pay a dime," Kevin Wright says. "It was a tortuous process, but it got him what he really wanted there—vindication. He didn't do anything wrong in the McCall transaction."

Wanting to talk with someone who could empathize with being a deep pocket and a constant target for someone looking to make a quick buck, Lewis called Michael Milken.

"Can you believe this?" he asked Milken. "Can you believe these issues? Can you believe that when you sell a business, you now have to depend on how well the people do after they buy it from you?"

At one point, Lewis talked to Ray LeFlore—the trial lawyer he'd briefly shared office space with at 99 Wall Street—about taking on the case. One afternoon they sat in Lewis's office analyzing different strategies they could resort to.

"Ray, this is duck soup," Lewis told his friend. "These guys are trying to take my money. Let me testify on the stand in front of a jury, let me testify. I'm the American Dream! I worked hard and this is real money and I can tell the jury that I did nothing wrong. I can show them that the reason this became a problem once I sold McCall is you had a bunch of guys in there who were like the gang that couldn't shoot straight. I handed them a beautiful deal and they just put it down the tubes."

But LeFlore was against the idea of the wealthy Lewis testifying on his own behalf. "You may think you're the American Dream and if you had different skin, you would be," LeFlore told Lewis. "From a litigator's point of view, I have no desire to put you on the stand and explain to a jury how this black guy could make this much money and do it honestly."

In retrospect, LeFlore says personal wealth "in most other instances is not a prima facie reason for thinking that something was wrong, but in his case it was."

Both cases were ultimately decided in Lewis's favor and he received a settlement in the last one, a minor consolation considering the angst and wasted time caused by the suit. Moreover, the McCall legal actions had another adverse side-effect: They strained the long business relationship and friendship that Lewis and Tom Lamia had enjoyed up to that point. "He always looked upon me as his protector, and I was his protector," says Lamia. "And I think he felt that I should have protected him from these lawsuits, that they should never have been brought. As far as I know, there's no way to insulate a seller from exposure to lawsuits." The last year of Lewis's life, 1992, he stopped calling Lamia and the two men drifted apart.

FOCUSING ON THE BOTTOM LINE

Again, it bears repeating that Lewis had an extraordinary ability to set priorities and not waver from them one iota. The McCall suits were a tremendous distraction, but Lewis would never allow them to interfere with his business objectives.

By 1989, he'd sold TLC Beatrice operating companies in Latin America, Asia, and Europe, enabling him to raise $867 million or 88% of the purchase cost of the acquisition. Toward year's end, Lewis met with his top executives in Manhattan. Quite pleased with themselves, they handed Lewis a game plan for 1990 that they believed would bump up operating income by 47 percent.

"No, that's unacceptable," answered Lewis, who was set on achieving something better than a 47 percent increase. "Go take another look and come back with something more reasonable."

The executives' jaws dropped when the Chairman and CEO of TLC Beatrice told them their plan wasn't ambitious enough, then they started huffing and puffing about how there was already a lot of stretch in their projections and that anything greater than 47 percent was pretty unlikely.

Ultimately, through dint of his business and management skills, and a weakened U.S. dollar, Lewis met his lofty expectations. TLC Beatrice produced $94.3 million in operating income during 1990, a 56 percent increase over the $60.5 million generated in 1988.

Lewis was rather methodical when conveying his vision to the troops. Before attempting to motivate or inspire anyone, he would first sit down and formulate a yearly plan. If it passed the acid test of being sufficiently aggressive when compared with the preceding year—and if it was realistic—then Lewis would sign off on it.

He would then use his yearly plan as a yardstick and would hold monthly management meetings to ensure that his objectives were being met. Once he'd told his managers in the field what his yearly plan was, the actual results—from the standpoint of capital expenditures, operating results and operating profit—were pretty much in the hands of operating management.

Naturally they could expect regular visits from the Chairman and CEO who made a habit of regularly visiting the different operations.

In 1990, we had a record year. We earned $1.5 billion in sales, close to $100 million in operating income, and $45 million after taxes. So on a buyout, we earned $3.62 a share on our common stock. You have to remember that the common stock had cost $1. In the meantime, we just continued to work on our operating needs. The principal focus of my activities has been running the business since that period. We closed the Chicago office and consolidated some of the functions that they had been performing into New York.

The sales total Lewis mentioned represented a 31 percent increase. By the end of 1990, Beatrice's debt-to-equity ratio had been sliced to 1.6 to 1, compared with 70 to 1 right after Lewis acquired the company. When the Berlin Wall fell, Lewis saw a business opportunity arise. At his urging, TLC Beatrice's ice cream operations in Germany expanded into the former East Germany, resulting in a 46 percent increase in sales.

As for shutting down the Chicago office, Lewis felt he wasn't getting sufficient value from TLC Beatrice's personnel in the Windy City, so the operations at 2 North LaSalle Street in Chicago were closed and Manhattan became the U.S. headquarters. TLC Beatrice had become a company principally centered in Western Europe, plus the greatest capital markets in the world are in Manhattan, Lewis reasoned. TLC Beatrice's president, Bill Mowry, decided to cash out his stock equity, netting him several million dollars. Several other Beatrice executives from Chicago followed suit.

TLC Beatrice subleased office space from RJR Nabisco at 9 W. 57th Street. The utilitarian, shopworn look of 30 Broad Street and 99 Wall Street was not revisited this time. Lewis's new office, with its Persian rug, bar, refrigerator, inset large-screen TV, executive washroom, and adjoining conference room, was a striking contrast to earlier offices.

But the most striking feature of all was a picturesque view of verdant Central Park 48 stories below. When Lewis looked down on Manhattan from his magnificent perch, it symbolized his unlikely, hard-fought ascent from working-class origins in Baltimore to an executive suite in America's largest city.

THWARTED AGAIN: THE IPO GLASS CEILING

An irony of TLC Beatrice's strong performance in 1990 is that in the last months of 1989 Lewis had been denied an opportunity to take the company public. The attempt marked the second time that he'd been denied a chance to guide a firm through an initial public offering. And as had been the case with McCall, the financial press again rained on his parade. Only this time, Lewis was personally singled out for disparaging coverage and second-guessing of his motives and scruples.

The TLC Beatrice initial public offering was supposed to accomplish two primary objectives. First of all, Lewis wanted to have his equity publicly traded so he would have what he referred to as "currency to make acquisitions."

Second, while he owned slightly more than half of TLC Beatrice's common stock, most of the other half was owned by Drexel executives and Drexel investors. Lewis had negotiated a price with Drexel that would have taken them out of the picture entirely. A successful IPO would have allowed him to execute that plan.

Plus, there may have been a personal side to Lewis's IPO attempt: He'd always hoped TLC Beatrice would be a New York Stock Exchange company, according to his boyhood friend Ellis Goodman.

Analysts noted that all proceeds from the IPO were to go to investors through special dividends and bond redemptions, and put out the word that Lewis might be looking to cash out of TLC Beatrice. That speculation, which happened to be inaccurate, made potential investors quite wary.

"The analysts pilloried the deal, saying Reg was being too greedy, there were problems getting cash back to the States—anything they could think of," Kevin Wright says.

Lewis had been courted assiduously by Merrill Lynch to do the IPO, which offered to sell 18.5 million shares at an estimated price of $9.75 a share. That represented 30 percent of TLC Beatrice and would have raised $180 million.

The IPO had to be done by the end of 1989, Lewis told Merrill Lynch, because he wanted to set a clear mission for the management of TLC Beatrice going forward into 1990.

The signs were ominous. That year, institutional investors bought significant amounts of public equity and many had experienced depreciation and gains and were looking to close shop toward the latter part of 1989. The TLC Beatrice filing took place late in the year, in mid-November, in the middle of the Thanksgiving and Christmas holiday seasons when many people take vacations and this diluted the pool of potential investors. And there had been a few IPOs in 1989 that had given investors pause, like one by Smith Corona Corp. that saw the company's stock drop more than $5 less than a month after its IPO.

The TLC Beatrice stock offering was also coming at a bad time because of repercussions from the 1980's orgy of acquisitions that were fueled by junk bonds. Companies acquired through leveraged buyouts were carrying tons of debt and many were struggling mightily to meet their debt service. There were predictions of massive junk bond defaults: The fact that Lewis had paid off most of TLC Beatrice's junk bond debt went unnoticed.

In addition, in mid-October of 1989, the stock market experienced a mini-crash with the Dow dropping several hundred points.

Finally, Lewis was being forced to swim upstream by the financial media. While initially receptive to Lewis's IPO, the press soon carried stories casting him as the king of avarice, in an era where his impressive wealth accumulation was a pittance compared with that of Michael Milken, Henry Kravis, and buyout specialist Ray Chambers, among many others.

On November 19, 1989, *Newsday* columnist Allan Sloan wrote the following story about Lewis's IPO attempt, under the headline, "A Feeding Frenzy at TLC Beatrice." Sloan wrote in part:

> When it comes to riding the leveraged buyout boom, few people have been more successful than Reginald Lewis . . . On the surface, becoming a partner of Lewis looks like something anyone in his right mind would want to do. After all, Lewis turned his $1 million McCall investment into more than $60 million, helping some of his co-investors and employees become very rich in the process. And the investors who bought 36 million TLC Beatrice shares for 25 cents each in the buyout now own a security that Merrill Lynch talks about selling to the public between $9 and $10.50 a share. That turns a $9 million investment into something in the neighborhood of $324 million to $378 million.
>
> So why haven't I run down to Merrill Lynch to be first in line to buy a piece of Lewis's action? Because some of the disclosures in Lewis's financial documents bother me. I'm not suggesting he had done anything illegal. But he has done things that seem to place his interests above those of his shareholders.
>
> Documents filed by Lewis's companies with the Securities and Exchange Commission show that while making a fortune for himself and his fellow investors, Lewis did some things that fall into the gray area where legitimate greed ends and excessiveness begins. To be fair, that's the same area where LBO stars have been known to dwell.

Sloan's column mentioned the then-pending Crowther McCall lawsuits against Lewis, suits where a federal court later twice vindicated him of any wrongdoing. Sloan also discussed the $11.3 million Lewis reaped after the sale of TLC Beatrice's Latin American divisions. Princely sums to be sure, but chicken feed compared to the tens of millions of dollars some LBO artists were fetching in greenmail—protection money paid by companies that didn't want to be taken over. Plus the money Lewis got appeared richly deserved in light of TLC Beatrice's financial performance the following year.

Still, when Lewis was trying to pull off the TLC Beatrice IPO in 1989, he was painted as a gouger and plunderer of companies.

But the final blow was delivered in a *Barron's* piece that noted TLC Beatrice's cash flow "was more apparent than real." After that story ran, Lewis's IPO was dead in the water. The top executives of TLC Beatrice viewed the *Barron's* piece as sensationalist claptrap and drafted a letter of protest that was signed by Everett Grant and sent to *Barron's* editor, for what it was worth.

An *Investment Dealers' Digest* story that ran in July 1990, referred to the *Barron's* article on the TLC Beatrice IPO as a "mugging."

Lewis was totally enraged, but his anger was directed at Merrill Lynch. In an argument that mirrors the one he directed at Bear, Stearns following the failed McCall IPO, Lewis blasted Merrill Lynch for their lack of resolve in pushing the TLC Beatrice public offering across the finish line. Merrill Lynch had done a great dog-and-pony show to get his business and had even sent a top executive to Lewis's Paris office to boast that "when Merrill Lynch says they're going to do something, they deliver." Only they didn't deliver, and they'd cost Lewis a lot of money.

"He'd always reflect back to the 1989 deal that didn't come off with Merrill Lynch and what it cost him from an opportunity lost perspective," one of Lewis's former top executives says. "I don't think he ever liked Merrill Lynch after that."

TLC Beatrice's Chairman and CEO also believed that if Drexel had been carrying the ball, his second IPO attempt would have reached the end zone. Never one to admit defeat, Lewis hadn't ruled out a third IPO attempt at some point in the future.

"I'm going to let a couple of years go by, because the next time we're ready to have an offering, the price will be even better," Lewis told Ellis Goodman. In 1991, Lewis toyed with the idea of going public at $50 a share, but decided against it.

Not wishing to be perceived a whiner and not wanting to jeopardize future opportunities when his 1989 IPO collapsed, Lewis never said anything about it publicly. However, privately he groused that his company was being held to a different standard.

Investment Dealers' Digest lent some credence to that point of view with an article on May 28, 1990. The story was about "reverse LBOs," a term for IPOs sought by companies acquired with leveraged buyouts: "The first glimpse of the new tough standards for reverse LBOs came last December. TLC Beatrice International . . . tried to go public with a $180 million offering. The deal was shelved, although Lewis had successfully concluded asset sales worth $854 million."

The piece went on to surmise that Lewis may have been thwarted because the expected price of TLC Beatrice's shares was almost 30 times earnings per share, when the norm was less than that.

Lewis endured other business disappointments as the leader of TLC Beatrice. He tried without success to acquire other businesses until shortly before his death in 1993.

ACQUISITION SHOPPING: EXPANSIONIST DREAMS

A major factor behind Reginald Lewis's acquisition push was his desire to have a U.S. leg to his empire, as a hedge against economic or currency fluctuations in Europe. In 1989, Lewis came within a whisker of buying AmBase, a diversified financial services company that at the time owned Home Insurance Co. and Carteret Bancorp. AmBase had hundreds of millions of dollars in debt because of junk bonds, but Lewis thought AmBase's problems obscured tremendous untapped potential. Lewis took a letter of intent to AmBase's headquarters and had Bear, Stearns lined up as his investment banker. But the deal was shot down at the last minute for unspecified reasons by AmBase's board.

That may have been a lucky break, because AmBase's stock price plummeted from $12.25 at the end of 1989 to 31 cents in 1990, while its debt soared to $738 million.

Lewis also took a run at the domestic operations of Beatrice Co., which were sold to ConAgra for $1.3 billion in June 1990, even though Lewis tendered a higher bid. If he had succeeded, the acquisition would have put such brand names as Peter Pan peanut butter and Orville Redenbacher popcorn under the TLC Beatrice umbrella. Kohlberg, Kravis, Roberts & Co. sold Beatrice Co. to ConAgra and Lewis felt Kravis never took his bid seriously. (Kravis declined to be interviewed for this book.)

Not only did a bid lower than Lewis's win the day, but the higher bid tendered by Lewis was never even acknowledged. "My price was higher and they didn't even call me. What do you think that was all about?" Lewis asked Tony Fugett.

"Hey, what can I say?" Fugett replied. "I think I know."

"Yeah, I think I do, too," Lewis said, dropping the matter.

It's important to note that Lewis never used race as a convenient excuse for failure. Nor did he seek or receive any special dispensation for being an African-American when he bought McCall or Beatrice. But there were times in his business dealings when his efforts had been thwarted and there just seemed to be no plausible explanation. His failed attempt to buy the domestic operations of Beatrice was one of those occasions.

Lewis also thought he was treated disdainfully by the Belzberg group, a business syndicate dominated by Canadian LBO artist Samuel Belzberg. He thought TLC Beatrice had given him a superb calling card, but that wasn't the case here.

Lewis had a letter of intent to buy the Scovill Apparel Fasteners Group, a zipper manufacturer, for $90 million. But the man who had successfully purchased an international company for $1 billion was taken lightly in his quest for a $90 million firm and accorded precious little deference or respect by Belzberg's syndicate. It goes without saying that the reception Lewis encountered scuttled that transaction.

Business associate Phyllis Schless last saw Lewis in November 1992, two months before he succumbed to brain cancer. They were looking at the possibility of acquiring a multimillion dollar firm Schless declined naming. She does say that Lewis took a hard look at possibly buying Capital Markets Assurance Corp. (CAPMAC) which was a subsidiary of Citicorp at the time Lewis was interested in it. CAPMAC is a financial guaranty company that insures fixed income securities.

First Executive, a troubled holding company for Executive Life Insurance that later turned into a tremendous moneymaker also got a once over from Lewis. "We always thought that we would have to take opportunities that were either half-baked, overlooked, or warmed-over and use our brilliance and genius to figure out how to make lemonade out of a lemon, which Reg was fond of saying," says his brother, Jean Fugett, Jr.

At one point in 1992, Lewis even gave some thought to buying the Baltimore Orioles baseball team before deciding it was overpriced. But by far the most fascinating company Lewis considered taking a run at in 1992 was Paramount. "I think his ideal job would have been running a movie studio, and we often fantasized about it," TLC Beatrice's Butch Meily says.

Lewis even made inquiries about buying one of the Big Three automakers. "We actually did look at Chrysler at a time when they were not producing the Jeep Cherokee and they were clearly under some financial duress," says Darryl Thompson, a special assistant to Lewis from 1991 to 1992. "He had some very high level meetings with senior people. But that acquisition attempt fizzled out, too."

STAFF TURNOVER, LOYALTY

With Lewis spending so much time in Paris, TLC Beatrice executives in Manhattan were seeing their Chairman and CEO infrequently.

After Bill Mowry left TLC Beatrice, Dumas Simeus became president in early 1991. He had been an executive with Beatrice Co. in Latin America. Simeus clashed with Lewis over how the company should be run and whether or not adequate results were being produced. Lewis responded by second-guessing Simeus's decisions and accusing Simeus of holding unauthorized staff meetings with employees.

Simeus left after about a year and filed a lawsuit in New York state court accusing TLC Beatrice of withholding stock options to which Simeus claimed he was entitled.

Lewis displayed a knack for being able to attract the best and the brightest, as well as a knack for occasionally having difficulty keeping such people.

Another was Darryl Thompson, a young man with a Stanford MBA who had worked with the mergers and acquisitions section of Morgan Stanley before joining TLC Beatrice in 1990 as a special assistant to the Chairman. Thompson left amicably after about a year because he and Lewis weren't in sync regarding the way acquisition opportunities should be pursued.

Robert Davenport, an investment banker who possesses a Harvard MBA and had been doing leveraged buyout work with First Boston, joined Lewis in 1989 as director of business development. Davenport also worked with Lewis for about a year before deciding to leave. His difficulties with Lewis mirrored Thompson's in that he felt stymied and frustrated because Lewis would never pursue acquisition projects that Davenport recommended.

"It's fair to say he was reasonably autocratic and had a fairly clear sense of what he wanted to accomplish and how, and really did view his employees as extensions of himself," Davenport recalls of Lewis. "I think he was interested in the input, but he was also very interested in making sure that whatever the ultimate strategy or tactic or end product of a given process was that it would have his initials firmly embossed in the middle and on the sides."

One of the more intriguing individuals to enter Lewis's inner circle was David Guarino, who was hired as a senior analyst at TLC Beatrice shortly after Cleve Christophe left in 1988. Hired to perform some of the financial modeling duties that Christophe had discharged, Guarino proved himself invaluable to Lewis through his financial analysis.

"David always finds ways to make himself useful," a former TLC Beatrice executive says.

Typical of Guarino's relationship with Lewis was an occasion when Lewis had just given a speech at a comptrollers conference in Brussels. Guarino came rushing up to the stage to greet his boss, gushing about how wonderful the speech had been. "That's what I like about David," Lewis said afterward. "He's always there, and he's always saying something supportive."

Guarino joined Beatrice in 1988, the same year as company spokesman Butch Meily. Both remained under Lewis's employ until his death.

Shortly before Lewis died, he granted stock options to four employees: Wright, Guarino, Meily and Lewis's executive secretary, Deidra Wilson. He also gave shares to the members of the board of TLC Beatrice, all of whom were his long-time friends.

14

A Door to a New Universe

Reginald Lewis's business accomplishments transformed him into something of a celebrity. He was besieged with offers to appear at various functions and with requests to do media interviews, which Lewis turned down. Among these were "60 Minutes," "20–20," "The Charlie Rose Show," and the "Oprah Winfrey Show." Strangers recognizing Lewis's distinctive profile would stop him on the streets of Manhattan to shake his hand or bend his ear.

Lewis, the onetime outsider, was now unquestionably a star in the firmament of American business, and one of the brighter ones at that. A move in 1989 by Jim Robinson, who was then Chairman and CEO of American Express, to make Lewis a member of the Business Roundtable further solidified his status.

Yesterday I went to this Business Roundtable meeting. The power in that room was just staggering. Richard Nixon addressed the group which was comprised of CEOs, including Bob Allen of AT&T and John Akers of IBM. Next to Akers was John Reed of Citicorp and also present was Mike Miles of Philip Morris. At the other side of the room were Charlie Sanford, the chairman of Bankers Trust, and John McGillicuddy, the chairman of Manufacturers Hanover.

It was enjoyable and interesting. Our company is one of the smaller ones, but $4 a share on a $1 stock isn't bad, when you consider where we started.

I really had to ignore the fact that, well I was the only black person in the room. Who gives a shit? I was just talking to guys who wanted to talk to me and who can relate to me. What's interesting, though, is the guys who are the most insecure were afraid to be seen with me.

In general terms, the decision to go on the Roundtable board after Jim Robinson invited me may have been a good decision, but Jim had to sell me on doing it because I was not interested in any sort of token stuff. But having gone to four or five meetings, the experience has proven useful.

It's an impressive organization and I'm convinced that everyone, believe it or not, wants to do the right thing by American industry and American business. People have their own agendas, as you might expect, in a group that lobbies on behalf of business. But in that room I got the feeling that a lot of good patriotic Americans were present. In general, I received an extremely warm and friendly reception.

One day, Bob Allen and I were chatting about football and I asked him if he played any sports in school. He said, "Yeah, I played football," so we had a nice conversation about that. He was a defensive and offensive end, before the days when players concentrated on either defense or offense. Bob's hands happened to be on the table, so I took a look at them and said, "Looks like you've got a good pair of hands." He allowed that once a jersey or football was in his grasp, "it was mine."

He asked if any sports franchises were available and I said, "Yeah, quite a number." At the time the Boston Red Sox, Detroit Tigers, Kansas City Royals, and Seattle Mariners could be had. There was also a possibility the Baltimore Orioles might be for sale.

We also talked about his company, which he is very pleased with. I asked him how things had been going since the NCR acquisition. Bob said he planned to let the other culture survive, to let them do their thing. I think he's a good corporate leader, a very good one.

And Richard Nixon is a classic example of how real men of power with intestinal fortitude operate. I think he's shown an incredible ability to look forward and not back—cut your losses and keep your chin up regardless of what happens. And he never admitted guilt; he only said he made mistakes. I don't think he's ever actually apologized to the American people. Over the long haul, I think people will perceive him to be an honest gentleman.

Nixon has also been very good at seeking out writers and columnists and people who felt Watergate was probably blown out of proportion by the left-leaning press, and he just kind of hung in there. He's also shown himself to be incredibly well informed on matters affecting the national interest. And by force of intellect and personality, he's managed to portray himself as a man of power and good will.

I came away not focusing on his improper conduct—the tapes and all that stuff—but on what he had to say. The man had a valuable perspective on how our country should be looking at certain issues. He had an interesting assessment of other presidents. He thought that Reagan had been a very good president and felt that Bush had been generally good. He felt Clinton wouldn't make a bad president and thought Eisenhower was probably superb.

He did not think Ross Perot would make a good president. As he put it, Ike was a good soldier and also a great politician. Reagan was a good actor and a great politician. Ross Perot is a great business-man and a very poor politician.

On the subject of Perot, I had an occasion to meet him once. I was down at The Wall Street Journal *talking to the editors and after about two hours the publisher, Peter Kann, got up and went out of the room and came back with Ross Perot. I deferred to him and let him hold court to some extent for the next 45 minutes or so. I had doubts about whether I should do that or not because it was arguably my show. I mean, I took the time to go down there and hadn't quite made all the points that I'd wanted to, but Perot was interesting. He was a little leery around me, but not that much.*

I am trying to figure out why people are a little leery around me. I guess it's a lack of knowledge or maybe hearing about how tough I can be and all that sort of thing.

The Business Roundtable is not truly my peer group in a sense. For one thing, some of the members have more traditional back-grounds in that they've started businesses from scratch. Then there's also the matter of personal wealth. And unfortunately, I think the ethnicity factor, so to speak, is there. And it's a reality. There remains sort of a preoccupation with race during any initial encounter in this country, but it fades quickly. In my career, I found the most important thing is not to be self-conscious about it and not to let it interfere with the way you think or the manner in which you operate.

In addition to rubbing shoulders with the heads of Fortune 500 companies and politicians like David Dinkins and Jesse Jackson, Lewis was on friendly terms with Bill Cosby and was a visitor to Cosby's townhouse in Manhattan. Lewis was also an admirer and friend of opera singer Kathleen Battle. Lewis got a kick out of putting on a black tie and taking his brother Tony Fugett with him to hear Battle sing in Manhattan. Battle later sang at his memorial service.

"Today" host Bryant Gumbel was also an acquaintance. They met, of all places, in an airport and wound up sitting next to each other on the same flight. That encounter led to a relationship where they would pick up the phone from time to time just to say hello.

"I think more often than not we wound up talking about society's perception of black men who are successful, more than anything else," Gumbel says. "And we would kind of commiserate with each other and share stories about how we were perceived, or different standards that we were held to."

"It was part and parcel of the whole deal of talking about being black and successful in this society and some of the things you have to do that most people don't think about."

Black men who are prepared or confident or willing to act aggressively are viewed as undesirables who are arrogant, uppity, and too big for their britches, Lewis would tell Gumbel.

In addition to being able to pick up the phone and call other celebrities, Lewis found that fame brought with it people who routinely suck up to the rich and powerful. On occasions when Lewis and his wife were besieged by sycophants, he would turn to Loida and utter quietly, "It's the car," causing both of them to burst into laughter. The remark was made famous in the Lewis household one afternoon when Lewis was driving his convertible 550 SL Mercedes with his oldest daughter, Leslie, seated beside him. Two beautiful women walking along the street as Lewis was approaching made a big show of giving him flirtatious looks.

Leslie, who has a dry sense of humor like her father, turned to him and said, "Daddy, it's the car." Her comment tickled Lewis to no end and gradually became a shorthand for people who seem friendly but are really motivated by ulterior motives.

THE JOYS OF FAMILY AND RELAXATION

Family and business were the dominant passions in Lewis's life. When business wasn't the topic of discussion with Lewis, his family was. Family members, friends, and business associates all remark that Lewis had a deep love for his wife and his daughters.

Tom Lamia and Lewis talked about their families all the time. "Gee, Tom, you're really lucky to have six children," Lewis told his colleague once. "I'd love to have six children."

However, the birth of Lewis's second daughter, Christina, had been a difficult one and Lewis feared that having additional children might put Loida Lewis's health—and possibly her life—in jeopardy. By all accounts, Reginald Lewis was a different man at home than in the business arena. He could still be demanding and a taskmaster, but he was also very nurturing and supportive. Home life brought out a side rarely displayed in the workplace.

"He was sort of a lion in business, but to me he had a completely different personality at home," says Alan Schwartz, the Bear, Stearns executive who befriended Lewis during the McCall days. "Reg clearly was the focal point of his house, but there was a very soft side to it. He clearly was very proud of his family and there was a softness to him that you wouldn't have seen in a business deal. I think Leslie just wanted to be a female Reg."

Of his two children, Leslie, 21, is most like Lewis in that she tends to be intense and analytical, can be eloquent or blunt depending on the situation, and tends to approach matters in a no-nonsense, focused way.

Christina, 14, who is attuned to things creative and artistic, is already an accomplished pianist and also displays a talent for creative writing. She seems to be more like her mother in that she has a spirituality about her and a quiet, inner strength.

Lewis spent as much time with them and with his wife on weekends and holidays as he could. But the week was devoted to business pursuits. It's not that he held business or his personal ambition above his family—realizing his dreams just took a lot of his time. It was that simple.

"He knew the tremendous sacrifice he had to make by being away so much, which always bothered him," says one of Lewis's brothers, Jean Fugett, Jr. who's also a lawyer and briefly worked with Lewis at 99 Wall Street. "That was something that he really hated about his job. But if he had to do it all over again, he would do exactly what he had done."

That meant that maximum enjoyment and gratification had to be extracted from time spent with his family. Easter was a time of year the family trekked to the Virgin Islands. Thanksgivings were spent on Long Island and later in Paris. Christmases were celebrated in Baltimore, and the New Year was traditionally ushered in while in the Caribbean. There were also weekends in the family home on Long Island and generally at least one week-long trip a year to some vacation spot.

Lewis was particularly close to his girls because he felt the love they had for him was unalloyed, totally pure and unconditional. At one point, like many young men, Lewis was hoping to have a boy, whom he would have named Reginald Scott Lewis. That dream vanished without a trace of remorse once his daughters were on the scene. Their self-worth, solid personalities, well-adjusted outlooks on life and even physical attractiveness were all sources of immense pride for Lewis. "I knew I was going to have daughters who were going to be lookers," Lewis was fond of saying.

"All I saw was the twinkle in his eye when he was talking about them," Michael Milken says. "And how proud he was of them and how different their life was going to be from his life."

Lewis was protective of his daughters; he shielded them from prying media eyes wanting to know more about the private Reginald Lewis. Although his relationship with his family was a love affair of the first order, business is a jealous mistress and Lewis found her siren song irresistible.

"We worked at things pretty much the same way, which meant that by definition our families were deprived of a lot of our time," Cleve Christophe says. "That just was kind of the way it was. So we would talk about it in terms of our destiny, what we're seeking to achieve, why it's right for us to do this. We recognized at the same time there were certain of life's experiences, particularly on the family side, that in a way were compromised in the process."

Lewis's happiest, closest times with his family were spent in Paris when he moved there after the acquisition of Beatrice. His focus shifted more toward family and he and his wife were probably closer than at any other juncture in their marriage.

On Friday nights, Reginald and Loida Lewis would usually go to the opera and have black-tie dinners at Maxim's, one of Paris's best known restaurants.

Lewis got a kick out of giving his wife unexpected surprises with a romantic twist. One time he materialized with tickets to the Vienna Philharmonic Orchestra and whisked her off to Austria in his private jet. They took in the concert, spent the night in splendor at the Imperial Hotel in Vienna, and flew back to Paris the next afternoon.

The Lewises savored their time in Paris and looked forward to growing old together, with Lewis spending his golden years as the dean of a major U.S. university.

Dinnertime in the Lewis household saw the dining room turn into a courtroom as soon as dinner was finished. The Lewises would hold mock trials with one family member filling the role of prosecuting attorney, while another was a defense attorney, a judge, and a defendant.

Reginald and Loida Lewis had serious objectives in mind when these mock trial sessions, ostensibly a game, were held. They wanted their girls to be capable of thinking quickly on their feet and able to make defensible arguments based on sound analysis. Not surprisingly, Leslie and Christina possess a better than average grasp of how the U.S. legal system operates. Leslie, in fact, has given some thought to attending law school, which would put her on the same path as her father and mother.

"It was always interesting to hear the legal conversations when you walked into the dining room," says Lucien Stoutt, the Lewis's butler in New York. "Sometimes you'd walk in and you'd hear the kids prosecuting Mommy and Daddy. And nobody would be getting angry, they'd just be doing what they had to do based on the legal process."

In Paris, Leslie began to exhibit the rebelliousness that has marked many a child's passage into the teenage years. A typical disagreement between Leslie and her father would be over what time she was supposed to return home from an outing in the Lewis's chauffeur-driven limousine. When differences between them would reach a head, Lewis resorted to an old-fashioned remedy and grounded his daughter for a week at a time. Lewis was tremendously relieved when at 18 Leslie outgrew the rebelliousness that caused them to butt heads on so many occasions.

It was terribly important to Lewis that his children not grow up to be sheltered and pampered and oblivious to the fact that few people enjoyed the life of privilege and wealth they were accustomed to. There were occasions in Paris when Lewis had Christina or Leslie personally deliver checks to an orphanage he made contributions to. As with his other goals, Lewis was successful; his daughters appear to be unpretentious and socially enlightened.

One accomplishment of which Lewis was tremendously proud was the fact that he never missed a parent-teacher association meeting or a play or recital at the international, multilingual school his girls attended in Paris. The same was true when they were living in New York.

Lewis was getting Leslie more and more acquainted with Beatrice and its operations. And he took Christina with him to visit TLC Beatrice's potato chip operation in Ireland and the soft drink bottling plant in Brussels. But there was no grand design to groom either Leslie or Christina. Lewis saw no pressing need to have a capable successor waiting in the wings.

Evenings at the Lewis household were marked by laughter. Leslie and Christina loved to tell their father jokes, and he often reciprocated with one of his own. Lewis and Leslie were both partial to lengthy, intricate jokes that had to be meticulously retold to reach the punch line.

The family devised its own version of Trivial Pursuit, with Lewis asking each person at the dining table a math, history, or literature question.

Initially, Christina's piano playing filled the Lewises' Paris apartment with discordant, stacatto notes, leading her father to close the door to his study.

But as her playing became more and more fluid and melodic, the door to Lewis's study stayed open more and more often. He even arranged for her recital to be held at the Hotel Meurice in Paris and often asked her to play her concert pieces for visiting friends.

It was terribly important to Lewis and his wife that their children grow up as normally as possible, given their sheltered and privileged lifestyles. When *Forbes* placed Lewis on its list of 400 wealthiest

Americans in 1991 and 1992, he made no mention of it to Leslie or Christina.

Lewis also taught them the value of a dollar, and how to hold on to one despite their affluence. It was one lesson the girls learned well at the master's knee. "Christina and Leslie are just as tight with a dollar," laughs their grandmother, Carolyn Fugett. "They do not spend to be spending, believe me. And don't owe them anything!"

During the period he was living in Paris, Lewis seemed to take more time to enjoy the fun and relaxing things that his enormous wealth made possible. During several Christmas holiday seasons, he and Tony Fugett jetted into Jamaica to decompress for a week while Loida and the girls went to the Philippines. As the brothers passed through Jamaican customs, they were asked if they had any firearms to check.

"Do we have firearms?" a bemused Lewis responded. "No. Why, do we need them?" His trademark belly laugh was soon booming through the customs section of the airport. The brothers chuckled about the exchange throughout their stay. After leaving the airport they traveled to a resort in Jamaica known as Tryall, where they'd rented a villa named Randolins.

"I saw a change in the man," Fugett says. "We did not have a phone and he did not read a paper. He read books and we swam together in a sea pool and we played tennis two times a day. It was unbelievable. There was a dog at the villa and he actually walked with the dog—this from a man who hated dogs!"

"He said he never relaxed as much as he relaxed at the Randolins. He was going to buy the place."

While in Paris the Lewis family had a peculiar immigration arrangement: Because they had tourist visas, the clan had to leave France every 90 days. That was no problem given the geography of Europe, where countries are in close proximity to one another. The Lewises were well traveled on the continent and tallied Rome, Madrid, Berlin, and Prague among the cities that they toured.

When living in Europe, the ability to glide effortlessly between cultures and languages comes in handy. After a time, the Lewises were all fluent in French, with Loida Lewis and Leslie going a step better by adding Spanish to their repertoire, and Christina topping everyone by taking on Spanish and Japanese.

For Leslie's eighteenth birthday, Reginald Lewis arranged for a black-tie dinner at the family's Paris apartment that was attended by 60 of Leslie's classmates. Her graduation present from dad was a snazzy Volkswagen Cabriolet convertible. When *Time* magazine asked why Leslie didn't receive a more expensive vehicle like a Porsche or Mercedes, Lewis replied, "So she'll have something to look forward to!"

One of Lewis's proudest moments in life was when Leslie was accepted to Harvard College in 1991. Lewis and his family flew from East Hampton to Boston aboard TLC Beatrice's corporate jet to accompany Leslie to Cambridge, Massachusetts, to begin her studies at Harvard. When it was time for the Lewises to leave and return to Paris, Leslie started to cry. Loida Lewis also got moist-eyed after the limousine began to pull away from the dormitory, affecting her husband.

With the Lewis household shrinking from four people to three, Reginald Lewis bought Christina two Labrador retrievers, named Gaston and Gilbert, so she wouldn't feel too lonely in her sister's absence.

With TLC Beatrice having its best year ever in 1991 despite a looming recession in Europe, and a home life that brought him endless joy, it was with eagerness that Reginald Lewis looked forward to the approach of 1992.

15

Connoisseur, Philanthropist, Citizen of the World

Reginald Lewis gave millions of dollars to charities and causes where he thought his energies and wealth could make a difference. He was involved with philanthropy long before he became rich and long before he knew about his brain cancer in late 1992.

If charity begins at home, young Lewis had a first-rate teacher in his grandmother, Savilla Cooper. She possessed one of the biggest hearts in East Baltimore and thought nothing of escorting a stranger to her dinner table if that person had hit a stretch of bad luck and was hungry.

The lessons of Savilla Cooper were further amplified by Lewis's mother, Carolyn Fugett, who urged her son to always deal compassionately with those less fortunate, something she did in deed as well as with words. She frequently gave monetary gifts to people. Clinton Lewis was also generous—in fact his restaurant business fell on hard times in part because he simply couldn't turn away anyone who was hungry and couldn't afford to pay for a meal.

Lewis possessed a mixture of toughness and tenderness akin to that of his mother. He turned away many of the endless proposals and requests for funding he was inundated with after he became one of America's wealthiest men. But he was sufficiently caring to funnel a constant stream of money to projects and institutions he thought could have a positive impact on things.

In 1987, Lewis created The Reginald F. Lewis Foundation to manage his philanthropic activities.

"The genesis of that was, he understood the law and he understood how the law and society interacted," Jean Fugett, Jr. says. "And he understood the role of institutions and he understood how historically we've been denied access to these institutions—political institutions, economic institutions, and philanthropic institutions. If you look at all these institutions that have a great deal of impact, some would say even a disproportionate impact, on the lives of people today and you look at society today, you can see that a way to attack it or approach it is institutionally."

An institutional approach allowed Lewis to have a continuing influence on causes he was interested in, he believed.

Lewis used the same mindset for philanthropy that he employed for business: What's the best way to maximize my power and influence? Early childhood education and pediatric preventative medicine were two of his pet issues. Lewis initially personally screened all proposals coming into his foundation, but that responsibility proved to be too time consuming and Lewis delegated it to his staff. He even appointed his oldest daughter, Leslie, to the board of The Reginald F. Lewis Foundation, on her eighteenth birthday to instill in her a sense of doing the right thing.

Within four years of its inception, the Lewis Foundation had donated roughly $10 million to a variety of educational, civil rights, medical, and artistic institutions in the United States and in France. The year after the foundation was created, Lewis gave a total of $2 million in grants, including $1 million earmarked for Howard University, a historically black school in Washington, DC.

Some people interviewed for this book have cynically suggested that Lewis's interest in charity was directly proportional to his interest in shaping his legacy and in wanting to buy a kinder, gentler image. That view is off the mark, because Lewis did much of his charity work without publicity. Also, the passion with which he addressed certain societal issues through philanthropy—particularly those affecting African-Americans—clearly came from the heart.

"Reg was concerned about the world in which he lived," says Cleve Christophe, longtime friend until their falling out during the Beatrice deal. "I knew him for too many years and we discussed it far too many times for me to believe that that was just a facade—it was not. I remember in 1986 he said, 'Cleve, I have a very deep concern about the direction of our society, particularly as it relates to black males.' That was long before the theme that is so prevalent today of, 'What's happening to black youth, the males in particular?' He felt we had important roles to play—by example as well as by dint of what our success might enable us to do, in terms of philanthropy and otherwise."

"When he gave the $1 million to Howard, I wanted a big press conference and a lot of publicity on it," says Butch Meily, the spokesman for Beatrice. "He absolutely refused." Instead, Lewis went to Howard without fanfare, handed over a check and did an interview with Howard's television station.

Many people were surprised to learn of the scope of Lewis's activities, which weren't fully disclosed until after his death. "As it turned out, I didn't know half the things he was doing," says Jill Slattery, a friend from Lewis's Harvard days. "One thing I remember him saying was that one way he could give back and help was to get to a certain point in life. I learned a whole lot at the funeral of how much he had given back."

"No one really knew the true Reginald Lewis, because he was private," his mother says. "He didn't brag that he paid this for somebody, or he did that for somebody. His foundation was truly all his money—it did not come from some foundation or from the company, it came from him. A lot of people give a whole lot of money, but it comes through their corporations and they feed it from a profitable corporation into a nonprofit organization, but he didn't do that. This is Reginald Lewis giving back, and the nicest thing about it is he did it while he was alive."

In later years, Lewis made a one-time donation to his wife's alma mater in the Philippines in memory of her late father. "The gift of $100,000 to the University of the Philippines, my university, was a complete shock," Loida Lewis says. "He never gave me any inkling that he was going to do that and that he was going to do it in my father's name and not his."

But Lewis's relatives, including his mother, knew better than to make charitable pledges under the assumption that he would subsidize them. "If you're talking about saying to Reginald, 'This is a charity I'd like you to support,' I didn't do that," Carolyn Fugett says. There was one occasion where Fugett had forgotten she'd promised to donate some money to a church group. As luck would have it, Lewis called shortly after she was reminded of her commitment.

"Mom, is there anything that you want to give something to?" he asked as though clairvoyant.

She told him about the pledge she'd made to St. Edward's Catholic Church in Baltimore.

"Is your name on the line?" Lewis asked.

"You got it," his mother replied.

"Well then, I'll do it out of discretionary funds," Lewis said, making $2,000 available to his mother. Lewis was a regular benefactor of St. Edward's, including a $10,000 donation in 1989 for a new piano and an upgrade to the church's sound system. St. Edward's had been looking for $7,500. Carolyn Fugett was able to present the check in front of the congregation to enthusiastic applause.

After Lewis's death in 1993, his uncle, James Cooper, insisted that Jean Fugett, Sr. go with Cooper to a Baltimore Lincoln-Mercury dealership. Sitting in the middle of the showroom floor was a new Lincoln Continental with a huge red ribbon wrapped around it. Loida Lewis, knowing that her late husband had wanted to surprise Jean Fugett, Sr. with a new car, carried out her husband's unfulfilled wish.

When Lewis lived in Paris, he arranged for the Fugetts to fly to France on the Concorde, then go on an all-expense paid tour of Paris and the surrounding countryside.

At Christmas, Carolyn Fugett could usually expect a box full of jewelry from Tiffany's from her son, while Jean Fugett, Sr. usually received Brooks Brothers suits, leather jackets, and the like. During one yuletide gathering, Jean Fugett, Sr. casually mentioned within earshot of Lewis that he'd like to operate a McDonald's fast food franchise.

"Do you want one—seriously?" Lewis asked his stepfather. "I backed off, but evidently he was serious," Jean Fugett, Sr. says. "He would have gotten me a franchise."

Every Christmas Eve, Beatrice spokesman Butch Meily would take a check for $10,000 from his boss to the Rev. Calvin Butts, a high-profile civil rights activist and pastor of the Abyssinian Baptist Church in Harlem. From Lewis's perspective, it undoubtedly didn't hurt that Butts was a member of Kappa Alpha Psi, the black fraternity Lewis joined at Virginia State.

The Kappa Alpha Psi New York Alumni Scholarship Foundation, Inc., is also a beneficiary of Lewis's. His foundation gives at least $5,000 a year toward a $25,000 scholarship fund for New York City high school and college students. Lewis personally made the first contribution in 1989. After his death, the awards ceremony for handing out the 10 $2,500 individual scholarships was named the Reginald F. Lewis Memorial Scholarship Luncheon.

In January of 1990, Lewis gave $1 million in grants to predominantly African-American educational, artistic, and arts institutions. Among the institutions that received money from Lewis were the Mother Hale House in New York, which takes care of babies born to drug-addicted mothers. He also supported the Dance Theater of Harlem, the National Association for the Advancement of Colored People, and the Schomburg Center for Research in Black Culture at the New York Public Library. "I am encouraged by the support of African-Americans to African-American endeavors, and want to be part of that," Lewis said. "I share that African-American heritage and these institutions represent the kind of philanthropy I choose to support."

TAKING TIME TO MAKE A DIFFERENCE

Lewis didn't limit himself to checkbook philanthropy. Appropriating money is easy if one is so inclined: It's more difficult to carve precious blocks of time out of a schedule already crammed full. Lewis would generally clear the decks without fail to take advantage of an opportunity to address African-American students. The practice paid an unexpected dividend: Lewis had such an inspirational effect on some of these students that they later sought him out in hopes they could work for him.

Robert Suggs, who would one day work for Lewis & Clarkson at 30 Broad Street, first encountered Lewis during a speech to black law students at Harvard Law School in 1972. Darryl Thompson, who became an executive with TLC Beatrice, met Lewis during a conference for black business students at Stanford University. "Hard work, discipline, being focused, and having your skill knitted together in terms of what's needed to get the job done are the keys to success," Lewis told the enthralled Stanford audience. He didn't mention the subject of race until a student asked what it was like to be the pre-eminent African-American businessman in the country.

"Colors and labels have a way of categorizing people and creating artificial constraints around people and the way they think about themselves," he gently informed his questioner.

A $3 MILLION EXPRESSION OF GRATITUDE

An institution Lewis had a big soft spot for was Harvard. He never forgot that Harvard had accepted him to the law school even though his application circumvented the traditional process, or that Harvard made money available for his expenses so he could concentrate exclusively on his studies. Also, Lewis appreciated the fact that at Harvard Law School he found that the professors and administrators were not patronizing or prejudiced.

One of his first charitable contributions was a $10 check Lewis wrote to Harvard in 1969 while he was a junior associate with Paul, Weiss in Manhattan.

During the late 1980s, Lewis came to Harvard Law School's Ames Courtroom to give a talk on corporate takeovers. One of those taking in Lewis's remarks was corporate law professor Robert Clark. "It was jam-packed," Clark remembers. "I think it probably had the largest turnout of African-American students of any event that year. He loved it."

A few years later, after Clark was made dean of the law school, he put the touch on Lewis for what was Lewis's most impressive contribution: A $3-million commitment to Harvard Law School.

Lewis belonged to the Harvard Law School visiting committee tasked with planning the facility's long-term future. "What I remembered most about him in those settings was that he kept urging us to take the big picture into account," Clark says. "Take a global perspective, don't neglect international studies, train your students to learn about international law, international business and tax. That's where the future's going to be," Lewis used to tell the council constantly.

Three years later, The Reginald F. Lewis International Law Center would grace the law school's campus following Lewis's gift to the law school, but not before a lot of groundwork had been laid by Clark. One never gets a gift unless you ask, and usually more than once, laughs Clark, who, together with Dean for Development Scott Nichols, approached Lewis several times before finally succeeding in their quest. Their first talk took place in Manhattan at the Harvard Club in early 1991. "It went on for a few hours," Clark recalls. "We went to some part of the Harvard Club and had a few drinks and just talked. Basically, he was trying to size me up. It went pretty well."

So well, in fact, that Clark decided to make his pitch. He casually asked Lewis for a $5 million gift for Harvard's law school. Lewis inhaled sharply, his eyes widened and he gave Clark a look reserved for fools and madmen. Then Lewis let loose a huge belly laugh at the sheer audacity of Clark's request. "Boy, you've got a lot of nerve!" Lewis told Clark. Things were left at that, because Lewis wasn't about to make a snap commitment for that kind of money. But by the time they met for the second time to discuss the donation, the size of Lewis's gift was slowly starting to crystalize in his head.

"You know, I'm going to do something and it's going to be big," Lewis told Clark. "But I've got to figure it out." Whatever he would decide on, Lewis was determined to get his money's worth. He shared some opinions with Clark regarding what the law school should be emphasizing. He wanted to know what the school was doing in terms of international law and business law. He also asked a lot of questions about minority students. He wanted to know how many were applying, how many Harvard was accepting and how minority students were performing academically once admitted.

Lewis was also very curious about a well-publicized flap involving African-American law professor Derrick Bell, who was protesting Harvard Law School's lack of minority professors. Lewis made it a point to call other black Harvard professors including Christopher Edley and see what their take on the situation was.

Clark and Lewis met next in Cambridge, Massachusetts, on June 14, 1991, during Harvard Law School's campaign kickoff. A dinner was held in the massive law school reading room, which is larger than a football field. After dinner, speeches were made by some of those in attendance, including Lewis, who introduced Clark.

"This guy Clark, you meet him and you think: 'Well, this is a book-ish guy,'" Lewis said, smiling. "He's calm and scholarly and so forth, but then he can look you in the eye and ask you for more money than you'd ever think was possible," Lewis said, pausing a second for the laughter to subside. "And he got to me," Lewis said, to even louder laughs.

After a good deal of deliberation, in late 1991 Lewis arrived at a minimum financial figure he would feel comfortable donating. He was quite pleased to be able to tell Clark and he looked as though a load had been lifted from his shoulders. "It will be at least $1 million," Lewis said. "I don't know if I can get up to $5 million, but you can absolutely count on me for $1 million." Lewis eventually decided on $3 million, to be paid in annual installments of $500,000. At the time, Lewis's donation represented the largest gift ever made to Harvard by an individual donor.

Most of the money had been earmarked for international studies, with at least $500,000 to be dispensed in consultation with a committee chaired by Professor Edley, an African-American. In his letter bestowing the grant, Lewis wrote, "I am particularly hopeful that this gift will help the school continue to expand and accelerate its efforts in faculty diversity and other areas." Lewis's contribution was announced in July, 1992.

A good friend of Lewis's from his Virginia State days, Carolyn Powell, was curious why Lewis would give a significant gift to already richly endowed Harvard, rather than a black college. "I mean, I was upset a couple of times," Powell says. "Why did you give Harvard so much?" Lewis made her understand over time how much it meant to be able not only to give money to one of the nation's premier institutions, but to give more than any man—black or white. Plus, Lewis felt that having a major campus building named after an African-American would have incalculable inspirational and motivational value on black students at Harvard.

Plus, in Lewis's mind, Harvard was simply the best. Period.

Virginia State, Lewis undergraduate alma mater, received some money from him, too. Lewis had contributed roughly $80,000 to Virginia State, not including the $5,000 annual scholarship for the graduating math major with the highest grade point average.

In the last full year of Lewis's life, his philanthropic work was becoming increasingly important to Lewis. Phyllis Schless, who was on his acquisition team for McCall and Beatrice, had a lunch with him in the summer of 1992 that lasted about four and a half hours. The subject of philanthropy came up several times. "You know, I am really thinking about taking a year off and really getting involved with volunteerism," Lewis told Schless. The business world, while still attractive and tremendously gratifying, had begun to lose a little of its luster for Lewis.

In the summer of 1992, he helped Harvard pin down another substantial gift. Several fundraisers for Harvard Law School were in Europe talking up alumni viewed as potential donors. The team stopped by to see Lewis at his office in Paris. Dean Robert Clark mentioned that it looked as though he and his colleagues were going to miss a flight to London, where a dinner with 10 ambassadors from Arab countries had been scheduled.

"What's the meeting about?" Lewis asked. Told that the law school had plans for an Islamic legal studies center, he said, "Well, why don't you ride in my corporate jet? I'd like to go to this dinner, too." The Islamic ambassadors, who were from Saudi Arabia and Kuwait, among other countries, were quite impressed that Lewis had accompanied the law school's fund-raising team to the dinner. Harvard wound up receiving a seven-figure gift from King Fahd of Saudi Arabia, which was earmarked for the Islamic legal studies center.

In the last months of 1992, it looked as though a dear old friend of Lewis's, Ben Chavis, might have a shot at becoming the executive director of the NAACP. Ever since their flight from New York to North Carolina to battle school desegregation, Chavis had an enthusiastic supporter in Reginald Lewis. He told Chavis he would do whatever he could to help.

According to Chavis, Lewis "made an unlimited commitment to help the NAACP" if Chavis were elected executive director. In January 1993, a few days before his death, Lewis dictated some thoughts on the matter to his wife. Lewis asked that a portion of his fortune go to charity, including $2 million for the NAACP. That pledge of $2 million was used to establish The Reginald F. Lewis Memorial Endowment, created with an objective of raising $100 million for the NAACP.

Lewis's $2 million gift to the NAACP was announced in July 1993, and prompted a young black entrepreneur who had befriended Lewis to make a $1 million pledge to The Reginald F. Lewis Memorial

Endowment a few weeks later. Alphonse Fletcher, Jr., the 27-year-old CEO of Fletcher Capital Markets, viewed Lewis as a role model and mentor. Lewis first contacted Fletcher after he read in *The Wall Street Journal* that Fletcher had filed a discrimination lawsuit against Kidder Peabody. Fletcher charged that racial bias had affected his pay while he was managing an investment group for Kidder Peabody, and was awarded $1.26 million in arbitration. A Harvard graduate like Lewis, Fletcher met with Lewis a number of times.

When Ben Chavis announced Lewis's $2 million gift during the NAACP's annual convention, which was held in Indianapolis in 1993, Fletcher was in the audience. "I was sitting there thinking about what I could do to help others," Fletcher told the *New York Times* after his $1 million pledge was announced. "This was an appropriate way to honor Reginald Lewis."

Another organization Lewis donated money to was WNET-TV, Channel 13 in New York City. Lewis was on the board of the Public Broadcasting System station, after being invited to serve by the board chairman Henry Kravis, from whom Lewis bought TLC Beatrice. Lewis made a commitment of $250,000 to WNET.

"When he made that commitment, he called me up and we talked about it," says George Miles, Executive Vice President and Chief Operating Officer of WNET. "We talked back and forth about what he should do, and what the other board members were averaging in their contributions. He wanted to make sure the gift was significant, but he also didn't want to over-give."

WNET sought out Lewis in hopes of getting him involved with the station. Lewis told Miles that the media—television in particular—have tremendous potential to make a positive difference in peoples' lives. At WNET, Lewis espoused several issues near and dear to him: Health care, the state of the African-American community and entrepreneurship.

Miles recalls that Lewis's first check for $50,000 arrived on January 20, 1993—the day after his death.

16

"I Am Not Afraid of Death"

The incredible demands of doing business and social activities on an international scale typically left Reginald Lewis feeling fatigued, but toward the middle of 1992 he felt more enervated than usual. As early as 1990, he had begun to tell close business associates like Kevin Wright, "You guys don't know how tired I am."

No wonder: On May 20, 1992, Lewis flew from Boston to London to meet with the Harvard Law School Association of the United Kingdom. On May 22, he flew from London to Paris to attend a VIP dinner. On May 25, he jetted back to London for another dinner. On May 26, Lewis flew back to Paris for a dinner at the French Senate. May 27 saw Lewis taking a train to Brussels for a VIP breakfast. The next day, May 28, Lewis flew to Turin, Italy, for a meeting with Giovanni Agnelli at the headquarters of automaker Fiat. On May 29 there was a flight from Rome to Istanbul, Turkey. Two days later, Lewis was on a plane headed for Boston to visit his daugher, Leslie, a freshman at Harvard.

In addition to his peripatetic lifestyle, Lewis routinely placed calls to the United States at 1 and 2 o'clock in the morning Paris time, in order to catch key U.S. executives at their homes in the evening. It was inevitable that his demon pace would catch up with a man a few months shy of 50.

In the past, Lewis could sit through lengthy meetings with no lapses in his impressive concentration and no need for breaks or interruptions. Now, he needed repeated rests just to get through a meeting an hour or two in length.

"I knew that he hadn't been feeling well—a lot of us in the family knew that, but we didn't know what it was," Jean Fugett, Jr. says. "I had a great concern for his lifestyle and his travel. I asked him to slow down. He was really exhausted and worn down."

Lewis looked elsewhere for answers. Figuring he might be carrying a pound or two too many, Lewis went on a diet, hoping that would invigorate him. He shed the weight successfully, but still couldn't shake the fatigue. In the summer and early fall of 1992, came other changes in Lewis's health. He started to become allergic to ice cream. Eating it made him hyperventilate, so he cut it out of his diet completely.

Then he became allergic to his beloved champagne, which would bring on the same physical symptoms as the ice cream. Described by close friends as someone who was a latent hypochondriac most of his life, now Lewis's maladies were all too real.

By the time summer rolled around, Jean Fugett, Jr. was concerned enough about his brother that he was making frequent calls to France from the United States.

Lewis visited TLC Beatrice's Manhattan headquarters in August. Robert Davenport, who worked briefly as Lewis's director of business development, dropped by briefly to see his old boss.

"He was sitting in his office and he didn't get up when I walked into the office. So I walked over to him and shook hands and he never stood up."

It was an uncharacteristically reflective Lewis that began talking to Davenport. "His death put into very sharp focus the conversation we had, which sounded a lot like a retirement speech," Davenport says.

Lewis told his former employee, "I just wanted to take the company public, but that didn't work out. I'm comfortable now and I don't need to make any lifestyle adjustments," Lewis said. "Things are on track and running well. I'm really sort of comfortable where I am and I'm really going to pull back a bit."

When it was time for Davenport to leave, Lewis got up to escort him to the door.

"Reg, goodness you've dropped a lot of weight!" Davenport exclaimed.

"Oh, a diet— I've really cut out all the meat and alcohol," Lewis responded.

In September an old schoolmate from Lewis's Virginia State days, John "City" Green, came to visit the head of TLC Beatrice in Paris. Chairman of the board of regents of Morgan State University, a historically black school in Baltimore, Green wanted to talk to Lewis about increasing his philanthropic aid to Morgan. Lewis's foundation had already given $50,000 to Morgan to establish the Reginald F. Lewis Scholarship.

"My god, City, I haven't seen you in years," Lewis said as he shook hands with, then hugged his Kappa Alpha Psi frat brother. "This is something I need to do more of."

In addition to admiring Lewis's classy charcoal brown suit, Green noticed something else about his old friend. "I came away with the feeling that he wasn't feeling well or was tired or something," Green recalls. " I just attributed it to the trans-Atlantic lifestyle. He didn't seem as intense as I would have expected him to be after remembering him from school. But then I said to myself, 'Maybe it's because he wasn't with people in business with him.'"

In October, Lewis flew out to California to visit Michael Milken in prison camp, where Milken was sent after being convicted of stock manipulation charges. As usual, Lewis was preoccupied with a potential business acquisition. "He was looking at Paramount independent of me," Milken remembers. "Paramount stock at the time was $40 to $41 a share. That was our last extensive conversation. We walked around the visiting area and there was a gleam in his eye and he was energized." Lewis also talked about his family. "He loved to talk about his girls," Milken says.

Milken also noticed subtle changes in Lewis's demeanor. "His voice didn't have the same ring to it," Milken remembers. "He then gave me a five- six-minute lecture on beauty. And art. The twinkle in his eye was there in late 1992 when I was with him. The twinkle in his voice was not there."

By Thanksgiving, something was undeniably amiss with Lewis's health. He was beginning to have vision problems in his left eye. He told a concerned Loida Lewis that he planned to fly to the United States to undergo a thorough physical exam, which had been scheduled for his 50th birthday. A battery of tests was conducted on Lewis, including a CAT scan. It revealed an ominous looking growth inside Lewis's brain.

As a doctor explained the test results to Lewis, he felt himself going numb with incredulity. And the somber expression on the physician's face filled Lewis's heart with trepidation. He sat for a minute in the examining room after the doctor had left, collecting himself. Then, he walked on leaden legs to a telephone and called his wife in Paris. "Something is wrong and they don't know what," Lewis said in a monotone. "A CAT scan showed something on my brain and they want to do a biopsy." Loida and Christina Lewis were on the next plane from Paris to New York.

The biopsy was performed and it confirmed the Lewises' worst fears: Reginald Lewis had brain cancer. Due to the size and location of the tumor it was inoperable. If left untreated, Lewis would have roughly six to eight weeks to live, the doctors estimated. Radiation treatment was the only treatment option, but the odds of eradicating the cancer were nominal, the Lewises were told.

His mind still sharp and his analytical approach to problem solving very much intact, Lewis wanted to know about the potential negative side effects associated with radiation treatment. He was told that his memory and powers of reasoning might be impaired, and there might be a loss of bodily function. Hair loss was pretty much a definite.

For a brief while Lewis toyed with the idea of undergoing radiation sessions. He even went through the motions of talking to a physician who would administer the radiation treatments. But in the end, he couldn't bring himself to do it. Under his risk/benefit analysis, the chances of radiation being successful were practically nil, but without it, at least his faculties would remain intact. He couldn't fathom the notion of having his mental faculties impaired and succumbing to cancer in a few months anyway.

On December 8, one day after Lewis's birthday, he received an award in Manhattan from the New York Urban Coalition, in what would be his last public appearance. Later that day, Lewis's butler received an unusual request from his boss. Lewis wanted Lucien Stoutt to cut the meat on his plate, because Lewis was unable to hold the fork in his left hand.

"Lucien, it's not like when we used to be at East Hampton, playing tennis," Lewis told Stoutt as the butler quietly sliced Lewis's meal into manageable pieces.

Four days after his diagnosis, an emotional, sobbing Reginald Lewis called his mother in Baltimore to break the horrible news. He simply told her that he'd had a CAT scan that showed a brain tumor.

"Well, let me come up and be with you," Carolyn Fugett said calmly, fighting to keep her own surging emotions in check.

"I don't want to take you away from the family," Lewis said.

"Well, look at it this way: Loida can be with you and I'll be with Leslie and Christina."

"Okay, Mom, that would be nice."

They got off the phone, ending one of the worst telephone calls any parent can get from an offspring.

"I felt that I had died inside, truthfully, when I heard him," Carolyn Fugett says. "Before the CAT scan, you could tell something was wrong. I guess the mother in me knew that he wasn't in the best of health."

Only a select group of family members were told of Lewis's malady. Tony and Jean Fugett knew, as did James Cooper, the uncle Lewis was particularly close to.

"He just said, 'I have cancer,'" Cooper remembers. "The reason I knew he didn't have long to live is because he said, 'I don't want you to see me, because you wear your feelings on your sleeve. I want you to pray for me, because it's serious.' When he said it that way, I knew it was serious."

"I KNOW I'LL BEAT THIS THING"

As the shock and disbelief gradually wore off, Lewis resolved to fight his cancer rather than surrender meekly to it. He was also determined not to let his illness derail his life.

"He was tired, but he'd talk in the car sometimes about future plans," says Lewis's chauffeur and bodyguard, Ed Gregg. "He'd talk about buying things—hotels, that sort of thing. I guess his mind was always going on a business cycle."

Indeed, the beat never stopped in terms of Lewis presiding over Beatrice and conducting its affairs. His mother says Lewis would wheel and deal over the telephone at home.

"He was taking care of business," Carolyn Fugett marvels. In the last few weeks before his death, Lewis initiated a currency swap that resulted in a tidy gain for the company.

Meanwhile, only two executives at TLC Beatrice were told that the chairman was seriously ill. Another person who figured it out after a phone call from Lewis was Charles Clarkson. On a leave of absence from TLC Beatrice at the time, Clarkson who suffered from a spinal tumor while under Lewis's employ some years back, was compassionately given plenty of time to recuperate.

"I just wanted to talk to you because I know you had been ill," Lewis said, prompting Clarkson to immediately suspect Lewis had cancer. Any remaining doubt Clarkson harbored was alleviated after Lewis said he might need to see Clarkson's brother-in-law, who is a radiation oncologist in a Manhattan hospital.

"Reg, do you want me to call him for you?" Clarkson asked.

"Well, maybe if I go I'll talk to you," Lewis said.

Without telling Clarkson, Lewis quietly saw the physician. He scheduled a number of appointments for radiation treatments, but never followed through.

Lewis did try to reach out to Kevin Wright, but because of the nature of their relationship and because Lewis was too private to discuss his illness, they missed a chance to connect one last time. "On a couple of occasions the message came back to me, 'Reg wants to see you.' But with Reg, I never just showed up—I waited until I was summoned. If I had known he was that ill, I would have just gone over."

Despite the hospital visits, it was becoming obvious to Lewis and those around that the malignant growth inside his head was starting to overtake him.

"In the space of about two weeks, you could see he was sick," Lucien Stoutt says. "He slept more than usual." Plus the bright smile and flashing eyes Stoutt had grown accustomed to were absent.

Ed Gregg says Lewis's children were very quiet and obviously upset as their father was fighting for his life. Loida Lewis, who possesses vast reserves of quiet inner strength, maintained her equilibrium. "You could see it wearing on her," Gregg remembers. "I guess he was such a dominant figure in their lives that to see him get sick was probably a big shock to them."

As if life weren't topsy-turvy enough, in December the Lewises moved from their brownstone on 22nd Street to a spectacular two-level, 15-room East Side co-op that once belonged to former automaker John DeLorean. In some respects, the distraction was a welcome one.

Lewis spent New Year's Eve hosting a black tie dinner party for close friends and the family. January 1, 1993—a Friday—was quiet. He stayed with his family. The brain cancer had now dramatically weakened his left side and he often needed assistance in order to move around. The vision in his left eye was also demolished. An independent and proud man, Lewis hated the vulnerability and dependence brought on by his illness.

"As he lost control of the left side of his body, I became his left side," Tony Fugett says. "No one else could touch him or watch him or be around him. In the morning I was there when he was up, and I was there when he went to sleep at night. I almost became like an extension of him."

However, Lewis resolutely refused to wallow in self pity, nor did his optimism wane. Shortly after New Year's Day, Lewis called up Charles Clarkson. "I want to wish you a Happy New Year," Lewis told his long-time colleague. "I'm still struggling, but I'm strong. I know I'll beat this thing." Lewis never did tell Clarkson what his malady was.

A PROMISE OF HOPE

Because Lewis's hospital treatments didn't appear to be working, Loida Lewis suggested that he try something outside the realm of conventional medicine. A faith healer who was famous in the Philippines could be flown to New York to see if he could arrest Lewis's illness. The healer claimed to have the ability to touch sick people and literally pull their maladies out of their bodies.

Lewis flatly rejected the proposal at first. But after some more thought, he figured it certainly couldn't hurt. So the healer was flown to Manhattan and put up in a hotel not far from the Lewises' new residence near Central Park. The mystic was supposed to conduct healing sessions in Lewis's home that were to take place over five days. The first session started during the first full week of January 1993.

"At the beginning, we thought it was for real, but it was fake," Loida Lewis says. "When we looked closely, it was just sleight of hand."

Tony Fugett, who was also present, told his brother that the healer was a fraud. "What!" exclaimed Lewis, who wanted to believe in the mystic's abilities.

Fugett, who can be hot-tempered like his big brother, was furious, but he held it in. "He was palming and he wasn't a fucking good palmer, either," Fugett says of the faith healer. "But my focus was more on Reg than this phony bastard. I was angry at his decision to go forward, because Reg still made all the decisions."

Yet, Fugett understands why his brother agreed to see the mystic. "He wasn't desperate, but he felt that there had to be some cure somewhere and he would do whatever he could to find something."

Even though Lewis, his wife, and his brother had seen through the faith healer, he was allowed to continue, though his sessions were cut from five days to three. Fugett asked his brother if he still intended to pay the man?

"Yes, Tony, I'm paying him. Why am I paying him? Because there was a promise of hope," Lewis responded philosophically. "Is this amount of money worth the promise of hope? Yes—give it to him."

Another promise of hope materialized in Canada. An experimental drug was being offered there that might have the ability to dissolve Lewis's tumor. However, the drug was not approved by the U.S. Food and Drug Administration, so Lewis would have to go to Canada for treatment.

Arrangements were made for Lewis to be seen in an oncology outpatient facility in Toronto. The day before he flew to Toronto, Lewis's secretary, Deidra Wilson, came to his co-op to take some dictation from her boss.

The following draft memo, which was dictated January 13, indicates that Beatrice's Chairman was still remarkably focused and lucid less than a week before his death:

To all shareholders:

In the next few days we will issue a press release announcing my retirement from day-to-day operations and the formation of an office of the chairman to assume many of my former duties.

Since the Lewis family will continue to own 51% of the company's common stock, I will, of course, stay involved to some extent. However, I shall relinquish all responsibilities for day-to-day management and turn these over to a group of young, but highly seasoned executives in whom I have great confidence.

The goal will continue to be to produce superior returns for all stockholders, while maintaining a solid balance sheet, stability and continuity in all of our operations. As you know, our principal holdings are in Western Europe, whose economies are feeling the effects of recession and high unemployment. I am confident, however, that the long-term future of Europe is strong, particularly in France, Germany, Spain, Italy, Holland, and the other markets where we do business.

I am also confident that we have made the necessary investments over recent years to ensure that our independent subsidiary companies can continue to compete effectively. I want to thank our many employees—5,000 worldwide—who have stood shoulder-to-shoulder with me since December of 1987 to produce what can only be described as fine results for all involved. I am particularly grateful to many of our senior executives in the field, Señor Delfin Suarez, Messrs. Jean and Jacques Baud and the Baud family, Vincent O'Sullivan, and to our organizations in Spain, Italy, Holland, Belgium, Germany, Denmark, and in other operating theaters around Europe.

They have given me their cooperation on an unfailing basis and have accepted my vision and leadership for this company from the very beginning.

To my board of directors, which has been a great source of moral support to me, I extend my thanks and appreciation.

The new team will be led by Jean S. Fugett, Jr., who is no stranger to this company or TLC's affiliates. Jean, who as many of you know is my brother, has been with me since the inception of TLC in February of 1984. He has worked very closely with me through the McCall acquisition, its revitalization and subsequent sale and was also an integral part in the acquisition and ongoing affairs of TLC Beatrice, with our emphasis on investments and rigorous review of operations. He has worked very closely with me over the past five years and I believe is in a unique position as a family member to understand the needs of the 51% majority shareholders. He also appreciates the manner and culture that I have tried to instill in the company, so that we can work for the benefit of all shareholders, applying the most rigorous standards of integrity and professionalism.

I have confidence that these policies will be continued.

In the future I have decided to devote the bulk of my personal time to my family and philanthropic activities, particularly in the area of social justice and civil rights.

Later, Lewis dictated the following public statement to his wife, Loida, as part of his expression of support for Reverend Chavis:

When I think about how I want to spend the rest of my life, the decision to devote it to the cause of social justice, to the area of civil rights, and to American cultural affairs is to me a stimulating and challenging assignment.

Even in my own career, a person of very modest means has been able—by dint of his own efforts—to achieve great wealth and financial independence, which therefore suggests that some progress clearly has been made. But in my view, it is all too little when we consider the day-to-day drama being inflicted upon many of our children who are of African or Hispanic descent and who are not yet fully included in the American Dream.

By working in this field in the future, I believe that I am working for all Americans, because I truly believe that our society is highly vulnerable unless we join together in seeing this not as a particular problem of any one ethnic group, but as something that the nation must address as part of its own spirit of renewal.

At no point in the memo or statement was the underlying reason for Lewis's abrupt retirement given.

On January 14, 1993, a Thursday, Loida Lewis called down to the front doorman of the family's apartment to have a wheelchair ready. The time had arrived to fly to Toronto. Flanked by his wife and Tony and Jean Fugett, Lewis walked haltingly to the elevator portico of his magnificent apartment.

The elevator door opened and Lewis entered slowly, grabbing Tony's arm for support. After descending a few floors, the elevator opened on an impressive foyer with a view of a central courtyard. Something else came into view—the wheelchair that his wife had requested for her husband. The doorman stood beside it attentively.

"No, please," Lewis said. "I will walk." With his brothers on either side of him, Lewis walked proudly—if somewhat unsteadily—past the wheelchair and out the front door of the building.

The Lewises chauffeur and bodyguard, Ed Gregg, sprang out of their Bentley to open the rear door to the vehicle. Lewis and his family members got into the car and Gregg immediately took off without first asking for a destination, which he customarily did when the constantly rushing Lewis was his passenger.

Gregg was instructed to head for Teterboro Airport in New Jersey. Teterboro serves as something of a corporate jetport for New York City, freeing heavily congested LaGuardia and Kennedy airports for commercial traffic. "That was the last time I saw him," Gregg says. "He was very weak."

The Chairman of Beatrice was assisted up the ladder of his plane. The pilots and flight attendant were stunned by Lewis's appearance. "They didn't know that the tumor had advanced to the state that the left side of his body was affected," Tony Fugett says. "I remember the crew trying to be cool and calm. They were professional throughout."

After their arrival in Toronto, Lewis, his wife, and two brothers booked themselves into a hotel. His cancer treatments were to be administered there, rather than at the out-patient oncology center. Lewis pretty much stayed in his hotel suite during the brief time he was in Toronto, taking his meals via room service and allowing health care workers to administer his anti-cancer medication.

He initially believed the treatment would help him whip his illness. But after about two days, Lewis sensed the drug wasn't the answer.

"Tony, it's not working," Lewis said matter-of-factly when the two of them were alone in his room.

Perhaps sensing the inevitable, Lewis—who believed in God, but was not a devout Catholic—had begun telling his wife, "Death does not frighten me—I'm not afraid of death. I surrender myself to Christ."

During a moment when just Lewis and his wife were in their hotel suite, he pondered the irony that of all the places to be afflicted with a fatal malady, it had to be his mind. "I know I have cancer of the brain," he told his wife, "I used my brain as a weapon to go forward and to disprove a lie about people of color, and I had no protection."

Jean Fugett, Jr., by that point the de facto CEO of TLC Beatrice, left Toronto for New York in order to run the business.

On January 16th, a Saturday, it was sunny in Toronto with a typically frigid, mid-winter Arctic air mass straddling the city. Lewis awoke that morning on a mission: He planned to "play" a particularly wicked game of tennis, and Tony Fugett was going to do it for him. Fugett, who hadn't brought any tennis gear sent the flight attendant out to fetch some. He was somewhat baffled by his brother's insistence that Fugett play tennis. Leisure activity was the furthest thing from his mind right now, but he dutifully carried out Reginald Lewis's request.

"Tony, I want you to go out and play a tennis game. I'm going to be your coach—you really need to get some exercise because you've been caught up in doing a lot of things," Lewis told his brother. "Now, what I want you to do is I want you to get 60 percent of your first serves in. I know you can hit that overhead, I want you to take that hitch out of your forehand and come to the net behind that powerful serve of yours."

Fugett promised Lewis he would go out and try to play a memorable tennis match. He left Lewis's hotel room and closed the door gently behind him. He called his brother, Jean Fugett, in New York.

"Jean, Reg wants me to go out and play tennis," Tony Fugett said. "And not only does he want me to play tennis, but to do what he wants, I have to play the best tennis of my life!"

Tony Fugett set out for a nearby indoor tennis club. He found a tennis pro willing to play and waged battle as though the Wimbledon championship were at stake.

Not long after Fugett departed, Loida Lewis entered her husband's room.

"Loida, it's like there's a shade falling over my eyes," Lewis told his wife. She went over to see what the matter was and finding her husband to be okay for the moment, went into another room of their hotel suite. Feeling totally helpless and frustrated, Loida sobbed quietly.

Lewis summoned a male nurse to come to his room and shave him. Lewis asked the nurse to dress him well, not in pajamas, but in a manner appropriate for a fancy dinner.

Over a meal of veal scalopini, Lewis reminisced with his wife about their life together and what a fantastic, improbable journey it had been. They did this not out of a sense of foreboding, but because it was something they normally did from time to time.

Tony knocked on the door and Loida let him into the hotel room. "Did you do the best you could do?" Lewis asked.

"Yeah," Tony said.

"Did you have fun?" Lewis asked. "Yes," Tony Fugett replied.

"That's all that matters," Lewis said, catching Tony Fugett by surprise. "Here's a man who kept track of the score in everything," Fugett says, thinking back to their post-game conversation.

On Sunday, January 17th, at about 3 A.M., Tony Fugett was awakened by a frantic call: "Come down to our room right away!"

Lewis was lying in his bed with rivulets of sweat pouring down his face when Fugett arrived. The first thing Fugett did was sit Lewis up in the bed and prop some pillows behind his back. He then took off his big brother's nightshirt and undershirt, which were soaked with perspiration, and then put a fresh Brooks Brothers nightshirt on Lewis.

Fugett then gently lowered Lewis back down on the bed.

"Tony, help me, I need you," Lewis said, then he began to convulse from a seizure before lapsing into unconsciousness.

"A coldness came over me," Fugett says. "I had frantic people around. It was take charge time—get him to the hospital. He was always a master of execution and I had to become one."

After getting his brother to a hospital, Fugett left to rustle up the crew of Lewis's plane and alert them that they needed to be ready to return to the United States at a moment's notice.

Back at the hospital, the family was informed that Reginald Lewis had suffered a massive cerebral hemorrhage brought on by his brain tumor. The Chairman of Beatrice was in a coma and had suffered irreversible brain damage, the doctors said. They added that there was practically no hope of recovery and that Lewis could pass away at any time.

A woman pastor from the hospital asked Loida Lewis if she wanted a Catholic priest to administer extreme unction—the ceremony where the priest prays for and anoints with oil a person who is dying or in danger of dying. She said she would like to have the sacrament performed.

"Lo and behold, the Catholic priest was an African," Loida Lewis recalls. "Because my husband is so fierce about race, God sends him an African in Canada to give the last rites."

She now faced a perilous decision: Should they remain in a Toronto hospital, or transport Lewis to a medical facility in Manhattan, a trip he might not survive?

Praying that she was making the right decision, Loida Lewis opted to move her husband to Manhattan. After she told the doctors of her decision, she noticed Reginald Lewis's head move slightly, as though he were nodding in the affirmative.

Hooked to portable life-support machines, a stretcher-bound Reginald Lewis was carried aboard his private jet for a final international flight.

Now that Lewis's condition was touch and go and his cancer could no longer be kept under wraps, his relatives were told his situation was bleak and that they should travel to the hospital Lewis was being transported to in Manhattan. On Monday, January 18th, the day before Lewis's death, his family was told Lewis's pulse was beginning to weaken.

"The day before Mr. Lewis died, I saw his mother look kind of sad," Lucien Stoutt says. "I could see something was wrong from the expression on her face."

Butch Meily was given permission to notify the press that Reginald Lewis had brain cancer, was in a coma, and the prior week had created an office of the chairman to be headed by Jean Fugett, Jr.

The next day, Tuesday, January 19th, a doctor checked Lewis, turned to the assembled family members and said, "His pulse is going." Everyone present, including Lewis's wife and mother gathered around his bed. Loida Lewis recited the Twenty-Third Psalm aloud, "The Lord is my shepherd," she started and continued to the end of the psalm. Then she whispered, "You may go now, my darling. I love you."

"Everybody was crying, including me," James Cooper says. Just then, the fire alarm sounded. Carolyn Fugett said in a loud voice, "The angels are welcoming him in heaven." Reginald Lewis was dead at the age of 50.

Cooper and Tony Fugett were responsible for getting Lewis's remains from New York to Baltimore for burial. Lewis would have gotten a chuckle out of the stunt they pulled to get his body out of the hospital without being detected by the press. They'd bribed an elevator operator to allow Fugett to accompany Lewis's temporary casket to the ground floor via the back elevator.

Acting as a decoy, Cooper went out the front door and hopped into a waiting limousine to draw away any reporters or photographers that might be lurking out front. As soon as the limo pulled away from the curb, Cooper ordered it to go to the rear of the hospital, where the casket was loaded into a hearse. Then Cooper and Fugett followed the hearse from Manhattan to Teterboro Airport in New Jersey.

Cooper and Fugett were both impressed by what they saw next: The crew of Lewis's aircraft had washed and waxed his plane to a mirror-like sheen. Even the landing gear and the tires were gleaming. "The plane was immaculate and the crew was impeccably dressed, like Reg would have wanted it," Fugett recalls. Several seats had been removed to accommodate Lewis's casket, which was placed gingerly, almost reverently, inside Lewis's beloved private jet. Fugett and Cooper, who had never flown before, boarded after the casket was loaded and flew off in a southerly direction. Their destination was Baltimore-Washington International Airport.

When the plane landed, a hearse was already on the tarmac, waiting to take Lewis's body to March Funeral Home in West Baltimore. Loida Lewis, who had never left her husband's side since she arrived from Paris last December, had asked Tony Fugett to stay with her husband until she arrived in Baltimore. The funeral home was devastatingly cold at night because its automatic thermostat couldn't be overridden. Cooper also stayed, because Fugett asked him to.

Lewis's many uncles took turns standing at his side, keeping him company, from January 19 until January 23, the day of his funeral and burial.

Epilogue

Dressed warmly to fend off a biting winter wind, relatives, friends, and those merely wishing to pay homage to a remarkable man began trickling into St. Edward's Roman Catholic Church in Baltimore around 9:50 A.M. on Saturday, January 23, 1993. The wake for Reginald Francis Lewis was scheduled for 10 A.M., with a Mass of Christian Burial to follow an hour later. St. Edward's is on Poplar Grove Street in Northwest Baltimore, literally around the corner from Mosher Street and the house and community that Lewis called home.

As the limousine carrying Loida, Leslie, and Christina Lewis glided up to the front of St. Edward's, Leslie Lewis felt compelled to remind her mother of something: "Okay, Mommy," said Reginald Lewis's oldest daughter, who had flown down from Harvard in the middle of taking exams. "We are the Lewis women."

In front of her husband's open casket, Loida Lewis greeted mourners with a firm handshake and a smile, belying her profound sorrow and sense of loss. She chose to submerge her pain and console others, instead of the other way around.

I had written a lengthy piece about Reginald Lewis for USA Today following his death and really didn't have to attend his funeral, because no coverage had been planned by my paper. Nor had I been tabbed to write this book. But I put on a tie and went anyway. I wasn't present when Jackie Robinson or Frederick Douglass were laid to rest, but figured I could at least tell my grandchildren I was at Reginald Lewis's funeral. Here was a fellow African-American from Baltimore who grew up in a neighborhood not far from mine and clawed his way to the summit of a billion-dollar business empire.

When I walked past Lewis's casket, Loida Lewis greeted me warmly, even though we had never been introduced. I was disappointed that an opportunity to meet Reginald Lewis when he was alive had never materialized, and thus chose not to view his body.

Loida, Leslie, and Christina all spoke before the overflow crowd gathered inside St. Edward's Catholic Church with dry eyes, conviction and strong, clear voices, as did all of Lewis's family members, including his mother, Carolyn Fugett.

Christina Lewis began by reading a passage from the Bible, the Book of Wisdom, Chapter Four, Verses 7–14: "The just man, though he die early, shall be at rest. For the age that is honorable comes not with the passing of time, nor can it be measured in terms of years. Rather, understanding is the hoary crown for men, and an unsullied life the attainment of old age. . . . Having become perfect in a short while, he reached the fullness of a long career, for his soul was pleasing to the Lord. Therefore, he sped him out of the midst of wickedness, but the people saw and did not understand, nor did they take this into account."

Leslie Lewis took a different tack: "My father never stopped moving forward, no matter what fate threw in his way. Whether racial stereotypes that would hamper him in his business, racial bias and prejudice, no matter what the world threw him, he didn't let it stop him. . . . As we traveled to the church this morning, we had a police escort. In their urgency, they stopped traffic at intersections and they played sirens, and I thought, 'Wow! They're really making a lot of noise.' Then I thought, 'My God, yes! Let them make noise. Let there be a commotion. Let there be a loud noise because we are sending off a great man today.'"

Finally, Loida Lewis spoke of a love that death would never dimish: "The foundation on which Reginald F. Lewis grew up is a foundation based on love. Not the love we see on television or the love in which you say, 'I love you,' and then forget it the next day. No! It's the love that St. Paul talks about in his letter to the Corinthians. Love that is patient, hopeful, expecting. Not nagging. It is love that is kind, not hurting with your tongue. It is love that is not conceited, or self-centered, or ego-based. It is not selfish; nor does it keep a record of wrongs. . . . True love never gives up. Its faith, its hope, its patience endures. So my darling, you had it in your early life, and I tried to give it to you in our marriage. I have loved you without conditions, without reservations. My love for you will never end."

Among those who sent messages of condolence was newly inaugurated president Bill Clinton. "Hillary and I are deeply saddened to learn of your husband's death," Clinton wrote. "Reginald Lewis's commitment to excellence, his life of achievement and his deep concern for his fellow man were an inspiration to me and to all who knew him."

"His generosity was boundless, enriching the lives of people around the world. We will miss him. You and your family are in our thoughts and in our prayers."

Bill Cosby wrote: "Reggie Lewis is to me, not was, is to me what Joe Louis is to me. What Jackie Robinson is to me. Regardless of race, color, or creed, we are all dealt a hand to play in this game of life. And believe me, Reg Lewis played the hell out of his hand."

Lewis was eulogized by his friend and soon-to-be head of the National Association for the Advancement of Colored People, Dr. Ben Chavis. Those in the church laughed heartily as Chavis recounted how he and Lewis had gone to North Carolina to fight school desegregation, and Lewis had had the moxie to ask a uniformed, white Southern sheriff to display identification.

Buried with Lewis at New Cathedral Cemetery in Baltimore are a box of his cherished Monte Cristo cigars, a bottle of Dom Perignon champagne—vintage 1985—and a graphite tennis racquet, should he encounter an old tennis foe in the great beyond.

A few days after the funeral, a memorial service was held for Lewis in Manhattan, at the Riverside Church in Harlem. Among those who addressed the 2,000 or so people in attendance were New York Mayor David Dinkins, Texaco Chairman James W. Kinnear, the Reverend Jesse Jackson, and Harvard Law School Dean Robert C. Clark. Opera star and friend, Kathleen Battle sang "Amazing Grace," Lea Salonga, who was starring in the Broadway musical "Miss Saigon," gave a rendition of "The Quest" (The Impossible Dream), and the Harlem Boys Choir—a benefactor of Lewis' philanthropy—also performed.

Looking back on the incredible life and times of Reginald F. Lewis, one of his favorite poems seems particularly appropriate. Written by Langston Hughes, it's titled, "Mother to Son":

Well, son, I'll tell you:
Life for me ain't been no crystal stair.
It's had tacks in it,
And splinters,
And boards torn up,
and places with no carpet on the floor—
Bare.
But all the time
I'se been a-climbin' on,
And reachin' landin's,
And turnin' corners,
And sometimes goin' in the dark
Where there ain't been no light.
So boy, don't you turn back.
Don't you set down on the steps
'Cause you finds it's kinder hard.
Don't you fall now—
For I'se still goin', honey,
I'se still climbin',
And life for me ain't been no crystal stair.*

*Used with permission by Vintage Books, a division of Random House, Inc.

Sources Interviewed

Finally, I would like to thank everyone who graciously agreed to talk to me about Reginald Lewis. Whether your name appears or not, you helped me draw a bead on a complex and fascinating man:

Mark Alcott
Earle Angstadt
Lee Archer
Jack Auspitz
Paulette Bacote-McAlily
Al Banks
Jean Baud
Robert Bell
Richard Brown
Tom Bourelly
Bill Cammer
Ben Chavis
Cleve Christophe
Robert Clark
Charles Clarkson
Elaine Cole Lewis
Mary Coleman
Alan Colon
James Cooper
Robert Cooper, Sr.

Samuel Cooper
Robert Davenport
Clarence David
Guy DeBrantes
Richard Dehe
Mathias DeVito
Lucious Edwards
Peter Eikenberry
Dominique Fargue
Hughlyn Fierce
Carolyn Fugett
Jean Fugett, Jr.
Jean Fugett, Sr.
Anthony Fugett
Joseph Fugett
Reg Gilliam
Elzee Gladden
Ellis Goodman
Reynaldo Glover
Everett Grant

John Green
Ed Gregg
Bryant Gumbel
Lynwood Hart
Norma Jean Harvey
John Hatch
Ray Haysbert
Dan Henson
Bob Hermann
Bertrand Hill
Duane Hill
James Hoyte
Ford Johnson
Orlan Johnson
Amalya Kearse
Joerg Klebe
Remmert Laan
Tom Lamia
Connie Langford
Diana Lee

Ray LeFlore
Christina Lewis
Loida Lewis
Arthur Liman
Louis Loss
Roger Lowenstein
Howard Mackey
Pedro Massanet
James McPherson
Richard McCoy
Butch Meily
George Miles
Michael Milken
Don Moore
Kermit Morgan
Laurie Nelson
Imelda Nicolas
Hanley Norment

Peter Offerman
Ricardo Olivarez
Sam Peabody
Carolyn Powell
Leonard Quigley
Delores Quiller
Timothy Roberson
Bill Robinson
Jim Robinson
Frank Sander
Fredi Savage-Eaton
Phyllis Schless
Alan Schwartz
William Scott
Bill Slattery
Jill Slattery
Joel Smilow
Edith Smith

Melvin Smith
William Smith
Hercules Sotos
Elie Souaf
Lucien Stoutt
Charlotte Sullivan
Robert Suggs
Angela Tillman
James Tillman
Darryl Thompson
Edgar Toppin
Doug Walter
Bryan Williams
Ralph Williams
Elias Wilson
Josephine Wilson
Robert Winters
Kevin Wright

Index

ABC News, 183
Ackerman, P., 142, 143, 144, 145, 146, 167, 170, 199, 204, 206, 208, 229
Acquisition Funding Corp., 144, 145
Adams, W., 111, 112
Aetna Life and Casualty, 77, 111
Agnelli, G., 293
Akers, J., 273
Albert, N., 73
Alcott, M., 71, 74, 260, 261
Allen, B., 273, 274
Allen & Company, 145
Allfresh Foods, 95
Almet, 113, 114, 116, 117, 118, 119, 125, 127, 133, 137, 141, 152
AmBase, 269
American Association of Minority Enterprise Small Business Investment Companies, 84
American Can, 163
Angstadt, E., 135, 138, 140, 141, 153, 161, 162, 163, 164, 165, 176, 177, 179, 180, 181, 182, 202
Archer, L., 84, 85, 181
Arctic, 253
Artigel, 252
Ashe, A., xv, 45
Ashley, L., 157
AT&T, 273
Auspitz, M., 82
Avis, 132, 134

Bacote-McAlily, P., 29
Balladur, E., 228
Ballve, P., 220, 221
Banco Popular, 129
Bankers Trust Company, 144, 145, 146, 147, 148, 149, 150, 151, 155, 166, 167, 169, 171, 172, 178, 179, 180, 181, 194, 273
Banks, A., 37, 39, 40
Barker, T., 181
Battle, K., xv, 276, 310
Baud, J., 224, 301
Bear, Stearns & Co., 130, 135, 136, 141, 143, 156, 171, 172, 176, 187, 268, 269, 277
Beatrice, 86, 87, 94, 182, 184, 185, 188, 191, 192, 193, 197, 200, 201, 202, 203, 205, 208, 210, 211, 212, 214, 215, 216, 218, 219, 220, 221, 222, 223, 224, 225, 226, 227, 228, 229, 230, 231, 233, 235, 237, 238, 239, 243, 254, 257, 264, 270, 279, 280, 284, 285, 291, 300, 303, 305
Beatrice Co., 269
Beatrice International, xiv, xv, 113, 123, 164, 187, 188, 189, 193, 195, 198
Beatrice International Foods, xiv, 199, 110
Beattie, R., 194, 215
Belafonte-Harper, S., 160
Bell, D., 289

Bell, R., 25, 26
Bell, T., 93
Belzberg, S., 270
Black Enterprise, 82
Black, L., 197, 226, 236
Bon Grain, 228, 238
Bourelly, T., 94, 95
Bouriez, P., 240
Bradley, T., 125
Brennan, J., 170
Brennan, W., 67
Broadcast Capital, Inc., 128, 129
Brody, C., 193
Bronson, C., 227
Brown, B., 167, 169, 170, 194, 195, 196, 197
Brown, D., 20
Brown, H., 64
Brown, L., 248
Brown, R., 60, 63
Buchan, J., 213
Burnham, 218
Burson-Marsteller, 184, 211, 214
Bush, G., 126, 249, 275
Butterick, 157, 163, 180
Butts, C., 45, 286

Cadbury Schweppes, 220, 229
Cain, B., 17
Callard & Bowser, 239
Callender, G., 74
Cammer, B., 113, 115, 117, 118, 125, 141
Campofrio, 222
Canadian Bombardier, 256

315

Capital Cities-ABC, 133
Capital Markets Assurance
  Corp. (CAPMAC), 270
Caribbean Basin Broadcasting,
  130, 131, 137
Carteret Bancorp., 269
CBS Sports, 128
Chambers, R., 266
Chase Manhattan, 95
Chavis, B., 90, 91, 92, 93, 291,
  292, 302, 310
Chemical Bank, 111, 114, 115
Christian, P., 113
Christophe, C., 93, 95, 189,
  190, 191, 192, 193, 200,
  203, 204, 205, 208, 210,
  214, 216, 217, 218, 219,
  220, 224, 225, 226, 229,
  230, 233, 235, 236, 240,
  241, 242, 243, 272, 278,
  284
Chrysler, 271
Chubet, B. J., 141, 144, 170
Citibank, 93
Citicorp, xv, 190, 270, 273
Claiborne, L., 157
Clark, B., 239
Clark, E., 256
Clark, R. C., 288, 289, 290,
  291, 310
Clarkson, C., 77, 78, 79, 87,
  88, 96, 114, 115, 116,
  118, 120, 124, 127, 139,
  142, 145, 147, 152, 154,
  156, 159, 163, 171, 173,
  174, 208, 219, 298, 299
Clayton, A., 133
Clinton, W., xvi, 275, 310
Clinton, H., 310
Coach Cain, 18, 19
Cole, E., 3
Coleman, 138
Colon, A., 40, 46, 47, 49
Coloroll, 260
Columbia Savings, 229
ConAgra, 269
Cooper, J., 2, 19, 26, 39, 61,
  83, 175, 286, 297, 306,
  307
Cooper, S., 2, 4, 6, 68
Cooper, S. S., 2, 5, 6, 283
Cora-Revillon Business Group,
  240
Cosby, W., xvi, 276, 310
Count Basie, 101
Cravath, Swaine and Moore,
  72, 75

Cuff, D. F., 183, 184
Cunningham, G., 193
CVC Capital, 129

D'Amato, A., 126
Daniels & Bell, 93, 94
Davenport, R., 271, 272, 294,
  295
Davidow, B., 167, 169, 196,
  197
Davis Polk, 75
Davis, C., 18, 19, 20
Davis, Jr., S., 67
De Jongh, R., 130
Dean Griswold, 57
Deloitte, Haskins and Sells,
  141, 208
DeLorean, J., xvi, 299
Dequase, C., 228
DeVito, M., 69, 70, 71
DeWind, B., 70, 71
Dickey, C., 73
Dinkins, D. N., 125, 126, 248,
  249, 276, 310
Disunno, D., 247
Douglass, F., 308
Drexel, Burnham, Lambert,
  141, 142, 143, 167, 169,
  170, 171, 193, 194, 196,
  198, 199, 203, 204, 205,
  206, 208, 218, 219, 220,
  226, 227, 235, 236, 240,
  265, 268
Dreyfuss, D., 126

Eaton, F. S., 44
Edley, C., 289, 290
Edwards, L., 46
Eikenberry, P., 121
Equico Capital Corp., 82, 83,
  85, 114, 153, 154, 178, 179
Equitable Life, 77, 83
Esmark, Inc., 132, 133, 134, 135
Executive Life Insurance, 270

Ferguson, J., 202
Fiat, 293
Fierce, H., 95
First Boston, 180, 271
First Chicago, 141
First Executive, 229
Flannery, B., 258
Fletcher Capital Markets, 292
Fletcher, Jr., A., 292
Ford Foundation, 77, 110
Forstmann Little, 236
Forstmann, T., 236

Fugett, A.., 11, 24, 28, 38, 89,
  202, 244, 246, 249, 269,
  276, 281, 297, 299, 300,
  302, 303, 304, 305, 306,
  307
Fugett, C., 11, 12, 14, 15, 27,
  28, 44, 103, 112, 201,
  209, 213, 281, 283, 285,
  286, 297, 298, 306, 309
Fugett, Joseph, 14, 249
Fugett, Jr., J. S., 11, 24, 28, 67,
  115, 124, 128, 130, 154,
  270, 278, 284, 294, 297,
  301, 302, 303, 304, 306
Fugett, Sr., J. S., 9, 10, 13, 15,
  26, 28, 67, 72, 286

Gant, H., 126
Garrison, L., 74
Gelati Sanson, 222, 234
General Foods, 77, 84, 202
Gladden, E., 16
Glass Containers Co., 134
Glover, R., 97, 98
Goldberg, A., 74
Goodman, E., 23, 111, 112,
  175, 202, 245, 265, 268
Grant, III, E. L., 160, 166, 189,
  201, 210, 226, 230, 235,
  238, 239, 249, 268
Graves, E., 82, 83
Green, J., 295
Gregg, E., 250, 297, 298, 303
Guarino, D., 272
Gumbel, B., 276
Gunter, P., 256

Haje, P., 73
Harding, C., 144
Harlem Boys Choir, 310
Hart, L., 3, 33, 34, 35, 36, 37,
  39, 42, 43
Hatch, J., 56, 59, 62, 64
Haysbert, R., 112
Helms, J., 126
Henson, D., 9, 13, 84, 103
Hermann, R. L., , 153, 162,
  163, 164, 165, 174, 177,
  179, 182, 183
Hertz, S., 73
Hill, B., 29, 30, 31
Hillsdown Holdings, 239
Home Insurance Co., 269
Hughes, L., 310
Hunt Wesson, 132, 134
Hurwitz, C., 135
Hutch, J., 197

Iacocca, L., 211
IBM, 202, 273
Icahn, C., 211
Ilagan, E., 248
International Playtex, 141

Jackson, J., 125, 276, 310
Jeep Cherokee, 271
John Crowther Group, 181,
    183, 259, 260
Johnson Publishing Co., 85,
    214
Johnson, J., 85, 214
Johnson, O., 123, 171, 172
Joiner, 92
Joseph, F., 197
Jux, D., 253

Kalise, P. L., 252
Kalish, A., 208
Kanga, D., 124, 224
Kann, P., 275
Kaye, Scholer, Fierman, Hays
    & Handler, 145, 155
Kearse, A., 77
Kehler, D., 197, 199, 204, 226,
    235, 236
Kelly, D., 132, 133, 134, 198
Kidder Peabody, 292
King Fahd, 291
Kinnear, J. W., 310
Kinney Parking Lot, 141
Kissam, P., 73
Klebe, J., 129, 139
Kohlberg, Kravis, Roberts &
    Co., 133, 208, 211, 236,
    269
Korman, E., 73, 105
Kravis, H., 198, 205, 206, 211,
    225, 226, 227, 234, 235,
    236, 266, 292
Kurosawa, A., 102

Laing, H., 239
Lambert, 218
Lamia, T., 114, 115, 116, 133,
    136, 137, 138, 139, 145,
    147, 149, 151, 152, 153,
    155, 156, 158, 165, 173,
    192, 193, 208, 210, 216,
    219, 221, 222, 223, 224,
    226, 227, 229, 230, 233,
    235, 236, 237, 241, 263,
    277
Lange, E., 8
Lasker, M. E., 261, 262
Laurence, C., 76

Lee, D., 77, 78, 79, 116
LeFlore, R., 121, 122, 262
Lehman Brothers, 112
Lelong, P., 258
LeMans Haberdashers, 86, 87
Leslie Fay, 177
Levine, B., 73
Lew, S., 188, 199
Lewis & Clarkson, 287
Lewis, C. C., 2, 3, 8, 10, 33,
    107, 283
Lopez, F., 107
Loss, L., 50
Louis, J., 310
Lowenstein, R., 69, 70
Luey, M., 73

McCall Pattern Company, xiii,
    85, 113, 125, 131, 132,
    133, 134, 135, 136, 137,
    138, 139, 140, 141, 142,
    144, 146, 147, 148, 149,
    150, 151, 152, 153, 154,
    155, 156, 157, 158, 159,
    160, 161, 162, 163, 164,
    165, 166, 167, 170, 171,
    172, 173, 174, 175, 176,
    177, 178, 179, 180, 181,
    182, 183, 185, 187, 189,
    192, 194, 195, 196, 197,
    198, 199, 200, 202, 210,
    214, 215, 219, 233, 238,
    244, 251, 252, 259, 260,
    262, 263, 265, 267, 268,
    270, 277, 291, 301
McCoy, R., 26, 28, 29
McDonald's, 286
McGillicuddy, J., 273
McPherson, J., 52, 63, 64
Mackey, H., 82, 83, 85, 86, 181
Mahoney, D., 133, 134, 142,
    202
Manalac, P., 106
Manufacturer's Hanover, 237,
    273
Martinez, A., 108
Meily, R. S., 183, 185, 211,
    214, 215, 221, 223, 224,
    243, 254, 256, 257, 258,
    259, 270, 272, 285, 306
Merrill Lynch, 259, 266, 267,
    268
MESBIC, 81, 82, 83, 84, 110,
    114, 122, 127, 243
Mifune, T., 102
Miles, G., 292
Miles, M., 273

Milken, M., 83, 143, 167, 168,
    169, 170, 171, 194, 195,
    196, 197, 198, 199, 200,
    204, 205, 206, 208, 262,
    266, 278, 295
Miller, D., 71
Minority Business Development
    Agency, 84
Minority Enterprise Small
    Business Investment
    Companies, 81
Moore, D., 71
Morgan, K., 86, 87
Morgan Bank, 153
Morgan Stanley, xiv, 187, 188,
    205, 207, 209
Moriarity, J., 204
Mowry, W., 200, 221, 224, 238,
    253, 264, 271
Moynihan, D. P., 126
Murphy, G., 200
Murphy, R., 76

NAACP, 90
Nelson, L., 122, 123, 126, 139,
    152, 159, 171, 172
Nestlé, 238
New York Stock Exchange, 94
NICFUR, 106
Nichols, S., 289
Nicolas, F. J., 106
Nicolas, I., 98, 104
Nicolas, M., 103
Nimitz, M., 200
Nixon, R., 81, 273, 274, 275
Norment, H., 46, 48, 49
North Street Capital, 84
Norton Simon, 77, 132, 133,
    160, 193
Norton Simon Industries, 132,
    202
NSI, 134

O'Sullivan, V., 301
Obi, J., 130
Offerman, P., 144, 145, 146,
    155, 194
Olivarez, R., 113, 130, 137,
    153, 179
Onex, 188, 199, 216, 217, 233,
    240
Organizacion Polar, 239
Oxendine, J., 128, 129

Paramount, 270, 295
Parks, H., 111, 112
Parks Sausage, 111, 113, 127

Parnall, T., 73
Patterson, B., 126
Paul, Hastings, Janofsky and
  Walker, 114
Paul, Weiss, Rifkind, Wharton
  & Garrison, 70, 71, 72,
  73, 74, 74, 75, 76, 97,
  104, 105, 193, 200, 208,
  230, 231, 233, 235, 237,
  238, 260, 288
Peabody, S., 137, 153, 179
Perelman, R., 206
Perot, R., 275
Philip Morris, 273
Piedmont Airlines, 91
Piper & Marbury, 69, 70, 71
Playtex, 132, 135, 137, 138, 147,
  148, 149, 150, 153, 154
Powell, C., xvi, 45, 186, 290
Price Waterhouse, 141, 160
Pryor, McClendon, Counts &
  Co., Inc., 86
Pulaski, P., 249

Quigley, L., 73, 74, 75

Reagan, R., xvi, 126
Reed, J., 273
Republic Furniture and Leisure,
  Inc. (RFL), 114, 137
RJR Nabisco, 265
Robinson, B., 56, 59, 62, 66
Robinson, J., 216, 273, 274,
  308, 310
Robinson, M., 36
Rochlin, M., 73
Rockefeller Foundation, 51, 54

Salomon Bros., 187, 193, 205,
  207
Salonga, L., 310
Sander, F. E. A., 50, 52, 54
Sanford, C., 273
Sanson, T., 222, 223, 252
Savage, F., 127, 129
SBA, 84
Schless, P., 130, 131, 135, 136,
  139, 143, 144, 145, 147,
  149, 152, 156, 193, 270,
  290

Schonwald, G., 73
Schumer, R., 200
Schwartz, A., 170, 176, 177,
  277
Schwartz, G., 199
Scott, R., 17, 20
Scovill Apparel Fasteners
  Group, 270
Shearson Lehman, 260
Sheehy, J., 170, 187, 193, 216,
  259
Shields, B., 161
Simeus, D., 271
Simplicity, 135, 141, 157, 162,
  163, 168, 180
Sinatra, F., 67
Slattery, B., 62, 65, 66, 89
Slattery, J., 66, 285
Sloan, A., 267
Smilow, J., 135, 136, 137, 138,
  145, 148, 149, 150, 154
Smith, E. M., 40
Smith, M., 38, 42, 44
Smith, R., 73
Smith, W., 24, 25, 43, 157, 185
Smith Corona Corp., 266
Somerset Imports, 134
Sorensen, T., 74
Sotos, H., 138, 139
Stoutt, L., 245, 246, 247, 248,
  279, 297, 298, 306
Strait, G., 51, 60
Strufe, H., 69, 99
Suarez, D., 301
Suggs, R., 79, 81, 287
Sutton, P., 45, 126
Swift, 132

Texaco, 310
The New York Times, 183
Thomas, A., 71, 73
Thomas, F., 110
Thompson, D., 271, 287
Thorpe, J., 76
TLC Beatrice, 78, 85, 124,
  125, 137, 150, 186, 206,
  217, 232, 234, 238, 240,
  242, 244, 247, 251, 252,
  253, 255, 256, 259, 260,
  261, 263, 264, 265, 266,

267, 268, 269, 271, 272,
  282, 287, 292, 294, 295,
  298, 301, 303
TLC Pattern, Inc., 133, 154
Toepfler, L., 53, 54, 56
Travelers Insurance Co., 260,
  261
Trowbridge, C., 134
Turner, E., 38

United Biscuits, 239
Urban Coalition, 77
USA Today, 183

Vanguard, 84
Vann, A., 126
Vogue, 157, 163

Walker, D., 246
Wall Street Journal, 183
Wallace, F., 74, 76
Wallace, Murphy, Thorpe and
  Lewis, 76, 96
Walter, B., 134, 135
Walter, D., 136, 137, 138, 139,
  141, 145, 147, 149, 150,
  151, 153
WCRN-FM, 127
Weinstein, M., 73
Wilder, D., 125
Williams, R., 27, 29
Wilson, D., 189, 219, 241, 272,
  300
Winters, R., 153
WNET-TV, 292
Wolfe, T., 180
Wong, J., 142, 146, 167, 170,
  196, 197
Woods, C., 177
Wright, K., 88, 122, 123, 139,
  142, 147, 148, 149, 150,
  152, 154, 155, 156, 158,
  159, 171, 172, 173, 174,
  179, 210, 212, 213, 214,
  219, 234, 238, 240, 255,
  256, 259, 262, 266, 272,
  293, 298
WSTX-AM, 127

Youngwood, A., 73